I never was in a worse station for writing Letters, than this, especially for writing to MD, since I left off my Journals; For I go to Town early and when I come home at night, I generally go to Ld Mashams, where Ld Tr comes and we stay till past twelve. But I am now resolved to write Journals again, tho my shoulder is not yet well, for I have still now a new itching Pimple and a little Pain now and then It is now high Cherry time with us, take notice is it so soon with you; & we have early Apricots, & Gooseberries are ripe. On Sunday Arch-deacon Parnel came here to see me. It seems he has been ill for grief of his wife's death, & has been 2 Months at ye Bath. He has a mind to go to Dunkirk with Jack Hill, and I perswade him to it, & have spoke to Hill to receive him, but I doubt he will not have spirit to go. I have made Ford Gazeteer, and got roule a year settled on the Employment by ye Secrty of State; beside the Perquisites. It is ye prettyest Employmt in Engd of its biguess: yet ye Puppy dose not seem satisfyd with it. I think People keep some Pollgys to themselves till they have Occasion to produce them He thinks it not genteel enough, & makes 20 difficultyes. Tis impossible to make any man easy. My salary is sd him every week if he pleases, without fines or Statuts. He has little to do for it, he has a pretty Office, well Coale, Candles Paper &c. can franc what Letters he will, and his Perquisites if he takes Care may be worth too a more. I have ye Bp of Cl is landing or landed in Engd; & I hope to see him in a few days. I was to see mrs Bradly on Sunday night. Her youngest Gle is marryd to somebody worth nothing, & her Daughter was kind to hear Dilly Ashe, because the Mother was striking up an Intrigue with a Frenchman, who plays well upon ye Flute. I think the mothers element of it. Yesterday ye old Bp of Worcester, who pretends to be a Prophet, went to ye Queen, by Appointmt, to prove to her Majesty out of Daniel and the Revelations, that 4 years hence there would be a War of Religion; that ye K. of France would be a Protestant and fight on their side, that ye Pope would be destroyd &c, and declared he would be content to give up his Bishoprick if it were not true, Ld Tr who told it me was by, and some others, and I am told, Ld Treasr confounded him sadly in his own Learning, wch made ye old Fool very quarrelsom. he is near ninety years old. Old Bradly is fat and lusty, and has lost his Party. Have you seen Toland's Invitation to Dismal? how do y like it? Let it is an Imitation of Horace, and perhaps y don't understand Horace. Here has been a great Sweep of Employments; and we expect still more Removicalls the Court seems resolved to make thorow work. mr Hill intends to set out to morrow for Dunkirk of wch he is appointed Governr. but he tells me to day, that he can not go till Thursday or Friday. I wish it were over. mr Secrty tells me he is no fear at all that ye French will play tricks with us, If we have Dunkirk once, all is

JONATHAN SWIFT

By the same author:

NON-FICTION

Trollope
Rebecca West: A Life
Vita: The Life of Vita Sackville-West
Edith Sitwell: A Unicorn Among Lions
Elizabeth Bowen: Portrait of a Writer
A Suppressed Cry
Hertfordshire

FICTION

Electricity
The Grown-Ups

VICTORIA GLENDINNING

JONATHAN SWIFT

HUTCHINSON
London

© Victoria Glendinning 1998

The right of Victoria Glendinning to be
identified as the Author of this work has been asserted
by Victoria Glendinning in accordance with the
Copyright, Designs and Patents Act 1998

All rights reserved

1 3 5 7 9 10 8 6 4 2

This edition first published in 1998 by
Hutchinson

Random House (UK) Limited
20 Vauxhall Bridge Road, London SW1V 2SA

Random House Australia (Pty) Limited
20 Alfred Street, Milsons Point, Sydney,
New South Wales 2061, Australia

Random House New Zealand Limited
18 Poland Road, Glenfield,
Auckland 10, New Zealand

Random House South Africa (Pty) Ltd
Endulini, 5A Jubilee Road,
Parktown 2193, South Africa

A CIP record for this book is available
from the British Library

Papers used by Random House UK Limited are natural,
recyclable products made from wood grown in sustainable
forests. The manufacturing processes conform to the
environmental regulations of the country of origin.

ISBN 0 09 179196 0

Typeset in Baskerville by MATS, Southend-on-Sea, Essex

Printed and bound in Great Britain by
Mackays of Chatham PLC, Chatham, Kent

FOR KEVIN

CONTENTS

LIST OF ILLUSTRATIONS

PREFACE

THE QUESTION THAT biographical writers are most frequently asked about their subjects is 'Do you like him?' What they in part mean is 'If I read your book, will I meet someone whom I will like?' There is no answer I can give that makes much sense about Jonathan Swift. He is extremely 'nice' in the eighteenth-century sense. He is not always 'nice' in our sense of lovable and pleasant. He is a disturbing person. He provokes admiration and fear and pity. All I can assure you is that in keeping company with Jonathan Swift you are not wasting your time.

Rather little is known by the general public – outside Ireland, at least – about Swift, except that he wrote *Gulliver's Travels*. Professional Swiftians and eighteenth-century specialists, on the other hand, have familiar recourse to sagging bookshelves of published documentation and research. They will want to know if I have seen anything new. It is worth noting therefore that the lost Cobbe copy of the autobiographical fragment is still in existence and in good hands, although I am not at liberty to say where; and that the records of C. Hoare & Co. are instructive about the financial dealings of some Tories in the last years of Queen Anne's reign. Private collections still harbour treasures, such as the first edition of Pope's *The Rape of the Lock* which Swift gave to Stella; and a notebook which has come down through the Acheson family, containing poems by Swift both in his own hand and in others', one of them unpublished. At the behest of the notebook's owner this remains, for the moment, unpublished.

In Swift's day it was customary to write common nouns with capital initial letters, and to italicize a great many words. Editions of Swift's works vary in what they do about this. Some modernize, some do not. The same is true of spelling. Since I have not had one uniform edition of all Swift's poetry and prose in my possession, and have consulted many editions of the different – and sometimes of the same – works, I have had to make my own decision.

Capitalization gives a gamy period flavour, for example in this paragraph from Swift's 'character' of Thomas Earl of Wharton:

> He is without the Sense of Shame or Glory, as some Men are without the Sense of Smelling; and, therefore, a good Name to him is no more than a precious Ointment would be to these. Whoever, for the Sake of others, were to describe the Nature of a Serpent, a Wolf, a Crocodile or a Fox, must be understood to do it without any personal Love or Hatred for the Animals themselves.

There is in that, for us, a quaint antiquarianism. If you experiment by writing out the sentence without the capitalization, you will see how the passage seems less charmingly mannered and more mordant. I have modernized most of the capitalization, some spellings, and some punctuation in the interests of clarity. Period flavour can be just too intrusively flavoursome. You might object that this is as perverse as saying 'Hold the mayo' when ordering lobster mayonnaise. But I would rather give proper attention to the lobster.

There is a problem concerning dates. Before the reform of the Gregorian Calendar in 1582, the beginning of the Christian year was 25 March, not 1 January. Various Protestant states declined for a long time to make the change. Denmark, the Netherlands and the Protestant German states switched in 1700. England stuck with the old calendar until 1752, thus putting herself out of synch with her European neighbours, and causing later writers to make errors in dating events which took place in the first part of a year: a date given as 17 February 1714 is, to us, 17 February 1715. The custom in Swift's lifetime was sometimes to acknowledge the problem by writing, for example, 17 February $17^{14}/_{15}$. Where I have given dates, they correspond with the post-1752 calendar.

There is also a problem concerning money. To translate early eighteenth-century costs, prices and salaries into current terms, it is probably safe to take a multiplier of 90. This calculation has limitations, in that the basket of goods was different. For individual transactions, different variables make comparison often meaningless. What were luxuries then are common items now, and vice versa. The cost of some commodities fluctuated during his lifetime, the pound in England did not always have the same value as the pound in Ireland, and contemporary statistics are unreliable. So any calculation is approximate.

For much of his life, as vicar of Laracor and its dependent parishes, Swift's income was around £250 a year, out of which he paid a curate. Curates had on average £50 a year; the shopkeeper class and tenant farmers lived on rather less. For those at the bottom of the scale the money economy was almost irrelevant, while the income of peers of the realm averaged between £3,000 and £4,000. When Swift became Dean of St Patrick's, his combined stipend rose to £650 (in today's values, a good professional salary, and better than that of most professional men in his time). But some English bishoprics, to which he vainly aspired, were worth more than twice that amount.

I would like to thank the many generous people who have helped me significantly with this book – by pointing the way, or saving me from errors (those that remain are mine), or sharing their special knowledge, or giving me access to materials in their possession, or facilitating access to privately held material, or providing hospitality and encouragement during the research – and in a few cases simply by some casual remark which serendipitously illuminated Swift for me:

Bruce Arnold, Margaret Atwood, Toby Barnard, Alain de Botton, Michael Bruford, Hugh Cobbe, John Coleman, Giles Fitzherbert, Professor Roy Foster, the Duke of Devonshire, Professor William R. Duncan, Bamber Gascoigne, Toby Glanville, Hugo Glendinning, Matthew Glendinning, Professor Nigel Glendinning, Professor Paul Glendinning, Dr Simon Glendinning, the Countess of Gowrie, the Very Revd V. G. Griffin (formerly Dean of St Patrick's), the Duchess of Hamilton (Jillian Robertson), Peggy Hill, Robert Hogan, David Hughes, Bruce Hunter, Professor W. Johnson, P. J. Kavanagh and Kate Kavanagh, Professor Hermione Lee, Melosina Lenox-Conyngham, Alison Lurie, John McBratney, Charles Moore,

Professor Bruce Redford, Professor Angus Ross, Tim Schadla-Hall, the Earl of Shelburne, Baron von Stauffenberg, Professor Greg Schirmer, Christine Shuttleworth (for the index), Professor David Singmaster and Deborah Singmaster, the Very Revd Maurice Stewart (Dean of St Patrick's), Stella Tillyard, Jeremy Trafford, Jenny Uglow, Julian Walton, Dr David L. Wykes. Also, the librarians or archivists of Bowood, Chatsworth, C. Hoare & Co., Knole, the Leicestershire Record Office, the London Library, Marsh's Library, St Patrick's Hospital, the National Art Library at the V&A, Trinity College Library, and the public and private collections and archives which provided the illustrations.

I have greatly benefited, while working on this book, from the investigations of Paul McQuail, formerly Deputy Secretary in the Department of the Environment, into the politics of the reign of Queen Anne. His analytical skill and his professional perspective on the dynamics of power gave me a focus I needed, and I am grateful for his sustained and sustaining interest. My special thanks also to Dr Nick Groom and to Richard Cohen, for their critical comments and suggestions.

My last and best thanks are to my husband Kevin O'Sullivan, who little imagined the extent to which he would be sharing his life with an ambitious, volatile, screwed-up genius in a clerical gown and a periwig. Unable to find a quotation from Jonathan Swift to express my gratitude for his perceptive input and patience, I turn to Swift's contemporary Anne Finch, Countess of Winchelsea, whom Swift admired, as do I. When she put in a verse request to 'indulgent Fate' for 'a sweet, but absolute retreat', she added:

> Give me there (since Heaven has shown
> It was not good to be alone)
> A partner suited to my mind,
> Solitary, pleased and kind.

I have had such a partner – in London, in France, in Ireland – while I was writing this book.

Chapter One

BEGINNING

I AM SITTING in the Manuscripts Room of Trinity College Library in Dublin, transfixed by a fragment of autobiography written by the author of *Gulliver's Travels* – the Dean of St Patrick's, Dr Jonathan Swift.

The fragment of autobiography was donated to Trinity on 23 July 1753, eight years after Swift's death, by his great-nephew and biographer Deane Swift (Deane, in this case, being a forename, not an ecclesiastical title).

The manuscript was given to Deane Swift by his mother-in-law Martha Whiteway, a cousin of Jonathan Swift's who looked after him in his last illness. Deane Swift, when he published it in 1755, said that it was written 'about six or eight and twenty years ago', that is, between 1727 and 1729. It may be relevant that Stella, the most important woman in Jonathan Swift's life, died in 1728. Deane Swift did not think Swift was aiming for anything very ambitious. He was trying to set down on paper 'a few memorials, for the instruction of any person that should write his life'.

The autobiographical fragment has been scrutinized by scores of Swift scholars and biographers before me. It has been transcribed, edited, glossed, expanded, discussed, deconstructed, and sometimes just paraphrased as if it were the gospel truth.

There is one other known manuscript version of it in existence – a contemporary copy, made for one of Swift's younger clerical friends, Dr Charles Cobbe, who became Archbishop of Dublin. John Forster saw this copy and used it for his Swift biography of 1875, after which it was apparently lost. Over a hundred years on, it has reappeared. (Its reappearance gives one hope that there are still more Swiftian letters or papers somewhere – in the attics of country houses, in the

1

back stores of lawyers' offices, in the unsorted boxes of museum collections . . .) In the Cobbe copy, whole paragraphs are included which Swift never wrote, and which were added by Dr John Lyon, the clergyman who managed Swift's affairs in his last years and did some genealogical research at Swift's request.

I have read books about Swift, I have read his work – including this fragment, with and without Lyon's additions to the Cobbe copy – in print. I have seen other examples of Swift's handwriting, which was neat, unfussy, and print-like, easy to read except when he was saving paper by writing small, in letters to Stella. But to have the original of the autobiographical fragment lying before you, and to turn its pages, is to slide out of linear time into a confrontation with the man who wrote it.

No. That is sentimentality. Jonathan Swift is out of sight, his step is clattering away down the wooden back stair of the Deanery, his mocking voice is hanging in the silent air. 'Swift haunts me', wrote the poet W. B. Yeats, 'he is always just round the next corner.' So are Vanessa and Stella, who loved him. On a woman's thin shoulder is the shadow of a bruise.

It is all so long ago. We can encompass the nineteenth century. The parents of people still living, as I write, were born as Victorians. We have photographs of them. But Jonathan Swift was born in 1667, the year after the Great Fire of London. In his youth, there were people still alive who had passed Shakespeare on the London streets, and he trails in the dusty hem of his clerical gown all the fanatic times – the 'fanatick times' as it was written in his day, and pronounced with the accent on the first syllable – of the disturbed seventeenth century. He cannot be seen as an Enlightenment figure. What we think of as eighteenth-century, in terms of architecture, furniture, painting and the decorative arts, came mostly after his heyday. He died in 1745 and was isolated by deafness and dementia from the late 1730s.

Nothing has prepared me for the impact of this manuscript. Handwriting betrays states of mind. When someone is upset, or depressed, or ill, it shows in the graceless formation of the letters, and in the awkward disposition of the lines. When Swift picked up his pen and wrote on these folded folio sheets of paper, he was neither calm nor happy. He was writing badly, uncertainly.

Sometimes he wrote on both sides and sometimes not. He started each line halfway across the page, leaving a wide margin on the left for second thoughts and additions. He cancelled out many of these marginal notes, scrawling round and round and over and over them to make quite sure that they were indecipherable.

In his main text too there are crossings-out, imperfect sentences, words and phrases written in between the lines, and ink-blots. This is not a finished manuscript, it is a draft, a try-out, something abandoned as hopeless or impossible.

He can't remember names and dates. He slips from the third to the first person and back again. The only flash of effective writing is a savage dig at Henry Sidney, erstwhile Lord-Lieutenant of Ireland and later Lord Romney, who had failed, decades earlier, to keep his promise to the young Swift that he would ask William III for a prebend for him – 'as he was an old, vicious, illiterate rake, without any sense of truth or honour'.

The autobiographical fragment is a sad and unreliable document. Swift would never have wanted the public to see it. When writing about other people or outside events, Swift's characteristic prose style, up to the end, was rigorous, lively, and frequently savage. In verse, as in the mock-autobiographical poems 'Life and Genuine Character of Dean Swift' and the 'Verses on the Death of Dr Swift', he was sharp about himself as seen by others. But here, in prose, his style has collapsed into ungrammatical imprecision.

In this fragment of autobiography Swift says that when he was a year old his nurse stole him away from his widowed mother and his uncle, and from Dublin, where he was born, and took him over the sea to her home town of Whitehaven.

Whitehaven is in Cumbria, on the north-west coast of England. The nurse, he says, was 'under an absolute necessity of seeing one of her relations, who was extremely sick, and from whom she expected a legacy'. The nurse was 'extremely fond' of Swift; and when his mother realized what had happened, 'she sent orders by all means not to hazard a second voyage, till he' – Swift is writing about himself in the third person – 'could be better able to bear it. The nurse was so careful of him, that before he returned he had learnt to spell; and by the time that he was three years old he could read any chapter in the Bible.'

I can believe that he was taken off to Whitehaven by the nurse. I can't believe that he could read any chapter in the Bible by the time he was three, but such prodigious claims were frequently made, in his day and later, for children who turned out to be exceptional in later life.

What rings false to me is that he was taken to England without the knowledge of his mother, and that it was her fear of the danger of the sea journey which prevented his return home. That sounds like a comforting fable.

It is like something written by Elizabeth Bowen, a twentieth-century writer poised, like Swift, between Ireland and England. She claimed that her mother, having hired a governess to organize her child's days, 'thought of me constantly, and planned ways in which we could meet and be alone'. The most far-fetched interpretation of adult behaviour is preferable to the possibility that your mother finds your constant presence inconvenient.

Swift's mother, Abigail Swift, née Erick, left Ireland and went to live in Leicester in England, where her parents came from and where she still had family. She went, according to Jonathan, soon after he was brought back to Dublin, leaving behind her two young children – Jonathan had an elder sister, Jane – with their Swift uncles and aunts. Not that we hear much about the aunts. Jonathan's childhood world was ruled by uncles.

Jonathan Swift's father – if he *was* Swift's father – died before he was born. Seven months before, according to the autobiographical fragment. He was only about twenty-five. Swift had no romantic picture of his parents' marriage. It was, he wrote in the auto-biographical fragment

> on both sides very indiscreet, for his wife brought her husband little or no fortune, and his death happening so suddenly before he could make a sufficient establishment for his family: And his son (not then born) hath often been heard to say that he felt the consequences of that marriage not only through the whole course of his education, but during the greater part of his life.

To say that you suffer the consequences of your parents' unwise marriage is to wish you had not been born to those parents, which is to say you wish you were someone else, or that you had not been born at all. Swift does not exactly confess to anything so painful. Feeling is characteristically distanced; he is reporting merely

4

what the Dean 'hath often been heard to say . . .'

Swift also was often heard to tell, at the dinner table, the story about the nurse carrying him off in his babyhood to Whitehaven. As Deane Swift wrote, the story 'gave occasion to many ludicrous whims and extravagances in the gaiety of his conversation'. He told it with variations and embellishments, sometimes saying that he was smuggled out of Ireland in a bandbox. Swift was to describe Gulliver, a finger-sized manikin among the giant Brobdingnagians, being parted from his giant nurse-girl, wafted in his carrying-box over the sea by an eagle, and dropped into the water to float on till he was rescued. I think, when he wrote that, the Whitehaven story was in the back of his mind.

Those who heard Swift tell the story to entertain his guests remembered different versions. One young woman recalled him telling her that the nurse was a Dubliner, not a native of Whitehaven, and that she went over to visit her husband. According to this version, the nurse was so fond of baby Jonathan that she could not bear to part with him; and she made no contact with the Swift family until she returned him safely three years later, to the great joy of his mother – a joy all the greater because it was clear that the nurse's only motive in stealing him had been 'pure affection'.

Another friend gathered that Abigail Swift went to her relations in Leicester only about two years after her husband's death, which means she would not have been in Dublin when his nurse brought him back, and would not have seen her son at all until he was grown up. Abigail Swift, apart from one documented visit to Dublin around the time her daughter Jane married, remained in Leicester for the rest of her life.

Jonathan sought out the mother he did not know when he himself first went to England at the age of twenty. It must have been a strange meeting.

The Whitehaven incident is just one of the mysteries in the life of Jonathan Swift. There are others. He was loved by two women, both of whom lived in Ireland so as to be near him.

Was he secretly married to Esther Johnson, the woman he called Stella? And if so, why did he not acknowledge her as his wife?

What was the nature of his relationship with the other, younger woman, Hester Vanhomrigh, whom he called Vanessa? He made her very unhappy.

Did he have some physical or psychological trait, or some family secret, which made it impossible for him to lead a normal life with Stella, or with any other woman? Who was his real father; who was Stella's real father?

Perhaps it is just a modern fad to regard a man who steers clear of intimate relationships as inadequate or in some other way problematic. In which case, we should just accept as the simple truth Swift's throwaway remark that 'he never yet saw the woman for whose sake he would part with the middle of his bed'.

What was the root of his peculiar and impertinent treatment of women, particularly young women, verging on cruelty? There was also something obsessional about his preoccupation with cleanliness and its opposite, filth – again, especially in connection with women.

He was a churchman but he was not a mystic, he was not having a love affair with God. So what powered him, in his professional, political and literary life? Worldly ambition? A craving to 'belong'?

'I remember, when I was a little boy, I felt a great fish at the end of my line which I drew up almost to the ground. But it dropped in and the disappointment vexeth me to this very day and I believe it was the type of all my future disappointments.' He was a disappointed man. Disappointed by the circumstances of his birth, which led to his youthful poverty. Disappointed by the powerful patrons who could have furthered his career and did not. He harboured grievances and resentments.

Swift felt that he never landed his great fish, though objectively speaking, he did. His career, for the son of an obscure couple in Ireland – a separate kingdom under the English Crown, but treated more like an off-shore colony – was extraordinary. His fame in his own lifetime would have been quite enough for most men.

If he had known how his fame would endure – how he has survived as an immortal 'character' in the minds of men and women – and that at least one of his works, *Gulliver's Travels*, would be firmly established in the canon of world literature; that the adjective 'Swiftian' would become a critical map-reference for a certain kind of dark imagery, would his disappointment have been assuaged?

Probably not. His disappointment, like his pride, was part of his nature.

After he died, people who had known him went public about their famous friend, filling their pages with anecdotes, vignettes, other people's memories, reported conversations, family lore, hearsay, rumours, gossip, along with first-hand and second-hand information.

These early books laid the foundation of what is called 'the tradition'. They unleashed a spate of speculation and analysis which continues to this day – not only in biographies and criticism, but in poems, novels and plays. Swift as a person is so elusive that the temptation to extrapolate and to fictionalize him is enormous. Maurice James Craig, in his *Dublin 1660–1860* (1952), wrote that Swift 'has been the occasion of more nonsense than any other writer except Shakespeare'. And once any anecdote or speculation about Swift appears in print, it becomes part of the confused and confusing tradition.

His exorbitant personality and satirical manner have been magnets for myth. Thomas Sheridan (son of Swift's close friend, and father of the playwright Richard Brinsley Sheridan), who knew Swift when he himself was a boy, observed in this context how often 'witty sayings, blunders, and things of humour, are constantly fathered upon the most remarkable Wit'. Sheridan well knew that some of the anecdotes, jokes and repartees credited to Swift came from the common stock. Even today, in Ireland, someone quoting a quip or maxim will tack 'as the Dean said' on to it. The Irish man of letters Stephen Gwynn, writing in 1933, noted that Swift was one of those great writers who 'so affected popular imagination in their lifetime that a ghost of them survives, vaguely familiar to thousands who in reality know nothing but the name'.

Gwynn recognized traces of Swift's mind and style in the Trinity College luminaries of his time. Dublin is alive with her dead. The electric energy of Swift's manner still runs, if less fiercely, in the wit and savagery of Dublin's literary and political life – in the insult disguised as a compliment, the compliment disguised as an insult, the outrageous joke delivered deadpan, the hyperbole, the telling anecdote, the irony that spancels the enemy.

It is a truism that those who make us laugh most are frequently prey to melancholy. Turning everything to wit or humour is a strategy for survival and a redeeming route to acceptance and popularity. Swift's wit is often shocking. It has a lash. He challenges the hypocrisies and received opinions which enable people to rub along together. He rarely indicates with any reliability what he might consider 'the truth' on any issue. In his polemical prose, you cannot always wholly count out, or count in, any expressed value or opinion.

If you insist on reading Swift in pursuit of 'real' propositions, you frequently sink deeper into the bog of paradox.

He despised pretentious prose, and long words where short ones would do. His imagery is full of insects, animals, and everyday objects. His idea of style was 'proper words in proper places'. Each sentence he writes is, on its own, perfectly easy to understand. Hemingway, with his short, declarative sentences, is not more transparent than Swift. The problem arises because the sentences, and the arguments they express – often, not always – undercut and contradict one another, weaving a web which he does not untangle.

This makes quotation tricky. Not so much in his poetry, which Leslie Stephen called 'a mere running of everyday language into easy-going verse'. (I assume he was using 'mere' in its eighteenth-century sense of pure, unmixed, entire.) Swift is a seductively quotable writer, and yet to quote from his published prose is dangerously problematic.

He often makes striking statements simply to demonstrate that such an opinion *can* be logically formulated. It may be demolished on the next page, or it may be left standing for the reader to grapple with unaided. 'But I suppose it is presumed', he once wrote, 'that common people understand raillery, or, at least, rhetoric, and will not take hyperboles in too literal a sense.' He is optimistic. My aim is to have a sufficiently firm grasp of the context of what I quote, so that I do not misrepresent him.

Swift warns critical writers against another danger of quotation: 'Whoever only reads in order to transcribe wise and shining remarks, without entering into the genius and spirit of the author' will end up traducing that author, out of a desire to cram in everything that has caught the eye and the imagination in the course of research. The result will be, in Swift's own words, 'a manifest incoherent piece of patchwork'. So I have tried to keep quotation within bounds, and have passed up more of Swift's 'wise and shining phrases', and more popular and colourful anecdotes about him, than I can well bear to remember.

Political satire at the expense of governments or institutions is one thing. Personal invective is another. Swift was an expert at both. He himself did not take kindly to being the butt of the wit or satire of others. Early in his close friendship with Dr Patrick Delany, Delany made some sally at Swift's expense, and laughed loudly at his own wit. He was reproved by Swift in verse:

If what you said, I wish unspoke,
'Twill not suffice, it was a joke.
Reproach not tho' in jest, a friend
For those defects he cannot mend;
His lineage, calling, shape or sense
If nam'd with scorn, gives just offence.

In this he is in agreement with the poet and dramatist John Dryden (a generation older than Swift, and the nephew of Swift's paternal grandmother, née Dryden). Dryden wrote that 'We have no moral right on the reputation of other men', and condemned personal satire – caricatures, libels, lampoons – as 'a dangerous weapon, and for the most part unlawful'.

Swift frequently endorsed this view. It cannot be said that he practised what he preached. He reversed the usual order of things by insulting the friends he wished to attract (especially if they were women). With his enemies, there were no holds barred. He attacked *ad hominem*, and *ad feminam*, shamelessly.

Swift was a man of the world who walked the world in his clerical gown as a man of God. In one of the descriptions he wrote of himself, he suggests an aspiration to be in the world but not of it:

Humour, and mirth, had place in all he writ:
He reconciled divinity and wit.
He mov'd, and bow'd, and talk't with too much grace;
Nor shew'd the parson in his gait or face;
Despis'd luxurious wines, and costly meat;
Yet, still was at the tables of the great.

'Perhaps there never was a man whose true character was so little known', wrote Thomas Sheridan the younger, in 1785. That is still true, though by now the life of the author of *Gulliver's Travels* is extremely well documented.

His poetry and prose is available to us in modern scholarly editions. A great mass of his correspondence has survived, and is published. Much research has been done on his life and writings, and on the life and writings of his English and Irish contemporaries.

It would, therefore, be possible to write a full and responsible biographical account of Jonathan Swift – to add to the other full and (mostly) responsible biographical accounts of him already in existence – while declining to confront the impossibly difficult questions, or to speculate about their answers. That is what the late Professor Irvin Ehrenpreis, American author of the standard three-volume biography of Swift, chose to do.

It is an honourable strategy, and indeed it is a Swiftian strategy. Swift thought that what we cannot determine by observation and common sense we are incapable of apprehending, so shouldn't try. But if one were to approach Swift in that spirit, there would be only a silence.

What I am writing is not a chronicle biography. It is more like an extended version of what was in Swift's time called a 'character' – a written portrait.

Lord Halifax, one of the Whig statesmen brought down by Swift's Tory friends, said that a 'character' differed from a portrait only in that 'every part of it must be like, but it is not necessary that every feature should be comprehended in it, as in a picture, only some of the most remarkable'. There is some pain in this method. Learning about Swift, every feature seems remarkable, and everything that I am unable to dwell upon grows in my mind like a reproach. One can never have finished with Swift.

Whatever the biographical method, there has to be a trajectory: a story. I'm going to set down now the main facts – in the sense of the verifiable or widely accepted events – of Jonathan Swift's life: the resumé of a biography.

He was born of Protestant, English parentage in Dublin, Ireland, on 30 November 1667. With his father dead, his mother in another country, he and his sister Jane passed their childhood amid a welter of cousins. There was, it seems, no one adult who particularly cared for Jonathan, or for whom he particularly cared.

In 1673 he went as a boarder to Kilkenny College, and in 1682 he entered Trinity College, Dublin. He was a troublesome and rebellious student. He was about to take his MA degree in 1689, when military and political events supervened.

After the Protestant monarchs William and Mary were crowned in London, the deposed Catholic monarch James II, who had fled to France, landed in Ireland with the intention of winning back his crown. William's armies definitively vanquished James's in Ireland at the Battle of the Boyne in the summer of 1690.

But before this, young Jonathan Swift had already fled, like many other Protestants, fearing the repercussions of a Jacobite victory. He went first to his mother in Leicester; and then found a position as secretary to the ex-diplomat and writer Sir William Temple, at Moor Park in Surrey.

It was in the Temple household that he first met Esther Johnson (Stella), who was then eight years old; he helped her with her reading and writing, and her company brought him solace and pleasure. She was to become the most important woman in his life.

With the Temples, Swift learned the ways of the great world, became fiercely ambitious for himself, and began seriously to write. It was with the Temples too that he had the first attacks of the giddiness and nausea which were to recur distressingly throughout his life. This illness has been diagnosed retrospectively as Ménière's syndrome.

Between 1689 and Sir William Temple's death in early 1699, Swift spent three periods at Moor Park as secretary. In between the second and third, he took holy orders in Ireland and was ordained priest, with a dead-end parish in Kilroot in the north of Ireland. There, bored and frustrated, he embarked upon a relationship with Jane Waring (Varina).

After Temple's death, Swift was appointed vicar of Laracor in Co. Meath. In 1701 Stella, now aged twenty, left England to settle in Ireland in order to be near him, with Rebecca Dingley as her companion.

In 1702, the year William III died, Swift took (by paying for it, as was perfectly usual) the degree of Doctor of Divinity from Trinity College, and was thenceforth known as Dr Swift.

He was in England off and on between 1704 and 1709, with an official mission from the Church of Ireland to Queen Anne. We have a painful glimpse of him in his early days in London as the awkward provincial, knowing no one, stared at and mocked by the wits in the coffee-houses. But in 1704, *A Tale of a Tub* was published – anonymously, though its authorship became known – and brought him his first public notoriety and the friendship and admiration of other writers. He met government ministers – Whigs, who were in power – and soon was on close terms with Addison and Steele. He published some political-religious tracts (notably *An Argument against*

Abolishing Christianity) but got nowhere with his mission and retreated to Ireland.

He was in England again between September 1710 and September 1714.

This was the most exciting period of his life. In the heady last years of Queen Anne's reign, Dr Jonathan Swift, a vicar from an obscure Irish parish, was manipulating English public opinion on behalf of the Tory party, who had won a landslide victory. He was on close personal terms with Lord Oxford, the Lord Treasurer and First Minister, and Lord Bolingbroke, the Chief Secretary. He was the government's publicist, writing pamphlets, verses and periodicals which were instrumental in discrediting the Whigs, bringing down the Duke of Marlborough, and turning public opinion against the war with France.

He formed lasting friendships with Pope, Gay, and Arbuthnot among other wits, writers and Court eminences. He worked hard and he played hard. He was at the centre of public life, in the confidence of great men, courted and feared by lesser men.

He sent copious and intimate letters about his life in London back to Stella in Ireland, later published as the *Journal to Stella*. He was also, in London, becoming involved with a new young woman named Hester Vanhomrigh (Vanessa), who later came to live near him in Ireland. This new friendship he kept from Stella.

He was never presented to Queen Anne. She and some of her advisers distrusted and disliked him because of the virulence of his personal satires and his apparent godlessness. Yet his ambitions, it seemed, must be realized. His friends at Court and in the ministry would surely put a fat bishopric in England his way.

Again, public events supervened. With the death of Queen Anne in 1714, the break-up of the Tory ministry, and the disgrace of the Tory ministers, Swift's intoxicating period close to the centre of metropolitan public life came to an end.

Swift did not want to return to Ireland. However, the best that the great men who were his friends could do before they were dismissed from office was to obtain for him the Deanery of St Patrick's in Dublin.

Queen Anne was succeeded by the Hanoverian George I. The Whigs under Robert Walpole were returned to power. Swift himself, linked to the discredited outgoing ministry and their covert Jacobitism (i.e. their connections with the exiled Catholic monarchy), was an object of official suspicion in both England and Ireland.

He returned to Dublin to take up his residence at the Deanery and his duties as Dean. A big fish in a small pool, he established a circle not of public figures but of convivial friends whom he dominated and sometimes bullied.

His secret friendship with the passionate Vanessa, who followed him to Dublin, was a source of anxiety. Stella was still there, and at the centre of his Dublin life. In 1716 he may secretly have married Stella, though they never lived together as man and wife. Vanessa died in 1723. Swift's ambiguous poem about his intense relationship with her, *Cadenus and Vanessa*, was published in 1726, the same year as *Gulliver's Travels*, which was an international success. Swift revisited England in 1726 and 1727, but then never again. He maintained his English friendships by means of increasingly creaking correspondences. Stella died in 1728, leaving him lonely.

His reputation as an Irish patriot was first established by the publication of *The Drapier's Letters*. Though he always saw himself as exiled in Dublin – doomed to die 'in a rage, like a poisoned rat in a hole' – he grew increasingly incensed by England's attitude to Ireland. *A Modest Proposal*, the work which first springs to mind when thinking of Swift the savage satirist, was published in 1729.

During the 1730s, the ageing Dean continued to write and publish prose and poetry, including the scatalogical poems – some of which were circulated privately, some of which were published, and which have puzzled and disgusted some readers and critics ever since.

In the late 1730s his temper, his memory, and his reason deteriorated. In 1742 he was found to be of unsound mind. He lived on, unable to read or write or care for himself. He died at the Deanery on 19 October 1745, having willed his money for the foundation of a hospital in Dublin for 'idiots and lunatics', which survives to this day as St Patrick's Hospital.

That is the outline, the portmanteau 'life'. Now I want to unpack some of what is in the portmanteau, beginning at the beginning, circling a little, gradually zooming in on the man himself, until the central questions about him can finally be confronted in close-up.

For some readers there will be too much politics in this book, and for others too little. I have not fully unpacked the political intricacies of the last four years of Queen Anne's reign, because they do not all concern Swift. I have not unpacked his relations with his London friends – Lord Oxford and Lord Bolingbroke, Pope, Gay, and Dr Arbuthnot – after he returned to Dublin never to see them again. His correspondence with them, combined with theirs with him, makes up the fattest volume of his published letters. They were all wordsmiths. Covering reams of paper was no problem at all. The survival, on paper, of these friendships is a book-length study in itself; though I find the correspondences self-conscious and laboured.

What is also not included represents the limitless, cloudy underside of all biographical writing. The reader will become familiar with the most important figures in the private and public life of Jonathan Swift. But he and they are to be seen and heard in the context of a great company of other faces and voices, familiar to him but mere voices off in these pages – agents, archbishops, artists, beggar-women, bishops, booksellers, carriers, courtiers, curates, deans, doctors, enemies, factors, friends, fixers, functionaries, grooms, ladies-in-waiting, landlords, middlemen, peers, poets, printers, rectors, relatives, scholars, servants, soldiers, speculators, spies, statesmen, tenants, tradesmen, vicars, dogs and horses (Swift liked lists), all playing their part in Swift's life and in his private letters or public writings, and many of them with stories of their own worth the telling.

There are a great many clergymen in this book. When we think of Church of England vicars and bishops, deans and archdeacons, we think of Anthony Trollope. Trollope's Barsetshire is further from Swift's world than a paltry hundred and fifty years would suggest. Churchmen in Swift's day were involved in matters of state, of life and death. The stakes were very high. Even though Trollope's clergyman are very milky tea in comparison with Swift's contemporaries, there is a succession. The rude and wrangling, political, place-seeking clerical types known to Swift are like Hogarthian caricatures of the characters created by Trollope.

'I could name certain gentlemen of the gown', wrote Swift, 'whose awkward, spruce, prim, sneering, and smirking countenances, the very tone of their voices, and an ungainly strut in their walk, without one single talent for any one office, have contrived to get good preferment by the mere force of flattery and cringing.' He is surely describing the Obadiah Slope of his age.

In some ways he is locked into the mind-set of his generation, or rather of the generation before him, because he was not, in many of his views, 'progressive' in his time. The established Anglican Church, in Swift's youth, had assumed considerable political power in both Britain and Ireland. All other denominations suffered from disabling legal discrimination. Swift would not have believed that the Roman Catholic Church would even have survived as a force in Ireland, let alone that it would become the majority religion and an arm of the independent Republic. And if he heard that Ireland had a woman president, and that Britain had had a woman prime minister, he might think he was hearing of an absurdity more grotesque than anything in *Gulliver's Travels*.

In other ways – in his loathing of a national politics organized along party lines, his attitude to monarchy, his unstable narratives, his love of transparency and insistence on calling a spade a spade (however revolting, and even though he might, had he written about a spade, have depicted it as a jam-spoon, or as a mechanical digger), his hatred of militarism, his concern for human rights, social justice and the natural world, his attitude to social welfare – he seems to have leapfrogged the Victorians and most of the twentieth century, and to stand as the moral true north not only for the millennium but for all time. His private life is another matter altogether.

Chapter Two

YOUNG

NUMBER 7 Hoey's Court, the house in which Swift said he was born, no longer stands. It was demolished in the course of redevelopment.

Hoey's Court was in the heart of the city between the two Church of Ireland cathedrals, Christ Church and St Patrick's, and in the lee of Dublin Castle, where the Lord-Lieutenant resided and the English administration had their headquarters.

Swift's early biographers, writing in the eighteenth century before the area became unrecognizable, naturally saw no need to describe the house or its environs. Fortunately, the physician William Wilde (Oscar Wilde's father, later Sir William), writing in the 1840s, left an account of what it was like in his time, a century after Swift's death.

If today you walk northwards up Great Ship Street, with the Castle wall on you right, you reach Castle Steps, leading up to Castle Street, through vestiges of the old city walls. In Swift's time there were not yet steps, just a slippery slope called Cole's Alley. To the left, off this steep passage, there used to be a few steps up into the small cobbled square called Hoey's Court, 'in the mouldering grandeur of the houses of which', wrote William Wilde, 'we still recognize the remains of a locality once fashionable and opulent'. The Lord Chancellor had one of these houses towards the end of the eighteenth century, and the Surgeon-General another. Eade's Coffee House, a fashionable meeting-place, was also in Hoey's Court.

On the far side, where the court narrowed into an alley opening westwards into busy St Werburgh's Street, stood what was then number 7.

As fashionable Dublin moved eastwards to St Stephen's Green

and the area around it – the streets and squares we admire as 'Georgian Dublin', and which the ageing Swift was to deplore as nasty speculative development – the Castle area was taken over by the fast-growing population of ordinary citizens. William Wilde reproduced a sketch of 7 Hoey's Court as it was in his day: a once-fine house of four storeys over a basement, with stepped gables. It is already dilapidated. S-shaped iron trusses hold the crumbling masonry together. The hall door, standing open, is topped by a simple lintel. Wilde noted that 'a handsome door-case a few years ago ornamented the front of this house, but some antiquary, it is said, carried it away'.

Before that, in 1809, when Sir Walter Scott was researching his life of Swift, the house was occupied by a woman who sold earthenware. Its social decline had already begun. By William Wilde's time it was in multiple occupation by several families of 'poor tradesmen'. But inside, 'the carved wainscotting and cornices, the lofty ornamented chimney-pieces, and the marble window-sills, which existed up to a very recent period, and some of which still remain, all attest the remains of a mansion of note in its day'.

It's a familiar Dublin story. The fate of 7 Hoey's Court foretells the fate of many of the Dublin town-houses built with such confidence in Swift's maturity and after, which fell in their turn on hard times and, in the twentieth century, became tenements in multiple occupation by poor families, their carved woodwork vandalized or stolen, their Italian plasterwork deteriorating sometimes beyond hope of rescue.

When Swift was born, 7 Hoey's Court was a fine house in a prime location. Such a house could not have belonged to Swift's impecunious young father, clinging on to a less than glorious legal career, dead in his mid-twenties. It belonged to his prosperous Uncle Godwin Swift, who took his pregnant, widowed sister-in-law Abigail under his wing.

Uncle Godwin was the eldest and most potent uncle, but he was just one of a phalanx of Swifts, all brothers, several of whom had come to live in Ireland by the 1660s. They were the sons of Elizabeth Dryden and the Revd Thomas Swift, the vicar of Goodrich in Herefordshire, an ardent royalist who suffered greatly from the persecutions and deprivations of Cromwell's troops in the time of the Commonwealth. All his boys became lawyers except Uncle Thomas, who was a clergyman.

17

There were fine pickings for lawyers in Ireland, a troubled country where lands were annexed, restored, sequestered, allotted, and fought over in retaliation or response to every rebellion of the native Irish, and every change of English administration, religious-political upheaval, or policy shift. And 'in those days Ireland was very moderately supplied with lawyers or attorneys of any tolerable reputation', as Deane Swift, Jonathan's biographer (the son of Swift's first cousin, another Deane Swift) discreetly put it.

For Ireland was a land of opportunity providing remunerative jobs, sinecures, and a high irresponsible lifestyle for British professional men, entrepreneurs, and swashbuckling chancers of all kinds who could tolerate or exploit the volatile political and social conditions. Daniel Defoe's fictional sexual adventuress, Moll Flanders, had an admirer who wanted her to go to Ireland with him. He assured her that a farm could be had there for £50 a year that would cost £200 a year in England, 'and that we were sure to live as handsomely upon it as a gentleman of £3,000 a year could do in England'. Moll was eventually transported to a more distant colony, Virginia, which offered the same kind of opportunity; and indeed in thinking of Ireland in the early eighteenth century it is important, as Roy Foster has written, to recapture its 'gamy' flavour – 'an echo of colonial Virginia, or even the Kenya highlands of the 1920s'.

Next in age after Uncle Godwin Swift came Uncle Dryden; then Uncle Thomas, then Uncle William, who was equally successful and rich, and worked his way through four wives. The youngest was Uncle Adam, whose daughter Martha Whiteway was to be one of the very few Dublin cousins who meant anything to Jonathan Swift in his declining years; and Martha's daughter Mary married her cousin Deane Swift, the biographer of Jonathan.

Jonathan Swift's father, Jonathan the elder, was the fifth brother, coming between William and Adam. In the fragment of autobiography, Swift said that his father had 'some employments and agencies' before becoming an attorney, which means that he tried his hand at various kinds of business. He was very young when he died; he had a respectable but lowly job as steward to the King's Inns, where his chief responsibility was keeping the minutes of benchers' meetings. He and Abigail, whom he married in 1664, probably had lodgings within the Inns.

All the Swifts, apart from Uncle Dryden and Jonathan, our

Jonathan's father, prospered exceedingly in Ireland. Uncle Godwin in particular made great display of his houses, furniture and equipage. Uncle Godwin was a man of substance in Dublin, with extensive business interests as well as his legal practice.

Uncle Godwin became 'intimately acquainted' with a greater grandee, the much older Sir John Temple. It was, said Deane Swift, 'a warm, sincere, disinterested friendship'; the two men would dine and 'pass the remainder of the day' at one another's houses.

Old Sir John Temple was a wily creature and a very big wheel in Dublin. His father had been Provost of Trinity College. He himself was Master of the Rolls in Ireland. He was flexible in his political allegiances, managing throughout (apart from a short spell in prison) to feather his own nest. He had been in Charles I's personal service, but became a sympathizer with the Parliamentary cause against Charles in the 1640s. His history of the Irish Rebellion of 1641, loaded with partisan anti-Irish accounts of the bloody massacres perpetrated by the rebels, caused a sensation and seemed to justify Cromwell's subsequent brutality in Ireland. (One of the first resolutions of the 'patriot' Jacobite Irish Parliament during the Troubles of 1689 was to order Sir John Temple's book to be burned by the common hangman.)

When he became acquainted with Godwin Swift in the 1660s, Sir John Temple was in charge of land allotments to 'adventurers', i.e. settlers, from England and Scotland. He allotted quite a lot of lands to himself and his family, chiefly in Co. Carlow (with estates at Ballycrath and Moyle, and his principal residence, Castletown) and in the neighbouring midland counties; but also in and around Dublin, including a large chunk taken out of Phoenix Park. Temple Bar, beside the Liffey in central Dublin, is named not for some ancient temple or inn of court, but for the influential Temple family.

Uncle Godwin was determined to make his family secure, remembering his youthful misery when his parents' Herefordshire home was stripped by the Roundheads. He had a lot of people to look after, producing fourteen children, eight of whom survived, by three wives. He was also responsible for his dead brother Jonathan's boy, left by their mother on the Swift clan's hands. The siblings were divided; Uncle William seems to have taken on Jonathan's sister Jane.

Swift aunts seemed not so large in Jonathan's consciousness as Swift uncles, perhaps because there was rather a rapid turnover, due

19

to death. No benign female figure, after the ambiguous nurse who carried him off to Whitehaven, can be discerned presiding over his childhood.

Jonathan was only six when he was sent as a boarder to Kilkenny Grammar School. His uncles probably felt they were doing right by him. It was considered the best school in Ireland. A first cousin, Thomas (Uncle Thomas Swift's son), was there with him, as was the future playwright William Congreve, two years younger than Jonathan.

He left no direct memories of his schooldays at Kilkenny. But writing in 1708 to his younger friend Charles Ford – a mainly absentee landlord with an estate called Woodpark in Co. Meath – he observed how people remembered the past falsely, recalling only the pleasant things:

> So I formerly used to envy my own happiness as a schoolboy, the delicious holidays, the Saturday afternoon, and the charming custards in a blind alley; I never considered the confinement ten hours a day, to nouns and verbs, the terror of the rod, the bloody noses, and broken shins.

This suggests that in maturity he did remember the negative aspects of school life; and indeed he never referred to his boyhood without resentment.

He complained that he had been given the education of a dog; whereas he was, on paper, given the best education that Ireland offered, and a better one than most of Uncle Godwin's own children. Swift's animal imagery is always precise. He was given the education of a dog, perhaps, in that both at home and at school he was adequately fed and watered; he had somewhere to sleep; and he was often ignored, given peremptory orders, and beaten when he disobeyed. The position he was in – a poor relation, fatherless, effectively motherless – was enough to make any boy unhappy and angry.

He went to Trinity College from Kilkenny School in 1682, when he was fourteen – a young, but not then abnormally young, age for a university student. He remained there for seven years. His cousin Thomas entered the college at the same time.

Trinity College and Dublin Castle were the twin poles of the intellectual and social life of Protestant Dublin. Trinity was also the hotbed of the Anglican Church in Ireland, all-male of course, staffed by clerics, and a training ground for clergymen on the fast track to Irish prebendaries, deaneries and bishoprics – though some of the bishoprics, much to Jonathan Swift's vehemently expressed disgust and disapproval in later life, tended to go to men from England of no distinction, who could be trusted to toe the Westminster line in the Dublin parliament.

Away from the centre of the city, half a mile south of the Liffey and enclosed by a wall, Trinity did not present the classical façade and imposing Front Square that we see today. These were not built until ten years after Jonathan Swift's death. His university consisted of the original Elizabethan block built round a court in the 1590s, with some modest additions in the direction of College Green and what is now Parliament Square. The buildings were of thin red bricks, two storeys high with dormer windows. The turreted hall and the chapel beside it were the remains of a priory that had once stood in that place.

Narcissus Marsh was Provost of Trinity when Swift first took up residence. Later, when Marsh was Archbishop of Dublin, Swift wrote a 'character' of him which displays a hearty disrespect: 'It has been affirmed that originally he was not altogether devoid of wit, till it was extruded from his head to make way for other men's thoughts.' In 1783 Marsh was succeeded by Robert Huntingdon.

More important for Jonathan than either of these was his tutor, about ten years his senior, who became his lifelong friend – the Revd St George Ashe, who later became Provost of Trinity, and finally a bishop.

Nearly all the teaching was oral, and in Latin. The chief subjects were Latin, Greek, and Aristotelian philosophy. The students had to talk Latin at meals. A new chapel and dining-hall were under construction when Swift was there, so the students had to eat in the library, with all the books piled up in other places. Lectures began at seven in the morning, following chapel at six. There was chapel again for morning prayers at ten, and evening prayers at four. There were fines for non-attendance – Swift's most usual reported offence. During dinner, there were Bible readings.

It sounds exceedingly spartan and dreary, but energetic young men will find a way of amusing themselves, legally or illegally.

Jonathan was already writing spoofs and parodies – among them the kernel of what was to be *A Tale of a Tub* – aided and abetted by his cousin Thomas. He scraped through his exams and took his BA degree in 1686, doing sufficiently well in the classical languages but poorly in abstract philosophy and formal rhetoric. His own preferred reading was history and poetry, which were not even on the syllabus.

In his fragment of autobiography, he wrote that on account of 'the ill-treatment of his nearest relations', he was so 'discouraged and sunk in his spirits that he too much neglected his academic studies'. Uncle Godwin had stopped subsidizing him financially.

In 1687 Jonathan was had up for neglect of duties and for 'frequenting the town' and 'causing tumults'. There was a consequent row with the junior dean, and his degree was temporarily suspended. He would nevertheless have taken his MA in the spring of 1689. But events supervened. Revolution in England exiled the Catholic King James, inviting in to rule in his stead his Protestant daughter Mary and her Protestant husband William of Orange, from Holland.

William and Mary automatically became monarchs of Ireland as well. Under James, power in Ireland had been transferred from Saxon to Celt in the Irish parliament and the army. King James planned to land in Ireland, with French support, to reclaim his crown, and the Protestant English in Ireland feared terrible depredations, even massacre.

Uncle Godwin's powerful crony Sir John Temple was by that time over ten years dead, and buried in Trinity chapel. Uncle Godwin could help no one, not even himself. He had been overstretching himself. 'He ran into a thousand projects, and consequently became the dupe of a thousand villains. He pursued fifty kinds of business in the city of Dublin, which he himself was wholly a stranger to', wrote Deane Swift. One of these businesses was an iron-works in Co. Cavan, in which he naively made a huge investment, and got cheated.

Swift very rarely wrote about his family. But in his late years, fulminating about the place-names of Ireland – either unpronounceably Irish, or inanely invented English – he mentioned a town 'where the worst iron in the kingdom is made, and it is called Swandlingbar'. Swift explained that the 'and' in 'Swandlingbar' stood for Sanders, the 'ling' for Davling, the 'bar' for Barry, and the initial 'Sw' for Swift (his Uncle Godwin): 'the witty conceit of four gentlemen, who ruined themselves with this iron project'.

After this failure Uncle Godwin's mind went. By 1689, the year of the Revolution, he 'had fallen into a kind of lethargy, or dotage, which deprived him by degrees of his speech and memory; and rendered him totally incapable of being of the least service to his family and friends'.

Meanwhile, Trinity too was in chaos. The teaching collapsed because nearly all the dons – including Swift's tutor St George Ashe – fled across the water to England during what were called, then as (*mutatis mutandi*) now, 'the Troubles'.

Uncle William and Uncle Adam went as well (though like St George Ashe and many others, they returned when times were favourable). In January 1689, two months before the deposed King James and his armies landed, Jonathan Swift and his cousin Thomas left Ireland too. When James and his forces reached Dublin, the remaining authorities in Trinity College, in keeping with the Anglican doctrine of passive obedience, greeted him and were assured of his good will. But the place was used as a barracks, the college silver sequestered, and the fellows and students forbidden to foregather in groups of more than three.

Jonathan, on arrival in England, went to Leicester, to the mother that he had not seen since he was a tiny child. He can have remembered her not at all, or hardly at all. Maybe she was a bright mystery to him.

Abigail Erick, mother of Jonathan Swift and of his elder sister Jane, is a bright mystery to me too. What I know about her makes me wish to know her better. But I know her rather little.

Leicester, where her parents came from, has since records began been full of families called Erick – or Errick, Ericke, Eyrick, Heyrick, or Herrick, as the name was variously spelled. The ones that rose in the world spelled it with an initial H. The poet Robert Herrick, born 1591, was one of the tribe.

Jonathan Swift's maternal forebears did not belong to the smart branch. They mostly lived in the city itself, and were respectable mercers, bakers, tailors, ironmongers, glovers. They were not artisans, or machine-knitters in the hosiery trade for which the area was becoming known. But they were not gentry, either. Swift, in his autobiographical fragment, claimed that they once had been; but 'declining every age, are now in the condition of very private gentlemen'. They were mostly of the superior tradesmen class from which aldermen, mayors, town bailiffs, churchwardens and stewards of the fair were drawn.

Some became clergymen, found livings in the villages around the city, and rose a little in the world. But they had no grand patrons; they were not the type who gained preferment in the Church, or who made a mark in the great world. The local vicarage or rectory represented the height of their ambitions.

With so many Ericks in the area, it is possible to deduce more than one family of origin for Swift's mother. She has, for example, been identified as the daughter of a butcher from the village of Wigston Magna. Having looked at the records, I agree with Irvin Ehrenpreis that her father was James Ericke (*sic*), from 1627 to 1634 vicar of Thornton, a village six miles west of Leicester on the edge of the old Charnwood Forest. Her brother Thomas was vicar of Frisby-on-the-Wreake, about ten miles north-west of the city.

So Abigail, soon after she lost her husband, went back to her own people. It was an odd thing to do because she had not been born and brought up in Leicester. If, as the records say, Abigail was seventy when she died in 1710, she was born in 1640. The baptisms of five children of James Ericke and his wife Elizabeth are recorded in his parish. But there is no record there of Abigail's baptism.

That is because her father had taken his family over to Ireland before she was born. The Revd James Ericke got into trouble with the church authorities. In 1734 he was arraigned for holding an unlawful conventicle: i.e., he conducted a religious service in the house of a brother-in-law in Leicester, in the illicit non-conformist manner. He was not deprived of his living at Thornton, but was put 'on trial' to see whether he conformed henceforth.

Later the same year, a report on his parish found that the churches under his care were in bad repair, and that he was not taking the services. A note explains that '*vertit solum in Herberniam*': he had emigrated to Ireland.

Thus Abigail was born in Ireland. Her marriage certificate describes her as 'of the city of Dublin spinster'. In Dublin, she met and married the young man from Herefordshire by the name of Swift who had also recently emigrated to Ireland.

Their families probably knew each other back in England. It has not been hitherto remarked by Swift's biographers that there were (and still are) also a great many Swifts in Leicestershire. The name frequently occurs, along with Erick, in the parish registers of the village of Frisby-on-the-Wreake, where Abigail's brother was vicar. Thirteen babies were born to couples by the name of Swift between 1699 and 1745. A John Swift was churchwarden there in 1700, and a William Swift in 1711.

John Nichols, a local historian, writing in the late eighteenth and early nineteenth centuries, categorically assumed that the Leicester-shire Swifts were connected with the Herefordshire Swifts to whom Abigail's husband belonged. 'It is an anecdote not generally known in the life of the Dean, that his relations John and Thomas Swift were, in conjunction with James Lee and Thomas Bass, the owners of the stage-waggons from Leicester to London.' This, Nichols thought, explained Jonathan Swift's preference for travelling between Holyhead in Wales (the disembarkation point from Dublin) and Leicester, and between Holyhead, Leicester and London, the hard way, mostly on foot, except when he went by waggon – with his kinsmen.

Either way, it was tough going. The roads, their lines unchanged since the thirteenth century, and along which the waggons lurched and rumbled, were straggling beaten-earth tracks with the holes filled in with brushwood and loose stones. That was true even of the old Roman roads which intersect around the city of Leicester; the Romans' gravel and paving stones had mostly been taken up and used for building materials.

Not that Jonathan Swift stuck to the roads. Deane Swift described the young man running 'like a buck' across country: 'Gates, styles, and quicksets [hedges], he no more valued than if they had been so many straws. His constitution was strong, his limbs active.' He only 'sprang into waggons' to escape the rain, or for fun, since he liked talking and joking with other travellers.

Deane Swift can only have this account from stories Swift himself told about his young days. It does nothing to weaken Nichols's case for a connection between the Herefordshire Swifts and the Swifts of Leicestershire. But Jonathan Swift, when he went into his father's family background, never mentioned any Leicestershire connection.

There is one other curious survival. In the book recording the marriages in the parish of Frisby-on-the-Wreake for the years 1754 to 1792 there are scribbles all over the back and front inside covers and on the flyleaf – sums, accounts, a list of the natural children of

Charles II, and the signature of Jame (*sic*) Wragge, a late-eighteenth-century vicar of Frisby. Among the notes and scribbles is the following:

> From Miss Van homrigh T Dr Swift Declaring her passion
>   for him
> and complaining of his neglect of her
> believe me it is with him.
> Vicar of Frisby in the County of Leicester
> Richard Winman Vicar

Since Richard Winman, or Wenman, was vicar of Frisby until 1755, and the marriage-register book was only started in 1754, this garbled note can be dated pretty precisely. Presumably it was provoked by the elderly Winman's reading of some of the accounts of Swift's life and loves which appeared in print from 1751 onwards. It could have been the local Erick connection which accounted for this prurient interest in Swift and Vanessa ('Miss Van homrigh'), or it could have been that the vicar knew something that posterity has forgotten – namely, that the famous Dean Swift was related to the numerous Swifts resident in his parish.

Either way, the amorous exploits of the man who caused gossip in Leicestershire in his youth in the early 1690s were still a subject of gossip there after his death.

And there was gossip in his youth. Jonathan's first cousin Jane Ericke married John Kendall, who became vicar of Thornton in succession to his father-in-law, Swift's uncle. Young Jonathan wrote to Kendall in 1692 justifying his behaviour towards a Leicestershire woman.

He was at this time employed off and on by Sir William Temple of Moor Park in Surrey, the son of Uncle Godwin's friend Sir John. Cooling his heels in Leicester on visits to his mother, he became involved with one Betty Jones, another local vicar's daughter. (She later married William Perkins, an innkeeper of Lutterworth, and the owner of the Lutterworth waggon.) The letter to Kendall may be about Betty, or it may be about another girl. In any case, Kendall had clearly reproached Jonathan for using or abusing her, and raising expectations of marriage.

Jonathan's reply, loaded with contained irritation, is revealing. His own 'cold temper, and unconfin'd humour', he said, could be relied on to prevent him from going too far with women. The very ordinary observations he had made within half a mile of the university, he told Kendall

> have taught me experience enough not to think of marriage, till I settle my fortune in the world, which I am sure, will not be in some years, and even then my self I am so hard to please that I suppose I shall put it off to the other world.

Someone in Ireland (an uncle?) had told him, he said, that he was like 'a conjur'd spirit' that would do mischief if he were not usefully employed. Restless boredom compelled him to turn everything to humour and to teasing when he was in female company; 'whether it be love or common conversation it is all alike, this is so common that I could remember twenty women in my life to whom I have behaved myself just the same way' – without any motive, he said, except his own entertainment when he had nothing else to do, 'or when something goes amiss in my affairs'.

Jonathan described himself to the reproachful clergyman as 'a man of the world'. He had known young and ignorant men to marry, he said, because they believed 'every silk petticoat contains an angel', or else from simple lust. 'I think I am very far excluded from listing under either of these heads.' Furthermore, 'a thousand household thoughts' of a dispiriting financial kind deterred him from matrimony.

'Besides', he said, in a sentence which is frustrating in its obscurity, not to say clumsiness, 'I am naturally temperate, and never engaged in the contrary, which usually produces these effects.' He must mean that he does not involve himself physically with women, and thus does not risk demands for marriage.

He was twenty-four when he wrote that letter. The self-awareness is impressive. What is less encouraging is that, with some exceptions, he never really developed past this point. With women, he got stuck with a 'manner'. You cannot quite call it flirtatious. There is aggression in it.

All his life his approach to women was teasingly intimate, but with a raillery that bordered on cruelty. As an older man, a famous writer, and a senior churchman with temporal and spiritual authority, he took outrageous conversational and even physical liberties with women which, exactly as when he was young, went some way towards easing his violent irritation, disappointment, and boredom with the life he was leading.

As for the gossip of which Kendall warned him, 'I should not have behaved my self after the manner I did in Leicester if I had not valued my own entertainment beyond the obloquy of a parcel of very wretched fools which I solemnly pronounce the inhabitants of Leicester to be, & so I content myself with retaliation.'

It remains hard to understand why Abigail left her two children in Dublin when, as a widow, she went back to England to live in Leicester. But the extended family was more deeply integrated then than now, and it was not so uncommon for children to be reared by relations other than their parents, for administrative or economic reasons.

Perhaps Abigail thought that the Swift uncles were better equipped to give them a start in life than she herself, even though that would have been no reason to absent herself entirely. If she kept in touch with Jane and Jonathan by letter from England, the correspondence has not survived.

She had not quarrelled with the Swifts, and they certainly bore her no resentment. Deane Swift, Jonathan's biographer, recorded that Abigail 'was greatly beloved and esteemed by all the family of the Swifts. Her conversation was so extreamly polite, cheerful and agreeable even to the young and sprightly that some of the family, who paid her a visit near fifty years ago [i.e., around 1705] at Leicester, speak of her to this day with the greatest affection.'

The feeling seems to have been reciprocated. Deane Swift reprinted in his biography a scrap from a letter of 1703 from Abigail to his father: 'Pray be pleased to present my best service to my good nephew [Willoughby Swift], and tell him I always bear in my heart a grateful remembrance of all the kindness he was pleased to show to my son.'

Willoughby was Jonathan's older cousin, Uncle Godwin's eldest surviving son. He was a merchant working in Lisbon. When Jonathan was in Leicester with his mother in the summer of 1694, he wrote to his cousin Deane Swift in Portugal, where he was visiting Willoughby. Jonathan had just departed, for the second time and with animus, from his employment with Sir William Temple at Moor Park. Sir William, Jonathan told his cousin, was 'extream angry I left him, and yet would not oblige himself any further than upon my good behaviour, not would promise any thing firmly to me at all'.

Jonathan asked for his 'best thanks' to be conveyed to Willoughby for his goodness and generosity. 'I wish and shall pray, He may be as happy as he deserves, and he cannot be more. My Mother desires her best love to him and to you . . .' Cousin Willoughby was the one male member of the Swift family of whom Jonathan spoke nothing but good. Willoughby contributed to the support of his young cousin when Godwin, his father, became unable to do so. One of Willoughby's daughters, Hannah, married the Revd Stafford Lightburne, who was Swift's curate at Laracor for eleven years from 1722.

It was in the same letter written from Leicester to the Swifts in Lisbon that the young Jonathan announced that he was going to be ordained a clergyman, 'and make what endeavours I can for something in the church'. Perhaps, he suggested, the Lisbon Swifts might make him chaplain to the expatriate commercial community out there. But nothing came of this.

Jonathan's mother, herself the daughter and sister of clergymen, would have been in favour of her son's ordination. The Deane Swift who was Swift's biographer was only four when Abigail died, and so had no first-hand knowledge of her. But he was informed that 'she was of a generous and hospitable nature, that she was very exact in all the duties of her religion', and went to church twice a day. She was always up and dressed by five o'clock in the morning, and her chief amusements were needlework and reading.

A list, compiled by himself, has survived of the letters Swift wrote between November 1708 and the end of October 1709. During this period he wrote to his mother twelve times, i.e. once a month. The letters themselves have not survived. When his mother died in Leicester, aged seventy, in April 1710, Swift was in Ireland, in his parish at Laracor. The news did not reach him until more than two weeks later, in a letter from his sister Jane, enclosing an account of their mother's death from Mrs Worrall, with whom she lodged in Leicester.

Swift wrote in his account book: 'I have now lost my barrier between me and death; God grant I may live to be as well prepared for it, as I confidently believe her to have been! If the way to Heaven be through piety, truth, justice, and charity, she is there.'

This is high praise of Abigail's character and conduct, with no hint of reproach. Whatever the reason for her departure from Dublin when he was small, he must have understood and accepted it. Elsewhere, he praised her prudence in connection with a warning she gave him about his involvement with the Leicester girl. The long early separation laid the foundations for his distrust, converted into disapproval, of any emotional dependence; but it did not destroy their adult relationship.

Sir Walter Scott was told an anecdote which persuaded him that Jonathan Swift's 'peculiar humour', but not his melancholy or his spleen, came from the Erick side of his genetic inheritance. Abigail Swift came back to Ireland just once, to see her grown-up children in late 1699. At that time her son Jonathan was employed as chaplain to the Earl of Berkeley in Dublin. Her daughter Jane, the elder child by eighteen months, was about to be married.

Abigail boarded in Dublin, in George's Lane, with a printer and his wife by the name of Brent. Clearly a playful lady – and also, perhaps, with an instinct to obfuscate her Dublin connections – Abigail pretended to Mrs Brent that she had come over 'to receive the addresses of a lover, and under that character received her son Jonathan's first visit', before disabusing her inquisitive landlady. Jonathan also boarded, later, with the Brents, and he stored his books and belongings in their house when he was in England. When as a clergyman he took on his first parish, Mrs Brent (presumably widowed) became his housekeeper, and remained in that post for over thirty years. When she retired, her daughter took over the position.

Jane, at the time of her marriage, was living in Bride Street, in Uncle William Swift's house. Senile Uncle Godwin had died four years before. Jonathan seems to have done his best for his sister. Lady Betty Berkeley, his employer Lord Berkeley's daughter, who became his friend, promised him that Jane would always be well received and welcome at the Castle. Earlier in 1699, Swift's previous employer, Sir William Temple, had died, and Jane had written to the Swift cousins in Portugal to say how sad and disappointing this was for Jonathan: Temple had promised to get him a living in England, 'but death came in between, and has left him unprovided both of friend and living'. Thus brother and sister were on good terms – until Jane's marriage.

She married Joseph Fenton, a tradesman, perhaps a currier. She was already thirty-three, with diminishing chances and choices. Jonathan was appalled by the idea of her marrying a tradesman, and is said by Deane Swift to have offered her £500 – which he certainly didn't have – to forgo the match. Swift's later friend Patrick Delany, always charitable in his interpretations, chose to believe that Swift had some personal knowledge of Fenton's bad character, 'for surely, he [Swift] could not be so ignorant, as not to know, that many families of higher rank than his, have not thought themselves disgraced by their alliance to tradesmen'.

Their mother Abigail, said Deane Swift, was 'equally fond of both her children, notwithstanding some disagreements that subsisted between them'. Her visit to Dublin was to attend the wedding, and to patch up the quarrel. Contemporary gossip does not suggest how far she succeeded. 'Whether his [Swift's] mother removed his resentment, in the journey she took from London, on that occasion, I cannot take it upon me to say', wrote Dr Delany. Deane Swift was equally cagey about the part Abigail Swift played in Dublin, seeing no point in seeking to unravel for the public 'little family quarrels of fifty or sixty years ago'. How much more difficult, then, to unravel them from a distance of three hundred years.

The Swift uncles were strongly in favour of the marriage, and one can see why. Joseph Fenton was said to be worth £5,000. The marriage would give Jane independence, and get her off their consciences. But Fenton turned out to be 'an old tyrannical vicious rake', 'an insolent brutal fellow', and had only half the money, if that, of which he boasted.

The Fentons parted in 1710, leaving Jane with two or three children. The family believed that her brother Jonathan gave her an allowance on condition that she lived in England.

Jane did go to live in England, and her brother, to judge from his correspondence with Stella, who was living in Dublin and knew Jane, made some rather ungracious gestures towards facilitating her new life. After their mother died, in late 1710, he was writing from London to Stella that he had another letter from Jane, 'who says you were with her. I hope you did not go on purpose. I will answer her letter soon; it is about some money in Lady Giffard's hands.'

Who is Lady Giffard? She is Martha, the widowed daughter of Uncle Godwin's grand friend Sir John Temple, and the sister of Sir William

Temple, in whose household Swift was employed as secretary, with intervals elsewhere, until the latter's death. Swift had entrusted Jane's money, left to her by their mother, to Lady Giffard, so that Joseph Fenton could not get his hands on it. Lady Giffard lived with her brother, while he lived, at Sheen near Richmond and then at Moor Park in Surrey.

Jane, like Jonathan, was taken on by the English branch of the Temple family. Like her brother, she had come to England before and sought her mother out – for the first time, so far as we know, in 1692, when she would have been twenty-six. She went to see her brother at Moor Park then, and met the William Temples and Lady Giffard for the first time. Jonathan, writing to Uncle William Swift after her departure, said that he had little news, 'for I am often two or three months without seeing anyone but the [Temple] family; and now my sister is gone, I am likely to be more solitary than before'.

On that first visit of Jane's to Moor Park, the child Stella (the eleven-year-old daughter of the housekeeper Bridget Johnson, and Jonathan's pupil and playfellow) waited upon her 'in the character of her little servant'. No one ever has a bad word to say about Stella – except Swift's sister Jane, who loathed her. In later years Stella was, wrote Deane Swift with unusual vehemence, 'that individual person whom she despised and hated beyond all the inhabitants of the earth'. Why?

It sounds as if Jonathan and Jane had some family traits in common – both ready to 'despise and hate' savagely, both beset by not dissimilar physical weaknesses. We have a description of Jane as 'of a middle size, finely shaped, and rather beyond what is called agreeable throughout her whole person. She was polite and well-bred, with at least a good share of understanding [i.e. intelligence]'. At the time of her marriage break-up, Swift told Stella that he was sorry for his sister, 'but her husband is a dunce, and with respect to him, she loses nothing by her deafness'.

It could be that Swift was using 'deafness' metaphorically. Jane may however have been deaf in actuality. She was delicate as well. When she came to England after the break-up of her marriage, she was given a post at Moor Park as Lady Giffard's waiting-woman – something between a companion and a personal maid – at £12 a year plus board and lodging. Not long after she began working for Lady Giffard, she had to leave and go into lodgings for a while because she was suffering from rheumatism.

'That lady', Swift wrote to Stella, referring to Lady Giffard, 'does not love to be troubled with sick people.' Actually he was finding Jane a nuisance himself, with her requests to him to get her son a place at Charterhouse, and her invitation to spend a week with her at Lady Giffard's. 'I will answer it with a vengeance', he told Stella. He had better things to do, and anyway he had fallen out with Lady Giffard.

We must become better acquainted with Lady Giffard, and Sir William and Lady Temple. Swift's time with them constituted his real education. And Stella, who loved him, was there from the beginning.

Chapter Three

TEMPLES

THE TEMPLE FAMILY are crucial. William Temple was the single most important influence on Jonathan Swift, and some Swiftians argue that Swift's relationship with the family was even closer.

William Temple married Dorothy Osborne in early 1655. Theirs is a famous courtship; her letters to him have been published. The sad irony was that Dorothy contracted smallpox before the marriage, and her beauty was destroyed by facial scars. The wedding went ahead. They spent the early years of their marriage in Ireland, in the house of Sir John Temple, William's father, in Dublin, and on one of his country estates in Co. Carlow.

William Temple lived with two women – his wife and his sister. The sister was Martha, ten years younger than he, who married Sir Thomas Giffard, a gentleman of Co. Meath, in Ireland in 1662. He died within a fortnight of the wedding. From then on Martha Giffard made her home with her brother, until he died. They had two other siblings, Henry and John.

William Temple's wife Dorothy was clever, and the ideal partner for a diplomat: discreet, cultivated, well informed. It was rumoured that some of Sir William's letters were drafted by Dorothy. But it was Martha Giffard who was most often with him as his companion and hostess in his diplomatic posts in the Low Countries, when his wife, prone to depressions and the spleen, remained in England with the children.

Martha Giffard was devoted to her brother and looked like him, with dark hair and large, heavy-lidded eyes. Both were conspicuously handsome. Later, in England, the Temples' widowed daughter-in-law and her two little girls joined the household. Apart from the usual roster of servants, there were also Bridget Johnson and her little daughter Esther (Stella), and young Rebecca Dingley, a poor relation of the Temples who made herself useful to Martha Giffard. All the Temples' children except two died in infancy. But throughout his life, William was surrounded by admiring females of all ages.

William Temple brought his wife and sister back to England in 1663. He could well, as a young man in Ireland, have known his father's entrepreneurial friend Godwin Swift, and maybe some of Godwin's brothers. Godwin Swift's family, perhaps facilitated by Sir John's influence over land acquisition, also gravitated in the direction of Co. Carlow. Godwin's son John had a place at Ballynunnery; Godwin junior lived at Swiftsheath, over the border in Co. Kilkenny.

There is also another Leicestershire link. Swift's mother, as a Leicestershire woman married to a Swift, would not have been an unknown quantity to the Temples. There had been Temples at Temple Hall – about five miles from Thornton, Abigail's father's Leicestershire parish – since the thirteenth century. 'Our' Temples had little claim on it, being descended from a younger son of four generations back. But in 1667, when William Temple was looking for a country house in England, he considered buying Temple Hall.

Old Sir John was against the plan, writing from Ireland:

> For first it is so ancient that it has quite lost the name, as well as the house, which is so ruinous, as a great sum of money will not repair; and it is only known now by another denomination, which I have forgot. Then the gentleman that bought it not long since and paid twenty years purchase for it, I believe will not part with it.

It sounds as if he had been there. Probably William had, too.

All in all, there is no mystery about why young Jonathan Swift, arriving from Ireland almost as a refugee, should be encouraged by his mother to apply to Sir William Temple, or why he should be found a place in the household. The Temples knew who he was. As Swift summarized it in the autobiographical fragment: 'The Troubles then breaking out, he went to his mother, who lived in Leicester; and after continuing there some months, he was received by Sir William Temple, whose father had been a great friend to the family.'

William Temple set up his English establishment just outside Richmond, on the river Thames west of London, in a hamlet called West Sheen, now swallowed up by modern Richmond. It was within walking distance of Richmond Palace – which, like many of the other royal palaces, was largely in ruins.

The former Charterhouse monastery on the Thames at West Sheen, linked eastward to Richmond Green by a lane, and abutting the Old Deer Park to the north, was also partly in ruins, with families perching in habitable sections of it, and new buildings being erected from the ancient materials.

In spring 1665, the year of the Great Plague, William Temple bought a lease on a house built within the sheltered precincts of this ruined monastery, in a great yard called Crown Court. He went off to the Low Countries on his first diplomatic mission, and moved his family into Sheen from Brussels the following year. Meanwhile he was made a baronet, as befitted his diplomatic standing, and became Sir William.

In the subsequent few years his family lived at Sheen when they were not with him abroad. He was already planning to enlarge his 'dominions' at Sheen, and to establish a garden within the sheltered monastery walls. He wanted to plant varieties of cherries to ripen right through from May to September, and to experiment with vines. He imported a new kind of apricot from Brussels.

After twenty years in public service, when he had fulfilled his final posting and served his term as ambassador at the Hague, he decided to 'retire to my corner at Sheen, and endeavour to pass the rest of my life as quietly and innocently as I can', as he wrote to his father, Sir John. He leased twenty acres of the Old Deer Park, south of the monastery walls, and bought two more houses in Crown Court. The diarist John Evelyn, dining in summer 1678 with Temple's neighbour, Henry Brouncker, noted how 'within this ample enclosure are several pretty villas, and fine gardens of the most excellent fruits'.

But Sir William had constant rows about party walls and private roads with Brouncker, whom Evelyn, his dinner guest, called a 'hard, covetous, vicious man'. Unwillingly, Temple agreed that Brouncker might open an access gate into Crown Court, breaking through the old wall. Several quarrels on, Brouncker claimed a right of way for carriages and carts through the court, thus ruining the quietness and privacy. This was in 1684, when Brouncker inherited his brother William's Irish peerage; and the year in which the Temples' beloved and only surviving daughter Diana died, aged fourteen. There was private grief and neighbourly unpleasantness among the villas and sheltered gardens.

When the Temples' son John married later that same year, Sir William, his wife and his household abandoned Sheen – with its orangery, and fruit trees, and espaliers, and hothouses, and many of his statues and paintings – to John and his new French wife, and moved to Surrey.

Sir William already had a home there, which he had bought in 1680. It was a red-brick Elizabethan house called Compton Hall, but he renamed it Moor Park after the house in Hertfordshire where he and his wife had spent their honeymoon, and whose formal gardens (later wiped out by Capability Brown) inspired him to create something along the same lines himself.

Gardening had became Sir William's passion. The light soil of Surrey was good for conifers. He made a bowling green against the south wall of his kitchen garden, and against the west wall he built his orangery, decorated with antique Roman heads and with a fountain flanked by heraldic dogs called talbots, the Temple family crest.

When Lord Brouncker, the horrible neighbour, died in early 1688, Sir William, with his wife and Martha Giffard, his sister, and their servants and retainers, came back to the house in Sheen. It was during this return to Sheen that the Temples' son John committed suicide. Shortly afterwards, Jonathan Swift, aged twenty-two, arrived from Leicester as secretary, at first for just a few months. It was at Sheen that Swift first met the eight-year-old Esther Johnson, known as Hetty, and to posterity as Stella.

It was at Sheen too that Swift first had an attack of the nausea, deafness and frightening giddiness which were to dog him all his life. The problem was probably Ménières disease, in chronic form. Since his sister Jane possibly suffered from deafness, there may have been some genetic predisposition. Swift went back to Ireland to see if he felt better in his native air. He did not, and returned to the Temples.

He ascribed his malady to eating a surfeit of fruit. One can see why he thought that. Sir William, who prescribed 'the eating of strawberries, common cherries, white figs, soft peaches, or grapes, before every meal', also favoured apples after meals. He recommended ripe fruit, in quantity; a portion of cherries for him was 'about forty cherries'. In later life Swift was wary about eating fruit at all, while retaining a passion for it.

Sir William had strong opinions about how one should live. Some of them stand the test of time. He was in favour of 'open air, easy labour, little care, simplicity of diet, rather fruits and plants than flesh, which easier corrupts, and water, which preserves the radical moisture'. He also recommended ground ivy as 'admirable in frenzies'; and dried millipedes, 'made up into little balls with fresh butter', for a sore throat.

Mostly, Sir William Temple gets a very good press. Lord Macaulay, writing in the 1840s, called him 'one of the most expert diplomatists and most pleasing writers of that age', and, as a public man, the one who had 'preserved the fairest character'. As a young man he sat briefly in both the Irish and English parliaments. His career as a diplomat began when he was already over thirty, in the reign of Charles II.

His most significant diplomatic postings were to the Low Countries, and his chief claim to fame is that he negotiated a peace between England and Holland and forged the Triple Alliance (of Sweden, England and Holland) in opposition to the territorial ambitions of Louis XIV of France.

William Temple and his wife also played a large part in fixing the marriage of Princess Mary, daughter of England's James II, to William of Orange: William, aged twenty-seven, came over to England briefly to marry the young princess. A good day for the Protestant succession and for the modernized, limited monarchy which Temple favoured; but a bad day for one unwilling sixteen-year-old girl.

As a writer, Temple has a distinctively emphatic voice and an easy, engaging prose style. For over a century after his death it was unthinkable, for anyone who read at all, not to have been familiar with Temple's histories and memoirs, and with his lively essays, published as a series of *Miscellanea*.

One of his literary ventures had repercussions for Swift. In the second volume of *Miscellanea*, in 1690, Temple included an essay 'Upon the Ancient and Modern Learning' which did nothing for his reputation. Temple was a cultivated man but his classical scholarship was superficial. He was conservative by temperament, and a loyal heir to the renaissance of classical learning. He believed that the civilizations of Greece and Rome furnished everything in literature, philosophy and science that humanity required; any thought worth thinking, every speculation worth pursuing, had already in his view been satisfactorily accomplished.

But there were two cultures. More muscular intellects were emancipating themselves from the straitjacket of classical learning and interesting themselves in the accomplishments of other civilizations and in the advances being made in natural philosophy – physics, physiology, and everything that we call science. Experimental 'improvements' in medicine, agriculture and technology were studied by groups of gentlemen meeting in Dublin and London in learned associations and societies. (Brouncker's brother William, a mathematician, had been the first president of the Royal Society.) Not that all moderns were scientists; the poet Dryden, Swift's kinsman, was on their side. Basically, the ancient–modern controversy was about whether human history was, or was not, a record of 'progress'.

Temple had an urbane distaste for all scientific treatises and similar 'pedantry', which he transmitted in full measure to Jonathan Swift. In his contentious essay, Temple championed writers of antiquity against the moderns, citing as an exemplar of excellence the Greek 'Epistles to Phalaris'. Sir William Temple did not know that serious scholars had proved the Phalaris letters to be spurious.

But members of the High Table at Christ Church, Oxford, were delighted with Temple's essay, since his traditionalist stance on the utter sufficiency of classical learning suited their own hidebound views. They commissioned Charles Boyle, a bright undergraduate from a distinguished family in Ireland, to prepare an edition of Phalaris, with the help of his tutor, the Revd Francis Atterbury. There was special piquancy in this, as young Boyle was nephew to a conspicuous 'modern', Robert Boyle, the great experimental physicist and chemist, who died in 1691. (Swift was to satirize Robert Boyle's methods in 'A Meditation upon a Broom Stick'.) Charles Boyle, the misled undergraduate editor, became fourth Earl of Orrery in 1703, and gave his name to an astronomical instrument invented by his protégé George Graham and christened an 'orrery' by Sir Richard Steele.

The Christ Church dons made fools of themselves over Phalaris. Two serious and distinguished classical scholars, Richard Bentley and William Wotton (both Cambridge men), rapidly went into print to demolish the pretensions of Temple, Boyle and Atterbury in a series of ripostes and counter-ripostes.

We would not be fretting over this academic controversy if Jonathan Swift, taking the side of Temple, his employer and mentor, had not in the late 1690s written *The Battle of the Books*, published with *A Tale of a Tub* in 1704 – 'perhaps the only valuable fruit', wrote Macaulay, 'of as silly a sally as ever diverted the mind of wits'. Dr Johnson thought that Swift did not properly understand the controversies, and misrepresented them. Wit, wrote Johnson, who admired Swift only moderately, 'can stand its ground against truth only a little while'.

But the essence of wit and polemic, and crucially of Swift's wit and polemic, is that it takes any argument to its logical conclusion and on beyond it – so that the argument topples over the edge into the absurd, and thus is outrageous, and unfair, and funny.

Swift was also, in his London years, a friend and sometime neighbour of the trouble-making Christ Church Tory (and covert Jacobite) Francis Atterbury, who was made Bishop of Rochester by Queen Anne – only because, some said, he was such a disastrous Dean of Christ Church. And in his years as Dean of St Patrick's in Dublin, Swift was a friend of the self-satisfied John, fifth Earl of Orrery, son of the editor of Phalaris. This Lord Orrery's first wife was a daughter of William III's squint-eyed mistress Lady Orkney; and he was to be one of Swift's early biographers.

No one has ever questioned William Temple's integrity, but many felt there was something missing in his character. Macaulay thought he was not a true patriot: 'He prized his ease and his personal dignity too much, and shrank from responsibility with a pusillanimous fear.' Cyril Connolly was among the later critics who found Temple's complacent epicureanism – 'practising moderation in a garden' – self-deceiving and suspect.

This can be seen in another way. One may admire Sir William Temple for valuing his private life – gardening, reading, writing, talking – more than his public life. At Moor Park he amassed his treasures – books, busts, paintings by Van Dyck, Titian, Holbein, Lely and Le Brun. He was too sophisticated to be any man's lackey, not even a king's. 'Bluntness and plainness in a Court', he wrote, was a sign of 'the most refined breeding. Like something in a dress that looks neglected, and yet is very exact.' It was better with great men to lean towards 'bluntness and coldness' than to flattery, which was artificial: 'Nothing so nauseous as undistinguish'd civility; 'tis like a whore, or an hostess, who looks kindly upon every body that comes in.'

This attitude is exactly that of Jonathan Swift, when he too was associating in his middle age with great men and women, though Swift characteristically took it even further. Swift adopted – and adapted to his more savage temperament and modes of expression – a great many of Temple's values and attitudes. Behaviours and opinions which are commonly characterized as uniquely Swiftian were picked up from Sir William Temple. Temple's views on the social order, on the ideal of national unity headed by a popular, limited monarchy, on the importance for stability of the landed, as opposed to the moneyed, interest, and on the necessity for Ireland to buy Irish manufactures instead of imports: all were taken on board by Swift, who in turn influenced the politicians of his maturity – particularly Lord Bolingbroke, in his book *The Idea of a Patriot King* (1738).

Sir William was bent on retirement. But he liked being consulted by King William, whom he had known since he was a boy in Holland, and he felt slighted if he were not. Temple was quick to express resentment at small mortifications. He was vain. He had an amorous temperament, and liked in old age to talk in a man-of-the-world way about his 'amours', boasting unattractively of 'his extraordinary abilities that way' which once upon a time 'had nearly killed him'.

Because of his family's formidable connections there, Temple was reckoned to be sound on Ireland. In context, this meant that Ireland should be ruled with a strong hand in the Protestant interest. (Under James II, restrictions on Roman Catholics had been relaxed.) Sir William was an autocratic father and it was without much enthusiasm that he let his only surviving son, John, enter the King's service. It was thought that, with his father behind him, the younger Temple would be also be sound on Ireland. John had already served in the Paris embassy, and had worked to get his wife's relations, imprisoned as Huguenots, released from the Bastille.

But Richard Hamilton, the distinguished Scottish military man whom John picked to negotiate in Ireland on behalf of William III with the Roman Catholic Lord Deputy, the Earl of Tyrconnell, ended up working alongside Tyrconnell for the Jacobite cause, in anticipation of James II's arrival in French ships and armed with French ammunition. When this disturbing news of betrayal reached London, neither the King nor anyone else blamed young John Temple in the least. Indeed, John's commission as Secretary at War was just being prepared.

But John Temple, overwhelmed by a sense of guilt and inadequacy, drowned himself. He took a boat at either Temple Stairs or Whitehall Stairs (accounts differ) and told the boatman to take him to Greenwich. Sitting in the boat, he wrote a few lines on a piece of paper with a pencil, and laid the paper on the seat along with the money for his fare. Then, as the boat passed under the central arch of London Bridge, he slipped overboard.

Various versions of his suicide note have survived. Macaulay's is 'My folly in undertaking what I could not execute hath done the King great prejudice which cannot be stopped – No easier way for me than this – May his undertaking prosper – May he have a blessing.' According to Sir William Temple's biographer, he wrote: 'From my father and mother I have had especially of late all the marks of tenderness in the world.'

Young John's will, made three years earlier, had a codicil: 'In case I die and my wife's fortune to be restored to her again, my Father must deduct the revenue of her estate in France, which I should have received for the time we were married, and did not and besides I paid for her at Paris things due by her before our marriage . . .'

I expect that William Temple contrived to extract the money from his daughter-in-law's estate. I find the Temples, as a family, to be pretty sharp about money, and at the same time emotionally extravagant. Sir William Temple, in his own will, directed that his heart be buried in a silver box under the sundial at Moor Park, and the rest of him in the south aisle of Westminster Abbey.

Sir William Temple moved back to Moor Park permanently at the end of this bad year. His sad wife – 'Mild Dorothea, peaceful, wise and great', as Swift apostrophized her – remained most of the time from now on in London, at a house owned by the Temples in Pall Mall. (She died in 1695.) When Swift came back from Ireland to Moor Park, Martha Giffard was to all intents and purposes the mistress of the house.

Temple's garden and greenhouses at Sheen fell into neglect; by

1693 he had sold all his holdings there. After his death, his sister Martha Giffard spent her winters in Dover Street in London and took for the summers an eleven-year lease on a house and garden at Sheen, probably part of the old family home. But all the houses in Crown Court were demolished by 1770. There is now a golf course on the site of the old Charterhouse.

The population of England was between five and six million; only about half the country was under cultivation. (The population of Ireland was something between a million and a million and a half.) The county of Surrey, where Sir William lived out the rest of his life, was a wild, uncultivated, thinly populated territory of unenclosed heaths, wooded hills and deep valleys. As Macaulay put it, 'his amusement during some years had been to create in the waste what those Dutch burgomasters, among whom he had spent some of the best years of his life, would have considered a Paradise'. King William, when he visited Moor Park to consult with Sir William, was well pleased to find in the wilderness a spot that looked as if it were transplanted from Holland, with its straight canal, terrace, rows of clipped trees, disciplined espaliers, and geometrically regular flowerbeds.

The politer corners of England, in fact, were going Dutch, and not just because William and Mary, like Temple at Moor Park, were laying out a formal Dutch garden at the mansion they had bought from the Earl of Nottingham in the village of Kensington, three inconvenient miles of muddy lanes away from Westminster. The United Provinces, or the United States – seven statelets combined for defence purposes – had huge significance for England, even before the Revolution. The Dutch were a major sea power and trading group, importing wine, tea and coffee, controlling the East European grain trade, and Baltic shipping.

The Dutch, now at the apogee of their power, were England's main commercial rivals. Armed naval confrontations in the 1650s and 1660s had been frequent. The awfulness of seeing Dutch ships impudently sailing up the Medway and throwing firebombs into the towns in 1667, the year of Swift's birth, was not easily forgotten. 'The State of Holland', wrote Sir William Temple in 1671, 'in point both of riches and strength, is the most prodigious growth.' The Dutch 'will ever seek to preserve themselves by an alliance with England against France, and by that of France against England'. There was, then, more than one reason for fostering an unbreakable bond between England and Holland.

William of Orange, England's William III, was not a king in his own country. Holland was a republic and William was the 'Stadholder'. England and Holland were not united under William; they remained wholly separate, linked by this strange man and by a common interest against the French.

Temple had liked the sociable, venal Charles II – his own contemporary – better than he ever liked James II, or William of Orange; but he admired William's seriousness. William's mother had been the eldest daughter of Charles I, but he was more Dutch than English and it was Mary, the Protestant elder daughter of the Catholic James II, who had the hereditary right to the throne of England. They ruled jointly as 'William and Mary', but she willingly conceded to him not only his regal title but the whole administration of government.

William of Orange was still in his thirties when he assumed the throne in England – but old for his age, never well, asthmatic, thin, weedy, beady-eyed, humourless, easily exhausted, short-tempered, charmless. His English was clumsy. He was not interested in the arts or the sciences. His one civilian passion was hunting, and riding dangerously. The English did not love him, but many respected his constitutional correctness, his military prowess and, of course, his unimpeachable Protestantism.

The English did not love the Dutch as a whole, either. They were stereotypically perceived in the 1680s and 1690s as big, greedy, vulgar, heavy-drinking (hence 'Dutch courage'), pipe-smoking, phlegm-spitting louts. Sir William Temple found them dull.

Yet there was another side to the story: Holland's astonishingly clean streets and canals, the scrubbed doorsteps and garden paths you could eat your dinner off, the obsessional (to the British) concern with laundry. Sir William Temple was amazed by their cleanliness – which tells you as much about English housekeeping as it does about the Dutch. As the Republic prospered, the rich Dutch evolved into a cultivated, bewigged upper class, creating a milieu at least as civilized as anything in England.

And now, the Dutch were in England, in what amounted to a peaceful invasion. After the 'Glorious' Revolution of 1689, many English and Irish acres, many named offices, and many hereditary titles were given to Dutch William's loyal Dutch officers who had brought about the rout of James II and his supporters.

The Dutchman William Bentinck became Earl and then Duke of Portland. He was also Groom of the Stole, a great office allowing access to the King's person at all times and commanding a huge salary. Zulestein was in charge of the Robes, Auverquerque was Master of the Horse. The new Earl of Athlone was the former General Ginkell, commander of William's forces in Ireland.

English aristocrats were mortified to find themselves preceded at Court by Dutch-speaking Dutchmen with English titles and estates. The Garters, Gold Keys, White Staves, rangerships and other ritual court sinecures that accrued to hereditary peers now went to Dutchmen. Some of these posts were for life. William van Huls, appointed Clerk to the Robes by William III in 1700, was still hanging in there throughout the reign of Queen Anne. With the top jobs came patronage, and the disposition of scores of lesser jobs, though to do him credit William III cut down on the number of sinecured hangers-on.

With the Dutch soldiers, administrators and functionaries came Dutch lawyers, doctors, cooks, gardeners and servants. It was said that the fire which destroyed the palace at Whitehall (apart from the Banqueting Hall, from which Charles I had stepped out to his execution) was started by a Dutch washerwoman. Two of the women who were close to Swift – Hester Vanhomrigh (Vanessa), and Laetitia Van Lewen (Mrs Pilkington) – had Dutch fathers. The Dutch also brought gin, and the techniques for distilling it. Within a generation, cheap gin was the grossly abused drug of choice for the English poor.

Some popular prejudice against the Dutch was inevitable. Pamphlets, broadsheets, news-sheets, periodicals – 'the media' in embryo – included attacks on 'Dutch favourites, Dutch guards, Dutch generals, a Dutch policy – everything Dutch – creeping in like the plagues of Egypt' and were passed around in the coffee-houses. Swift disliked the Dutch. (He disliked the Scots even more. He was not keen on the Germans or the Italians either.)

But Daniel Defoe, Swift's contemporary, published in 1701 a mordant poem called 'The True-Born Englishman', pointing out how 'That vain ill-natured thing, an Englishman' was but the mongrel descendant of previous waves of predatory foreigners – the Romans, the Vikings, the Normans – 'rascals' who were enriched and ennobled, as now were the Dutch. A Turkish horse, said Defoe, had a better pedigree than a so-called 'true-born Englishman':

> These are the heroes who despise the Dutch
> And rail at new-come foreigners so much;
> Forgetting that themselves are all deriv'd
> From the most scoundrel race that ever liv'd . . .

William and Mary's successor, Queen Anne, in retrospect, seemed 'good' by reason of her Englishness.

William and Mary had no children, and all Anne's children were stillborn or died young. By the Act of Settlement of 1701, the crown should have passed from Anne to James I's granddaughter, Sophia of Hanover. She died four months before Queen Anne; in the interests of a Protestant succession, and in spite of a flurry of intrigue among English and Scots Jacobites, the monarchy passed peacefully to her son George. On his accession, George brought over German favourites and German mistresses and German servants. He sacked Anne's English cook.

George I spent much of his reign back home in Hanover, and understood the English language so poorly that it was not worth his while, when he was in London, attending Cabinet meetings – thus setting a precedent that was sustained by all subsequent monarchs.

Modern England's grass-roots suspicion of a federal Europe may be accounted for by resentments which long ago became separated from any conscious memory of their origins.

The most important of William III's Dutch officers was Bentinck, Duke of Portland – a blunt, surly, loyal creature, who never learned to speak English well. He was the King's favourite. Their extreme closeness caused unease and speculation. In 1700 Portland married as his second wife Lady Berkeley, née Temple, niece to Sir William Temple and to Lady Giffard.

In the late 1690s Portland went as ambassador to France, where he lived with all the magnificence and ostentation of a small monarch. Meanwhile he was being supplanted at home in William's favour by young Arnold van Keppel, who had nicer manners, and got on better with the English, and who was also given an English title: he became the Earl of Albemarle. Swift thought the friendship was a sexual one, and that King William was 'male and female'.

Portland never got over the loss of his special relationship, but he did not suffer materially. When forfeited lands in Ireland were being redistributed, a fair amount went back to the ancient Catholic proprietors, in conformity with the Treaty of Limerick. But an area larger than many an English county was divided between Portland's eldest son and the Earl of Albemarle.

William III had a mistress, one of his wife's ladies-in-waiting. Several of the Temple nieces also waited upon Queen Mary; Martha Giffard too had taken her turn. But the King's choice fell on Elizabeth Villiers, whose husband he ennobled as the Earl of Orkney. (Lord Orkney was given the high-sounding title of Governor of Virginia; he governed this distant colony by proxy and never went there at all.)

Like James II, William III preferred plain women. Maybe, being less courted, they were felt to be more trustworthy. Lady Orkney, according to Macaulay, had many fine qualities but was 'destitute of personal attractions, and disfigured by a hideous squint'. She also was rewarded by a large chunk of Ireland. Swift, in his London years, was to grow very fond of her.

The English Parliament, resenting royal mistresses, Dutch incomers, and the right of Catholics in Ireland to own land, questioned all these land grants, much to William III's annoyance. The anti-Williamite pro-Jacobite pamphleteers added their voices too, after press censorship was ended in 1694 – a circumstance which was to be greatly advantageous to Swift's special talents.

William III had to watch his back. When in 1692 the idea of fixed three-year parliaments was under debate, he could not determine whether the arrangement would be to his personal advantage or not. So he sent Lord Portland down to Moor Park to consult his old mentor, Sir William Temple.

Sir William pronounced in favour of the bill for three-year parliaments. Portland was not convinced. Neither was his master. Sir William was not well enough, or said he was not well enough, to go up to London for further discussion with the King himself at Kensington Palace. Instead he sent his twenty-five-year-old secretary – Jonathan Swift.

Swift's physical energy was, in spite of his recurrent nausea and giddiness, phenomenal. Violent exercise was a necessity to him. At Moor Park, he would rise at intervals from his secretarial work and run up a hill behind the house and down again – half a mile each way.

He thought exercise was beneficial to his malady. It was also part of his natural assertiveness. Thirty years later he had a letter from William Flower, later Lord Castle Durrow, and a young relative of the Temples', recalling an incident of his childhood. The young Swift had been put in charge of the schoolboy Flower for the journey from Sheen to London by river. The boatman was 'very drunk and insolent' and refused to go further downriver than Hammersmith, while insisting, 'with very abusive language', on his full fare – which Swift 'very courageously refused'. A crowd gathered to hear the row. Flower expected Swift to be beaten up, but 'by your powerful eloquence you saved your bacon and money, and we happily proceeded on our journey'.

When Swift, on his first political commission, went to Kensington from Moor Park, he walked the thirty-eight miles there, and all the way back. At the Palace he was admitted into the closet – the King's private office – and gave the King a letter from Temple. He spelled out for his Majesty the essentials of its contents.

Temple's arguments for short, fixed-term parliaments favoured the King in that it made it easy for him to be rid, by statute, of ministries hostile to himself; but equally, it would force him to dissolve the ones that favoured him. It was this latter argument that prevailed with suspicious, touchy William, and Swift failed to convince him otherwise. In his autobiographical fragment, Swift wrote in the margin: 'This was the first time that Mr Swift had ever any converse with courts, and he told his friends it was the first incident that helped to cure him of vanity.'

When Swift left Moor Park for the second time, in 1694, it was after a serious quarrel with his employer. Swift felt becalmed at Moor Park. He wanted his real life to begin; he knew Sir William could use his considerable influence in getting him a position in the wider world. But Sir William wanted him to stay and go on making himself useful at Moor Park. In his capacity as absentee Master of the Rolls in Ireland, Temple did offer Swift a post in that office in Dublin, which was spurned.

Before he went back to Dublin Swift spent some time with his mother in Leicester, whence he wrote to his cousin Thomas: 'He [Sir William] was extream angry I left him, and yet would not oblige himself any further than upon my good behaviour, nor would promise anything firmly to me at all; so that every body judged I did best to leave him; I design to be ordained September next, and make what endeavours I can for something in the Church.' He only made this decision – not a vocation, a career decision – after he had turned down Temple's suggestion; he needed to take his destiny into his own hands.

Cousin Thomas immediately replaced him as Temple's secretary. Sir William Temple did more for Thomas, already ordained, than he did for Jonathan; he used his influence to have Thomas appointed rector of Puttenham, not far from Moor Park, soon after he arrived in Surrey. Thomas was milder, less eccentric, more amenable.

Before Swift could be ordained in Dublin, the Archbishop of Dublin – now Narcissus Marsh, previously Provost of Trinity – demanded a reference from Sir William 'of my conduct in your family', as Swift said in a long, careful, respectful letter regretting 'the many troubles' that he had caused his employer.

Duly ordained, Swift was appointed vicar of the seaside parish of Kilroot in the north of Ireland, near Belfast and the coastal town of Carrickfergus.

It was a dismal appointment. The little church at Kilroot was in ruins, though its dependent churches at Templecorran and Ballynure were usable. It was a strongly Presbyterian area. Swift's congregations were minuscule. If he had been frustrated at Moor Park – where at least there was gracious living, and a well-stocked library he could use, and intelligent conversation – he was even more frustrated in rural Kilroot.

The elderly Richard Dobbs, who lived at Castle Dobbs half a mile away, was Swift's most interesting contact there, a strong Protestant and 'a stern and upright man who suffered a good deal from the gout' – as did Sir William Temple. Swift spent much time at Castle Dobbs, and read in its library.

In 1689, five years previously, during the Troubles, this corner of Co. Antrim had been the scene of epic drama. William's general, the German mercenary the Duke of Schomberg, had marched on Carrickfergus, and Dobbs, then the mayor, had been briefly put in jail by the (Catholic) governor. When Schomberg prevailed, Dobbs had been the one joyfully to hand over to him the town's regalia. Later in the year William III himself landed at Carrickfergus, and Dobbs had presented him with a loyal address. These were stirring tales to be retailed to the new vicar of Kilroot, Jonathan Swift.

Schomberg had been killed at the Battle of the Boyne in 1690, when the Williamite army definitively overcame James II's forces. Swift had been in Ireland then, on his first brief absence from Sir William's household: he wrote two ponderous odes celebrating King William's victories. Years later, as Dean of St Patrick's, Swift had a memorial stone to Schomberg erected in his cathedral, after vain attempts to persuade the Schomberg family to fund a monument themselves. The inscription reads, reproachfully (in Latin): 'The renown of his valour had greater power among strangers than had the ties of blood among his kith and kin.'

In the peace, there seemed only stagnation. Richard Dobbs described Swift's parish, with the exception of his own family 'and some half-dozen that lie under me', as being 'all presbyterian and Scotch, not one natural Irish in the parish, or a papist'. Swift's animosity towards Scottish Presbyterians was reinforced by Dobbs and by the lonely futility of his own ministry in Kilroot; all his life, Swift disapproved vehemently of dissenters and non-conformists, protesting bitterly against all and any moves towards tolerance and inclusion.

Dissent always seemed to him a far greater threat to the Anglican Church than did Catholicism. Catholics in Ireland, he later wrote, were 'altogether as inconsiderable as women and children. Their lands are almost entirely taken from them, and they are rendered incapable of purchasing any more.' The result was that Catholicism 'will daily crumble away':

'Tis agreed among naturalists that a lion is a larger, a stronger, a more dangerous enemy than a cat; yet if a man were to have his choice, either a lion at his foot, bound fast with three or four chains, his teeth drawn out, and his claws pared to the quick, or an angry cat in full liberty at his throat; he would take no long time to determine.

The cat represents dissenters and non-conformists. Swift's convictions in this area verge on bigotry. In the light of the subsequent history of Ireland, the views of the sensible second wife of Swift's friend Lord Orrery have a prophetic quality (though neither she nor Swift could have conceived of the twentieth-century marginalization of the Anglican Church in Ireland). She wrote to her husband in 1751: 'Swift's bitterness against the Presbyterians I am confident did a great deal of harm in keeping up the spirit of division amongst us, so unworthy in X-tians, and sowing dislike in the breast of one honest man to another honest man.' Lady Orrery herself had used to abhor Presbyterians and Catholics equally, 'yet I have so far got the better of these wrong prejudices as to see the merit of persons in both these sects, and to pray to God Almighty that he will be pleased mercifully to break down the middle wall of partition between us'.

Swift, bored and disappointed in Kilroot, did what most young men in such a situation would do, and what he said he always did when 'something goes amiss in my affairs'. He got involved with a woman.

Chapter Four

THE LADIES

WHAT SWIFT DREADED was nothingness, and nothing happening. He had written to cousin Thomas from Moor Park in 1693 that he 'was never very miserable while my thoughts were in a ferment for I imagine a dead calm to be the troublesomest part of our voyage thro the world'.

Swift had known Jane Waring's brother and cousins at Trinity, and his uncle Adam Swift, who lived in the north of Ireland, was a friend of the family. Jane was a local archdeacon's pious daughter, seven years younger than himself – i.e. about twenty-one when he became involved with her. She was in delicate health. He made up his own name for her – 'Varina', a feminine Latinization of 'Waring'.

All we know about this affair derives from the two long, uncomfortable, hectoring letters to her which have survived. He abandoned Kilroot after only a year, leaving behind his books and papers, and debts to a tailor and an innkeeper. He decided that the distinguished devil he knew, at Moor Park, was temporarily preferable to the isolation and sterile ministry of his Ulster parish – or, as he put it to Varina: 'I am once more offered the advantage to have the same acquaintance with greatness that I formerly enjoyed, and with better prospect of interest.' Sir William Temple wooed him back with hints of obtaining for him a Church appointment in England.

Before Swift left Kilroot, he proposed marriage to Varina. The first letter we have is a follow-up to his proposal: 'You have now had time to consider my last letter, and to form your own resolutions upon it.' He told her of this plans for leaving Ireland, 'and how far you will stretch the point of your unreasonable scruples to keep me here, will depend upon the strength of the love you pretend for me'.

He is reproaching her for prevaricating. She makes him 'restless and uneasy', for 'a violent desire is little better than a distemper, and therefore men are not to blame in looking after a cure. I find myself hugely infected with this malady . . .' This is the only known instance of Swift admitting himself to be in sexual thrall to a woman.

He tries to persuade her that marriage will cure her own maladies also: 'Varina's life is daily wasting, and though one just and honourable action would furnish health to her, and unspeakable happiness to us both, yet some power that repines at human felicity has that influence to hold her continually doating upon her cruelty, and upon me the cause of it.' He did not want to live on her money, he assured her, and she could live wherever she liked while he established himself in the world 'with all the eagerness and courage imaginable'. All their friends, he said, wished to see them married. 'Is it possible you cannot be yet insensible to the prospect of a rapture and delight so innocent and so exalted? Trust me, Varina.' To deny the violence of her own inclinations might pass as a virtue, but it was 'folly as well as injustice'.

He ended with an ultimatum: 'Only remember, that if you still refuse to be mine, you will quickly lose, for ever lose, him that is resolved to die as he has lived, All yours, Jon. Swift.'

Varina was unable to make up her mind either to marry him or to forget him entirely. His successor at Kilroot, the Revd John Winder, kept him abreast of local gossip. 'You mention a dangerous rival for an absent lover', Swift wrote to Winder early in 1698. 'If the report proceeds please inform me.'

During his first two sojourns at Moor Park, Swift was a young man marking time. When he returned in 1696, remaining until Sir William's death in 1699, he was a twenty-nine-year-old clergyman. His position in the Temple household was still not illustrious; but it was not untypical.

The lower ranks of the clergy were not, until stipends improved in the middle of the eighteenth century, filled by younger sons of the aristocracy, moving smoothly from ordination to smart chaplainships to fashionable parishes and on to deaneries and bishoprics. The lower reaches of the Church did, however, provide a career ladder out of the tradesman class (as in Swift's mother's family). If a newly ordained young man lacked the connections necessary to obtain a curacy in a desirable parish, then attaching himself to a gentleman's household was one of the pleasanter ways of keeping body and soul together.

A clergyman in a private house at this time, according to Macaulay, was expected to say grace before and after meals, read prayers, provide conversation for bored and boring guests and insufficiently occupied ladies, give spiritual or literary assistance and advice, or occupy the children and young people, in return for his keep and a small stipend.

A clergyman thus employed sounds like a Victorian governess, or a poorly treated au pair girl of today: 'Sometimes the reverend man nailed up the apricots; and sometimes he curried the coach horses. He cast up the farrier's bills. He walked ten miles with a message or a parcel. He was permitted to dine with the family; but he was expected to content himself with the plainest fare. He might fill himself with the corned beef and carrots' – but was expected to leave the table before the desserts appeared, and only returned to say grace after the meal, 'from a great part of which he had been excluded'.

Swift's duties were not inconsistent with this version. From the beginning, they had included reading aloud to Sir William, keeping the household accounts, writing and copying letters, and transcribing Lady Giffard's translations from the Spanish. During his last period at Moor Park he also copied Temple's English correspondence from his diplomatic days, and translated the French correspondence, for publication.

Hetty Johnson (Stella), by then a bright teenager, helped him with the copying. A devoted and exigent tutor, he helped her with her reading and writing. He and she created a world of their own, bent over their books and papers, by means of a private, allusive baby-language; Swift was verbally ingenious and agile. He had a great liking for codes, riddles and puns.

He did not act as chaplain; Sir William himself read the daily family prayers. He was occasionally sent up to Kensington Palace with further messages. At the end of 1698 Martha Giffard wrote to her niece Lady Berkeley (the one who was later to marry Lord Portland) that she had sent 'the secretary' with 'another compliment from Papa to the King, where I fancy he is not displeased with finding occasions of going'. (Lady Giffard always called her brother 'Papa'.) Swift may also have sat in on conversations between the King and Sir William at Moor Park. 'I heard King William say', he reminisced years later, 'that if the people of Ireland could be believed in what they said of each other, there was not an honest man in the kingdom.'

In the same letter, Lady Giffard discussed with her Berkeley niece the servant problem, in her case a servant surplus. She had turned away one waiting-woman, as '3 gentlewomen had bin a little too much state as I make use of my cousin Dingley whenever I am in want. Hetty's place being the height of her ambition!' Hetty Johnson, a servant's daughter, enjoyed a privileged position closer to Lady Giffard's person than her own young cousin, Rebecca Dingley.

It is possible to see Swift as Temple's admiring disciple, and Temple as a unique, unforgettable, and hugely influential father-figure in his life.

There is also evidence that the relationship was scratchy and explosive, and that Swift resented his ambiguous position in the house and Temple's treatment of him. William Temple's nephew, Jack Temple, was at pains to stress how Swift was never admitted into the heart of the household, on account of his boorishness and ill-breeding: 'Sir William never favoured him with his conversation, because of his ill qualities, nor allowed him to sit at table with him.' Young Jonathan's 'bitterness, satire, moroseness' made him 'insufferable both to equals and inferiors, and unsafe for his superiors to countenance'.

Jack Temple is a hostile witness. He was Lady Giffard's favourite nephew, and her executor. He was never much at Moor Park when Swift was living there. He took his cue, and his information, from Lady Giffard, who had her own reasons for disliking Swift. Jack Temple's hostility was reciprocated. In London in 1710, Swift wrote to Stella, 'I thought I saw Jack Temple and his wife pass me to-day in their coach; but I took no notice of them. I am glad I have wholly shaken off that family.'

Swift's asides in later letters to Stella also confirm the prickliness of his relationship with Sir William. In April 1711, when he was in London and working with and for the government, he took offence at Mr Secretary St John's sudden coolness towards him, and wrote to her:

I made him a very proper speech, told him I observed he was much out of temper; that I did not expect he would tell me the cause . . . and one thing I warned him of, never to appear cold to me, for I would not be treated like a schoolboy; that I had felt too much of that in my life already, meaning from Sir William Temple, that I expected every great minister, who honoured me with his acquaintance, if he heard or saw any thing to my disadvantage, would let me know in plain words, and not put me in pain to guess.

Looking back the next day over what he had written, he expanded on it: 'Why, I think what I said to Mr Secretary was right. Don't you remember how I used to be in pain when Sir William Temple would look cold and out of humour for three or four days, and I used to suspect a hundred reasons.'

No daily contact between a clever, touchy, ambitious young man and an equally clever, self-satisfied, worldly-wise old one, accustomed to monopolizing the conversation and having his own way, could ever run smoothly. But each had a lot to give the other. Swift had a curiosity about how the great world worked, a mental agility and a literary gift which were both exploited and nurtured by living alongside Sir William. At Moor Park there was a fine library and endless talk. Swift acquired his political and literary education there. He wrote in his 'Ode to Sir William Temple':

> Shall I believe a spirit so divine
> Was cast in the same mold as mine?
> Why then does Nature so unjustly share
> Among her elder sons the whole estate?

I don't think he was being either sarcastic or sycophantic, but was expressing frustration at his own lack of achievement. He wrote to his cousin Thomas, of Sir William, that 'I never read his writings but I prefer him to all others at present in England, which I suppose is all but a piece of self love, and the likeness of humors makes one fond of them as if they were one's own.' Swift himself was desperate to be a poet; he *was* a poet, though at this stage of a heavy-handed and conventional kind.

He first saw his work in print in 1691, when his 'Ode to the Athenian Society' was published. Odes were what he wrote. He worked at his poetry for two hours in the early mornings, 'and that only when the humor sits' – sometimes he managed two stanzas a day, sometimes two stanzas took a whole week, 'and when all's done I alter them a hundred times'.

He was not trying to be innovative. His model was his boyhood favourite, Abraham Cowley, who died the year he was born. Late in life he quoted (but with ironic intent) two lines of Cowley's love poetry, 'which I thought extraordinary at fifteen'.

He was 'over-fond' of his own writings and read his work over and over again, he told Thomas, adding, 'I know 'tis a desperate weakness and has nothing to defend it but its secrecy'. He was, he said, like a baboon praising her own young, 'and indeed I think the love in both is much alike'. But he suspected he was on the wrong track. 'I cannot write anything easy to be understood tho it were in praise of an old shooo.'

Meanwhile in 1693 William Congreve, two years his junior at Kilkenny School and at Trinity, was already famous and fêted in London for his successful play *The Double-Dealer*, which made Swift's social and literary obscurity even more painful. He wrote a long poem to Congreve, warning the younger man, from his own rustic perspective, to stay clear of the world's corruption, and stressing 'the mighty gulph' between their two worlds. I don't think Congreve ever saw the poem.

But Swift can hardly have been so boorish as Jack Temple made out, or Sir William would not have sent him as his personal emissary to the King. He may have eaten his meals in the steward's room during his first, short period of employment, but later he was treated with respect by the servants. When Temple and his sister were away for several months in London in 1698, with Stella, her mother, and the rest of their retinue in attendance, Swift wrote to Stella from the solitude of Moor Park. He told her that Lady Giffard's parrot was pining, 'the miserablest creature in the world; and if his finger does but ake, I am in such a fright you would wonder at it'. He affected to be delighted by the family's absence: 'for now I live in great state, and the cook comes in to know what I please to have for dinner: I ask very gravely what is in the house, and accordingly give orders for a dish of pigeons, or, etc.'.

His value to Sir William Temple is incontrovertible. On Swift's brief return to Ireland in 1690, Sir William had written a recommendation for him (in the vain hope that he might land a secretarial post or a Trinity fellowship), in which he both expressed confidence in Swift's qualities and confirmed the Temples' close association with the Swift family: 'He has Latin and Greek, some French, writes a very good and current hand, is very honest and diligent, and has good friends though they have for the present lost their fortunes in Ireland and his whole family having been long known to me obliged me thus far to take care of him.'

When Sir William died in 1699, Swift travelled to the funeral in one of the three family coaches, with William Dingley – a young cousin on the Temple side, and Rebecca Dingley's brother – as his companion. Sir William, in a codicil to his will, left £100 to William Dingley, then an Oxford undergraduate; and to Jonathan Swift, 'now dwelling with me', exactly the same sum. More importantly, he made Swift his literary executor, with instructions to publish the latter part of his memoirs.

Yet Swift felt, with some justification, that Temple promised much, and delivered little. Temple said he would secure a position in the Church for Swift from King William. Swift overestimated not only Temple's goodwill but his influence. Temple was old, he was yesterday's man. Ambitious young parsons and would-be writers needed a powerful patron. That was the accepted system. All Swift had from Temple was the literary executorship.

His mature if defensive appraisal, expressed a quarter of a century later to Lord Palmerston (Sir William's ennobled eldest nephew, son of his brother John), was that he owned himself 'indebted to Sir William Temple for recommending me to the late King, though without success, and for his choice of me to take care of his posthumous writings'. He had remained at Moor Park only in order to profit from Sir William's 'conversation and advice, and the opportunity of pursuing my studies. For, being born to no fortune, I was at his death as far to seek as ever, and perhaps you will allow that I was of some use to him.'

The literary executorship was a mixed blessing. It was Swift's editing and publication of the Temple memoirs which occasioned the row with Sir William's sister Martha Giffard. Her hostility, conveyed to her influential acquaintances, did him lasting harm.

Lady Giffard was adamant that she did not want the last volume of her brother's memoirs published until Lady Essex was dead. The memoirs gave a critical picture of the old lady's late husband, the Earl of Essex, who in 1683 was accused of plotting against Charles II, and was sent to the Tower, where he cut his own throat with a razor.

His widow then sank into a depression, from which Sir William Temple had tried to raise her with an alarmingly bracing letter. This sad lady was a close friend of Lady Giffard's, and even pressed Lady G. to live with her after Sir William's death.

There were other family connections: the Duchess of Somerset, a close friend of Sir William Temple and Martha Giffard, was a niece of the unfortunate if treacherous Lord Essex; Martha had shown the manuscript to the Duchess, who had agreed that it should certainly be suppressed.

The Duchess of Somerset was a dangerous enemy to make. She was the daughter of the Duke of Northumberland, and a wealthy and startlingly attractive redhead twice widowed before she was sixteen; by the time the memoir was published she was high in the favour of William's successor, Queen Anne, and on intimate terms with her. Another complication was that a son of Lord Essex had married a daughter of Lord Portland, already related by marriage to the Temples.

Temple's memoir had been written in hot blood before this web of friendship and kinship had been fully woven, at a time when he felt Lord Essex was playing a double game not only with the King but with himself. This humiliation and resentment had been one of his reasons for retiring from public life. 'I had learn'd', Temple wrote in this volume, 'by living long in courts and public affairs, that I was fit to live no longer in either. I found the arts of a court were contrary to the frankness and openness of my nature.'

Swift published the memoir in 1709, ten years after Temple's death. His preface proves that he knew he was behaving equivocally in putting before the public what was perhaps a private, too-personal account: 'It was perfectly in compliance to some persons for whose opinions I have great deference, that I so long withheld the publication of the following papers. They seem'd to think, that the freedom of passages in these memoirs might give offence to several who were still alive.' He airily disassociated himself from such scruples, 'since I am not of an age to remember those transactions, nor had any acquaintance with those persons whose counsels or proceedings are condemn'd, and who are all of them now dead'.

Lady Giffard was furious, and her friends and relations rallied behind her. Sir John Danvers, a cousin, expressed no surprise in this day and age to find someone 'sacrificing their deceased friends to their present pecuniary interest. This I presume was the motive that induced Dr Sw—— to expose all your brother's papers that would yield him money.' (Swift received £40 from the printer for his volume.) 'Indeed this behaviour is inexcusable and may be remembered longer than any of his good qualities.'

The Duchess of Somerset too had her say, writing to Lady Giffard: 'I remember we both agreed with you that it was not proper to be made public during my Aunt Essex's life and I am sure Doctor Swift has too much wit to think it is, which makes him having done it unpardonable and will confirm me in the opinion I had before of him that he is a man of no principle either of honour or religion.' She no doubt transmitted this opinion to the Queen, whose confidante she was.

A couple of years later, in 1711, Swift, having found his voice as a polemicist, was to strike back at the Whig Duchess, ostensibly in the Tory cause, with the one weapon he had – his cruel and biting wit. His scurrilous squib ('The Windsor Prophecy') played on her lecherous and devious nature, albeit veiled in coded references – easily crackable. This did much for his fame and notoriety and nothing at all for his reputation with the Queen or the dignitaries of the Church of England, on whom he depended for preferment.

Swift also wrote a stiff letter to Lady Giffard after she put an advertisement in a newspaper 'in order to ruin my reputation', accusing him of having printed the memoir from an unfaithful copy:

> Those memoirs were printed by a correct copy exactly after the same manner as the author's other works were: he told me a dozen times, upon asking him, that it was his intention they should be printed after his death, but never fixed anything about the time. The corrections were all his own, ordering me to correct in my own copy as I received it, as he always did.

He had not consulted her in advance 'on purpose to leave you without blame'.

The repercussions of his decision to publish Temple's memoir was one among many contributions to his failure to land 'the great fish' of ecclesiastical preferment in England which he so much wanted and always expected.

On one level he did know the connection between his reckless actions and their consequences. In an undated sermon, he spoke about the common sight of seeing a man running headlong into 'sin and folly': 'Tell him that what he is going to do . . . will blacken his reputation, which he had rather die than lose', and still he 'rusheth into the sin like a horse into battle'. Such a man imagines that all he has to do is 'like a silly child to wink hard', expecting 'to escape a certain and infinite mischief, only by endeavouring not to see it'.

The scurrilous personal invective that Swift was so often to let loose upon the world may not, in the terms of his sermon, always have been a sin; the men and women he targeted sometimes deserved everything they got. But it was certainly, given his temporal ambitions, a perverse kind of folly – and part of his peculiar genius, which was not to be denied expression. That was his dilemma.

Our dilemma is that this particular sermon, 'On the Difficulty of Knowing One's-Self', cannot be categorically said to be by Swift. It was published as his, because it was in a bundle with his others, and the handwriting, said its editor in 1745, bore 'a great similitude to the Dean's'. But the title page, on which the Dean always wrote a memo as to when and where it was preached, was apparently missing. The original is lost. I believe, from the form and structure, that it is his. If it isn't, it was written with Swift in mind by some astute fellow-cleric who understood him very well, and Swift preserved it.

For ten years after Sir William Temple's death, Swift divided his time between Ireland and England. He attempted, via Lord Romney, to obtain from King William the prebend he thought he had been promised at Canterbury or Westminster, without success.

He felt Romney had not really tried, and this lasting grievance was what elicited the outburst about the 'old vicious illiterate rake' over a quarter of a century later, in the fragment of autobiography. Grievance against Romney also inspired Swift's poem 'The Problem' – not for publication, but passed around in manuscript – which has the promiscuous peer, unnamed but identifiable, farting uncontrollably during sexual intercourse.

It was not that Swift wanted only and absolutely to succeed in the Church; that was just one of the possibilities. Bishops sat in the House of Lords and were instrumental in legislation. Hopes of a literary career and/or some civil position were equally present in his mind. He wanted to make his mark on the world. He wanted fame and a name, and above all a platform.

He returned to Dublin a couple of months after Temple's funeral as secretary and chaplain to Charles, the second Earl of Berkeley, who was appointed a Lord Justice. He never went back to Kilroot, and imagined the position with Lord Berkeley to be a lasting one.

It was not, and again he was disappointed. He felt that Lord Berkeley, in recompense, should have used his influence to have him appointed to the vacant deanery of Derry. He was not even considered by Archbishop Narcissus Marsh. There was absolutely no reason why he should have been. He had no track record in the Church. Nevertheless, it was another disappointment. Swift's ambitions and expectations were completely unrealistic. He thus effectively courted disappointment.

He remained friendly with the Berkeleys, and especially with the Earl's pretty young daughter Lady Betty, with whom he played cards and wrote silly rhymes, including one, while he was still the family chaplain, for her maid Frances Harris, in Frances's persona:

> So the chaplain came in; now the servants say
> he is my sweetheart
> Because he's always in my chamber, and I
> always take his part . . .

One of his duties, as chaplain, was to read improving books aloud to Lady Betty. She liked the *Meditations* of the great scientist Sir Robert Boyle, which Swift did not. He inserted one day in the volume a few mock-solemn pages of his own entitled 'A Meditation upon a Broom Stick', and gravely read it out to his young pupil: 'But a broomstick, perhaps, you will say, is an emblem of a tree standing on its head; and pray what is man, but a topsy-turvy creature, his animal faculties perpetually mounted on his rational, his head where his heels should be . . .'

Lady Betty was taken in; and the trick, when 'smoked' (contemporary slang for 'getting' a joke), was much appreciated by the household.

Lady Betty later married Sir John Germaine, thirty years older than herself and reputed to be an illegitimate son of King William. Widowed, Lady Betty spent much of her life as a permanent guest with her own apartments at Knole, the great house in Kent belonging to the first Earl of Dorset (with whom Swift had uncomfortable relations when he was Lord-Lieutenant of Ireland). Lady Betty was said to be the particular friend of the Duchess.

Lady Betty also remained the particular friend of Swift. A fine portrait of him in plump and healthy-looking early middle age still hangs at Knole, and belonged to Lady Betty. Although she was a Whig and he attached himself to the Tories, they exchanged gossipy letters and sent each other presents, and they met when they were both in London. 'Lady Betty Germain and I were disputing Whig and Tory to death this morning', he told Stella in 1711. 'She is grown very fat, and looks mighty well.' Swift was also fond of Lady Betty's companion Biddy Floyd, much scarred by smallpox; he wrote a graceful verse tribute to her qualities:

> These Venus cleans'd from ev'ry spurious grain
> Of nice, coquet, affected, pert, and vain.
> Jove mix'd all up, and his best clay imploy'd,
> Then call'd the happy composition, Floyd.

The relationship with Varina had continued, inconclusively, throughout his last years at Moor Park, though their correspondence has not survived. The last long letter he wrote to her from Dublin, in 1700, implies that it was now she who was keen on marriage; and that she was agitated by the changed tone of his letters.

He explained to her rather formally and laboriously that her health, his lack of money, and her attitude accounted for the change in him. He had over the years pleaded his cause in every way possible. 'All I had in answer from you, was nothing but a great deal of arguing, and sometimes in a style so very imperious as I thought might have been spared, when I reflected how much you had been in the wrong.'

He told her that his uncle Adam Swift had asked him what his intentions were – put up to it, he was sure, by Varina herself. He had told his uncle 'that if your health and my fortune were as they ought, I would prefer you above all your sex; but that, in the present condition of both, I thought it was against your opinion, and would certainly make you unhappy'.

A complaining discontent seems to have been Varina's usual state. He set her some hard questions. Was she ready to live on perhaps less than £300 a year? Would she 'comply with my desires and humor'? Would she improve her mind at his direction 'so as to make us entertaining company for each other, without being miserable when we are neither visiting nor visited'? Could she guarantee to be always good-humoured? Could she put up with 'the cross accidents of life', and be happier with him, wherever he was, than in courts and cities without him?

If she could say yes to all this, 'I shall be blessed to have you in my arms, without regarding whether your person be beautiful, or your fortune large. Cleanliness in the first, and competence in the other, is all I look for.'

Honour demanded that he gave her this chance. But he wrote as if expecting a negative response to all his questions, and by their chilliness he ensured it. I think he felt too abused by her treatment of him to expect any radical change, and that the 'distemper' of his desire had burned itself out. Besides, there was Stella. He had plans for her.

Disappointed of a deanery, he had just been appointed to the parish of Laracor, a mile out of Trim – and near the site of the Battle of the Boyne – in Co. Meath, and within twenty miles, or a short day's ride on horseback, of Dublin. Laracor was within the Protestant pale, but as in Kilroot his congregation was small.

There were fewer than twenty Protestant families in this largely Catholic area, most of them wealthy gentlefolk. He was very busy, he was to write to the rector of Trim, John Stearne, 'being to preach today before an audience of at least 15 people, most of them gentle, and all simple'.

He took – by paying for it, as was the way – the degree of Doctor of Divinity at Trinity. He was Dr Jonathan Swift. With his appointment to Laracor and its associated smaller benefices came a plum: a prebend in St Patrick's Cathedral in Dublin. This put him in touch with the centre of Irish ecclesiastical life and ecclesiastical politics, while the only duties of a prebendary were to attend meetings of the cathedral chapter and to preach in the cathedral at rare intervals.

There was no vicarage house for him at Laracor; and, as he told Varina discouragingly, 'there is no other way but to hire a house at Trim, or build one on the spot; the first is hardly to be done, and the other I am too poor to perform at present'.

Some months later Stella (aged twenty), and her close friend from Moor Park, Rebecca Dingley (aged thirty-five), uprooted themselves and came over to Ireland, and to Trim. Apart from one trip back in

1707, the two women never saw England again for the rest of their lives.

Sir William Temple had left Stella leases in Ireland which brought in an income, and money went further in Ireland than in England. That was the explanation that Swift gave for her emigration in his autobiographical fragment, and I think it need fool no one. He wanted her presence and her company. If, at this stage, he wanted anything more, only he could know; I don't believe he did really know. But with Stella (known by the courtesy title accorded to all adult women, married or not, as Mrs Johnson) and Rebecca Dingley in Ireland, he had a sort of family.

Swift lodged at first in Trim, and became a close acquaintance of John Stearne, Trim's rector. Stearne was appointed Dean of St Patrick's in 1703 and was succeeded in Trim by John Raymond, 'a man of learning and fine address, with the advantage of a tall, handsome and graceful person', according to Swift's later friend Lord Orrery. Swift liked Dr Raymond (though he was utterly disgusted by the number of children he and his wife produced), and Dr Raymond became a particular ally of Stella and Rebecca – the Ladies.

The Ladies did not share a household with Swift. That would not have done. There was initially some interested speculation about the real reason for their arrival. Deane Swift, reflecting family lore, stated categorically that Stella had come to live in Ireland not for the economic reasons given in the autobiographical fragment, but 'to captivate the heart of Dr Swift'. Swift never denied that the move had been his idea. And yet, they remained single and separate. The Ladies took their own lodgings when they were in Dublin, and in the country they stayed with the Raymonds or in a cottage on the Percival estate.

A pleasant way of life evolved of constant informal visits and small entertainments and hospitalities, with much card-playing and backgammon. Swift liked to imagine them all at it when he was away. 'Stella, you lost three shillings and fourpence t'other night at Stoyte's, yes you did, and Presto [Swift himself] stood in a corner, and saw you all the while, and then stole away. I dream very often I am in Ireland . . .'

Stella's position as Dr Swift's protégée and special friend was so potentially ambiguous that she and Rebecca Dingley neither sought nor gained the acquaintance of society ladies. She lived 'among books and men', wrote Lord Orrery. The Ladies were emphatically accepted among Swift's friends – mostly fellow-clergymen, whether bachelors or married to comfortable, un-smart wives, and including, when they were in town, the bachelor William King, the Archbishop of Dublin. The Ladies' demeanour and the decorum of their life – alongside but not with Dr Swift – reassured these divines as to the utter respectability of the connection.

He visited them in their lodgings often enough. In bed on a freezing morning in London in 1711 he wrote to the Ladies: 'Starving, starving, uth, uth, uth, uth, uth. Don't you remember I used to come into your chamber, and turn Stella out of her chair, and rake up the fire in a cold morning, and cry uth, uth, uth? etc. O faith I must rise, my hand is so cold I can write no more.'

The two Ladies went everywhere and did everything together. The permanent members of what Swift called their 'gang' or their 'club', in Dublin, were John Stearne, as Dean of St Patrick's – 'your Dean', as Swift referred to him with a hint of anxious jealousy (Stearne was unmarried); Archdeacon and Mrs Walls in Queen Street; Alderman Stoyt and 'good, kind, hearty Mrs Stoyt', and Mrs Stoyt's spinster sister Catherine, out at Donnybrook; and Mr and Mrs Isaac Manley (he was postmaster-general). Sometimes, in later years, Swift worried about the narrowness of the circle. 'Have you got no new acquaintance? poor girls'; no one, he wrote, knew their 'good qualities'.

Swift referred to the two women frequently and freely in letters to their friends when he was away, and in terms which show that the pupil–teacher relationship established when Stella was a little girl still obtained: 'I am mightily afraid the Ladies are very idle, and do not mind their book. Pray put them upon reading', he wrote to the Revd William Tisdall, three years after the Ladies' arrival in Ireland, 'and be always teaching something to Mrs Johnson, because she is good at comprehending, remembering, and retaining . . . It is a pleasant thing to hear you talk of Mrs Dingley's blunders, when she has sent me a list with above a dozen of yours . . .'

Just a few weeks later this same William Tisdall announced himself to Swift as a suitor for Stella's hand in marriage, asking him to speak to her mother in England on his behalf. This came as a bit of a shock. Swift must have answered sharply; for Tisdall's next letter says: 'You have got three epithets for my former letter, which I believe are all unjust; you say it was unfriendly, unkind, and unaccountable.' Tisdall suspected an ulterior motive. Swift replied with what he called 'the naked truth' about his interest in the matter:

> First, I think I have said to you before, that if my fortunes and humour served me to think of that state [marriage], I should certainly, among all persons on earth, make your choice; because I never saw that person whose conversation I entirely valued but hers; this was the utmost I ever gave way to. And, secondly, I must assure you sincerely, that this regard of mine never once entered my head as an impediment to you; but I judged it would, perhaps, be a clog to your rising in the world.

He had, he said, spoken to Stella's mother:

> Nor shall any consideration of losing so good a friend and companion as her, prevail on me, against her interest and settlement in the world, since it is held so necessary and convenient a thing for ladies to marry; and that time takes off from the lustre of virgins in all other eyes but my own.

Again, he praised Stella, defining *en passant* the differences between Tisdall and himself:

> I have nowhere met with a humour, a wit, or conversation so agreeable, a better portion of good sense, or a truer judgement of men and things, I mean here in England; for as to the ladies of Ireland, I am a complete stranger. [Not true: what about Varina?] . . . I wish you joy of your good fortunes, and envy very much your prudence and temper, and love of peace and settlement, the reverse of which has been the great uneasiness of my life, and is likely to continue so.

As for himself, 'I am resolved suddenly to retire, like a discontented courtier [like Sir William Temple?], and vent myself in study and speculation, till my own humour, or the scene here, shall change.'

Thus Tisdall was given permission. But Stella turned him down. He married someone else, and remained an acquaintance of both Swift and Stella. Swift always found him a tiresome puppy. 'Do his feet stink still?' he asked Stella, nine years later.

On his church land at Laracor he soon had a single-storey cottage built – little more than a cabin, with an earth floor, and a 'field-bed' to sleep on. This he improved and enlarged with time. He planted his garden with a grove of cherry, holly and apple trees. He planted willows on the banks of the small river – 'my canal' – on his property. Later, he had a walk made from the house to the river. He repaired his parish church. He acquired at his own expense more glebe land.

For the first time in his life, Swift had a modest establishment of his own to enjoy. He employed a steward, who also collected his tithes, Isaiah Parvisol. He employed Joe Beaumont, a local linen merchant, to look after his financial and administrative affairs. He was frequently absent from his parish, in London or Dublin, furthering his political and literary aspirations, and then he left a curate in charge.

From his letters to Stella and Rebecca Dingley, when he was away at a later period, between 1710 and 1714, one gets a picture of life at Laracor. 'I should be plaguey busy at Laracor if I were there now, cutting down willows, planting others, scouring my canal, and every kind of thing.' He hoped to be back in the summer 'that we may have another eel and trout fishing; and that Stella may ride by and see Presto [Swift] in his morning gown in the garden'.

Laracor, which he retained for the rest of his life, was a place of refuge to him. On a return visit in 1713 he described it to Vanessa, his friend in London, who had never seen it: 'My river walk is extremely pretty, and my canal in great beauty, and I see trout playing in it.' On that same visit he told Archbishop King that 'it is one felicity of being among willows, that one is not troubled by faction'. Laracor was hardly Moor Park; but one hears again the echo of Sir William Temple.

As much as he often longed, when away, to be among his willows, to be vicar of Laracor was not enough for Jonathan Swift. He was not at all ready to retire 'like a discontented courtier'. His gnawing ambitions were reinforced by the modicum of security at home, and by the glimpses of the great world that he caught on his visits to London.

He wrote wistfully from Laracor in 1709, describing himself as 'cultivating half an acre of Irish bog', to one of his new London friends, the poet Ambrose Philips, asking him to 'remember me sometimes in your walks up the park'. He added: 'I reckon no man is thoroughly miserable unless he be condemned to live in Ireland.'

Chapter Five

QUESTIONS

IN 1952 Elizabeth Bowen wrote of Anglo-Ireland: 'With Swift came the voice.' She meant it both literally and figuratively. Since we cannot hear it, it is on paper that 'the voice' crackles across two centuries with unmistakable energy.

What did he sound like? Contemporary attempts to convey an Irish accent and Irish-English syntax in print prove that the Irish-English spoken then would be recognizable as such today. English was a second language, the language of government, bureaucracy and the majority of propertied people. Irish-English evolved as it were in simultaneous translation, with Gaelic intonation, syntax, idioms and imagery superimposed on English. It became the idiom even of those who knew little or no Gaelic.

Swift, an Englishman born in Ireland, would not have talked like an Irishman, even though, at Kilkenny school and at Trinity College, he would have heard every kind of country and city accent spoken by his native Irish companions, and adopted some of their intonations and usages as protective colouring – and lost them again, in his years with Sir William Temple. For in England, he wrote, 'what we call the *Irish brogue* is no sooner discovered, than it makes the deliverer in the last degree ridiculous and despised'. And 'the bad consequence of this opinion affects those among us who are not in the least liable to such reproaches, farther than the misfortune of having been born in Ireland, although of English parents'.

The tones of the cultivated (and, until recently, generally Protestant) man or woman in Dublin, which became known as the 'Trinity accent', would not yet have evolved. (This is the voice that sounds English in Ireland, and Irish in England.) The term 'Anglo-Irish' did not exist either. The English in Ireland, as all but the earliest settlers still thought of themselves, were anxious to preserve their Englishness, and deplored and corrected Irishisms in their children's speech and writing.

Both Swift's parents were born in England. Since he was apart from his mother during his childhood, whatever of Leicestershire she had in her speech is irrelevant. The uncles who supervised his boyhood were born and reared in Herefordshire, and would have retained the intonation of their home county.

The pronunciations and even meanings of some common English words in Swift's lifetime were, in any case, different from ours.

A 'bite' was a joke or a trick. Swift, in London in 1703, wrote to William Tisdall in Ireland: 'I will teach you a way to outwit Mrs Johnson [Stella]: it is a new-fashioned way of being witty, and they call it a *bite*. You must ask a bantering question, or tell some damned lie in a serious manner, and then she will answer or speak as if you were in earnest: and then cry you, "Madam, there's a bite."'

This was before he realized that Tisdall was a serious contender for Stella's love. He merely teased Tisdall for being so high in the Ladies' good graces, 'especially of her you call the *party*'; and in the same paragraph told Tisdall a crude story about a rejected mistress who told her rival she was welcome to keep their lover 'and stop him in your a[rse]'; the successful mistress said that would be inconvenient; 'however, to oblige you, I will do something that is very near it'.

Contemporary assertions that Dr Swift was never indecent in his conversation may be protective pieties. And in the early 1700s, at least, the thought of Stella was not in a different compartment of his mind from the thought of sex. In this context Swift's turgidly high-minded remarks to Tisdall only six weeks later, after Tisdall's proposal to Stella, smack somewhat of refinement.

'Refinement', in his time, was pedantry or pretension: what we would call 'bullshit'. (Swift hated refinement, as he hated all cant, false sentiment and hypocrisy.) A 'maggot' was a whim or conceit, as well as a maggot. 'Nice' had a stronger meaning, approximating to 'fastidious' or, depending on context, 'exact'. 'Disgusting', on the other hand, had a much weaker meaning, more like 'disagreeable'. Where we would say that a man was intelligent, they would say that he was 'of good understanding'.

'Serve the Lord' was pronounced, in the mouths of smart clergymen, as 'Sarve the Lard'. 'Gold' and 'Rome' were pronounced 'goold' and 'Room'; 'wind' was often pronounced to rhyme with 'bind'. 'Tea' was 'tay'. The polite pronunciation of short 'a' was short 'e', as, for example, 'fescinating'. In modified form, this last pronunciation survived in upper-class English speech until the mid-twentieth century.

Swift deplored what he saw as a slovenly falling-off from proper standards in the speech of his contemporaries. During his London years he presented to the Lord Treasurer, Lord Oxford, in an open letter, a proposal for 'Correcting, Improving and Ascertaining the English Tongue', envisaging the establishment in England of something like the Académie française in France. He was particularly against the religious 'jargon' of the non-conformists, and fashionable slang. After he had been out to dinner, or to a coffee-house, or to the Court, he would note down the 'choicest expressions' which he had heard; and he wrote three facetious dialogues, entirely composed of modish clichés, originally under the title *A Complete Collection of Genteel and Ingenious Conversation*, more generally known as *Polite Conversation*.

He was particularly offended by the modern manner of clipping and abbreviating syllables, eliding the vowels – these 'mangling abbreviations', as he put it in his proposal to Lord Oxford:

What does your lordship think of the words drudg'd, disturb'd, rebuk'd, fledg'd, and a thousand others everywhere to be met with in prose as well as verse, where, by leaving out a vowel to save a syllable, we form so jarring a sound, and so difficult to utter, that I have often wondered how it could ever obtain?

He found the clumped consonants intolerable. The correct and natural pronunciation, for Swift, was drudgèd, disturbèd, rebukèd, fledgèd. But the clipped version did obtain, and has survived. Nor did Lord Oxford take him up on his proposal.

The only reports we have of Swift's diction refer to the way he spoke as a clergyman, in church. Lord Orrery said that when as Dean he took services in St Patrick's Cathedral he read the prayers 'rather in a strong nervous voice, than in a graceful manner'. ('Nervous' meant energetic, i.e. 'sinewy'.) Swift's friend Dr Patrick Delany, who would regularly have heard Swift take divine service, confirmed this: 'And let me add, in a voice sharp, and high-toned, rather than harmonious.'

71

Swift, said Delany, had no ear for sounds, only for rhythms. Delany may be wrong; Swift was a good mimic. He seems to have used in his clerical duties that conventional high-pitched utterance which Thomas Sheridan the younger, who as well as being one of Swift's early biographers was a theatre manager and a teacher of elocution, condemned as being too often the error of clergymen. Since the voice becomes strained, the speaker falls into a 'disgusting monotony', nowhere more observable, wrote Sheridan, 'than in the usual manner of reading Divine Service . . . not have I heard many in my life who read the service in their proper pitch'. This clerical manner too survived into the twentieth century.

We may infer that Swift's 'proper pitch' in ordinary life was different. But though we know that he greeted visitors with the words 'What news? what news?' we cannot quite hear him. One of the elocution pupils of Thomas Sheridan – who strongly advocated a 'natural' way of speaking – recorded Sheridan's own pomposity and his 'trick of hemming, to clear his throat . . . "Cannot you deliver your words, hem-hemm-heiugh-m-m-m, with a perspicuous pronunciation, Sir?"' I think Swift's diction too would sound very strange to modern Anglophones. Stand in St Patrick's, amid the monuments and memorabilia, where his once-familiar voice still hangs in the air, and it is still, to us, irretrievable.

What was his manner, in company? Like the white rabbit in *Alice in Wonderland*, Swift was always taking his watch out of his fob-pocket to look at it, and to check its time-keeping against others – never entirely at ease in the unmeasured moment.

He talked a lot and he talked well, timing his remarks perfectly, contriving to dominate the conversation in a 'blaze of politeness', as his friend Patrick Delany put it. His theory was that everyone round a table had the right to talk for a full minute. If, after a few seconds' pause, no one else took over, the first speaker had the right to continue for another full minute. He much preferred to have women included in the group, and to determine any argument he would appeal for judgement to the youngest person present.

His friend Dr Thomas Sheridan, after praising Swift as the best story-teller he knew, wrote that if anyone at table took longer than six minutes to tell an anecdote, or hummed and hawed, or threatened to tell another when he had finished the present one, or spoke one word more than was necessary, the company had the right to take out their watches and make broad hints; and if that did not suffice, the offender was to have 'a glove, or a handkerchief, crammed into his mouth'. From this we may deduce that Swift was not long-winded, and that he did not tolerate long-windedness in others.

Yet this most witty and beguiling of men, this lover in his leisure time of puns, jokes, anagrams, doggerel, riddles, wordplay, 'bites', and everything that came under the heading of what he called 'la bagatelle', seldom smiled and almost never laughed. When he had said something funny or outrageous, or had stated, for effect, a shocking proposition with which no sane person could concur, he sucked in his cheeks and looked particularly serious. This made it disconcertingly hard to know whether he was making a joke or not. (The same is true of much of his prose writing.)

The playwright and parliamentarian Richard Brinsley Sheridan (son of the elocution teacher) employed the same sly technique in his oratory. I have known modern Irishmen to do it too. One might conclude that this deceptive deadpan delivery was a strategy evolved in Ireland, the rhetorical reflection of Ireland's long-standing political situation vis-à-vis the alien English: a sophisticated package of self-concealment, defensive deference, and covert mockery.

Alexander Pope's manner was similar: when he told a funny story, 'he was always the last to laugh at it', and seldom went 'beyond a particular easy smile'. Pope was thoroughly English; but he was also a Roman Catholic, and subject by law, like Irish Catholics, to a whole range of political, civil and geographical exclusions in his own country.

It was not only jokes that were processed for one's own protection, but all political discourse. Even in mainstream English public life, when a false step or a 'treasonable' view could land you in the Tower, language was manipulated to conceal what it expressed. This was the climate in which Swift moved and spoke and wrote. He could do it brilliantly. But the drama of Swift is that he continually broke the rules.

Swift's theatre could be a theatre of cruelty. He wooed with insults, 'testing' new acquaintances. He had, wrote Lord Orrery, 'a natural severity of face, which even his smiles could scarce soften, or his utmost gaiety render placid and serene'. When he was angry, this natural severity became frightening: 'it is scarce possible to imagine looks, or features, that carried in them more terror and austerity'.

Vanessa, who loved him, suffered from this cold, inexpressive anger. Pert Laetitia Pilkington, who stood up to him, suffered from his physical violence. If he was violent towards her, it is possible that he was violent to other women, who left no testimony. Orrery seems to have known something about this. The 'despotic power', he wrote, that Swift wielded over the 'constant seraglio of very virtuous women' who frequented his house when he was Dean of St Patrick's, unleashed 'passions that ought to have been kept under a proper restraint'. We shall look at this accusation more closely in a little while.

What did he look like? Thomas Sheridan the younger told a story about Swift and Ambrose Philips which gives an idea of Swift's build and height, and his habitual dress, in Swift's own words.

Swift met Philips (known from the soppy nature of his poetry as Pastoral Philips, and also as Namby-pamby Philips) on one of his earliest incursions into the London literary world. Philips, some seven years younger than Swift, was a protégé of Joseph Addison, and a Whig; he and Swift, after an early warm friendship, fell out over politics, and when in 1729 Philips turned up in Dublin as secretary to the newly installed Archbishop Boulter, the Dean of St Patrick's chose not to meet him.

Apparently Philips on one occasion, in Swift's company, was wondering aloud what sort of man the great Julius Caesar was, and imagined him to be 'of a lean make, pale complexion, extremely neat in his dress; and five feet seven inches high'. Philips, a vain man and a natty dresser, was identifying with Caesar and describing himself.

Swift heard Philips out, and then said: 'And I, Mr Philips, should take him to have been a plump man, just five feet five inches high; not very neatly dressed, in a black gown with pudding-sleeves.' (Pudding-sleeves were loose, full sleeves gathered in a band at the wrist.)

To make a point at Philips's expense, Swift had described himself. He always wore his clerical gown, even though in *A Project for the Advancement of Religion* he wrote that it would be 'infinitely better' if all clergy apart from bishops were to dress 'like other men of the graver sort' except when 'doing the business of their function'.

But fashionable coats would have cost more than his black gowns. He would not have liked to appear at a disadvantage, and he did not like to part with money; and the gown set him apart, in high society, in a way which preserved his integrity and his distaste for show. 'But what is man but a micro-coat?' he wrote in *A Tale of a Tub*. 'Is not religion a cloak, honesty a pair of shoes worn out in the dirt, self-love a surtout, vanity a shirt, and conscience a pair of breeches which, though a cover for lewdness as well as nastiness, is easily slipped down for the service of both?'

Ambrose Philips also gave an account of the eccentric impression Swift made when, in his early days in London in 1703 or 1704, already in his late thirties, he first braved Button's coffee-house, where Joseph Addison held court with his group of cronies and lesser 'wits'.

But before that story – what did it mean then, exactly, to be 'a wit'?

At its loftiest, wit was a self-conscious literary aesthetic. Wit implied the perfect expression of an insight. Wit required liveliness of phrase, but that wasn't enough. Wit was 'deep thought in common language', according to Swift's kinsman John Dryden. Swift's clerical friend Dr Francis Atterbury said in a sermon that wit 'implies a certain uncommon reach and vivacity of thought . . . very fit to be employ'd in the search of truth'. According to Pope:

> True wit is Nature to advantage dressed,
> What oft was thought, but ne'er so well expressed.

Swift, in the 'Apology' attached to the 1709 edition of *A Tale of a Tub*, wrote that 'as wit is the noblest and most useful gift of human nature, so humour is the most agreeable', and that the two together made any work 'acceptable to the world'. And, in a poem 'To Mr Delany':

> For wit and humor differ quite,
> That gives surprise, and this delight.

Satire is wit with teeth and a purpose. As Pope wrote, satire 'heals with morals what it hurts with wit'. That is exactly what Swift's satire did. Not many people have the ability. In Swift's words, again:

> All human race would fain be wits,
> And millions miss, for one that hits.

To qualify as a wit at the less lofty coffee-house level, however, a man needed an inventive mind, a facility for epigrams, a sprightly manner, a real or pretended insider's knowledge of the latest political, literary and sexual gossip, and a malicious streak.

This type of wit may be specifically eighteenth-century, but we all know him. A twentieth-century commentator on the social scene has said that humorists are mostly their own subjects, and therefore lovable. Wits have an object at whose expense they are witty, and are not lovable. They are funnier, but feared.

The coffee the wits drank was spiced with ginger, cloves or cinnamon, and sweetened with honey; but the coffee-drinking was secondary to the main business. Coffee-houses were informal social and political institutions, and by the time Swift was coming and going from London in the early 1800s every man of the upper and middle class went nearly every day to 'his' coffee-house to hear the political and social gossip, place bets, read the latest pamphlets and periodicals, receive and write letters, and show off to one another.

The wits made their reputations in the coffee-houses; and members of Parliament who might be silent in the House of Commons 'were loud in the coffee-house, where they nightly adjourn to chew the cud of politics, and are encompassed with a ring of disciples who lie in wait to catch up their droppings', as Swift wrote in *A Tale of a Tub*.

Coffee-houses were male preserves. Both women and men went to chocolate-houses. Only women went to India houses, which served tea and also sold prints, fans, china, and decorative small furniture. Being a wit was mostly a male thing too. *The Female Tatler*, a nicely sarcastic scandal-mongering periodical for ladies, complained in 1709 about the relentlessness of it all: 'Wit is entertaining, but people are not oblig'd always to be on the grin'; and 'the greatest wits are generally the greatest fools'.

Each coffee-house had its presiding genius, who sat in the best chair by the fire and held forth. At Will's in Bow Street, until his death in 1700, John Dryden made and unmade literary reputations. On one of his visits to London from Moor Park, Swift had sought out his eminent relative, and shown him his work. Dryden is said to have told 'Cousin Swift' that he would never make a poet. Swift described the scene in verse:

> At Wills you hear a poem read,
> Where [Dryden] from the table-head,

Reclining on his elbow-chair,
Gives judgment with decisive air.
To whom the tribe of circling wits,
As to an oracle submits.
He gives directions to the town,
To cry it up, or run it down.
(Like courtiers, when they send a note,
Instructing Members how to vote.)

Old William Wycherley, the Restoration playwright, introduced a young and ambitious Alexander Pope into literary society through this group.

Coffee-houses were democratic, and rank was left behind at the door. No one who could put down his penny at the bar was excluded, but the coffee-houses were highly specialized politically or by profession, and each attracted a regular clientele. Will's literary reputation did not long survive Dryden. Steele's *Tatler* asserted in 1710 that 'Where you used to see songs, epigrams and satires in the hands of every man you met' at Will's, 'you have now only a pack of cards.'

Literary supremacy had passed just across the road – to Russell Street, and to Button's, where Addison was the star. The proprietor, Daniel Button, was a former footman of the Countess of Warwick whom Addison was to marry in 1716. This was where the new wits first set eyes on Jonathan Swift.

At Button's, said Philips, over several successive days they observed 'a strange clergyman' come in, obviously unacquainted with anyone there. He would put his hat down on a table, 'and walk backward and forward at a good pace for half an hour or an hour, without speaking to any mortal'. The he picked up his hat, paid for his coffee, and left without having said a word to anyone.

Addison and his little knot of regulars amused themselves watching him, and nicknamed him 'the mad parson'.

One day they saw the mad parson staring at 'a gentleman in boots, who seemed to be just come out of the country, and at last advanced towards him as intending to address him'. The group of insiders were so eager to hear what the 'dumb mad parson' had to say that they 'immediately quitted their seats to get near him'. They overheard Swift saying abruptly to the country gentleman, 'Pray, sir, do you remember any good weather in the world?' The country gentleman, a simple soul, was taken aback and replied that he could remember a great deal of good weather in his time. 'That is more', said Swift, 'than I can say; I never remember any weather that was not too hot, or too cold; too wet or too dry; but, however God Almighty contrives it, at the end of the year 'tis all very well.' Then he picked up his hat and walked out without saying another word, 'leaving all those who had been spectators of this odd scene staring after him, and still more confirmed in the opinion of his being mad'.

This is a spiteful little story and it rings true. As a writer, Swift has lasted better than any of the smooth coffee-house wits. The 'mad parson' was already Dr Swift, the vicar of Laracor, the friend of the Ladies, and a published writer. But he is seen in Ambrose Philip's vignette as what he also was, the awkward provincial outsider, finally breaking his silence by barking out a question, couched in a characteristically oblique manner, to the only unthreatening person he had yet seen, and not making a success of it.

Witnessing this, we may think Jack Temple's brutal account of Swift's lack of social polish in the cultured ambience of Moor Park gains some credence; and that Swift gains much sympathy. But Swift was within a few months to be an intimate of the distinguished Button's coffee-house group.

They were more socially privileged than he, and Whigs. Addison, five years younger than Swift, was phenomenal, with 'something more charming in his conversation than I ever knew in any other man', according to Pope. The son of a dean, he was a scholar, poet, playwright, essayist and politician. He was a secretary of state in 1706 and an MP from 1708 onwards.

He and Swift may have been introduced by Sir Andrew Fountaine, with whom Swift sometimes stayed when in London. Fountaine was ten years younger than Swift, and had met him in Dublin when Fountaine – an asthmatic, hard-drinking, dilettante young man, a collector and connoisseur of art, with an estate in Norfolk – was one of Lord Pembroke's officials at Dublin Castle. When Swift came over to England in 1707, he travelled on the boat with Lord Pembroke and Fountaine, who in Dublin was part of Swift's Trinity-based circle, which included St George Ashe (now Bishop of Clogher), and St George's brothers Thomas and Dillon, who were also friends of the Ladies.

Addison too was to know Swift's Dublin world; in 1709 he went to Ireland as chief secretary to Lord Wharton, then Lord-Lieutenant. Swift by that time was in a position to give Addison introductions, and to write to Archbishop King of Dublin that Addison was 'a most excellent person, and being my most intimate friend, I shall use all my credit to set him right in his notions of persons and things. I spoke to him with great plainness upon the subject of the Test.' (The Sacramental Test excluded all but communicants of the Anglican Church from holding public office. There were Whig moves to abolish the Test. Swift – with his prejudice against Dissenters rather than against Catholics – was hotly in favour of retaining it. It was something of an obsession with him. 'I am every day writing speculations in my chamber', Swift told Ambrose Philips in 1708. He was writing tracts, 'remarks' and 'arguments' in favour of established religion and the Church of England – and, repeatedly, against repealing the Test Acts.)

Addison, who lodged in St James's Place, first asked Swift to dinner in London in March 1708, and Swift kept the letter of invitation for ever after. He valued this friendship. 'That man has worth enough to give reputation to an age', he told Ambrose Philips. The warmth of feeling was reciprocated. Addison's letters to Swift are respectful and affectionate. 'I long to see you', he wrote from Ireland. Patrick Delany reports that in later years, Swift used to say that on the many evenings he and Addison spent together, 'they neither of them ever wished for a third person, to support or enliven their conversation'. The two became attached to one another extremely fast, which necessitated a slight distancing for re-adjustment, but they remained friends even when differences in politics came between them.

Addison's old schoolfriend and sidekick, the good-natured Sir Richard Steele, was also at that first dinner. Swift described them in these warm early days of the friendship as a 'triumvirate', but they met in twos more often than as a threesome: 'I often see each of them, and each of them me and each other.' The friendship between Swift and Steele did not survive Swift's later support of the Tories.

Fountaine was delighted by the lionizing of Swift in the London circle, and wrote to him when he was back in Ireland in 1709: 'May your half acre turn to a bog, and may your willows perish; may the worms eat your Plato, and may Parvisol break your snuff-box. What! because there is never a Bp with half the wit of St George Ashe

[Bishop of Clogher], nor ever a secretary of state with a quarter of Addison's good sense, therefore you can't write to those that love you as well as any Clogher or Addison of 'em all.'

It was at St James's coffee-house, the one most frequented by gentlemen from Ireland, and another Whig establishment, that Swift often met Addison and Steele when he and they were in London, and where some numbers of the *Tatler*, to which he contributed, were written. Addison, who was imperious, revised Swift's poem *Baucis and Philemon*, making him, in a poem of two hundred lines, 'blot out forescore, add forescore, and alter forescore'.

Yet as early as 1705, Addison inscribed one of his books to Swift as 'the most agreeable companion, the truest friend, and the greatest genius of his age'; and in 1711, in the *Spectator*, writing up Swift's ideas for improving the English language, described Swift *en passant* as 'one of the greatest geniuses this age has produced'.

'Genius' had a milder and less absolute meaning than it does today, and one might also assume some amicable, hyperbolic jocularity in Addison's assessment; but nevertheless, a genius – on what evidence?

Swift had 'genius' – that is, a characteristic bent – for conversation and good company. But Addison and his friends had also read *A Tale of a Tub*, which became scandalously popular. Even though it was published anonymously, its authorship became known. The *Tale* made Swift's name.

A Tale of a Tub, in traditional fable form ('Once upon a time, there was a man who had three sons'), is a mock-treatise, and a parody of Grub Street garrulity and pseudo-science. The fable that holds it loosely together is an allegory of Christian religion. The three sons, Peter, Martin and John, were clearly understood by contemporary readers to represent Roman Catholicism, the established Church of England, and Protestant Dissent. Their father (God) gives each a coat, which will grow as they grow, with instructions how to care for them. The coats represent doctrine, 'fitted to all times, places, and circumstances', as Swift explained in a later edition. No prizes for guessing that the Church of England man is the least ridiculous and depraved, and pleases his father best.

Swift was writing, he said in his 'Apology', 'only to men of wit and taste'. It was, as he knew, his irreverent levity about sacred subjects that seemed shocking. In the long aftermath of the violence and persecutions of England's Civil War, politics and religion were still coterminous, and a matter of life and death. England and her allies, from 1702, were once again waging war with France. In both Britain and Ireland, archbishops and bishops of the established Anglican Church, sitting in a dominant House of Lords, wielded real power and intended to hold on to it.

The war was religion-based, with implications for the thrones of Europe and for the British monarchy. If France won, James II's Roman Catholic son – living in France, supported in great state as the rightful King of England by the French King Louis – would oust or succeed Queen Anne, and bring loss of office and property, and imprisonment or even death, to those currently in power in England.

Any whiff of Jacobitism – loyalty to 'the King over the water' – spelled danger to the current establishment. Of course, there were Jacobites in Britain; and a network of spies and informants to smoke them out.

The perilous resonance which Swift's risky fable had for his politically aware readers is largely lost on us. The reader of today, like the idle reader then, enjoys the *Tale* for its discursive observations on the extravagant vagaries not only of the three sons and their adherents, but of all human behaviour, and for its startling and often scatalogical imagery. There are 'digressions' on madness, and on critics; and a digression on digressions. Dr Johnson called the *Tale* 'a wild work' and he was right. It is a rich Swiftian ragbag.

The *Tale* became notorious and went into five editions in six years. It was the book people talked about whether they liked it or loathed it, and was mentioned more than once in *The Female Tatler*: 'How much better do arts and sciences become a lady than salves and potions? What a figure does *A Tale of a Tub* make on a toilet [dressing-table] beyond a herbal, which, with a book or two of devotions, used to be our allowance?' Congreve, before he knew Swift had written it, was among the dissenting voices: 'I confess I was diverted with several passages when I read it, but I should not care to read it again.'

It was not in essence a new work. The *Tale* had been sketched out in Swift's student days at Trinity, in collaboration with his cousin Thomas, and there seems little doubt that Thomas's contributions survived in the published version, even though Swift was infuriated by the claims made by his 'little parson cousin'. Swift had worked on the *Tale* at Moor Park (while struggling with odes), when cousin Thomas was nearby at Puttenham. But whatever the humourless

Thomas's input, the comic inventiveness and the savagery are Swift's.

Swift gave or sold the manuscript to a printer, who then owned not only the work but the right to sell or hand it on to another; this was the usual practice. It was first published in early 1704, just before 'the mad parson' left London again for Leicester and then Ireland, where he remained for three years. Included in the volume was *The Battle of the Books*, his fable defending Sir William Temple's position in the ancient-or-modern controversy, and those arguments are reheated in the *Tale*.

He never claimed the *Tale* as his; he prevaricated, even with his close literary friends. Always afraid of his letters being intercepted and read, as they were, he referred to it as the '*you know what*' even to Stella. But the word spread and, he thought, did no harm at all. 'They may talk of the *you know what*; but, gad, if it had not been for that, I should never have been able to get the access I have had.'

Another high-spirited piece, which led to a whole string of sequels in periodical form, appeared in 1708. Swift amused himself by parodying and outrageously rivalling the predictions of a popular astrologer called Partridge, calling himself 'Isaac Bickerstaff'. (The name is from Leicestershire; there were Bickerstaffs in the village of Frisby-on-the-Wreake, where his relations lived.) This pseudonym was flatteringly adopted by Steele in the *Tatler*. The frisky 'Bickerstaff Papers' seemed funny at the time (but not now) and, again, their success did him no harm at all.

Swift only began his 'real' life in London in 1710, when he became a figure in the great world. There is quite a lot more that we know about his appearance from that time on, from descriptions and from portraits. He was sitting for his painter friend Charles Jervas (pronounced Jarvis), an Irishman from Offaly who had studied in Italy, almost as soon as he arrived, intending to get one copy done for the Ladies, and to persuade Andrew Fountaine to buy another.

He was squarely, solidly built. His ears were set close to his head. He had a high-domed forehead, a strongly curved nose and a cleft chin; a small well-shaped mouth – 'an exceeding agreeable mouth' according to George Faulkner, his Dublin printer – with a fine regular set of teeth, most unusual for the time, which he cared for with a quill and a brush. He had a darkish, stubbled complexion; he complained that the hair on his chin was 'as hard as a hog's bristles'.

His eyes were expressive, protuberant, and bright blue, under bushy eyebrows. 'Though his face has a look of dullness', remarked Pope, 'he has very particular eyes: they are quite azure as the heavens, and there's a very uncommon archness in them.' In a portrait in Trinity College alleged to be of the adolescent Swift at the time of his graduation, his wide, lustrous, defiant eyes – delinquent eyes – seem to be dark; but the coat of varnish is very heavy.

It is still hard to grasp the actuality of him because portraits of the period make so many men look the same. Swift, as portrayed repeatedly by Jervas and by Francis Bindon, seems the epitome of them all – short-legged, barrel-bodied, the long waistcoat taped so tightly behind (waistcoats were designed to be fitting) that the fabric creases in front and gapes between the buttons over the belly. The face is jowly, the eyes heavy-lidded. The features are hard to read – for over all, leaching the individual significance from the face, distorting the proportion of head to body, soars the imposing falsity of the dressed and powdered wig. Wigs for men had been in vogue since before Swift was born. Samuel Pepys, for example, began wearing one after a great deal of anxious deliberation in the 1660s.

There were advantages in wearing a wig, when hair worn long was the norm. Keeping long hair clean, groomed and louse-free, in contemporary conditions, was a nightmare. The custom of powdering the wigs, so that they all looked much the same greyish-white, was adopted in the first years of the new century. 'Periwig' was a general term for versions of the elaborate wigs which were the height of fashion during the period of Swift's maximum social activity and public prominence.

Periwigs were parted in the middle, with high puffs of curls around the temples, and a mass of hair down to the shoulders. It became unthinkable for any man of position or aspiration to appear wearing his own hair, especially if it was cut short. Short hair was the mark of the apprentice and artisan class.

Swift wore full periwigs, but most middle-class and professional men tended to wear bob-wigs, short or long, which were thickly curled all over and not divided into sections. There were scores of different designs to choose from. Wigs were expensive items. London's pickpockets not only stole gentlemen's valuable watches and snuff-boxes. As Swift's friend John Gay described in *Trivia; or,*

The Art of Walking the Streets of London, little children were trained to snatch wigs off heads:

> Nor is thy flaxen wig with safety worn;
> High on the shoulder, in a basket born,
> Lurks the sly boy; whose hand to rapine bred,
> Plucks off the curling honours of thy head.

Wigs required constant maintenance. On an everyday level this was the manservant's job, but they needed from time to time specialist attention as well. Swift recorded in his account book the occasions and the amounts spent on having his wigs repaired or dressed. You needed to have at least two. If cared for, they lasted for years.

Swift noted that he spent ten pence on a wig-box in 1709, having bought a new periwig for £2. 10s. 0d. in London before returning to Ireland. In 1711 he wrote to the Ladies from London: 'It has cost me three guineas today for a periwig. I am undone! It was made by a Leicester lad, who married Mrs Worrall's daughter, where my mother lodged; so I thought it would be cheap . . .' He bought another periwig (for £3) in the autumn of 1718. Late in life, in Dublin in 1732, he bought two periwigs for £5. 5s. 6d., plus a wig-block to stand them on for eighteen pence. The following year he spent 1s. 1d. on getting one mended, and three times that amount on getting it, or another, mended again a couple of years later, acquiring a new but cheaper wig-box at the same time.

Wigs were made of human hair, or horse hair, or goat hair. 'Living hair' was preferred, as – with memories of the plague of the 1660s still alive – it was feared that 'corpse hair' could carry infection. To sell one's hair was a useful source of income for poor women and children. The chalky wig-powder was bought in bulk. Men had their heads shaved regularly – Swift had his face and the front and top of his head shaved by his manservant every other day – in order to make the wig sit well, and to avoid itching and discomfort. Hats only fitted easily over the more modest wigs, so periwigged gentlemen carried their hats as often as they wore them. Swift wore beaver hats, of which he thought highly enough to make specific legacies of three of them in his will.

In bad weather wigs were grotesquely inconvenient. No wonder Swift, a tireless walker through the streets and suburbs of London, dreaded the rain. It meant he had to pay for a sedan chair or coach home – to protect his wig. A wet, soggy, odorous wig, its powder caking, was a horrible, and possibly a ruined, object. When it rained, as Swift wrote in his poem 'A City Shower', everyone rushed for shelter:

> Triumphant Tories, and desponding Whigs,
> Forget their feuds, and join to save their wigs.

While Gay in 'Trivia' advised:

> When suffocating mists obscure the morn
> Let thy worst wig, long us'd to storms, be worn.
> Or like the powder'd footman, with due care,
> Beneath the flapping hat secure thy hair.

(There were umbrellas, but they were chiefly used by women. Addison wrote in the *Spectator* about umbrellas, after which Defoe equipped his fictional Crusoe with one.)

Wigs were worn indoors only when there were formal visitors. Gentlemen, shaved bald as coots, generally wore 'nightcaps' of some attractive material lined with lighter fabric, not only in bed, but all day when at home. Swift's were always in need of mending, or replacing. They were an acceptable gift to gentlemen from ladies, who often sewed them themselves. 'Patrick [manservant] tells me my caps are wearing out', Swift told the Ladies in 1711. 'I want a necessary woman strangely; I am as helpless as an elephant!' He bought four new ones, 'very fine and convenient, with striped cambric, instead of muslin'. Patrick, he said, could have his old ones.

To discover Swift's true features from his portraits it helps to obscure the wig with the hand; or to look at the portraits of him wearing a cap, or bareheaded and bald, when he seems defenceless and vulnerable; or at his dignified deathmask.

Swift was frequently ill during his long visits to London, with attacks of the giddiness and nausea that had become chronic. In 1709 he spent some time with his mother in Leicester, on his way back to Dublin, in order to recover.

He was still trying to catch his great fish – church preferment in England – or was it his great fly? 'It is a miserable thing to live in suspense; it is the life of a spider.' His new friends in London connived with him in hoping and plotting.

From Leicester, leading the life of a spider, he wrote to old Lord Halifax, who, like Lord Wharton, was one of the Whig group in power known as the Junto (though Swift, familiar with Spanish because of Lady Giffard's expertise in that language, always wrote it, correctly, as 'Junta').

He asked semi-facetiously to be considered for a prebend of Westminster with 'a sinecure in the country . . . which my friends have often told me would fit me extreamly'. He had some claim, he wrote, 'since the late King [William] promised me a prebend of Westminster, when I petitioned him in pursuance of a recommendation I had from Sir William Temple'.

Sir William had been dead ten years. Queen Anne had succeeded King William in 1702. Lord Romney had failed Swift as an intermediary in this matter a decade earlier, and Lord Halifax had no reason to resuscitate ancient hazy obligations.

Swift lowered his sights from English to Irish appointments. Archbishop King in Dublin was keeping him abreast of possible preferments at home, which somehow never came to anything, and Swift wrote to Halifax another and excessively conciliating letter from Ireland late in 1709. He said that Lord Somers (another member of the Whig Junto) had 'considered' him the previous year for the bishopric of Waterford, so perhaps now he might be considered for that of Cork, 'if the incumbent dies of the spotted fever he is now under'.

The incumbent did die, and nothing was offered to Swift. In spite of never formally acknowledging his authorship of *A Tale of a Tub*, knowing that its levity on religious matters would threaten his chances of preferment, he had dedicated it to Lord Somers, thus drawing that influential lord's attention to the work and increasing the likelihood of creative guesswork. Again, Swift was unrealistic, having undermined his own ambitions by his provocatively risky writings.

He never saw his mother again, after leaving Leicester on that occasion. She died the following spring, of 1710, when he was at Laracor.

It is possible that her death released him into being more fully himself. When he returned to London in the autumn of 1710 it was not to a prebend or a deanery or a bishopric but to the central drama of his life: four years of political and personal excitement and involvement.

'Whoever hath an ambition to be heard in a crowd must press, and squeeze, and thrust, and climb, with indefatigable pains . . .' There is a change in tempo.

Chapter Six

TEAPOT

DR WHITE KENNETT, the Bishop of Peterborough, made a diary note after observing the intriguing Dr Jonathan Swift in action when they were both at Court at Windsor Castle in the summer of 1713. His first sentence betrays his hostility: 'Dr Swift came into the coffee-house, and had a bow from everybody but me.'

In the antechamber to the Queen's drawing-room, wrote the Bishop, 'Dr Swift was the principal man of talk and business, and acted as master of requests. He was soliciting the Earl of Arran to speak to his brother the Duke of Ormonde, to get a chaplain's place established in the garrison of Hull for Mr Fiddes, a clergyman in that neighbourhood, who had recently been in gaol.'

Dr Swift promised another gentleman that he would 'undertake with my Lord Treasurer, that, according to his petition, he should obtain a salary of £200 per annum, as minister of the English church at Rotterdam'.

He stopped a minister who was 'going in with his red bag to the Queen, and told him aloud that he had something to say to him from my Lord Treasurer'.

He spoke to a gentleman who was going abroad 'and took out his pocket book and wrote down several things, as memoranda, to do for him'.

Dr Swift then turned to the fire, took out a gold watch, and complained that it was very late. Someone told him his watch was fast. 'How can I help it', said Swift, 'if the courtiers give me a watch that won't go right?'

Then he told a young nobleman that 'the best poet in England was Mr Pope (a papist)', who had begun a translation of Homer to which they must all subscribe. Finally, 'Lord Treasurer, after leaving the Queen, came through the room beckoning Dr Swift to follow him'; and the two went off together.

Swift was worried that summer because his political friends were in deep trouble, though no one would have guessed it from his demeanour. This vignette of a confident political operator is just as malicious as Ambrose Philips's account of the awkward, embarrassed and embarrassing 'mad parson' of Button's coffee-house. The transformation, however, is extraordinary.

How, in so short a time, had that become this?

Travelling alone, Anthony Trollope was to write, is only tolerable if one has a job to do, 'even a teapot to convey'. Dr Swift had his teapot, from 1707.

He had being doing more in London during those early visits than making literary friendships and a name for himself as a controversial author. He had an official reason to be there: a commission to negotiate on the Irish Church's behalf with Queen Anne's Whig-led ministry for the repeal of ancient taxes on Irish clerical incomes known as the First Fruits and the Twentieth Parts.

He had therefore every reason to seek access to Lord Godolphin, Lord Treasurer and party manager of the Whigs, and the leading member of the long-standing Whig Junto which included the Lords Halifax, Somers, Wharton and Sunderland; Swift had known Sunderland since Moor Park days. These lords were all getting on in years. Godolphin, an easy-living man, keen on racing and card-playing, had served every monarch since Charles II.

Swift sent progress reports back to Archbishop King in Dublin, who addressed his replies, at Swift's request, to St James's coffee-house. (Mail displayed in the glass-topped box advertised his name to the clientele, and gave him reason to call in.) Lord Sunderland promised to introduce him to Lord Godolphin, 'but either the one or other was always busy, or out of the way'.

He did get to see Godolphin, 'in a private room, and I told him my story'. Godolphin replied that he was 'passive in this business'. In fact he was to require a quid pro quo which was totally unacceptable to Swift: the support of the Irish Church for the repeal of the Test Acts. Swift met Somers and Halifax, and was advised to speak to Lord Wharton, who was to go to Ireland as Lord-Lieutenant, 'but I did not find him at home'. It went on, and on. Swift could not have been more assiduous.

Lord Wharton took the affair in hand. Swift, sidelined, felt bitter. But the thing had not gone through when the Whig ministry began to totter.

In the autumn of 1710 Swift returned to London, armed with a new commission from the Irish bishops to try again with whatever ministry should prevail after the forthcoming general election. Lord Wharton, anxious for his own political future, sailed for England on the same boat.

The word 'Tory', first used in Charles II's time, was originally a term of abuse for Irish rebels. The word 'Whig', first used for the group plotting to exclude the Catholic James II from the succession, was originally a term of abuse for Scottish rebels.

Tories historically included those who believed in the divine right of kings and in inherited succession. Tories were old money and the old landed interest. Some were strongly for the Anglican Church and against Catholics and Dissenters; some favoured religious tolerance. Some had a residual loyalty to James II's heir in exile. Such English Jacobites as there were were Tories.

Whigs historically included former Roundheads who hated the Court and former Cavaliers disillusioned by Charles II. Whigs engineered the Williamite Revolution of 1688. Whigs believed that the consent of the people was the source of political authority and that the monarch ruled only by that consent. Sir William Temple had been a Whig.

Whigs were in favour of the war against France, fearing a return of the Stuarts. Whigs included urban radicals and Dissenters. Whigs were new money, made after the Williamite Revolution and by profiteering from the grossly expensive war with France. It was the cash-and-credit exigencies of this war which gave rise to the development of financial institutions in Britain, and to the alliance of government with speculators, bankers and business.

Whigs and Tories were not homogeneous groupings. They were split into factions among themselves. Tories who put loyalty to the Anglican Church before loyalty to the monarch were a bit Whiggish. On other issues, a Whig might be something of a Tory. A man might go over to the other party whenever self-interest or single-issue conviction demanded. Ministries and oppositions were mixed Whig and Tory. Godolphin, for one, preferred it that way. Neither grouping had a cut-and-dried manifesto. An aspiring man attached himself to an influential individual, rather than to a set menu of party policies. But this was changing, and most thinking people deplored the change – except those at the top, who profited by it. As Alexander Pope wrote to his close friend Martha Blount in 1714, party spirit is 'at best but the madness of many for the gain of the few'.

Archbishop King had (as Dean of St Patrick's) bravely remained in Ireland at the time of the invasion of James II in 1689 – being, as he said 'never much frightened by any alterations', and 'never a favourite of any government'. (As a result, he was briefly imprisoned by James's forces.) He was not a party man, though he was Whiggish. 'But pray by what artifice did you contrive to pass for a Whig?' he had asked Swift in February 1709. Swift was naturally cultivating those in a position to facilitate his mission, who happened to be Whigs. King was equally sceptical when Swift became, with the change of ministry, immediately friendly with the Tories.

Archbishop King had more Christian tolerance than Swift. He kept company with 'Papists, Protestants, Dissenters, Whigs, Tories, tradesmen, gentlemen, even loose and wicked men as well as religious and devout', as he assured Swift. But Swift was equally appalled by a politics that was determined by party, a disease that he diagnosed in Ireland in 1706, in an unusually amiable letter from Dublin to Jack Temple at Moor Park: 'But Whig and Tory has spoil'd all that was tolerable here, by mixing with private friendship and conversation, and ruining both.'

Before 1710 he did not know anyone much in English politics except the Whig lords. For him the shifting political allegiances were coffee-house gossip. 'I never in my life saw or heard such divisions and complications of parties as there have been for some time; you sometimes see the extremes of Whig and Tory driving on the same thing.' During the icy winter of January 1709, when his mission was getting nowhere, he had 'amused himself' writing 'projects for uniting of parties, which I perfect overnight, and burn in the morning'. In a two-party system, 'without any hopes left of forming a third with better principles . . . it seems every man's duty to choose a side, though he cannot entirely approve of either'.

A man should 'unbias his mind as much as possible'. He consistently deplored the knee-jerk categorizing of people on party lines, when 'in order to find out the character of a person, instead of inquiring whether he be a man of virtue, honour, piety, wit, good sense, or learning; the modern question is only, whether he be Whig or Tory, under which terms all good and ill qualities are included'.

He had already been aware in 1707 how shaky the Whig-dominated administration was, and reported to Archbishop King that Mr Harley, with the help of his cousin Mrs Masham, one of the Queen's dressers and 'a great and growing favourite, of much industry and insinuation', had tried to get Godolphin put out of office.

Robert Harley was a career politician and party manager, an ex-Whig and ex-Dissenter who held together a mixed opposition bag of Tories and some Whigs. He had a strong power base in the Commons (composed in part of his own relations). He was until 1708 Secretary of State in the Whig-led administration. As the Whigs weakened, he saw his chance and how to exploit it by aligning himself with the Tories.

The powers of the monarchy had been limited since the Revolution. But the hiring and firing of ministers remained the monarch's prerogative, and Queen Anne exercised it, sometimes without consultation.

The Queen was forty-five years old in 1710. Her husband, the handsome but unremarkable Prince George of Denmark, died in 1708. Charles II is reported to have said of him, 'I have tried him sober, and I have tried him drunk, but there is nothing in him.' Anne was the daughter of the Catholic James II and of Anne Hyde (daughter of the ferociously anti-Catholic Duke of Clarendon). She was raised as a Protestant, and had little sympathy for her deposed father; when William of Orange landed in England, Anne's husband was among those who rode to welcome him.

Queen Anne was fat and unhealthy, not clever, and obstinate. A historian sympathetic to the Jacobite tendency found Anne's reputation for mildness and decency ill-founded; she was, he thought, 'a venomous, vulgar-minded woman'. She was con-scientious, and always attended Cabinet meetings. She had favourites. It was vital for those seeking their own advancement or the downfall of others to cultivate both the Queen and those who were close to the Queen.

Her new waiting-woman, Abigail Masham, formerly Abigail Hill, achieved huge influence, although she was only a bedchamber-woman – a menial position. Bedchamber-women did the work, while bedchamber-ladies handed the Queen her fan, and, if they were present, did anything that involved touching the royal person: 'shifting the Queen', for example. If a bedchamber-lady were present, the bedchamber-woman passed her the shift, who then put it on the Queen.

Until 1708 the greatest influence in the Queen's private life was the formidable Sarah, Duchess of Marlborough. For years she had enjoyed a cosy, intimate relationship with her monarch. They called one another 'Mrs Morley' and 'Mrs Freeman' – at first as a code, in letters, and then as a private game.

Not only Mrs Masham but the Duchess of Somerset (no friend to Swift, one must remember) was part of the Queen's household, and one of her intimates. The Duke of Somerset was a Harley supporter, though a Whig. The Whig Duke of Marlborough, currently the hero of the French war, victor of the battles of Blenheim, Ramillies and Oudenarde, briefly prevailed with the Queen to retain Godolphin.

In 1710 the Queen did, peremptorily, dismiss Godolphin – and Sunderland, and Somers, and Wharton, and her Lord Chamberlain (the Marquess of Kent, known as the Bug because he stank), giving the latter office to the malleable Lord Shrewsbury at Harley's suggestion.

The overweening Duke of Marlborough shocked the Queen and some of his supporters by demanding to be appointed Captain General for life. His Duchess, cold-shouldered by the Queen, became garrulously hysterical, accusing her royal mistress of a lesbian romance with Abigail Masham, who was not only related to Harley but was a poor relation of her own; it was she who had got Mrs Masham her job.

A High Tory, the Revd Henry Sacheverell, gave an inflammatory sermon in the new, not-quite-finished St Paul's Cathedral against the 'false brethren' of Dissent, against the so-called Glorious Revolution of 1688, and in favour of the divine right of kings. He touched a reactionary nerve in the populace. There were appalling riots in support of Sacheverell, and Dissenters' meeting-houses were burned down.

This resurgence of High Church Anglicanism, and a desire to put an end to Marlborough's cripplingly costly war with France, were suddenly in the centre of the frame. Parliament, in the autumn of 1710, was about to be dissolved. Could the Tories dominate in a new Harley-led ministry – preferably with Whig support? Both the Queen and Harley preferred to divide and rule.

Marlborough was clinging on, even after the humiliation of his wife, because he was desperate to maintain the state funding of the outrageously expensive palace he was building for himself, to be called Blenheim. Harley wanted to humiliate Marlborough slowly. He needed him on board until he could negotiate a satisfactory end to the war.

This is where Dr Jonathan Swift came in, rising forty-three, returning to London in September 1710, before the dissolution of Parliament, with his growing literary reputation and his new, improved commission from the Irish bishops for the repeal of the First Fruits.

Robert Harley is a key figure not only in national politics but in Swift's personal life. He was older than Swift – aged fifty, in 1710. The second most significant person in Harley's now-hopeful opposition party, equally important to Swift, was another wily political animal: the gifted, glamorous young Henry St John.

St John had long been a rivalrous and resentful ally of Harley's, and Secretary for War in the Whig-led administration. It was he who said that 'the greatest art of a politician is to render vice serviceable to the cause of virtue', and he had some vices himself.

St John was more keen than Harley on making a clean sweep of the Whigs. In the event, the leading Whigs declined to play ball. The adversarial two-party system familiar to modern British politics was hardening, with the Lord Treasurer taking on the chief-executive function of a modern prime minister – a term which Swift himself used – to the further diminution of the power of the monarchy.

Harley and St John wanted Swift for their own purposes, and found in the event that they had recruited a true and congenial friend. They attached him to themselves, eliciting in him an unconditional loyalty which withstood all reverses. Because of this close connection, and because of the covert Jacobitism in which they dabbled for strategic reasons, and which they kept from Swift (and from each other), he became implicated by association with the wilder reaches of the Tory party. This did him a lot of harm after their downfall.

Harley was given a peerage by the Queen in 1711, and became the Earl of Oxford. St John was elevated shortly afterwards, and became Lord Bolingbroke. This was another cause of resentment between the two. Bolingbroke was a viscount, which is a lesser thing than being an earl. He blamed his colleague's influence with the Queen for this act of discrimination.

A lot of paper can be covered in attempting to determine whether Jonathan Swift was 'really' a Whig or a Tory. It is a non-question.

He addressed himself to the Tories in connection with the First Fruits in 1710 for the same good reason that he had previously addressed himself to the Whigs: they were the party in power, who could bring the matter about.

An enthusiast for the Williamite Revolution and reared on Sir William Temple's theories, he believed with the Whigs in a limited, Protestant monarchy ruling by consent of the people. His primary concern for the support of the Anglican Church, and his hatred of Dissent, was Tory. So was his support of the landed as opposed to the new-moneyed interest.

Once he allied himself with the interests of Harley and St John, their enemies were his enemies and 'Whig' became a term of abuse with him. But his innate dislike of what was called 'rage of party' mirrored his individualism.

He was conservative in many respects and he was radical in many respects. Even his support of the Anglican Church was binary. He was to fight like a wildcat for the rights, privileges, properties and emoluments of the Church against any encroachments from the laity, however reasonable. At the same time, he was perpetually and vocally at odds with his Church superiors. He cannot be pigeonholed.

Lord Orrery was right: 'He was neither Whig nor Tory, neither Jacobite nor Republican. He was DOCTOR SWIFT.'

After the general election of October 1710 the Tories had a majority of 200 in a House of 558. Such a large majority is intoxicating. It is also dangerous, since it breeds false confidence, and leaves too many government back-benchers without jobs, and with leisure to form internal factions and plot against their own ministers. The full story of the next few years explains a great deal about how the discourse, the models, and the systems of modern British politics have come to be as they are. But what matters here is what happened to Swift.

There are five interlocking layers to Swift's public and private life in London between late 1710 and Queen Anne's death in the summer of 1714.

The first is his familiar friendship with Harley and St John, the worlds of Court and 'kitchen cabinet' to which these friendships gave him access, and the part he played in furthering their political aims. This involved a great deal of talking, and intense hours of rapid writing for the press. It emphatically did not involve taking money.

The second layer is his makeshift domestic life in bachelor lodgings with his servant Patrick, where he did his writing, and struggled with his illnesses, a world away from the grandeurs of his life outside.

The third is his close and immediate friendship with other writers in London, especially John Arbuthnot, Alexander Pope and John Gay. The fourth is his ongoing relationship with the Ladies, particularly Stella, back in Ireland. His letters, written at night or in the early morning, often in bed, and sent off in batches, constitute his London diary. They also serve as a mirror, in which he observes his own meteoric progress while clinging on to the only familiar affection he knew.

It is astonishing how he packed so much varied activity into so short a space of time. There is also the fifth layer: the new and dangerous relationship he was forming with the young woman called Hester Vanhomrigh, whom he called Vanessa.

Chapter Seven

PUBLIC

SWIFT FOUND on arrival in London that Robert Harley had been appointed Chancellor of the Exchequer. He was the best person to apply to in relation to the First Fruits business. The general election, which the Tories were so decisively to win, was in the offing. 'I found myself equally caressed by both parties, by one [the Whigs] as a sort of bough for drowning men to lay hold of.' He found the Whig Lord Godolphin 'short, dry and morose'. Grub Street was pouring out polemics: 'the pamphlets and half-sheets grow so upon our hands, it will very well employ a man every day from morning till night to read them'.

He sent in his memorial about the First Fruits to Harley, and was received by him 'with the greatest marks of friendship and esteem'. On this first occasion Swift had two hours with him in company, then two hours with him alone. Harley 'had heard very often of me'. He invited Swift to dine with him, and wished to introduce him to the Queen, and to Mr Secretary St John. (He never introduced him to the Queen.)

'All this is very comical if you consider him and me', Swift wrote to Stella. 'He knew my Christian name very well.' Swift did not quite know what to make of this reversal of the usual state of affairs. Harley was courting *him*.

At this stage Swift was sceptical. 'I am not yet convinced that any access to men in power gives a man more truth and light than the politics of a coffee-house.' He felt that the 'schism in politics' by party had 'cloven our understandings, and left us but just half the good sense that blazed in our actions'.

Through Harley, the Queen agreed in principle to the remission of the First Fruits. But still nothing concrete was done, and the affair rumbled on. When it was finally achieved, Swift got very little of the credit. By then the Tories were in power, with Harley and St John in control, and Swift had other things on his mind. As he told Archbishop King, 'the ministry have desired me to continue here some time longer, for certain reasons . . .'

Erasmus Lewis, secretary to the second Secretary of State, Lord Dartmouth, brought Swift to dinner with First Secretary Henry St John. Swift was dazzled by him. 'I am thinking what a veneration we used to have for Sir William Temple', he wrote to Stella, 'because he might have been Secretary of State at fifty; and here is a young fellow, hardly thirty, in that employment.'

A year later, when he knew St John better, and knew of the difficulties between him and Harley, he was still dazzled: St John was 'the greatest young man I ever knew; wit, capacity, beauty, quickness of apprehension, good learning, an excellent taste'. His only faults, for Swift, were his complaints about having too much work to do, which was an affectation; and his attempts to 'too much mix the fine gentleman, and the man of pleasure, with the man of business'. St John was for ever slipping away to 'pick up a wench' or, with a euphemism that signified the same thing, to 'go to his devotions'. The Revd Dr Swift was indulgently noncommittal in the matter, being impressed by St John's 'prodigious application' when necessary: 'for he would plod whole days and nights, like the lowest clerk in an office'.

St John told him at their first dinner that Mr Harley complained he could 'keep nothing from me, I had the way so much of getting into him. I knew that was a refinement; and so I told him.' He confessed to Stella that he could not assess how much of 'truth and sincerity' there was in St John. It was strange to find these great men treating him as if he were one of their betters, while in Ireland he was scarcely regarded. 'But there are some reasons for all this, which I will tell you when we meet', he told Stella. After he had been two months in London his hints grew broader. 'I am involved with the present ministry in some certain things.'

He was seeing Harley and St John, separately, nearly every day. Only on a few occasions were all three together on a purely social basis. Other regulars at the meetings and dinners were the Lord Keeper Lord Harcourt, and the poet, diplomat and MP Matthew Prior, three years older than Swift and his good friend. Swift met Harley's family, and attended family dinners. After gambling at cards with them one evening, Swift reported to Stella how Harley gave each person a shilling to begin with: 'It put me in mind of Sir William Temple.' Being so much in with ministers and public affairs put him in mind of Sir William Temple rather often.

He dined as frequently with St John as with Harley. Sometimes, capriciously, he declined their invitations, saying he did not care for the company they kept. Or he left early, or said he would only come if he could choose his fellow-guests. By early 1711 he was being invited to Harley's unofficial inner cabinet meetings. These 'kitchen cabinet' dinners were held on Saturdays, and at first they were for 'four or five most intimate friends', as Swift wrote to Stella. Sometimes he stayed on late when the others left, for further talk. Later in the administration, the Saturday dinners were larger and less select, and lost their charm for Swift. He had grown grand. He wasn't interested in being a minor figure in such a 'rabble'.

Sometimes, just to put him in his place, either Harley or St John was unavailable when he called, or temporarily cool towards him, and he didn't like it. He told Stella he warned St John 'that I would not be treated like a schoolboy'.

Right from the beginning, with both Harley and St John, Swift was facetious, familiar, deliberately under-awed. After knowing St John only a few weeks, he was writing, apropos of a dinner, that even if the Queen were to give St John both a dukedom and the Garter, 'I would regard you no more than if you were not worth a groat'.

He made this part-coquettish, part-aggressive lack of deference his personal trademark. He read his verses aloud at their dinners (the first, a lampoon on Godolphin, was a great success with the company), and could rally (joke) more safely, he told his Archbishop, with a great English minister of state than he could with a Dublin attorney. 'I say things every day at the best tables, which I should be turned out of company for, if I were in Ireland.'

Antoine de Guiscard, a Frenchman living in England who had entered into treasonable correspondence with France, was arrested and brought before a committee of council in Henry St John's office. He made a lunge at Harley and stabbed him with a penknife he had picked up in an outer office. The knife struck a rib and the blade broke. Harley was hurt, but not mortally.

Swift was not present, but the incident made a huge impression on him. It gave him a 'pain of mind . . . greater than ever I felt in my life'. On very short acquaintance, he had conceived a disproportion-ately deep regard for Harley – who, he told Archbishop King in his account of the attack, 'hath always treated me with the tenderness of a parent, and never refused me any favour I asked for a friend'.

Shortly after the attack, in May 1711, Harley was appointed Lord Treasurer (the first minister, or prime minister: the brass plate on 10 Downing Street today says 'First Lord of the Treasury'). He was also made a peer – henceforth, the Earl of Oxford.

The newly created Earl of Oxford made a present to Swift of the offending weapon, the penknife; Swift had the broken end of the blade attached to the main portion with a chain, and it became one of his most treasured possessions. He used to show it to favoured visitors when he was Dean of St Patrick's, and Dr John Lyon, sorting through Swift's things, found it after he died.

'I took care of that knife', Dr Lyon wrote to Deane Swift in 1783, 'and also of the first plaster that was taken off the wound, both of which the good Dean had preserved, and did afterwards wrap them together in a paper.' Dr Lyon gave the knife to Lord Oxford's grandson in 1760. He did not say whether he passed on the dressing, with its fifty-year-old bloodstains, as well.

Another attempt on the Lord Treasurer's life came in a primitive parcel-bomb: a box containing two pistols with artificial barrels, and two large ink-horns, all filled with explosive. This time Swift was there, and opened the box himself without mishap.

'They call me nothing but Jonathan; and I said, I believed they would leave me Jonathan, as they found me; and that I never knew a ministry do anything for those whom they make companion of their pleasures . . . but I care not.' He did care, whatever he said to Stella. His attachment to Oxford and St John was bound up with hopes for his own advancement. 'My ambition is to live in England, with a competency to support me with honour', he told the Earl of Peterborough, who was amiably assiduous in looking out for Church appointments for him.

'I should think [Oxford] loves me as well as a great minister can love a man in so short a time', he told Stella. Oxford and St John needed Swift for a specific purpose. But great men also have need of familiar friends who are 'theirs', with whom they can relax and who are not in any way their rivals for office. 'No job description is needed. Many people less talented than Swift have had positions of this kind; but not many of his genius.'

Swift played many roles with the great men who took him up. Court jester and confidant were among them. With him, as he told Stella, they were generally 'as easy and disengaged as schoolboys on a holiday'. He also saw them in low moods. Harley, before his elevation to the peerage, 'confessed to me that uttering his mind to me gave him ease'. Swift dined with St John and found him 'terribly down and melancholy'. He was upset to realize by April 1711 that St John 'stands a little ticklish with the rest of the ministry', and tried to persuade him to return to the Saturday dinners. But the two colleagues were growing further and further apart, and St John never dined in Oxford's house again.

Swift's prankish lack of ceremony and manifest pleasure in their company disarmed both men, and most of their associates. Surrounded by political enemies, they liked being liked so apparently artlessly. 'How came you', Lord Peterborough asked Jonathan Swift, 'to frame a system (in the times we live in) to govern the world by love?'

What the ministry wanted from him was his pen and his wit and his talent. Dr Swift became their spin-doctor, writing propaganda for the ministry's policies, satirizing the opposition, testing opinion by flying kites and by judicious leaks. The Lord Treasurer, a modern man, understood the importance of managing the press. Public opinion was swayed by the floods of newspapers, broadsheets and periodicals pouring out of Grub Street and distributed throughout the country.

The *Examiner* was a weekly, consisting of a single unsigned article, often in the form of a letter. Henry St John had been managing it and writing some of it. Swift took it over.

The first issue that he wrote appeared only four weeks after his first meeting with Harley, and around the time that Harley was, secretly, opening peace negotiations with France. Swift wrote *Examiner*s for six months before handing the job over to Mrs Manley: Mary de la Riviere Manley, a playwright, a scandalous and erotic novelist, and editor of *The Female Tatler*, who deserves more notice than she gets from posterity. Swift deplored her spelling but told Stella that he was sending her five pamphlets, to all of which he had contributed 'except the best', which was by Mrs Manley. She had 'very generous principles for one of her sort; and a great deal of good sense and invention: she is about forty, very homely, and very fat'. (All the women whom Swift liked were fat.)

101

Swift's technique, in his first *Examiner*, was to present the author of the piece as a dispassionate observer with no partisan views (his own position, more or less, before he was beguiled by Harley and St John): 'It is a practice I have generally followed, to converse in equal freedom with the deserving men of both parties.' Only in judicious examination of the practices and policies of the previous and the present administrations will the writer find the Tories always in the right, and the Whigs always in the wrong.

The *Examiner* was chiefly addressed to the Tory party faithful and to moderate Whigs who wavered in their support for the government from fear of Tory sympathy with the Stuart cause. Swift poured contempt on whispers that the Lord Treasurer was unsound in this respect, and that the Tories might bring back the Pretender on the death of the Queen. The Glorious Revolution and the Protestant Succession were irreversibly sacrosanct for the moderate Whigs whose support the ministry still needed, and for most of the electorate. If the ministry were to survive, it had to be trusted on this issue.

The ministry's dilemma, as Swift saw it, was the undesirability of continuing the expensive war with France, and the danger of making an unfavourable or unacceptable peace. He quoted to Archbishop King a saying of Lord Oxford's: 'that wisdom in public affairs, was not what is commonly believed, the forming of schemes with remote views; but the making use of such incidents that happen'. That might have taught him something about Oxford's opportunism. Swift idealized Oxford as 'the greatest minister I ever knew; regular in life, with a true sense of religion, an excellent scholar, and a good divine, of a very mild and affable disposition, intrepid in his notions, and indefatigable in business, an utter despiser of money for himself . . .'

Oxford was a collector and connoisseur of art, books and manuscripts. Swift did not mention to Archbishop King that Oxford was also a drunk. Swift learned to drink at his table. Oxford 'drank more and more, grew stouter and stouter, more and more evasive; but Anne's tolerance of his almost continuous drunkenness suggests that it was, in part at least, a pose. Behind the obese, mumbling, lethargic bulk of the Earl of Oxford lurked cunning, weasel-toothed, sharp-sighted Robin Harley.' Oxford was a manipulator and a whisperer, a great user of backstairs methods, and an able party-manager.

Swift saw that the continuance of the ministry depended on three key people remaining in agreement – Lord Harcourt the Lord Keeper, Lord Oxford the Lord Treasurer, and Mr Secretary St John, 'and so I have often told them together, between jest and earnest, and two of them separately with more seriousness'. He believed they did 'love one another' sufficiently. 'They vary a little about their notions of a certain general.'

To make a peace popular, the great general the Duke of Marlborough would first have to become less popular, and be got rid of. St John had been a protégé of Marlborough's; he was less happy about bringing him down. The growing prickliness between Oxford and St John was not just personal. St John retained some allegiance to his old friends and to discontented factions of the Tory party. The two men were always uncomfortable as political partners, and differed in temperament. Oxford, Swift thought, was too reserved, and St John too free – 'not from any incontinency of talk, but from the mere contempt of multiplying secrets'.

In September 1711 Matthew Prior was in Paris negotiating a peace, and in October Swift was telling Archbishop King that 'all matters have been arranged between France and us', but England's allies – Holland, Hanover and Austria – still had to be brought on side, as did the British public. Home propaganda was Swift's job. 'There is now but one business the ministry wants me for; and when that is done I will take my leave from them', he assured Stella.

His pamphlet *The Conduct of the Allies*, approved by St John and published in November 1711, was designed for a purpose. It would 'open the eyes of the nation who are half bewitched against a peace', he explained to Stella. 'Few of this generation can remember anything but war and taxes.' It was read by everyone who mattered, and reprinted six times.

With this and supportive pamphlets Swift discredited the war and brought into question Marlborough's popularity, and his honour, and the honour of England's allies. Swift was able to tell Stella that 'the House of Commons have this day made many severe votes about our being abused by our allies; those who spoke drew all their arguments from my book, and their votes confirm all I writ'.

The ministry was afraid of the continuing influence of the Whig Duke and Duchess of Somerset with the Queen; and that the House of Lords would vote against the peace, and bring the ministry down. The Queen was persuaded to turn out the Duke of Somerset; and in order to ensure a Tory majority in the Lords, no fewer than twelve new peerages were created. Such an outrageous step has never been taken by any British government before or since.

One of the new peers was Samuel Masham, an ex-page, husband of the Abigail Masham who was one of the Queen's waiting-women and her Majesty's latest dearest friend. The new Lord Masham had already been appointed Comptroller of the Queen's Household in place of the sacked Whig Lord Godolphin.

Abigail Masham's position remained a little ambiguous. Hired as a waiting-woman, not a lady of the bedchamber, the Queen had initially been unwilling to turn a 'useful servant', however well loved, into 'a great lady' by ennobling her husband. As Lady Masham, however, this shrewd woman played a key role in discrediting the Whigs with her royal mistress. Swift dined often with her. Her apartments were, he told Stella, 'my best night place'. She kept getting pregnant, and her children sick, much to Swift's irritation. He never wished her to be away from the Queen's side for one moment.

Lady Masham moved into the apartments of the ousted favourite the Duchess of Marlborough (who, in her fury, had taken with her even the mantelpieces and doorknobs), and became Keeper of the Queen's Privy Purse. Lady M. ran the Queen's allowance from the Exchequer of £500 per week through an account at Hoare's Bank in Fleet Street. She drew on the account in her own name. The Duchess of Marlborough had darkly predicted that Lady M. was not to be trusted with money, and indeed very large payments were made from the Queen's account to Lady M.'s husband in the last year of the Queen's life. Quite apart from what seemed to be Lord Masham's regular and generous screw of £537. 10s. a month, there are in that year three separate payments to him of over a thousand pounds each.

Swift was to have just £400 a *year* as Dean of St Patrick's. In London he was mixing with astute people who knew very well how to feather their own nests in ways he never conceived of. When, early in their association, the Lord Treasurer sent him £50 for his services, he was extremely offended, and sent it back via Erasmus Lewis with a stiff letter.

'I have never got a penny from them nor expect it', he told Stella. The slipping to Swift of £50 was a rare error of judgement on the part of the Lord Treasurer, who instinctively sensed early on that what Swift wanted in return for services to the ministry was to be accepted into friendship and intimacy – with the further carrot of an English deanship or bishopric eternally dangled before him.

Swift did not expect or seek to make money, either, out of his pamphlets, broadsheets and satires, all published anonymously. (It was the printer-publisher who made the profit; which was fair enough in that it was the printer who went to prison if the anonymous work was prosecuted. Eighteenth-century printers are the heroes and villains of the history of publishing.)

Swift was by no means the only propagandist used by the ministry. He himself gave 'hints' – a much-used word at the time, meaning guidance, or rough notes, or suggestions for topics – to other pamphleteers. Harley had been employing Daniel Defoe, seven years older than Swift, for years. Defoe was in Newgate Prison in 1703 for his satirical pamphlet *The Shortest Way with Dissenters*. Harley had him released, and made him his creature. Defoe was hugely prolific. He produced, possibly, as many as five hundred political pamphlets.

Defoe was Harley's spy as well as his hack. He assessed public and private opinion in his travels throughout Britain, especially in Scotland, and reported back. His letters to Harley were prolix, obsequious, and loaded with religious reference.

His relations with the ministry were not a bit like Swift's. Defoe and Harley did not meet socially. Defoe came as it were to the back door while Swift went in at the front. The Lord Treasurer gave each what he needed. Defoe – always in debt – just wanted money. He was a butcher's son from Cripplegate, a thin, hook-nosed man who had fought well in his youth for William III and become acquainted with him. His twelve-book satire *Jure Divino*, dedicated to 'Reason, First Monarch of the World', contains memorable lines:

> Nature has left this tincture in the blood,
> That all men would be tyrants if they could:
> If they forbear their neighbours to devour,
> 'Tis not for want of will, but want of power.

Swift and Defoe – both working for the administration, both destined to be authors of immortal and not unrelated novels – shadow one another curiously. They both had an odd relationship with their sexuality. Defoe wrote an extraordinary treatise 'Concerning the Use and Abuse of the Marriage Bed', against conjugal lewdness. His target was not marital rape (though that came into it) but 'matrimonial whoredom'. So anxious was Defoe not to fall into the lubricity he was excoriating that it is hard to tell quite what he means. But he thought that 'irregular desires in the matter of carnal and sensual pleasure' left indelible marks on the innocent progeny of the marriage, whose faces were 'blotched and spotty'. It sounds as if Defoe blamed himself for his children's adolescent acne.

Swift may not have known that Defoe was in the ministry's employ, and they never met. Swift referred to him once to Stella, hazily – 'the fellow that was pilloried I have forgot his name'. In an *Examiner* he called Defoe and his rival hack, Tutchin, 'two stupid illiterate scribblers'. Oxford had to arrange for Defoe's release from prison three times during 1713. Defoe had business interests – among them a wholesale hosiery operation – which invariably failed. He helped to found the South Sea Company, a financial venture in which booming shares blew up in the 'South Sea Bubble' and multiple bankruptcies. (Swift had invested £1,000 in the company, and seems not to have lost it. John Gay acted as Swift's agent in London when he was back in Dublin, depositing his interest in Hoare's Bank.)

If Defoe wanted money, Swift wanted to be in the ministers' confidence, and to be 'in the swim' in the great world. He had the personal qualities to make a splash.

Harley told Swift soon after they met not to bother to attend the levées he held in his own house in York Buildings, by the river near Charing Cross. 'That was not a place for friends to come to.' This was a great compliment. Lady Mary Wortley Montagu thought the levées of great men 'a farce', and mocked 'the cringes, the grins, and the fawning countenance of the thoroughbred levée-haunter'. No one was more aware than Swift, his own life transformed by the friendship of great men, of the customary contract between patron and sycophant. Hence his proud refusal to cringe and fawn.

Having the confidence of a great man did not only mean one could advance oneself and one's friends and family. It meant one could dash an enemy's prospects with a raised eyebrow, and damn a rival with a whispered word. Those familiar with the nepotism and personal-political power-relations in emerging countries at the close of the twentieth century will find much that they recognize in early eighteenth-century England. When Swift wrote the following lines he was thinking of the backbiting literary world, but it was as true of social and political life:

> So, nat'ralists observe, a flea
> Hath smaller fleas that on him prey,
> And these have smaller fleas to bite 'em,
> And so proceed *ad infinitum.*

Swift himself, because he was intimate with the leaders of the administration, became the target of place-seekers and those looking for favours for family members. He was bombarded with flattering requests to 'put in a word' with the great men. 'I am now envied, and thought in high favour, and have every day numbers of considerable men teasing me to solicit for them', as he told Stella.

He encountered his friends and contacts in St James's Park, in the lobby of the House of Commons and at the Court of Requests (a large room in the Palace of Westminster whose only function now was as a meeting-place). He met ministers and officials at the Cockpit, an elegant octagon built by Henry VIII for cock-fights. The Cockpit had survived the fire at Whitehall Palace and was now Secretary of State Lord Dartmouth's office, where Swift's friend Erasmus Lewis worked. Other of the remaining buildings on the westward side of the sprawling site of the palace were being converted into apartments (John Gay had one rather later) or into ministerial offices. Old Whitehall was being transformed into a district of government departments.

Swift also attended Court. He went to Court for the gossip and the contacts, and also in the hope, often fulfilled, of 'picking up a dinner', as he put it, for free. He sounds to be always sponging. But he was a poor man living among rich men on equal terms, which is a difficult position to be in.

'Going to Court' meant attending regular gatherings at whichever palace the Queen was presently inhabiting. Court was like a formal reception of today, without the drinks. A dinner was provided in a private room for officials and their guests, and the Queen's ladies. This was called dining 'at the Green Cloth'. Swift picked up a dinner at the Green Cloth whenever he was able. 'I fancy I am better known than any man that goes there', he boasted to Stella.

For men in public life, and their wives, it was a slight to the monarch not to be a regular attender, a 'courtier'. For place-seekers, it was equally essential. It was an opportunity to buttonhole an influential person (such as Swift became), or to disassociate yourself from a discredited figure by declining to acknowledge his bow. In December 1711, when the Whigs were about to be turned out, Swift went to Court and told Stella that he found it 'mightily crowded; both parties coming to observe each other's faces. I avoided Lord Halifax's bow until he forced it on me; but we did not talk together.' Just before the Duke of Marlborough was dismissed he appeared in the drawing-room 'and hardly anybody took any notice of him'. Court manners were as merciless as farmyard manners.

London society was small, and concentrated into a tight geographical area. Attendance at Court made an introduction to anyone worth knowing relatively easy. Just a few thousand men and women, of whom only a few hundred were significant, ran social and political life. As Swift wrote to Stella, 'The court serves me as a coffee-house; once a week I meet acquaintance there, that I should not otherwise see in a quarter.' The anterooms were open every day, even when there was no 'drawing-room'. People came to see and be seen, the women whispering the latest rumours behind their fans, as the Duchess of Shrewsbury did to Swift when the Somersets were about to be dismissed by the Queen.

The Queen generally held her drawing-rooms on Sunday afternoons. She herself spoke to few people. She never spoke to Swift. He saw her, and she presumably saw him. He never was presented to her, in spite of many hints and promises.

No invitations to Court were issued, and there were no formal rules about who could attend. The ticket of admission was the right appearance. A good coat, a clean shirt, and a nicely powdered wig sufficed to get you past the footmen and gentlemen ushers. (Marginal cases could offer a bribe.) Courtiers were self-selected. Simple folk would never think of going, and would not have the right clothes or demeanour. Trouble-makers would not get past the guards.

When the Court was at Windsor in the summer, ministers went down there for the weekends. Swift was taken to Windsor by the Lord Treasurer for the first time in July 1711. But it was much the same routine whether at Windsor, St James's, Kensington Palace or

Hampton Court. Up the grand staircase, through the guard chamber and on through a series of small anterooms until you reached the place of general assembly, the drawing-room.

Beyond that were the private apartments – a smaller drawing-room, closets (small offices) and the royal Bedroom. Like previous monarchs, the Queen – attended by her ladies – frequently received courtiers in the Bedroom, where Swift was sometimes among those standing awkwardly around. She was seldom well, and often did not emerge into the drawing-room at all.

St James's Palace, never an adequate substitute for the burned-out Whitehall Palace, was a warren of small rooms and apartments. Although Queen Anne had a new drawing-room made, the approach to it, round corners and up and down steps, was not smooth. Each room had a different set of staff, each with a ceremonial title, for whom there was very little to do, though Queen Anne had continued William III's policy of cutting down on the number of salaried drones standing around.

The greatest Court day was the Birthday – the Queen's, in February – when the courtiers arrayed themselves in new and extravagant clothes in her honour. 'The great folks never wear them above once or twice', Swift told Stella. Swift, who always wore his clerical gown, did not generally attend the Birthday. But coming from dining with Lord Masham on the Birthday in 1712, he met 'all the company coming out of Court; a mighty crowd'. They had, he told Stella, to wait around a long time for their coaches; 'I had an opportunity of seeing several lords and ladies of my acquaintance in their fineries.'

He saw Lady Wharton, 'as ugly as the devil, coming out in the crowd all in an undress'; she had been watching the parade with the Duke of Marlborough's daughters from a window in St James's Street. The womenfolk of men on the way out did not show their faces at Court any more.

The convivial Dr John Arbuthnot was Queen Anne's favourite physician. He was also a scholar, a mathematician, a wit, a Fellow of the Royal Society, and a gamy writer of lampoons. His allegorical *History of John Bull* was written in support of Tory efforts to end the war with France. He had a house in Cork Street, but he and his family were living in apartments in St James's Palace, in order that he might be on call for the Queen. He was close to the Mashams.

Abigail Masham's younger sister Alice Hill, also in the employ of the Queen, was a great favourite with both Arbuthnot and Swift, and one of their frequent dinner companions. Mrs Arbuthnot was kept in the background.

Dr Arbuthnot was an important friend for Swift, the only Scot he ever liked, and his exact contemporary. When the Court was at Windsor, he took Swift riding in the great park with the Queen's maids of honour – saucy young girls much appreciated by bored courtiers for idle flirtations.

Arbuthnot was a member of the dining club that was formed in the summer of 1711, with Henry St John as the moving spirit (so Lord Oxford was excluded, though his son belonged) and Swift a founder member. The other members were Matthew Prior, the Dukes of Shrewsbury and Ormonde, and the Irish poet Thomas Parnell – a charmer and a drinker, whom Swift had introduced to Oxford and St John. (He later became Archdeacon of Clogher.)

'The end of our club', Swift announced to Stella, 'is to advance conversation and friendship, and to reward deserving persons with our interest and recommendation. We take in none but men of wit and men of interest; and if we go on as we begin, no other club in this town will be worth talking of.'

Lord Treasurer promised to provide 'money and employments' for them to bestow. The Society met in coffee-houses and taverns, members taking turns to host the dinner. When it was Swift's turn, at the Thatched House Tavern in St James's Street, he complained to Stella that it would cost him five or six pounds, even though St John was providing the wine.

When it was Dr Arbuthnot's turn, he provided a dinner cooked in the Palace kitchens, which was brought over to the group at the nearby Ozinda's Chocolate House. 'We were never merrier, nor better company, and did not part till after eleven', Swift told Stella in March 1712. Rank was of no account at the club. Members, whether dukes or indigent poets, addressed one another as 'brother', and the club was the Brotherhood, or the Brothers' Club.

Swift had renewed his friendships with Addison and Congreve. Dr Arbuthnot already knew Alexander Pope, who had been publishing since 1709 but in 1713 was becoming famous. 'Mr Pope has published a fine poem, called Windsor Forest. Read it', Swift told Stella.

He himself had just met the twenty-five-year-old poet – a delicate, deformed, stooping creature, only four feet six inches tall. Pope had been crippled as a boy by tuberculosis of the bone, which stunted his growth. He had breathing problems, poor sight, constant headaches and joint pains. He was always cold, and wore layers of waistcoats and three pairs of stockings. He couldn't get dressed or undressed without help, and wore stiff corsets to support his weak spine. He suffered from colds, indigestion, piles. In a poem 'Epistle to Dr Arbuthnot' he referred to 'This long disease, my life'.

Pope lived with his mother at Binfield in Berkshire. When he was in London he stayed with the portraitist Charles Jervas – Swift's Irish friend – in Cleveland Place off St James's. Pope loved his mother, his dogs (called, serially, Bounce), his close friends in the country, Teresa and Martha Blount, and his artistic and literary friends in London. Pope had genius as a writer, and half his energy went into his work: an enlarged version of *The Rape of the Lock* followed closely on *Windsor Forest*. The other half of his energy went into his talent for friendship.

He and Swift, a strangely assorted pair, took to each other strongly straight away. Pope was a hero-worshipper, and Swift became one of his idols. (Henry St John, as Lord Bolingbroke, became another.) Pope was also a professional author in the modern sense. Writers above the Grub Street level did not write for money but for fame. But Pope (like Defoe) wanted and needed to make money. His ill-health and his Catholicism disqualified him from the strategies employed by other authors to make ends meet.

These strategies included secretaryships, battening upon rich patrons, and the acquisition, through influence, of salaried public offices which were frequently sinecures. The state, one might say, was subsidizing literature. Steele, for example, was Commissioner of the Stamp Office, Surveyor of the Royal Stables at Hampton Court, Governor of the Royal Company of Comedians, and Commissioner of Forfeited Estates in Scotland. Congreve was, among other things, Commissioner for Licensing Hackney Coaches, Commissioner for Wine Licences, and Secretary for Jamaica. Swift, as a clergyman of the Anglican Church, made do with his paltry stipend.

Pope's literary friendships were woven into his work, and he considered his correspondence with his friends to be part of his literary capital, and realizable. Serious poetical works as well as 'poems on purpose', as Pope called them – occasional poems – by Pope and his friends, including Swift, were spattered with personal allusions and one another's names, not altogether unconsciously binding them together in immortality on the printed page.

Pope already had a close friend and ally in the young poet John Gay. Gay was an attractive personality, and clownish – lumbering, overweight, accident-prone, improvident. He came to London from the West Country and was apprenticed to a draper in the New Exchange – two floors of fashionable drapers' and mercers' shops, like a modern mall, in the Strand.

Gay was keen to discard his origins and operate in the smart sector of the literary world. He was known as 'honest John Gay', but he was shamelessly opportunistic in his cultivation of wealthy patrons – Lord Burlington, Sir William Pultney, Lord Queensberry. He perched in the mansions of his patrons, and rarely had lodgings of his own. His sycophancy just bordered on irony, as if he were holding on to his own integrity without ever overstepping the mark and endangering his advantageous position. In writing, he was a natural collaborator. Swift, Pope and Gay formed a triumvirate in which individual authorship cannot always be disentangled.

Yet another Tory club was established, in spring 1714: the Scriblerus Club, presided over by Swift, with Gay, Pope, Arbuthnot, Parnell, and Lord Oxford as a frequent guest. The Queen's health was worsening. The Scriblerians met in Dr Arbuthnot's rooms at St James's Palace, so that he would be available when called for by the royal invalid. Pope's plan for a satirical periodical was abandoned in favour of collecting material for a collaborative volume, the biography of Martin Scriblerus. This was to be a mockery of 'learned' idiocy and folly, alchemy, millenarianism, quackery, critics, bad writing – the usual targets.

Swift's *Gulliver's Travels* owed much to the satirical scribblings of Scriblerus. Eating, drinking, and the reading aloud of celebratory doggerel took up much of their meetings. Swift's invitation to Lord Oxford, 'From the Doctor's chamber, past eight':

> The Doctor and Dean, Pope, Parnell and Gay
> In manner submissive most humbly do pray,
> That your Lordship would once let your cares all alone
> And climb the dark stairs to your friends who have none:
> To your friends who at least have no cares but to please you
> To a good honest Junta that never will teaze you.

The fun, the glow, and the effect that Swift, Pope, Gay and Arbuthnot had upon one another bore fruit for many years – in letters, in their verse and prose, and in Gay's *Beggar's Opera*, which was a phenomenal success.

It was Swift's idea. Discussing projects with Pope in a letter from Ireland in 1716, he was musing that 'a porter, footman, or chairman's pastoral might do well. Or what think you of a Newgate [prison] pastoral, among the whores and thieves there?'

Gay took the idea up, but not for another decade. His low-life musical play was a hit by reason of its slightly shocking originality; his scheming, wittily articulate whores and thieves, presented in all their whoredom and thievery, provided juicy entertainment in marked and mocking contrast to the 'noble' characters and subjects of the Italian opera which it parodied. Gay's was an *English* opera; the tunes were traditional airs. Swift and Pope may have provided some of the lyrics. Swift and his friends found the vogue for Italian opera insufferable.

Not that Swift ever went to the Italian opera. Ironically, he never saw the *Beggar's Opera* either. He was in Dublin when it finally hit the London stage in 1728, to be followed by a spate of imitations and what we would now call 'merchandising', though Gay derived no direct profit from it – playing-cards, fans, firescreens, toys, representing scenes from the opera.

Swift, as Dean of St Patrick's, did not go to the Dublin production either. He was puritanically opposed to clergymen attending public theatres and concerts. But he wrote about it in the *Intelligencer*, a Dublin periodical he was co-producing at the time, justifying its morality, its efficacy in satirizing 'Italian effeminacy and Italian nonsense', and the democratic quality of humour – 'not a talent confined to men of wit or learning; for we observe it sometimes among common servants, and the meanest of the people, while the very owners are often ignorant of the gift they possess'.

As his sociable literary life in London grew more vivid, political life lost its gloss. Three weeks after the creation of the twelve new peers, the Duke of Marlborough was dismissed from all his offices and employments. Whatever his greed, peculation and self-aggrandizement, he had won major victories for his country. Swift, influenced by Bolingbroke's pity and admiration for him, had never wanted to destroy Marlborough. 'I really think they will not do well in too much mortifying that man, although indeed it is his own fault', he had written to Stella soon after he became involved with the ministry. Marlborough was 'covetous as Hell, and ambitious as the prince of darkness', yet 'he has been a successful general, and I hope he will continue his command'. Again, a few months later: 'I think our friends press a little too hard on the Duke of Marlborough.' He sometimes softened the attacks on the general in the 'hints' for articles and pamphlets given him by the ministry.

After Marlborough's disgrace and dismissal, Swift was anxious for him to know that 'those things that have been hardest against him were not written by me', he told Stella. Marlborough went to France, to the Court of the Pretender. Swift sent the Duke a message that he had 'hindered many a bitter thing against him . . . and I desired everything should be left him, except power'. The Queen, who now hated Marlborough, as did Lord Oxford, had dismissed him peremptorily with a letter so offensive that he threw it on the fire.

The Peace Conference opened at Utrecht, and the Treaty of Utrecht was signed in March 1713. Henry St John was the chief negotiator of the peace, and was made a viscount as a reward. He took the title 'Bolingbroke'. Swift told Stella he could hardly persuade him to take it, 'because the eldest branch of his family had it in an earldom'. Swift was growing proud and weary. He still saw constantly the two enemies who were his friends but could do nothing more. They complained that he neglected them.

Having achieved a main purpose of their ministry, the Lords Oxford and Bolingbroke began to fall out openly. In their struggle for control over the ministry they clashed violently in Cabinet across the sometimes recumbent person of the sick Queen. Sir Richard Steele accused the ministry of Jacobite sympathies, and was expelled from the Commons as a result. The split between the factions in Cabinet widened. Oxford and Bolingbroke were finding reasons to discredit one another, uncovering sleaze.

By early 1714 both Oxford and Bolingbroke, separately, were involved in secret negotiations with the Pretender. The Elector of Hanover, the heir to the Protestant Succession, was already in contact with the Whigs. He was not specifically anti-Tory but he did not trust Oxford or Bolingbroke. He had not approved of the peace negotiations with France. If he came over as king, Oxford and Bolingbroke would be ruined.

Swift had written to the always-apprehensive Archbishop King in March 1712, 'I do not think any one person in the court or ministry here, designs any more to bring in the Pretender, than the great

Turk.' But Oxford and Bolingbroke – and the Duke of Ormonde – had always hedged their bets.

They did not tell Swift, since his job was to persuade the voting public that the Succession was safe with the Tories. No man in power ever tells everything that he knows, or all that he intends, to any one other person. He spreads his net wide, always keeping something back from each favoured confidant. To this extent Swift was used and duped; but no more than any other person in politics is used and duped by his masters. Lord Orrery put it more cruelly:

A man always appears of more consequence to himself than he is in reality to any other person . . . [Swift] was elated with the appearance of enjoying ministerial confidence. He enjoyed the shadow; the substance was detained from him. He was employed, not trusted . . . he was suffered only to sound the shallows near the shore, and was scarce admitted to descend below the froth at the top. Perhaps the deeper bottoms were too muddy for his inspection.

Swift knew the score, in everything except the Jacobite contacts. He wrote that he never knew anyone who was so much a master of secrecy as to 'wholly conceal his opinions' among those to whom he talked most closely. 'This I say, upon a supposition that they would have held the mask always before me, which, however, I have no reason to believe.'

It is safer to say he knew that no one person knew the score. As he wrote to Lord Peterborough in May 1714, 'I thought myself twenty times in the right, by drawing conclusions very regularly from premises which have proved wholly wrong. I think this, however, to be plain proof that we act altogether by chance; and that the game plays itself.'

He was unimpressed by what he had seen. He had never known a minister, he wrote when he was back in Dublin, who did not wish it to be thought that government was a 'profound science'. 'Whereas it requires no more, in reality, than diligence, honesty, and a moderate share of plain common sense.' He had sometimes felt inclined to say to great and high-minded persons that 'a small infusion of the *alderman* was necessary to those who are employed in public affairs'.

He knew what he had been wanted for. Years later, in his *Memoirs relating to the change which happened in the Queen's Ministry in the year 1710*, he wrote that Harley told him 'that their great difficulty lay in the want of a good pen, to keep up the spirit raised in the people, and to assert the principles, and justify the proceedings of the new ministers'. Bolingbroke wrote to him in later life that 'we were determined to get you; you were the only one we were afraid of'. Swift would have done well to re-read Sir William Temple's words on quitting public life. Sir William had had 'enough of the uncertainty of princes, the caprices of fortune, the violence of factions, the unsteadiness of counsels, and the infidelity of friends, nor do I think the rest of my life enough to make any new experiments'.

Swift had a price put on his head for rash words about the Duke of Argyll and other of the Scots nobility in a pamphlet entitled *The Publick Spirit of the Whigs*. After he returned from his trip to Ireland in the autumn of 1713, he made some last attempts to heal the breach between Oxford and Bolingbroke, and save the ministry. He contrived to have them both asked to dinner with the Mashams, at the Palace. The Mashams left the three alone together. Swift's arguments and pleadings had no effect. The next day he contrived, again, to put them together in a coach to Windsor, himself following in another vehicle, 'expecting them to come to some eclaircissement'.

There is something touching in Swift's faith in the effect of a coach ride to Windsor. He was always exhilarated by fast vehicles on good roads. The first time he ever went to Court, in 1710, with doomed Lord Halifax, 'We left Hampton Court at sunset, and got here [to London] in a chariot and two horses time enough by starlight.' That was what he loved about London, he told Stella: 'that you go dine a dozen miles off in October, stay all day, and return so quickly; you cannot do anything like this in Dublin'.

Later, travelling to Windsor with Lord Treasurer or St John (never the two together) were always light-hearted times. In September 1711, on the way to Windsor, Swift's chariot overtook another in which he recognized Lady Giffard and his sister Jane, 'going, I suppose, to Sheen'. Swift's companion was Lord Treasurer's brother; Lord Treasurer caught them up in another chariot, and Swift changed vehicles and travelled on with him. So 'those people', as he told Stella, never actually saw him with Lord Treasurer. Perhaps he was sorry they had not.

They always gossiped and played childish games of the 'I Spy' variety on the way. Lord Oxford

> Would take me in his coach to chat,
> And question me of this and that
> As 'What's o'clock' and 'How's the wind?'
> Whose chariot's that upon the road?

On this final occasion, when they all reached Windsor, Bolingbroke told Swift that it was no use, no miracle of reconciliation had taken place.

Having failed, and knowing that he must soon return to Ireland, Swift – unwell and dispirited – fled from the political débâcle in May to an old friend, the rector of Letcombe Bassett, near Wantage, in Berkshire.

Gay wrote to him at Letcombe about the goings-on at the latest Scriblerus meeting, and referred to the many favours received 'purely out of your love for doing good'. Gay was off to Hanover as secretary to the British Ambassador, the Earl of Clarendon, a post obtained through Swift's recommendation. Dr Arbuthnot wrote telling how Gay was dancing attendance on Lord Oxford for money for shoes and linen to go to Hanover in. Swift wrote advising Arbuthnot to keep Scriblerus under his own control, as he had the best ideas of all of them. Pope 'has no genius at all to it, in my mind. Gay is too young; Parnell has some ideas of it, but is idle.' Pope wrote about translating Homer, and always with affection: 'Of all the world, you are the man (without flattery) who serves your friends with the least ostentation.'

Pope and Parnell came down from London, in the rain, to visit him. Swift 'talked of politics over coffee, with the air and style of an old statesman, who had known something formerly; but was shamefull ignorant of the three last weeks', as Pope reported to Arbuthnot. (Swift had another visitor too: a young woman.)

From Letcombe Swift wrote to Lord Oxford that 'in your public capacity you have often angered me to the heart, but, as a private man, never once'. Charles Ford reported that 'the Dragon and his Antagonist' (Oxford and Bolingbroke) still met every day for government business, and were civil, 'and when they part, I hear they give one another such names, as only ministers of state could bear without cutting throats'.

117

Five days later the Queen, mortally ill, dismissed Oxford. She did not appoint Bolingbroke in his place, but the adventitious Lord Shrewsbury.

Queen Anne died on 1 August. Swift, far from the centre of things, heard the news from the vicar of Wantage, who sent word. The Elector of Hanover was proclaimed George I. In September, Robert Walpole's first administration was formed. The Whigs had triumphed.

The intense literary friendships, though revitalized by Swift's return visits in 1726 and 1727, were – in the flesh, as opposed to the spirit – pitifully brief. Between June and September 1713, soon after he had met Pope, Swift was away in Dublin being installed as Dean of St Patrick's. The Scriblerus Club was founded only a couple of months, if that, before Swift left London to bury himself at Letcombe Bassett prior to returning to Dublin to take up his duties as Dean. He had known Pope for just over a year, and Gay for rather less.

The London friends, literary and political, were to be faithful to Swift by correspondence to the end of his life or theirs, but there is a bleak finality about Swift's letters from Letcombe.

'I have said enough', he wrote to Lord Oxford, 'and like one at your levée having made my bow, I shrink back into the crowd.'

And to Arbuthnot: 'You are a set of people drawn almost to the dregs; you must try another game; this is at an end.'

The death of the Queen, the fall of the ministry, his exile to Ireland marked the conclusion of the public life of Jonathan Swift. The drama of his private life, which he kept very private indeed, remained unresolved.

Chapter Eight

PRIVATE

SWIFT WROTE to Stella and Rebecca Dingley almost daily during this time in London, and they wrote to him on the same basis. His letters were his diary. He sent several days' chronicles off in batches. In print, they make up a sizeable book. The title *Journal to Stella* was first used by Thomas Sheridan, when he published the letters in 1784.

They were indeed chiefly for Stella; but Swift addressed the letters to 'Mrs Dingley, at her lodgings over against St Mary's Church near Capel Street' in Dublin, and she as well as Stella is present in his mind as he writes ('For God's sake be good girls'). He wrote to both women together, and addressed the letters to Dingley, both for reasons of discretion and because Dingley generally had to read the letters aloud to the weak-eyed Stella. And perhaps, also, he was fearful of establishing too intense an epistolary relationship with Stella.

The subsequent history of these letters is complicated, and important. After Stella died they were returned to Swift, presumably in the 'strong-box' which was all that she bequeathed to him apart from her gold watch.

In 1738 he gave the first forty of them, as part of a bundle of papers, to his cousin Martha Whiteway. He was then already failing and probably didn't know what was in the bundle, though at some previous point he himself had censored the letters, erasing some private phrases with his particular round-and-round scrawls.

The remaining twenty-five were discovered by Dr John Lyon, sorting through Swift's papers after his death, and were published in 1766 as the tenth volume of John Hawkesworth's edition of Swift's works. The trouble is that Hawkesworth did not publish them as they stood. He edited them heavily, and 'translated' the intimate code of made-up words and baby language which Swift used when writing to Stella. But luckily the originals of these last twenty-five letters ended up, after many vicissitudes, in the British Museum. Otherwise we would have the whole correspondence only in falsified versions.

In 1768 Hawkesworth also published the forty letters that had been casually handed to Mrs Whiteway; Deane Swift, who had married Mrs Whiteway's daughter, claimed that he saved them from being thrown away. Deane Swift prepared them for Hawkesworth's edition, adding some useful notes. But he too edited out a lot of the intimate language, making the letters less spontaneous and more literary than they really were.

It was Deane Swift too who cavalierly substituted the name 'Presto' for Swift referring to himself. 'Presto' was what the Duchess of Shrewsbury called him. She was Italian, and 'could not say my name in English, but said Dr Presto, which is Italian for swift', as he told Stella. In the originals, Swift calls himself 'Pdfr' (perhaps, judging from the prevailing idiom of the letters, standing for 'poor dear foolish rogue').

Swift did not use the name 'Stella' in the letters either. No one ever called her Stella until Swift began using that name for her in poems 'To Stella' on his return to Dublin after the Queen's death. This is another of Deane Swift's interventions. Swift referred to her in his letters as 'Ppt', commonly interpreted as 'poppet'. When referring to Stella and Rebecca Dingley together, he wrote 'MD' – 'my dears'.

In the letters that have survived exactly as they were written, some of the little-language code is easy to interpret. 'All melly Titmasses – melly Titmasses', he wrote on 25 December 1712, and ended up another section of the same letter-batch: 'Nite two dee logues.' ('Goodnight two dear rogues.')

Sometimes he signed off with strings of capital letters and secret words: 'Nite deelest richar MD [erasure] dee MD MD MD FW FW FE ME ME ME Lele Lele Lele. My second cold is better now. Lele lele lele lele.' 'Deelest richar' is 'dearest little'. Reading the letters, you acquire an ear and an eye for interpreting nearly all the little language. The signing-off litanies remain impenetrable.

This is Swift in a uniquely private mode. Nothing in his social or professional presentation of himself, and nothing in his writings except the word-games of 'la bagatelle', prepares one for it.

This was not only how he wrote to Stella, it was clearly how they talked to each other in private, too – a continuation of the playful and conspiratorial intimacy between the little girl and her tutor at Moor Park. 'Do you know that every syllable I write', he told her in April 1711, 'I hold my lips just for all the world as if I were talking in our own little language to MD. Faith, I am very silly; but I can't help it.' And again: 'When I am writing in our language I make up my mouth just as if I were speaking it. I caught myself at it just now.' This is from the edited sequence of letters; the original would itself have been couched in 'our little language' or, as he rendered it, 'ourrichar grangridge'.

He must have destroyed the letters that the Ladies wrote to him, after Stella died. Mrs Whiteway remembered him having burned a great many papers in the early 1730s. (His own were earmarked as aides-memoire for the events of those years.) Deane Swift noted that Stella's handwriting was very like Swift's, but 'she writ more legible and rather better'. When Harley saw a letter from Stella addressed to Swift awaiting collection in the glass case at a coffee-house, he thought Swift was writing to himself; Charles Ford, who forwarded it, thought the same, Swift told her. 'I remember others have formerly said so too. I think I was little MD's writing master.'

He listed her spelling mistakes, allowing her six in each missive without censure. He urged her to read, ride, walk, eat sensibly. She was still his pupil, still the little girl of Moor Park, in this tender fantasy game. He infantilized her. He infantilized himself too. 'MD' were 'saucy girls'; he was a 'good boy'.

The reader may find this kind of thing embarrassing. Cyril Connolly did not like the *Journal to Stella* for its intoxication, its boasting, its facetiousness – 'the most unpleasant, the most morbid of his writings'. I rather favour the gentlemanly sentimentality of an Edwardian introduction to the *Journal* by Frederick Ryland, who in 1908 wrote that the impenetrable litanies of coded letters and syllables 'doubtless had an earnest intensity of meaning for the strange, grim, middle-aged lover and his mistress, but for us they are dumb, and like shrivelled petals found between the leaves of some old romance we can only dimly wonder what was the message they carried to the eyes which brightened as they saw them'.

When he began spending his time with government ministers, Swift told the Ladies not to send their letters to the coffee-house any more: 'you must enclose your letter in a fair half sheet of paper, and direct the outside to Erasmus Lewis, Esquire, at my Lord Dartmouth's office at Whitehall'. He no longer frequented the coffee-house, 'and they will grudge to take in my letters'.

He wrote to 'MD' in bed in the early mornings ('I must say something to MD when I wake, and wish them a good morrow; for this is not a shaving day, Sunday, so I have time enough'). He made believe Stella was with him: 'Come, sit off the bed, and let me rise, will you?' He continued the letters in bed again late at night: 'I cannot go to bed without a word to them; I cannot put out my candle until I have said goodnight.' When he was sleepy, he made 'blunders and blots' and wrote crooked: 'I cannot write straighter in bed, you must be content.' He tidied away MD's letters to him 'in the letter partition of my cabinet . . . Method is good in all things. Order governs the world.'

When he first arrived in London in 1710, he lodged in Pall Mall, then moved to Bury Street, near St James's Street and the Palace. 'I have the first floor, a dining-room and bed-chamber, at eight shillings a week; plaguey deep [expensive], but I spend nothing for eating.' He told MD where and what he ate and drank (he learned to drink in London, and was often hungover). He always ate out, if possible at someone else's expense, and used his dining-room as a sitting-room. His servant Patrick got drunk three times a week, and sometimes got beaten for it. Swift was always on the point of dismissing him.

It was Patrick's job to procure coals and candles, and to make up the coal fire in the dining-room early in the morning. He 'wakes me five or six times, but I have excuses, though I am but just awake'. Swift did not get up until the room had warmed.

Is there a good fire, Patrick? Yes, sir, then I'll rise; come take away the candle. You must know I write on the dark side of my bed-chamber, and am forced to have a candle till I rise, for the bed stands between me and the window, and I keep the curtains shut this cold weather.

If 'the extravagant whelp' built the fire up too high in the evening, Swift would pick off the coals before he went to bed. 'I have got some loose bricks at the back of my grate for good husbandry.' Coals cost him a shilling a week. There was no fire in his bedroom, but woollen curtains round his bed. It was also Patrick's job to deliver notes, and to admit Swift's visitors, and sometimes to lie to them that Swift was out.

Patrick looked after Swift's clothes, and helped him to dress, and held Swift's keys, and was always locking up his pen and ink in the chest of drawers, and then going out, so that Swift could not write; or filling the ink-pot too full, so that Swift spilled it; or sending Swift's clothes on to Windsor when he was just returning, so that he had to borrow a shirt from Mr Secretary St John at Windsor, and a night-gown from his landlady when he got back. Patrick finally left of his own accord, 'to my great satisfaction'.

There was little security in a lodging house. When Swift moved to Leicester Fields, he had iron bars put on the windows of his two rooms, 'and I hide my purse in my thread stocking between the bed's head and the wainscot'. He moved again, to a cheaper single room up two flights of stairs in Little Rider Street, near Bury Street.

He told MD all his dreams, and about his colds, and his attacks of piles, and his 'fits' – his recurrent malady: 'sitting up in bed, I had a fit of giddiness; the room turned round for about a minute, and then it went off, leaving me sickish . . .' He told them about the remedies he tried: vomits, purgatives, asafoetida pills (asafoetida is a resinous gum, used as an anti-spasmodic), 'steel drops', a 'steel bitter drink', brandy for breakfast, no snuff, simple food (though he was growing 'stout' nevertheless), lots of walking. He had a longing for fruit but believed it made his head worse. 'I envy people maunching and maunching peaches and grapes, and I not daring to eat a bit.'

He missed the Ladies, especially at first. Nothing gave him 'any sort of a dream of happiness' except a letter from them or, failing that, the expectation of one. 'Yes, faith, and when I write to MD, I am happy too; it is just as if methinks you were here, and I prating to you.' He was homesick: 'O that we were at Laracor this fine day! the willows begin to peep, and the quicks to bud.' 'I will say no more', he wrote in May 1711, 'but beg you to be easy, till fortune take her course, and to believe that MD's felicity is the great end I aim at in my pursuits.'

Right from the beginning, Stella had been instinctively suspicious about one of his new female friends in London.

This young woman's father was born a Dutchman, naturalized

English – Bartholomew Van Homrigh, a revenue commissioner in Dublin who rose to be Lord Mayor. Her mother had been a Miss Hester Stone, of Dublin, daughter of another revenue commissioner.

By the time Swift knew the family, the name was generally written Vanhomrigh, and pronounced Vanummery. Their eldest child and first daughter was Hester – Swift's Vanessa. He made up his name for her from the 'Van' of her surname combined with 'Hessy', which was what she was called at home. Sometimes he called her 'Missessy'.

Back in 1707, the widowed Mrs Vanhomrigh brought her young family – two daughters and two sons – over to live in London. In the small Protestant society of Dublin, Swift could have met, and certainly would have known of, the Vanhomrighs. Crossing on the same boat – along with Lord Pembroke and Sir Andrew Fountaine – they were thrown together when the coach passengers from Holyhead stopped for refreshments at an inn in Dunstable, probably the Saracen's Head.

Hessy/Vanessa would then have been about nineteen, twenty-one years younger than Swift and nearly seven years younger than Stella.

It was a memorable encounter at Dunstable. Five years later, after stopping at the inn again, Swift wrote to Mrs Vanhomrigh: 'I could not see any marks in the chimney at Dunstable of the coffee Hessy spilt there.' In the course of their long involvement, Swift, especially when under stress, would list the key moments of their secret history, in his letters to her. These litanies often began with 'Dunstable'.

Stella and Rebecca Dingley were briefly in London during 1707 too. It was the last time they would ever leave Ireland. If Stella met Vanessa it would have been then, when the Vanhomrighs were nothing more than amusing new friends. Mrs Vanhomrigh was a sociable and well-connected widow. She came to London in order to settle her children in the world, and probably to seek husbands for her daughters. The Duke of Argyll was godfather to her son Ginkel (who died in 1710). She sent her other son Bartholomew to Oxford.

Swift called on the Vanhomrighs almost as soon as he arrived in London in September 1710. The family were in lodgings in Bury Street, and so was he: 'I was so lazy today that I dined next door.' Just as Stella and Rebecca Dingley constituted his family in Ireland, so the Vanhomrighs became his family in London. They and their lady friends fussed over him, giving him a new scarf, 'and Lady

Abercorn is to get me another, to see who does best; mine is all in rags'.

In January 1711, after walking into the city and shopping with Charles Ford ('I laid out one pound five shillings for a Strabo and Aristophanes, and I have now got books enough to make me another shelf'), he had a message from Mrs Vanhomrigh that 'her eldest daughter was taken suddenly very ill, and desired I would come and see her.' But he found on arrival it was just a 'silly trick' to get him to call in.

The fourteenth of February was that eldest daughter's real birthday – 'and Mr Ford and I were invited to dinner to keep it, and we spent the evening there drinking punch. That was our way of beginning Lent; and in the morning, Lord Shelburne, Lady Kerry, Mrs Pratt and I, went to Hyde Park, instead of going to church.' He had a hangover, and it would be 'so silly and troublesome' to get sick in church. Andrew Fountaine was another regular diner at the Vanhomrighs', as were Charles Ford and Erasmus Lewis.

By the end of February 1711 Stella must have been getting irritated by hearing quite so much about the Vanhomrighs, for Swift wrote with defensive facetiousness: 'You say they are of no consequence; why, they keep as good female company as I do male; I see all the drabs of quality at this end of the town with them.'

He moved out of London to Church Street in Chelsea for a couple of months at the end of April 1711, travelling 'in the stage-coach with Patrick and my portmanteau for sixpence, and pay six shillings a week for one silly room with confounded coarse sheets'. He stored some of his possessions at the 'Vans', as he called them, and also the Tuscan wine given him by Chief Secretary Henry St John. The wine was to be his contribution to dinners with the Vans, though it was bad and sour, 'at least the first two flasks were so, and hardly drinkable. How plaguily unfortunate I am! and the Secretary's own is the best I ever tasted.'

He liked being out of town, though Chelsea was no longer properly rural. The hayfields smelled sweet, 'but the hay-making nymphs are perfect drabs, nothing so clean and pretty as further in the country'. His lodgings were opposite the Atterburys' house, and Mrs Atterbury sometimes sent him in a dinner. He took the sixpenny coach into town from Chelsea when it was 'bloody cold' or 'bloody hot', and sometimes a boat (except on Sundays, when there was no river transport).

Generally he walked back to Chelsea, at sunset: 'My way is this: I leave my best gown and periwig at Mrs Vanhomrigh's, then walk up the Pall Mall, through the Park, out at Buckingham House, and so to Chelsea a little beyond the church.' It took him just under an hour. 'It is a good two miles, and just five thousand seven hundred and forty-eight steps; so there is four miles a day walking, without reckoning what I walk when I stay in town.'

In the morning, on returning to town, he would call in at Mrs Van's, 'at whose lodgings I always change my gown and periwig' or, again, 'where I keep my best gown and periwig to put on when I come to town and be a spark'. He washed and shaved there too sometimes. Calling in at the Vans' twice a day, he was assiduous in reiterating to Stella the practical reasons for doing so.

On the thirtieth of May 1711: 'I am so hot and lazy after my morning's walk, that I loiter at Mrs Vanhomrigh's, where my best gown and periwig was, and out of mere listlessness dine there very often, so I did today.' He had called on Erasmus Lewis in Lord Dartmouth's office in Whitehall, to collect MD's letter, 'and I read it in a closet they lend me at Mrs Van's, and I find Stella is a saucy rogue and a great writer, and can write finely still when her hand's in, and her pen good. When I came here tonight, I had a mighty mind to go swim after I was cool, for my lodging is just by the river, and I went down with only my night gown and slippers on at eleven, but came up again; however, one of these nights I will venture.'

He did so venture:

I am just this minute going to swim. I take Patrick down with me to hold my night-gown, shirt, and slippers, and borrow a napkin of my landlady for a cap. – So farewell till I come up; but there's no danger, don't be frighted – I have been swimming this half hour and more; and when I was coming out I dived, the napkin fell off and is lost, and I have that to pay for. O faith, the great stones were so sharp, I could hardly set my feet on them as I came out.

Another time it was less pleasant. 'I was every moment disturbed by boats, rot them; and that puppy Patrick, standing ashore, would let them come within a yard or two, and then call sneakingly to them.'

Chelsea figures later in Swift's litanies of special times and places with Vanessa, which means she visited him there. Maybe that was somewhere in the back of his mind when in *Gulliver's Travels* he described the young female Yahoo conceiving a passion for Gulliver on seeing him bathe naked (as Swift did not) in a stream.

Any excuse would do to spend time at the Vans'. It was somewhere, as he said, where he 'could be easy'. One summer day he stayed to dinner because it was raining; 'and there I did loiter all the afternoon, like a fool, out of perfect laziness, and the weather not permitting me to walk. But I'll do so no more.' But it was still raining next day, 'and I struck into Mrs Vanhomrigh's, and dined, and stayed till night very dull and insipid'. Sometimes he makes it seem a chore: 'Mrs Van made me dine with her.'

Sometimes he went round to Mrs Van's after dining with the Lord Treasurer, and stayed for the evening, drinking coffee and eating an egg for his supper. Mrs Van knew how to make him feel welcome, and gave him the sort of simple food he liked. In default of any better invitations, or of 'picking up a dinner' at Court, he just went round to the Vans'. Often there was smart and amusing company, though sometimes he described himself as dining 'gravely' there, making it sound dull.

He built fantasies about Stella having her own dinner at the same time, in Ireland: 'I dined with my neighbour Vanhomrigh, and MD, poor MD, at home on a loin of mutton, and half a pint of wine, and the mutton was raw, poor Stella could not eat, poor dear rogue, and Dingley was so vexed . . .' In July 1711 he moved from Chelsea back into town. He went to Suffolk Street and then (because his landlady needed the room for her own family) moved again, to Leicester Fields.

The first extant letter from Swift to Vanessa herself is dated 18 December 1711. The real reason for his visits becomes clear. He enclosed what he called 'a starched letter' for showing to her family. The other one was for her eyes alone. The forty-four-year-old Dr Swift is capable of deception: 'See what art people must use, though they mean ever so well. Now are you and Puppy lying at ease . . . Adieu, till we meet over a pot of coffee or an orange in the Sluttery, which I have so often found to be the most agreeable chamber in the world.'

So that is where he had been whiling away those rainy afternoons and evenings. The Sluttery was the upstairs sitting-room used by Vanessa and her younger sister Mary.

Christmas, a family time, was always difficult for Swift. He spent Christmas Day 1711 at the Vans', feeling poorly with his 'new cold' and a bad back. His 'Windsor Prophecy' – the particularly nasty squib about the Queen's favourite, the Duchess of Somerset – was about to be published. 'I believe everyone will guess it to be mine', he told Stella with mingled pride and unease. He was expecting the Duchess to be dismissed, as later she was. But when he went to see Mrs Masham on Boxing Day, she urged him to withdraw the piece, 'for fear of angering the Queen'. He made only half-hearted attempts to stop it circulating, and it was twice reprinted.

Another difficult time in London was his first August, when the Court was at Windsor and he did not follow. His home-from-home was cut off from him too: 'I found Mrs Vanhomrigh all in combustion', he told the Ladies, squabbling with her rogue of a landlord; she has left her house, and gone out of her neighbourhood a good way. Where shall I dine tomorrow? can you tell? Mrs Vanhomrigh boards now, and cannot invite one; and there I used to dine when I was at a loss; and all my friends are gone out of town.'

'In lodgings', one ordered meals and had service provided in one's own quarters, which might be one room, or several. 'Boarding', as the Vans now did, one generally ate at a common table with other boarders, and the proprietor. To take lodgings cost more, and had more status, than boarding. Swift was always in lodgings. He had fobbed Stella off about an early probing about the Vans, only two months after he arrived in London: 'What do you mean "That boards near me, that I dine with now and then?" I know no such person: I do not dine with boarders.'

Swift did in desperation dine at Mrs Van's, with 'her damned landlady, who, I believe, by her eyebrows, is a bawd'. After two months Mrs Vanhomrigh and her family moved again. Swift had been quite right about the eyebrows. The new place was better. 'I dined with her today, for though she boards, her landlady does not dine with her.'

The Vans were ordering herrings for dinner rather often. Luckily Swift liked herrings. Herrings were cheap. All these flittings were because Mrs Van was strapped for cash and unable to pay her bills. Her husband's very considerable property in Ireland was in trust until the children should all be of age. Bartholomew and Mary were still under twenty-one. Swift put himself out and used his contacts to help Mrs Van and Vanessa with a petition to the House of Lords for a private bill which would empower them to break the trust and realize the Irish assets.

(Until the end of her life, Vanessa was struggling with the law over her inheritance. Mrs Van was an indiscreet spender. But if what Lord Orrery heard was true – that when Vanessa and her younger sister Mary did leave London for Ireland they travelled secretly, on a Sunday, 'to avoid the interruption and importunities of a certain fierce kind of animal called bailiffs' – it was only because they could not get hold of the family money: £5,000 from their father, with another £5,000 to come from the estate of Mrs Vanhomrigh. Vanessa was potentially an heiress.)

The petition to the Lords stated that 'Hester the daughter is now come of age, and in prospect of marriage, but cannot receive her portion'. Dr Swift, acting for the family in this private matter, was in the family's eyes the prospect in prospect. It's no coincidence that after the submission of the petition he was laid low with three colds in a row, followed by a severe attack of shingles. He complained to Stella that he had horrible pain in his neck and shoulders, 'great red spots', and small pimples 'full of corruption'. He ended that letter with a spate of code and little language:

> I have been in no danger of life, but miserable torture. I must not write too much. So adieu, deelest MD MD MD FW, ME ME ME, Lele. I can say yet lele, oo see. Fais, I don't conceal a bit, as hope saved [i.e. as I hope to be saved].

He may not have been concealing anything about his health. But he was concealing a good deal else; though he had let fall that there was a plan for Mrs Van's 'eldest daughter' to go to Ireland 'to look after her fortune, and get it in her own hands'. (That is one of the three times that Swift actually referred to Vanessa when writing to Stella; and he never mentioned her by name.)

The ageing Lady Orkney, William III's plain, squint-eyed mistress, grew fond of Swift during his London years. She lived at Clevedon, a great house on the Thames near Taplow. Swift met her at Windsor in 1712, and dined with her frequently in London. 'She is the wisest woman I ever saw', he told Stella. 'She is perfectly kind, like a mother.'

If Swift ever confided in anybody about the complications of his

129

private life, I guess it was to motherly Lady Orkney, in the autumn of 1712. 'I dined yesterday with Lady Orkney, and we sat alone from two till eleven at night', he told Stella. That is nine hours' solid talking. On another occasion 'we had a long discourse with her about love', and she repeated a saying, 'which I thought excellent, that *in men, desire begets love, and in women, love begets desire*'.

Lady Orkney had a writing-table 'of her own contrivance' made for him: 'I heartily thank your ladyship', wrote Swift, 'for making me a present that looks like a sort of establishment. I plainly see, by the contrivance, that if you were First Minister, it would have been a cathedral.' She also gave him a 'bed nightgown', and sent him medicine when he was ill. She gave him a portrait of herself, by Kneller. 'He has favoured her squint admirably', wrote Swift to Stella; 'and you know I love a cast in the eye.'

(Lady Orkney was a stayer, and her appearance did not improve. Lady Mary Wortley Montagu described her at George II's coronation in 1727. She 'exposed behind a mixture of fat and wrinkles, and before a considerable pair of bubbys greatly withered, a great belly that preceded her; add to this the inimitable roll of her eyes, and her grey hair which by good fortune stood directly upright, and 'tis impossible to imagine a more delightful spectacle'.)

Swift reports dining with the Vans on more than fifty occasions during the period covered by the *Journal*, which ends in 1714. After 5 February 1713 there are no more references to them at all.

Swift wrote to Anne Long, an acquaintance of the Vanhomrighs of whom Swift became very fond, that there was not 'a better girl upon earth' than Vanessa.

> I have a mighty friendship for her; she had good principles, and I have corrected all her faults; but I cannot persuade her to read, tho' she has an understanding, memory and taste, that would bear great improvement; but she is incorrigibly idle and lazy; she thinks the world made for nothing but perpetual pleasure.

Vanessa's current favourites, he told Mrs Long, were 'Lady Ashburnham [the Duke of Ormonde's daughter], her dog, and myself'. She treated him with so little respect 'that it almost distracts me'.

Swift's relationship with Vanessa was of the familiar kind in which he felt stimulated, confident and comfortable. He was the teacher, and Vanessa was the pupil. Swift was, wrote Deane Swift, 'a man beyond all others upon earth, whose delight was to give instruction to young people, especially to young women'. What's more, he wanted submission. He wanted, sometimes, abasement. He reproached her for laziness. He pressed her and her younger sister to

> walk as often as you can in the park, and do not sit moping at home, so that you can neither work nor read, nor play, nor care for company. I long to drink a dish of coffee in the Sluttery, and hear you dun me for secrets and: Drink your coffee – why don't you drink your coffee?

Coffee meant something more than just coffee to Swift and Vanessa. Some hot-eyed students of Swiftiana have supposed the references to coffee to stand for the sexual act. Horace Walpole, aesthete son of Sir Robert, was one of the first to give it this interpretation: 'I think it plain he lay with her . . .' Another who assumed the apparently obvious was the Walpoles' friend Lady Mary Wortley Montagu, who wrote in 1730:

> So when Vanessa yielded up her charms,
> The blest Cadenus languish'd in her arms.
> High on a peg, his unbrush'd beaver hung,
> His vest unbutton'd, and his God unsung,
> Raptur'd he lies . . .

That was in her 'Epistle to Mr Pope', and it would be interesting to know what Alexander Pope made of it. He had with Martha Blount the same kind of ambiguous close relationship that Swift had with Stella. Pope's unhappy physique made sexual activity difficult, if not impossible. Of a rumour that he had visited a brothel, he said that it was 'a lie as to the main point . . . and I had so few things of that kind ever on my hands that I could scarce have forgot it'. Yet he liked to project a 'gay dog' image. He wrote to women with what a biographer has called an 'exaggerated teasing style of gallantry', and had written contrived and mannered love letters to Lady Mary before they fell out.

Coffee was exotic and smart, and a stimulant. In late life Swift

131

gave up both tea and coffee, as 'unwholesome'. Pope versified ecstatically about coffee:

> While coffee shall to British nymphs be dear;
> While fragrant steams the bended head shall cheer;
> Or grateful bitters shall delight the taste;
> So long her honour, name, and praise shall last!

And again:

> For lo! the board with cups and spoons is crown'd,
> The berries crackle, and the mill turns round.
> On shining altars of Japan they raise
> The silver lamp; the fiery spirits blaze
> From silver spouts the grateful liquors glide,
> While China's earth receives the smoking tide.
> At once they gratify their scent and taste,
> And frequent cups prolong the rich repast.

Coffee was specially exciting for and with women, since coffee-houses were male preserves. In private houses, the coffee was sometimes made in the kitchen, though it was unlikely to be made well. Swift, in his comic *Directions to Servants* (in which he highlights servants' shortcomings by instructing them how best to cheat and abuse their employers), tells the footman that 'if you are ordered to make coffee after dinner, and the pot happens to boil over while you are running up for a spoon to stir it, or thinking of something else, or struggling with the chambermaid for a kiss', he should wipe the coffee-grounds off the sides of the pot, carry it up boldly, and 'when your lady finds it too weak, and examines you whether it has not run over, deny the fact absolutely'.

More usually coffee was made in the dining-parlour over the fire or a spirit lamp; just as tea was brewed at the table by the lady of the house, until the end of the nineteenth century.

I think it was like this: Dr Swift and Vanessa were certainly left alone together. He told Mrs Long that she would, in his presence, tell her sister to run away downstairs because she had 'some private business with the Doctor'. I think they made coffee together in the Sluttery, bent over the fire or spirit lamp, making their private jokes, their heads close, their hands touching as they managed the kettle and coffee-pot; and then sat back in their chairs, and talked, forgetting the coffee, reminding one another to drink it. This became a cherished ritual, carrying a sexual charge heightened by anticipation and repetition. We may think about this again hearing Laetitia Pilkington describing Swift making coffee at the Deanery, later.

From the internal evidence of Swift's poem *Cadenus and Vanessa*, Vanessa declared to Swift in London that she had fallen in love with him. From the internal evidence of his letters (and of *Cadenus and Vanessa*), he protested against her passion, which meant entering fully into her feelings, and thus met her halfway, since the way they felt about each other became the main topic of conversation. If he had no intention of marrying her, he was abusing his position – he was so much older than she – and her mother's hospitality. Whether he was abusing Vanessa herself is a moot point. The situation was not without piquancy, for both of them.

Attending the Court in Windsor, in August 1712, he wrote to Vanessa of his weariness. He had been to the Duchess of Shrewsbury's ball, 'looking a little singular' in his clerical gown 'among so many fine ladies and gentlemen'. He returned briefly to London to see her and look for new lodgings, 'pretty near where I did before and dine with you thrice a week; and will tell you a thousand secrets, provided you will have no quarrels with me'.

When he was again in Windsor, Vanessa and her brother Bartholomew came down for a few days. That visit marked another significant episode in the litanies of their secret history.

In April 1713 Swift heard through Erasmus Lewis that his name was not on the new list of senior clerical appointments. This was a humiliating blow. He had kept a watching brief on every English deanery and bishopric that became vacant, and let his hopes be raised every time. Archbishop King of Dublin, not anxious to have him back in Ireland, had been urging him all along to get himself some preferment in England: 'Pray lay aside your modesty and push it', and 'Consider that years grow upon you; and, after fifty, both body and mind decay.' Lord Peterborough had repeatedly put in a good word for him with the Lord Treasurer, Lord Oxford.

Swift told Lord Oxford now that he could not stay on in London 'unless I had something honourable immediately given me'. Oxford muttered about getting him a prebend at Windsor. Nothing happened. 'I confess I thought the ministry would not let me go', he told MD, who had gone oddly silent. It was by another route – the appointment was in the gift of the Duke of Ormonde – that he was offered the deanery of St Patrick's in Dublin.

When he told Stella about his appointment as Dean of St Patrick's he did not pretend to be pleased about it, and warned that he would be returning to London soon after his installation. 'I shall be very busy. Short letters from henceforward.' They were not to take lodgings for him. 'I can lie somewhere after I land, and I care not where, nor how.' The Ladies had not been writing to him at all, recently. He was 'vely akklee [angry]'.

The night he left on horseback for Chester and the boat, he wrote to Vanessa promising to write yet again during the journey – 'a common letter to you all' but 'directed to you'. 'Pray be merry and eat and walk. And be good . . . and so adieu brat.' He wrote again from St Albans. She was writing too. 'I am very impatient to hear from you at Chester', she told him. 'It is impossible to tell you how often I have wished you a cup of coffee and an orange at your inn.'

At his inn in Chester, exhausted after six days' riding, the claims of both women pressed upon him. He heard at last from Stella on arrival, and wrote to her, appreciative of some acerbic sally in her letter: 'I said aloud – agreeable b-tch.'

Vanessa was flooding him with fluent, unpunctuated letters – 'if you think I write too often your only way is to tell me so or at least to write to me again that I may know you don't quite forget me for I very much fear that I never employ a thought of yours now except when you are reading my letters which makes me ply you with them . . .' – which suggest she talked fast and a lot, a match for Swift: 'I find no conversation upon earth comparable with yours', she wrote, 'so if you care I should stay do but talk and you'll keep me with pleasure.'

Once in Ireland, having endured the installation ceremony in St Patrick's in melancholy mood, he wrote to Vanessa from his 'cabin' at Laracor, preferring 'a field-bed and an earthen floor before the great house there, which they say is mine . . . I am now fitter to cut hedges than meddle with affairs of state. I must order one of the workman to drive those cows out of my island . . .'

By the end of September 1713 he was back in London, emotionally involved in the last fight to save the Tory ministry and his vain attempt to reconcile Oxford and Bolingbroke. It is not known how his reunion in Dublin with Stella and her companion had turned out. There are no more letters to Stella surviving.

But something had changed. His centre of gravity, during his brief return, had shifted back to Ireland. On his return to London he wrote to Archdeacon Walls: 'I protest I am less fond of England than ever. The Ladies tell me they are going to live at Trim, I hope they will pass their Christmas at Dublin.' And in November, also to Walls, he expressed anxiety about the health of the 'Black Lady' (Stella) and sent instructions about money due to Mrs Dingley.

When he went off to bury himself in retirement at Letcombe, and Queen Anne was dying, he wrote immediately to Vanessa about the boringness of his routine. His host, the Revd John Geree, was 'a melancholy man'. Swift was melancholy too. They dined between twelve and one, had some bread and butter and ale at eight, and at ten Geree went to bed. Mr Geree's wife was away. The Pretender or the Prince of Hanover might both have landed, 'and I never the wiser', he told Vanessa. (Within a few days he was being bombarded with letters from London friends.) Vanessa's mother was ill. Swift offered to lend Vanessa money to offset the family debts.

Swift read, walked and wrote letters. Then Vanessa paid him a visit, unannounced. The 'Berkshire surprise', as it became known between them, was a bold move (though not so bold if she considered that they were affianced). Afterwards Swift scolded her for it, and especially for showing herself in Wantage, the nearby small town, where he was known to the vicar. 'I think, since I have known you', Swift wrote to her, 'that I have drawn an old house on my head. You should not have come by Wantage for a thousand pound. You used to brag you were very discreet. Where is it gone?'

He ordered her not to address her letters to him in her own handwriting, and to write 'nothing that is particular, but which may be seen'. He was agitated about her idea of returning to Ireland with her younger sister, and gave her a brutal warning:

If you are in Ireland while I am there, I shall see you very seldom. It is not a place for any freedom, but where everything is known in a week, and magnified a hundred degrees . . . but it is probable we may meet in London in winter, or, if not, leave all to fate, that seldom cares to honour our inclinations. I say

this out of the perfect esteem and friendship I have for you . . .
I would not answer your questions for a million, nor can I think
of them with any ease of mind.

This is unpleasant. It is the letter of a man disentangling himself. The
new Dean of St Patrick's, with cathedral business already pressing on
him through the mails, had enough to worry about without the
threat of a possessive and ardent Vanessa at the Deanery door. He
was anxious to be back on terms with the Ladies.

He did not return to England that winter; he did not return for
twelve years. But Vanessa, constant by nature, and committed to
him as the love of her life, was not going to be dislodged so easily.

Chapter Nine

DEANERY

THE DEANERY still stands within its high enclosing walls on the edge of St Patrick's Cathedral close, though much altered since a fire in 1781, which did serious damage to the west side of the house. Later alterations have been made for the convenience of modern incumbents. There was no entrance porch when Swift lived there, and more steps than there are now leading up to the hall door; the ground has been raised.

The Deanery fronts on to Kevin Street. Its back windows look out over the walled garden and the burial ground, on to St Patrick's Cathedral. Marsh's Library, endowed by the archbishop who was Provost of Trinity when Swift first went there as a student, is next in line eastwards. Beside the library and also fronting on to Kevin Street was St Sepulchre's, the palace of the archbishops of Dublin, occupied in Swift's day by his ambivalent colleague Archbishop King, and stretching back far enough for Swift to see its rear portions from his side windows.

Furniture and objects that Swift inherited or brought into the house have necessarily mostly been lifted, or borrowed, or thrown out, over the decades. Others have been brought back. Yet you feel his presence, or is it his absence? There is in the house one of the four portraits of him that Francis Bindon painted, this one done in 1739, when his health was already beginning to fail – very baggy under the eyes, heavily double-chinned.

His high-backed upholstered chair is still there, and the patent for his deanship, done freehand on parchment in a welter of ornamental scrolling. There is the pastel portrait of Stella with a feather in her hair, and a chunky wooden rushlight said to have been hers. There is a gate-legged drop-leaf table, which belonged to Robert Lindsay of Cookstown in Co.Tyrone, on which Swift had worked when he stayed there, and donated by the Lindsay family. There is Swift's Chinese cabinet, on a stand, with carrying-handles, inlaid with mother-of-pearl; and inside the doors are five rows of little drawers, with a lock on the bottom left-hand one. Swift kept in this cabinet the small objects he bought or was given: antique seals set in gold, commemorative medals of modern monarchs in gold and silver. There is a pinchbeck snuffbox inscribed 'CELER AT FERENDUM', a Latin pun signifying 'Swift to Boyle', Boyle being the family name of the Earl of Orrery. On the inside of the front door, the heavy rectangular wooden lock-case with its curling decorative brasswork is probably the one Swift knew.

Swift took over the Deanery from John Stearne, his old friend the former rector of Trim. Stearne was made Bishop of Dromore by the good offices of the Duke of Ormonde and Lord Oxford, only in order to make a place for Swift, and with Swift's active connivance.

Swift was not going to get anything better. He was out of the great game of musical chairs played by career clerics for the Church of Ireland bishoprics of Derry and Down, Kilmore and Cloyne, Clogher and Clonfert, Killaloe, Killala, Ferns, Elphin and Raphoe . . . twenty-two dioceses in all, out of all proportion to the numbers of their flock, being based on pre-Reformation divisions. In many dioceses there were only ruined bishop's palaces, or no house at all; though an orgy of episcopal palace-building was getting under way towards the end of Swift's life, following a requirement that bishops reside part of the year in their dioceses.

The deans of St Patrick's had not had a decent house to live in either, until now, since the Reformation. The deanery house lay 'waste and ruinous' in the mid-sixteenth century, and though repaired in the interim it was still dilapidated in the mid-seventeenth. When John Stearne became Dean in 1705, he built a brand-new house on the site, with a sixty-eight-foot frontage, and stretching forty-four feet from front to back. It took him years.

Swift followed its progress ironically, little thinking he himself would ever live there. Stearne had built a small house as a temporary home for himself, to one side; this was to become the porter's lodge, balanced on the other side by the stables. The Ladies,who, on most Fridays when Swift was away, dined, and played cards, and roasted oranges over the fire with Dean Stearne (whom they found very kind) and their clerical friends, would have visited him in the small house; and observed the ongoing slow progress of the building operations.

Stearne spent virtually the whole of his deanship getting the house built. He also left his deanery with plans designed by himself to build a spire on the north-west tower of St Patrick's Cathedral. Archbishop King pressed Swift to look into the practicality of realizing it, but nothing was done in Swift's lifetime.

The Deanery seemed to be nearing completion in 1708. 'I reckon by this time you have done with masons and carpenters', Swift wrote to Stearne from London in April that year, 'and are now beginning with upholsterers . . . But pray keep the garden till I come.' From the time he had his own little demesne at Laracor, Swift took a keen and jealous interest in his friends' garden projects. A couple of months later: 'I long to know what is become of your new house, whether there is yet a union between that and the little one, or whether the work stops for lack of money; and you pretend that it is only that the boards may have time to season.' Four years later, in 1711: 'I reckon your hands are now out of mortar, and that your garden is finished.' Dean Stearne can only have lived in his 'big' house for a couple of years before he moved out again and Swift moved in.

The Deanery garden is small, and later Swift acquired the lease of a rectangular three-acre field on the other side of Kevin Street, which he named 'Naboth's Vineyard'. He had an eight-foot stone wall built round it, 'which will ruin both my health and fortune, as well as humor', he told Charles Ford in summer 1724. It cost him £400, and he took an obsessional interest in its construction. In 1730 he reminisced to Bolingbroke: 'I built a wall five years ago, and when the masons played the knaves, nothing delighted me so much as to stand by while my servants threw down what was amiss.' He had the interior south-facing side lined with brick, against which he grew fruit trees. He planted elms, and laid down gravel walks. It was never much of a garden, more of an exercise ground, and a place of excursion with visitors, or the Ladies, 'who come every afternoon to the Deanery as to a country house' from their lodgings. He sometimes put out his horses there.

Stearne was afraid of fire, and in his new Deanery of three storeys over a basement there were four flights of stairs for ease of escape – one grand, main one, rising out of the entrance hall, two narrow flights from different ends of the basement to the ground floor, and one set of back stairs to the upper floors. The stairs gave Swift exercise in wet weather. He liked chasing any guest who had the stamina up and down and round and round. Swift had a manic streak.

The stone-vaulted kitchen, the barrel-vaulted scullery, the pantry, a warren of larders, and the wine and beer cellars were in the basement. Swift bought forty-six wine bottles soon after he moved in 'and want nothing but the circumstances of wine to be able to entertain a friend'. He did not feel able to go away at all until his 'great vessel' of Alicante wine was bottled, 'and till my horse is in a condition to travel and my chimney piece made. I never wanted so much country air, being plagued with perpetual colds and twenty ailments, yet I cannot stir at present as things stand.' Swift's wine-bins were still in place as late as the 1930s. Also in the basement was a room which served as the servants' hall. Swift's living-in servants slept down there too.

On the ground floor was the blue-painted dining-parlour where he entertained his friends, the butler's pantry, Swift's study (at the back), and the 'street-parlour' – the housekeeper's room, where Mrs Brent had her domain. On the first floor, there was a drawing-room at the front, and at the back a large room over the dining-parlour, with a fireplace each end. This had been Dean Stearne's library; Swift had offered to acquire books for him in London while the collection was being made, and Stearne amassed far more volumes than Swift ever did. Swift sent over just six boxes of books from England to add to those which had been stored with Mrs Brent and the Ladies in Ireland. He was a reader but not a book-collector, writing to Pope in 1729: 'I hate a crowd, where I have not an easy place to see and be seen. A great library always makes me melancholy, where the best author is as much squeezed, and as obscure as a porter at a coronation.'

Stearne, like Swift, was unmarried, but he had built a considerable house. Swift, who had few possessions and little furniture, was too proud and poor to take any of the outgoing dean's. 'I shall buy Bishop Stearne's hair as soon as his household goods', he told the Ladies. 'I shall be ruined, or at least sadly cramped, unless the Queen will give me a thousand pounds. I am sure she owes me a great deal more. Lord Treasurer rallies [teases] me upon it, and I believe intends it; but, *quando* [when]?'

The Deanery, its windows uncurtained, its wooden floors

uncarpeted, was echoingly large for him. But houses were customarily thinly furnished, and he acquired good pictures to hang in his drawing-room. He had a set of thirteen small Persian paintings; and there was a large painting of birds, the gift of the Earl of Pembroke whom he had known as Lord-Lieutenant in 1707. Pembroke had disappointed Swift in his early efforts for the remission of the First Fruits levy; but Pembroke was convivial and a fellow-punster, and gave him the bird picture. There was a miniature of Lord Oxford by Zincke, which Swift left in his will to Pope, 'my dearest friend', and a portrait of Charles I said to be by Van Dyck, which Swift believed to be an original.

Lady Orkney had given him a half-length portrait of herself by Kneller. (Swift left it to Lord Orrery in his will.) Women did like to give things to Swift. Lord Oxford's daughter-in-law, Henriette Harley, gave him a snuff-box when he was moving back to Ireland. He squashed it: 'I put it in a close pocket, when I was on horseback, and forgot to remove it when I alighted, and so overlayd it as a mother does a child she is too fond of.' The Harleys replaced it with another, made of tortoiseshell inlaid and lined with gold.

The writing desk, which is in the Deanery, was a later present from Lady Worsley. She was the mother of Lord Carteret, who was three times Lord-Lieutenant of Ireland, a scholar, a lover of 'la bagatelle', and the only Castle grandee who ever became part of Dean Swift's intimate circle. In 1730 Carteret's daughter-in-law gave Swift a tea-caddy which she had decorated with seashells – 'which I take to be malicious', Swift told Carteret's mother, 'with design to stand in your place. Therefore I would have you to provide against it by another, and something of your own work, as hers is. For you know, I always expect presents and advances from ladies.' Lady Worsley riposted generously, not with 'something of her own work' but with the writing desk. Swift was to leave this writing desk and the Harley snuff-box to Deane Swift's wife Mary.

It was in the crowded downstairs study that Swift had his books, his letter collections, his manuscripts, the Chinese cabinet and the writing desk with his silver desk-set and ink-pot. He also had a less elaborate desk made by Mrs Brent's son-in-law Ridgeway, a cabinet-maker. He slept in one of the rooms on the first floor (next to the unused large room, Stearne's former library), at the back of the house and overlooking the cathedral.

*

Swift fell into a depression on arriving in Dublin in late August 1714, oppressed by 'perfect laziness, and listlessness', and unable to write anything, as he told Charles Ford in a letter about a week later. 'I hope I shall keep my resolution of never meddling in Irish politics.' He did not even read the newspapers.

> 'Tis true, – then why should I repine
> To see my life so fast decline?
> But why, obscurely here alone?
> Where I am neither lov'd nor known.
> My state of health none care to learn;
> My life here is no soul's concern.
> And, those with whom I now converse,
> Without a tear will tend my hearse.

He had thought to take refuge in his little property at Laracor, and had dreamed, while he was huddling in Letcombe, of being back there, or somewhere reassuringly like it:

> I often wish'd, that I had clear
> For life, six hundred pounds a year,
> A handsome house to lodge a friend,
> A river at my garden's end,
> A terrace walk, and half a rood
> Of land set out to plant a wood.

He wanted the Dean's salary – £400, in addition to the £250 he had from Laracor – but not the Dean's house. But as he wrote to Bolingbroke, his little house at Laracor was in a bad state. 'The wall of my own apartment is fallen down, and I want mud to rebuild it, and straw to thatch it. Besides, a spiteful neighbour has seized on six feet of ground, carried off my trees, and spoiled my grove.' He hadn't yet been up there: 'I have not fortitude enough to go and see these devastations.' In Dublin he was seeing no one except Archdeacon Walls, Stella and Rebecca Dingley, and other old friends.

His Scots groom got in hay, but stacked it on a rainy day so that it fermented and steamed and 'my stable is a very hospital for sick horses', as he told Knightly Chetwode in early October 1714. The joiner making bookshelves in his study was taking twice as long as he said he would. Swift did not have the money to put everything in order. The promised £1,000 never materialized, his friends having fallen from office before the grant was negotiated.

His one victory in those first weeks was getting rid of 'a great cat, that belonged to the late Dean, and almost poisoned the house'. Stearne returned from Dromore specially to collect his cat, 'who by her perpetual noise and stink must certainly be a Whig'. Swift also had to find a way of saying goodbye to an old woman servant, whom Stearne had left in the house along with the cat. Then the Scots groom ran off, 'having robbed me and several of the neighbourhood'.

Away from Dublin in November, Swift charged Archdeacon Walls with overseeing the work in the study, urging economy: 'Why the whole room painted? is it not enough to have only the new panels and edges of the shelves painted; do what you will, but pray let it be done before I come, that the smell may go off. Is the chimney-piece up, or only finished at the man's house?'

The study was the only room that he made truly his own. After ten months in the Deanery, he wrote to Pope: 'You are to understand that I live in the corner of a vast unfurnished house; my family consists of a steward, a groom, a helper in the stable, a footman, and an old maid, who are all at board-wages, and when I do not dine abroad, or make an entertainment, (which last is very rare) I eat a mutton-pie, and drink half a pint of wine.'

Bad horses and unsatisfactory servants continued to bother him, though he made a lasting accommodation with a new cook, 'as old and ugly as that the Bishop [Stearne] left, for the ladies of my acquaintance would not allow me one with a tolerable face though I most earnestly interceded for it'. He called this cook, with grim affectionate irony, 'Sweetheart'. His friend Patrick Delany remembered her as 'of very large size, and very robust constitution; and such a face, as in the style of ladies, would be termed plain; that is, much roughed by smallpox, and furrowed by age'.

Someone pinned some verses on the cathedral door when it was announced that Swift had been appointed dean:

> Today this Temple gets a Dean
> Of parts and fame uncommon
> Us'd, both to pray and to profane:
> To serve, or God, or Mammon . . .

Look down, St Patrick, look we pray
On thine own church and steeple;
Convert the Dean, on this great day;
Or else God help the people.

And now, whene'er his deanship dies
Upon his stone be graven,
A man of God here buried lies
Who never thought of Heaven.

The someone was the Revd Jonathan Smedley, a busy Whig, four years Swift's junior, who spent much time in London though he was then the vicar of a parish in Co. Cork and later achieved serial deanship. In a sycophantic poem to the Lord-Lieutenant in 1726, angling for a bishopric, Jonathan Smedley referred maliciously to 'the dextrous shift' in feathering his nest

Of t'other Jonathan, *viz* Swift,
But now, St Patrick's saucy Dean . . .

To which the aforesaid saucy Dean riposted with a sarcastic mock-reply from the Lord-Lieutenant, published as a broadside, which began:

Dear Smed I read thy brilliant lines
Where wit in all its glory shines . . .

Smedley continued to write sneering verse attacks on Swift, and Swift continued to reply in kind.

Smedley published his cathedral-door verses, along with a spoof of Swift's diary for the year 1714. This item is quite eerie. The idea was to lampoon the alleged diarist as a sponging, trimming, godless, unprincipled Jacobite; Jacobitism apart, it is pretty near the knuckle:

Thursday: Wak'd with a headache. Said no prayers that morning. Dressed immediately. Look'd confounded rakish. Repeated verses while I was washing my hands. Resolv'd (whilst I was putting on my gowns) to ridicule the orders of bishop, priest, and deacon. After dinner at my Lord B———s. Went to drink tea in York Buildings [where Lord Oxford lived]. The

Earl look'd queerly. Left in a huff . . . Drove to the Cocoa-Tree. Sat till one, musing and thinking of nothing . . . Damn'd the cook, lik'd the wine. No wit. All politics. Settled the succession. Fix'd the place and time and manner of his landing . . .

Friday: . . . Walk in my room for two hours. Loll on my couch for two hours. Take a manual for devotion in my hand, but say extempore prayers. Mightily given to ejaculations . . . Give a farthing to a poor man. Put on a pair of new gloves. Go to St James's. Don't like things. Confirm'd concerning animosity between the Earl and Lord Harry. In a quandary . . . Some wit. Much impiety. Am treated. Expenses one shilling. *Mem*: This day month I had clean sheets.

The manner and matter constitute so accurate a parody of Swift's manner and matter in the *Journal to Stella* that it seems impossible Smedley had not been shown some of his diary-letters: proof that Swift's fears were justified about his letters being intercepted. Archbishop King had authorized this perlustration of the mail.

Swift had several reasons for being depressed. There was Vanessa. There was Stella. Smedley was just one example of many exterior irritants, symptomatic of the suspicion in which Dean Swift was held by the Whig ministry under Sir Robert Walpole in England, and by Walpole's Whig appointees in Dublin. He knew his letters were still being intercepted.

Because of his close identification with Lords Oxford and Bolingbroke, and with their (previously covert) connections with the Pretender, Swift too was tainted with Jacobitism. Stories that he was pelted with mud on the streets of Dublin may be apocryphal. But he recorded being set upon by unknown assailants as he took his exercise on horseback on the strand at Clontarf, accompanied by two servants. He never rode or walked out alone. 'My amusements', he told Pope, 'are defending my small dominions against the Archbishop, and endeavouring to reduce my rebellious choir.'

The cathedral hierarchy over which the Dean of St Patrick's presided consisted, working downwards, of the Dean and twenty-three others, including the Precentor, the Chancellor, the Treasurer, two archdeacons, a clutch of prebendaries, and the Dean's Vicar, who was his personal assistant. Most of them, Swift told Francis

Atterbury, 'have taken a fancy to oppose me upon all occasions in the Chapter House'.

Even though he spent long periods away, Swift was a conscientious and authoritarian dean, involving himself deeply in every detail of the cathedral's ritual and routine: the quality of the music (in spite of being unmusical), the training of the choir, the quality of the preaching, the demeanour of his clergymen when 'outside'. He revived what was then considered the primitive practice of consecrating, administering and himself receiving the Sacrament of Holy Communion on Sunday. (In this, as in other High Church gestures and practices, he was considered a little Romish.) He was jealous of his authority, challenging Archbishop King on appointments and preferments over which they both had influence, and testing his own privileges, and his rights of decision and veto in his Chapter House, to their legal limits. It took him about six years to get his empire under control.

His fiefdom extended beyond the cathedral close, spanning the five acres of narrow city streets and courts which constituted the Liberty of St Patrick's, over which the Dean and Chapter had jurisdiction and the civil authorities did not. This area of old Dublin was known as 'the Liberties' in the plural; the Dean's Liberty lay within the Archbishop's larger one, while remaining free of of its jurisdiction.

Swift's relations with his next-door neighbour and ecclesiastical superior, Archbishop William King, had always been prickly. They had known one another ever since Swift took orders as a young man, and were constantly in communication when Swift was negotiating for the repeal of the First Fruits. King had been sceptical of Swift's ability to negotiate the remission of the First Fruits with the Tories, because he had been on good terms with the Whigs. The Duke of Ormonde was asked to solicit the Queen separately, which was galling for Swift. King had also constantly reminded Swift, once he allied himself with the possibly Jacobite-tinged Tories, of the terror among the Protestants in Ireland of the return of the Stuarts.

The Archbishop, who came from Antrim in the north of Ireland, was seventeen years older, a sound churchman, not much of a writer or scholar, never sycophantic to any English ministry, and a patriot for Ireland in that he cared deeply about the poverty of the general population and resented English interference with Irish affairs. St Sepulchre's was his official residence. He also had a country place at

Mount Merrion, where, like Sir William Temple at Moor Park, he cultivated melons, peaches and apricots. By his own account he had 'but an awkward way of address to ladies'.

Archbishop King's letter to Swift on hearing of his appointment as dean was cool. 'This is to welcome you to my neighbourhood of St Sepulchre's. I have a very great loss in the removal of the Bip of Dromore [Stearne] who was not only a neighbour but a bosom friend.' Swift and King had endless 'little brangles', as Swift called their quarrels.

King, in earlier years, could have obtained for him some desirable Church appointment in Ireland. But he was not prepared to put himself out for the unpredictable Dr Swift. King offered Swift some sober advice in 1711, when Swift was at the height of his London excitement. The Archbishop wrote counselling him to set himself to some 'serious and useful subject in your profession', by which he meant a learned book of divinity or theology. 'Assure yourself, that your interest, as well as duty, requires this from you.' He may have been right. One would say he did not know his man, were it not that we know he had been reading Swift's private letters.

The two fell out now over what Dean Swift saw as Archbishop King's meddling with the affairs of the Dean and Chapter of St Patrick's. From the moment of his appointment, Swift wrote to King in 1727, 'your Grace hath thought fit to take every opportunity of giving me all sorts of uneasiness, without ever giving me, in my whole life, one single mark of your favour, beyond common civilities'.

Yet like two snarling but companionable old dogs they always managed, as Swift had said back in 1711, to 'go on as before'.

Swift kept on a minor canon, the Revd John Worrall, as Dean's Vicar, and used him as a dogsbody, writing him when away letters full of household instructions for Mrs Brent.

It was Worrall too who had to deal with a threat from the past. Betty Jones was Swift's girlfriend from the time when, as 'a lad', as he said, he first went to his mother in Leicester: the one his clergyman cousin had warned him about. Betty subsequently married an inn-keeper. 'My mistress with a pox', as Swift said to Worrall, had been writing him letters. She had a widowed daughter who was in Dublin and needed a loan to set herself up in a shop. The daughter had already written to Swift.

There is a bad smell of blackmail about this, which Swift does not quite acknowledge to Worrall. 'The errand is so romantic, that I know not what to say to it. I would be ready to sacrifice five pounds, on old acquaintance, to help the woman; I suspect her mother's letters to be counterfeit, for I remember she spells like a kitchen maid. And so I end this worthy business.' He suspected that the woman in Dublin might not be Betty Jones's daughter at all. He gave Worrall her Dublin address and asked him to use his judgement.

Patrick Delany thought John Worrall was 'low', and unworthy of the Dean's intimacy. Mrs Worrall, however, was 'a woman of great vicacity, good-nature, and generosity; remarkably cleanly and elegant in her person'. She kept a good table. Swift often ate at the Worralls', treating their house in Big Sheep Street (later Ship Street) like a tavern, paying his way and sometimes inviting guests. After Mrs Worrall died, he had far less time for her husband.

It was with Worrall that he often took his walks around his Liberty, speaking to all and sundry, exchanging witticisms with the people in the lanes and alleys. His true mistresses, said Delany, were the poor women selling plums, nails, tapes, or gingerbread, or knitting and mending stockings, or cobbling shoes. 'One of these mistresses wanted an eye: another, a nose: a third, an arm. He bought their wares, and overpaid, and called each by her own name, invented by him: Cancerina, Stumpa-nympha, Pullagowna.'

When, in the 1720s, famine struck Ireland and the population of beggars escalated, the Dean inaugurated a system of badges (to be sewn on to the shoulder of their garments) for the beggars of his own Liberty, to distinguish them from the swarms of 'foreign' beggars who should go back to whence they came. He was irritated because many were too proud to wear their badges, but kept them in their pockets.

Swift gave away about a third of his income to charity, but never parted with money without a groan. The weavers of Dublin mostly lived in his Liberty, and in 1721 they were workless, owing to the economic depression following the bursting of the South Sea Bubble. The starving families came to see the Dean. He did not only write about their distress and its reasons, he inaugurated a scheme of small loans – £5 or £10 – from his own pocket, to enable any small tradesman to get back on track by buying tools or materials, or to start up in some other line. Mrs Brent kept the accounts.

The money had to be paid back in regular weekly instalments, plus interest. He was adamant about the repayments, and was on this

Left: Portrait of Jonathan Swift as a student at Trinity College, Dublin.

Above: Lady Giffard, *née* Martha Temple. This portrait was in Swift's possession at the Deanery in Dublin for many years.

Left: Sir William Temple in youth, *circa* 1660. He was in his retirement Swift's employer and mentor, and a dominant influence on his life.

Esther Johnson, Swift's 'Stella': 'Believe me,' he wrote when she was dying, 'that violent friendship is much more lasting, and as much engaging, as violent love.'

Presumed portrait of Hester Vanhomrigh, Swift's 'Vanessa', who wrote to him:
'I was born with violent passions, which terminate all in one – that inexpressible passion
I have for you.'

Right: Queen Anne in 1705, when Swift was making his first political contacts in London. Ten years on, when he was attending Court, she had become a good deal fatter.

Above: Henry St John, the First Secretary, portrayed on his elevation as Viscount Bolingbroke. For Swift he was 'the greatest young man I ever knew; wit, capacity, beauty, quickness of apprehension, good learning, and excellent taste.'

Right: Lord Treasurer Robert Harley, Earl of Oxford. On the day in 1714 when he fell from office he wrote with emotion as 'a private person' to Swift: 'I believe in the mass of souls ours were placed near each other.'

Left: John Arbuthnot, Queen Anne's doctor and, with Pope and Gay, Swift's convivial dining-companion and literary collaborator.

Below: John Gay.

Above: John, fifth Earl of Orrery, the friend of Swift's later years and his most critical early biographer.

Left: Alexander Pope, portrayed by Swift's friend and his, Charles Jervas.

Right: Uncle Godwin's fine house and Swift's birthplace, 7 Hoey's Court, Dublin, sketched in a state of dilapidation in the 1840s.

Below: A house in Armagh which may be the Achesons' Markethill, where Swift stayed for long periods. During Swift's lifetime, before being built or rebuilt in the classical 'Georgian' style, Irish country seats generally consisted of several separate low buildings.

Bottom: Pope's villa on the Thames at Twickenham, where Swift stayed in the late 1720s.

A
LETTER
TO THE
Shop-Keepers, Tradesmen, Farmers, and Common-People of IRELAND,
Concerning the
Brass Half-Pence
Coined by
Mr. Woods,
WITH
A DESIGN to have them Pass in this
KINGDOM.

Wherein is shewn the Power of the said PATENT, the Value of the HALF-PENCE, and how far every Person may be oblig'd to take the same in Payments, and how to behave in Case such an Attempt shou'd be made by WOODS or any other Person.

[Very Proper to be kept in every FAMILY.]

By M. B. Drapier.

Dublin: Printed by J. Harding in Molesworth's-Court.

Far left: Swift as the 'Hibernian Patriot': frontispiece to Vol IV of Faulkner's edition of the *Works*, Dublin 1735.

Left: Cover of the first of the Drapier's *Letters*, Dublin 1723.

Engraving, 'The punishment inflicted on Lemuel Gulliver…', late 1720s: the incident depicted does not occur in *Gulliver's Travels*, and is an indication of the work's immediate notoriety.

Engraving, 'Scene in a Madhouse', ie, Bedlam: from Hogarth's *A Rake's Progress*. Note the two fine ladies on a sightseeing visit.

Left: Swift in his London heyday, in his late forties, one of several done by Charles Jervas. This one belonged to Swift's old friend Lady Betty Germaine.

Above: A version of this curious line-engraving of Swift bareheaded was chosen by his friend Lord Orrery as the frontispiece for his *Remarks on the Life and Writings of Dr Jonathan Swift*, so he presumably considered it a fair likeness.

Left: Informal pencil drawing of Dr Jonathan Swift, Dean of St Patrick's, done in 1730, when he was 63.

account considered by some to be harsh. His system, now known as 'micro-credit', involving small sums from $2 to $100, is successfully practised in our own time by Muhammad Yunus, founder of the Grameen Bank in Bangladesh. Yunus's theory is that handouts destroy initiative and help maintain poverty. That was what Swift thought too.

His friends in Dublin were men – and their wives, when they had wives – whom he had known at Trinity, or who were currently fellows of Trinity, or in the professions, or fellow-clerics: educated, English, or Anglicized. Among them were the seven hospitable Grattan brothers, 'men of open hearts, and free spirits'; their cousins the Jacksons, another cheerful tribe; the Rochforts, the Ludlows, 'men of parts, men of humour, men of wit and men of virtue', wrote Dr Delany, refuting Orrery's charge that Swift surrounded himself with unworthy people.

He kept, and was kept, well away from the aristocracy and most of the Whig-English administrators up at the Castle. His two best friendships, through whom most of the others were made, were with two men who were just over thirty years of age – almost a generation younger than himself – when he met them: Dr Thomas Sheridan, who kept a school in Dublin and later in Co. Cavan, and Dr Patrick Delany, both ordained clergymen.

Lord Orrery was scornful about Dr Sheridan, saying he was 'slovenly, indigent, and cheerful. He knew books better than men: and he knew the value of money least of all.' Orrery describes Swift latching on to Sheridan 'as upon a prey with which he intended to regale himself, whenever his appetite should prompt him'. Not so, said Sheridan's son. On their first meeting, Swift said: 'I invite all here present to dine with me next Thursday, except Mr Sheridan' – but with a look 'which expressed that the invitation was made wholly on his account'. They became inseparable, all the more so because Sheridan and Stella took to each other strongly. Sheridan was brilliant, high-spirited, extravagant, susceptible, irresponsible, indiscreet; he was a good foil for the Dean, who advised him and scolded him and enjoyed his vagaries. 'Sheridan is still the same', he wrote to Charles Ford in 1724, 'I mean in the sense that weathercocks are still the same.'

Sheridan played the fiddle. He was also a true scholar and had genius as a schoolteacher. He refreshed Swift's liking for reading the classics (though failed to interest him in mathematics), and was his best companion in 'la bagatelle'. Swift and Sheridan composed and exchanged reams of riddles, enigmas, doggerel invitations and insults, and verses and letters in schoolboy codes or in mock-Latin which reads as English, viz. 'Mi de armis molli' for 'My dear Miss Molly' – exercises that are nowadays dignified by the term 'recreational linguistics'. Dr Delany took no part in this, considering it a fearful waste of time.

Patrick Delany was a fellow of Trinity who was Professor of History, Chancellor of St Patrick's and later Dean of Down. He had an urgent interest in polygamy, against which he preached and wrote continually, apparently alarmed that certain episodes in the Old Testament might be interpreted as advocating the practice. Though as Lord Orrery wrote to Mary Barber (one of the Deanery circle), on receipt of 'his new book on polygamy', 'Surely the Dr has given himself an unnecessary trouble, for this is an age when we are so far from taking two wives that we can scarce be prevailed upon to keep one.'

In 1732 Delany married a wife with £1,600 a year – upon which the Dean joked to Gay that he himself, as Delany's ecclesiastical superior, could not possibly consider marrying anyone with less than £2,000. Swift used to complain about Delany's uxoriousness, which kept him from the Deanery. He wrote to Mrs Pendarves that 'Dr Delany lives entirely at Delville, the town air will not agree with his lady, and in winter there is no seeing him . . .' Delany had a house in Dublin in Stafford Street, as well as Delville out at Glasnevin.

The Mary Pendarves to whom Swift was writing became (widowed) Delany's second wife; they were married two years before Swift died. She found Dublin more agreeable than London, for reasons with which modern Londoners will concur: 'This town is grown to such an enormous size, that half the day must be spent in the streets, going from one place to another.' This is the bluestocking Mrs Delany who became known for her published autobiography and letters, and for her decorative shell-work and cut-paper flowers. Visiting Dublin friends a decade before he became her husband, she described Delany as 'as agreeable a creature as I ever met with, and one who condescends to converse with women, and treat them like reasonable creatures'. Delany was 'a perfect courtier' according to Swift. To judge from his bust in Trinity college, he was attractive as well as agreeable.

The Ladies, still living in lodgings (with two maids and a manservant), shared the Dean's social life. Swift invited friends to the Deanery every Thursday and Sunday. They did not come for the food. Dr Delany, encouraged by Stella, scratched a verse on a window at the Deanery comparing the hospitality of the former Dean with that of the present incumbent:

In the days of good John, if you came here to dine,
You had choice of good meat, but no choice of good wine.
In Jonathan's reign, if you come here to eat,
You have choice of good wine, but no choice of good meat.

The indifferent meat, burned or raw, sent up by 'Sweetheart', was served on silver plates. Swift's one luxury was a complete silver service, worth at least £1,000 – dishes, plates, domed dish-covers, claret-coolers, and 'monteiths' (punch-bowls with scalloped brims on to which glasses were hooked). Stella organized Swift's parties for him, and although at the table she conducted herself like any other guest, the friends knew of her special position in his life and invited the Ladies to their entertainments when they invited the Dean.

Stella was good company. She was a man's woman, 'the usual topics of ladies' discourse being such as she had little knowledge of, and less relish', as Swift said in the painful piece he later wrote about her when he was grieving for her death. She did not interrupt, or laugh at anyone's mistakes, 'but helped them out with modesty; and if a good thing were spoken, she would not let it fall, but set it in the best light to those who were present'.

But if anyone offended her by indecent talk, she 'gave full employ-ment to her wit, her contempt, and resentment, under which even stupidity and brutality were forced to sink into confusion'. And in any evening's conversation, 'she never failed, before we parted, of delivering the best thing that was said in the company'. Swift was biased; but no other observer materially contradicted this assessment.

The Ladies moved into Swift's house when he was away, making it 'their villa', as Swift said. A punster friend wrote in 1726, when Swift was in London: 'I have called twice at the Deanery about one a clock, but have been told both times that noncompos-stella was not stirring.' Stella, watched over tenderly by Dr Sheridan, was not well. Swift fretted because she did not eat. But he must in his heart have known what was gnawing at her. Vanessa.

At the end of 1719 the Dean's deafness was worse, he had banged his shin and the wound would not heal, and he felt like an old has-been. (He was fifty-two.) He told Lord Bolingbroke: 'I have gone the round of all my stories with the younger people, and begin them again. I give hints how significant a person I have been, and nobody believes me. I lay traps for people to desire I would shew them something I have written, but cannot succeed . . . If I boast of having been valued three hundred miles off, it is of no more use than if I told how handsome I was when I was young.' In April of the next year he was complaining to Charles Ford of 'a foolish importunate ailment that quite dispirits me' – piles. He does not sound like anyone's lover. But Vanessa did not give up.

He had his literary friends in London, but few political ones now. Bishop Atterbury had been one of the casualties of the discredited Tories. His fervent Jacobite sympathies were discovered, he was tried and sent to the Tower; he went into exile, became part of the quarrelsome circle around the Pretender in France, was sidelined, and died in unhappy circumstances.

Lord Oxford had been imprisoned in the Tower for two years, and was disgraced. Warm contact with Swift was maintained by letter. 'Two years retreat', Oxford wrote to the Dean, 'has made me taste the conversation of my dearest friend with a greater relish, than ever at the time of my being charmed by it in our frequent journeys to Windsor.'

Bolingbroke fled to France in 1715 – for a time, like Atterbury, to the Pretender's court, becoming Secretary to the Pretender. He, like the Duke of Ormonde, was involved in the abortive armed attempt of the Pretender's supporters to regain the Crown for the Stuart dynasty in late 1715. Bolingbroke did not return from exile (with a French wife) until 1723.

Oxford and Bolingbroke exchanged long, sad letters with Swift – they had a lot of time for writing – loaded with philosophical musings, reminiscences, health worries and professions of faithful affection and esteem (for Swift, not for one another), with never a mention of the proven Jacobitism that was the principal cause of their discredit with Walpole's administration.

I think Swift preferred not to face up to that. He remained, in obstinate good faith, partisan. In 1736 he made moves to publish his book-length account, *History of the Four Last Years of the Queen*, mostly written back in 1713. There was a terrific flurry in London from Erasmus Lewis and the second Lord Oxford (son of Swift's friend, who had died in 1734) to stop him publishing, at least until they had vetted it. 'I loved my lord your father better than any man in the world', protested Swift to the son. He insisted that his only aim was to defend Oxford's ministry, and Oxford's honour, and to refute all accusations that Oxford wanted to bring in Popery and the Pretender.

This was precisely what they were afraid of. It was deeply embarrassing. Erasmus Lewis, without explicitly compromising Oxford or Bolingbroke, tried to persuade Swift that the scene had changed, and 'what was sense and reason then, is not so now . . . It is now too late to publish a pamphlet, and too early to publish a history.' The spate of discouraging communications was humiliating. Swift gave up. The work was not published until thirteen years after his death.

Swift was not, however, finished as a force, nor as a writer, after he became Dean of St Patrick's. In the 1720s there were secret and potentially shaming tensions in the private life of this public man. It is not yet quite time to confront the passionately demanding presence of Vanessa, and the repercussions on his relationship with Stella. Then there was Vanessa's death, and a strange fugue on his part; and Stella's, which was a far more terrible blow.

Anguish and anxiety were dispelled, as with his 'great prince' in the 'Digression on Madness', in hyperactivity on other fronts. He had been writing since he was a student. He already had a sufficient body of work published to have ensured a lasting literary reputation, from *A Tale of a Tub* to the poems, lampoons, pamphlets and periodicals of his time in London. Verses still came easily from his pen. But his inventiveness, powered by disgust at the world's ways, was to have its mature and best flowering in prose. *Gulliver's Travels*, the distillation of all the conversations, obsessions, fantasies, word-mongerings, entertainments, arguments and disillusionments of his life, was still to be written. The actual writing of it was done in the early 1720s.

Even while he was composing *Gulliver*, he was restless. The Deanery and its routines could not hold him. Once Stella had gone, he made desperate and sometimes desperately silly gestures towards pale re-enactments of the tutor–pupil intimacy which had always eased his heart. And although he had been determined never to meddle in politics in Ireland, he became too angry to keep that resolution.

Chapter Ten

CUCKOO AND PATRIOT

S WIFT, IN HIS restlessness, liked to stay in his friends' houses in Ireland. He was sometimes the third party in a marriage, a demanding and indulged cuckoo in the nest. Playing happy families, he was sometimes a wild card in the pack, and caused ructions.

He had after all no family life of his own. Sir William Temple had put into words this pattern of behaviour, writing with understanding of 'something like home that is not home, like alone that is not alone, to be wished, and only found in a friend, or in his house'.

Swift took his own manservant, and sometimes two, and his dogs. He organized the clearing of some land in Queen's County, at Knightly Chetwode's Woodbrook – it became inevitably known as 'the Dean's field' – and supervised the making of a river walk. He stayed with Charles Ford at Woodpark in Co. Meath, and with the Rochforts at Gaulstown in the same county, telling Vanessa in 1721 that he was as busy with plantations and ditching 'as if they were my own concern'. He was a bit worried that he might have overstayed his welcome. He had been there from June until October.

He stayed with the Grattans at Belcamp, just outside Dublin at Raheny; with the Ludlows at Ardsallagh, near Trim and his own Laracor; with the Robert Copes at Loughgall in the north of Ireland. He went with Sheridan to the enormous house of the Mathews family at Thomastown, Co. Tipperary, where the (Catholic) host, whom Swift had never met, allotted guests their own set of apartments, and ran his dining-parlour like a coffee-house. Swift and Sheridan were there four days before they even saw Mr Mathews, and then only because Swift was so impressed by the 'improvements' on the estate that he sought him out.

He stayed very often with the Sheridans, along with the Ladies while Stella was alive, at Quilca near Kells in Co. Cavan, where the schoolmaster and his family spent the summers. And in 1728, two years after Stella died, he made the first of three annual visits to the Achesons at Markethill (later called Gosford Castle) in Co. Armagh.

The visits to the Achesons were so long – in the first year eight months, the second four, the third three – that they almost constitute a moving-in. A closer look at his intervention in the domestic lives of the Achesons and the Sheridans shows Swift at his most creative, and most destructive.

Sir Arthur Acheson, aged forty in 1728, was the deeply respectable MP for Mullingar, and Sheriff of Co. Armagh. His wife Anne was more fun. Swift had known her father, a former Chancellor of the Exchequer in Ireland. His reason for staying on (plus his two dogs and two horses), he told Sheridan during his first visit, was that he wanted to be there for 'planting and pruning time, etc. I hate Dublin, and love the retirement here, and the civility of my hosts.'

Sheridan was to ask Mrs Brent to send on a periwig, and a new gown and cassock, more money, and papers he needed, while John Worrall was chided for being 'a bad packer of bad grapes' (a gift for his hosts), and Mrs Worrall praised for the work 'of her fairest hands in making me two night-caps'. The periwig, procured and sent by Worrall, was a disaster, second-hand and second-rate, 'so long I cannot wear it, and the curls all fallen. I just tried it on my head, but cannot wear it.'

Sir Arthur, he reported to Pope from the Deanery after this first stay, 'is a man of sense, and a scholar, has a good voice, and my Lady a better; she is perfectly well bred, and desirous to improve her understanding, which is very good, but cultivated too much like a fine lady'.

The special attraction of Anne Acheson becomes clear: 'She was my pupil there, and severely chid when she read wrong.' He made her read Bacon and Milton for hours every day, and veered between raging violently at her ignorance, and being

> . . . so indulgent, and so mild,
> As if I were a darling child.

What with reading, and chiding, 'and walking and making twenty little amusing improvements, and writing family verses of mirth by way of libels on my Lady, my time passed very well and in very great order; infinitely better than here, where I see no creature but my servants and my old Presbyterian housekeeper [Mrs Brent] . . .' When he was ill with his recurrent deafness and giddiness at Markethill, he was looked after, and the family were 'so kind to speak loud enough for me to hear them'.

'My Lady is perpetually quarrelling with Sir Arthur and me, and shews every creature the libels I have writ against her'; Pope, knowing his friend's unusual way of showing affection, replied that if Swift was libelling and abusing her, then she must indeed be a 'valuable lady'.

From the mass of occasional and more than occasionally scatalogical verse that Swift reeled off at Markethill, mostly written in the assumed voice of Anne Acheson, one learns that she was very small and very thin. She wore six-inch heels under wide hooped skirts, causing Swift to joke about her costing her husband extra in silk-lengths.

> From shoulder to flank
> I'm lean and I'm lank;
> My nose, long and thin,
> Grown down to my chin . . .

Her elbows are so sharp that

> To 'scape them, Sir Arthur
> Is forc'd to lie farther,
> Or his sides they would gore
> Like the tusk of a boar.

Swift gave her names: Skinnibonia, Snip, Snipe. The 'tyrant Dean' pre-empted criticism by depicting himself as the guest from hell:

> After a week, a month, a quarter,
> And day succeeding after day,
> Says not a word of his departure
> Tho' not a soul would have him stay.

He complained about the cooking, interfered in the wine-cellar and the dairy, gave orders to servants and gardeners without referring to his hosts.

Swift was a stirrer, and it energized him. It was during his Markethill period that he wrote most of *On Poetry, a Rapsody* – a rhapsody indeed, but of fluently sarcastic verse-instruction to aspiring critics and talentless poets – hacks, jobbers, dunces, dullards, poseurs and flatterers. *On Poetry, a Rapsody* sprints over ground traversed more laboriously in Pope's *Dunciad*, and climaxes in an illustration of how to flatter: an exemplary verse-effusion of outrageous sycophancy to George II and his family, which pleased his Queen mightily until someone explained to her the concept of irony, upon which she joined the ranks of Swift's enemies.

Swift bought some land from Sir Arthur Acheson on which to build a house. He changed his mind. The celebrated Dean ceased to charm or amuse Sir Arthur, who was an introspective, ungregarious, indoor man. Too courteous or too depressed to complain about the antics of Swift and his wife, he withdrew into himself. Swift described in embarrassingly graphic terms a host

> Whose uncommunicative heart,
> Will scarce one precious word impart:
> Still rapt in speculations deep,
> His outward senses fast asleep;
> Who, while I talk, a song will hum,
> Or, with his fingers, beat the drum;
> Beyond the skies transports his mind,
> And leaves a lifeless corpse behind.

'The frolic is gone off', Swift wrote to Pope. That last summer at Markethill, Swift inscribed a green notebook: 'Anne Acheson 1730.' He and Anne copied into it some Markethill poems that were to be published, and one that has never been published.

Swift continued to see Lady A. in Dublin in the early 1730s, telling Charles Ford: 'She is a perfect Dublin rake, sits up late, loses her money, and goes to bed sick.' She had left her husband. I do not think the Dean of St Patrick's did anything to help that marriage. She lived with her mother on the north side of Dublin Bay at Baldoyle, and entertained merrily for a few short years. She died in 1737.

*

Staying at Quilca with the Sheridans was very different. Markethill was a well-ordered household, and grand in so far as old Irish country houses – mostly two-storeyed, with the domestic offices in wings each side, or in detached small buildings – were grand. Quilca was small, and a shambles, 'the dirtiest place I ever saw'. Swift in 1724 made a long list of the 'Blunders, Deficiencies, Distresses, and Misfortunes of Quilca', of which this is a selection:

> But one lock and a half in the whole house.
> The key of the garden door lost.
> The vessels for drink few and leaky.
> The door of the Dean's bed-chamber full of large chinks.
> The Dean's bed threatening every night to fall under him.
> The little table loose and broken in the joints.
> The large table in a very tottering condition.
> But one chair in the house fit for sitting on, and that in a very ill state of health.
> The kitchen [which was a separate cabin] perpetually crowded with savages.
> Not a bit of turf in this cold weather; and Mrs Johnson [Stella] and the Dean in person, with all their servants, forced to assist at the bog, in gathering up the wet bottoms of old clamps.
> A great hole in the floor of the Ladies' chamber, every hour hazarding a broken leg.

At Quilca Swift allied himself with the husband against the wife. It was perfectly understood between Sheridan and Swift that Mrs Sheridan was a disaster: a 'harpy', a 'monster', a 'serpent'. (She bore her husband at least four children, one of them the Thomas who was to write about Swift, and was his godson.)

Sheridan was burdened *cum uxore neque leni neque commoda* (with a wife neither agreeable nor useful), as Swift frankly told him. Sheridan agreed. Praising Mrs Worrall, Sheridan wished 'my spouse were but half as good'; he had been 'linked to the Devil' for twenty-four years, he said. He and his wife were 'perfectly easy, for we never see one another but by chance'.

It may have been in part a game and a pose, but it is ugly, especially as there is every evidence that Mrs S. welcomed Swift's visits warmly. Sheridan and Swift were thick as thieves, and the younger man's vitality and uninhibited verbal facility were a stimulus to Swift. At Quilca they hobnobbed together in the dining-parlour at the far end of the house and made up nonsense rhymes and riddles. Swift finished *Gulliver's Travels* there, and tried bits out on Sheridan. The two men took their meals separately from the family. Swift insisted on their having slices of meat brought in on plates; he could never bear to see a whole joint. I can't think how the Ladies occupied themselves at Quilca when they were there. (Sheridan had a great tenderness for Stella.)

'I wish Mrs Sheridan were dead out of the way', Sheridan wrote to Swift's cousin and companion Mrs Whiteway in November 1736. It was he who died.

He moved his school from Dublin to Co. Cavan. Swift hated to see the preparations for removal, stepping aside into a small room to hide his tears. The Cavan school failed. Sheridan came back to Dublin and stayed with Swift at the Deanery, as he frequently had before, this time in order to look for a new Dublin house. He fell ill at the Deanery, and had every reason to think that his fond old friend would be happy for him to stay till he recovered. As a matter of form, he apologized to Swift for the expense and inconvenience.

But Swift was becoming increasingly erratic in his behaviour. Mrs Whiteway, who happened to be present, said briskly to Sheridan: 'It is in your power, Doctor, easily to remedy this, by removing to another lodging.' Swift was silent.

Dr Sheridan was 'quite thunderstruck'. Swift's silence told him that Mrs Whiteway was acting under instruction. Humiliated, in anguish, he left the Deanery and never entered it again. He died soon after, in October 1838, 'of dropsy and asthma'.

The 'character' Swift wrote of Dr Sheridan after his death betrayed the drying-out of his emotional roots. He praised Sheridan highly as a teacher – 'doubtless the best instructor of youth in these kingdoms, or perhaps in Europe'.

But he wrote about him without affection as a 'dupe', easily fooled by tradesmen, completely inept at 'worldly management'. The marriage came in for another bashing: 'from hence proceeded all the miseries of his life'. Swift criticized the way Sheridan brought up his daughters as grand ladies instead of training them to 'housewifery and plain clothes'. He described with regret how Sheridan's clever son Thomas was sent to Westminster school in London, where he won a scholarship which left his father with only £14 to make up for the year – which he did not have, so the boy was brought back to Dublin, and was, when Swift was writing, at Trinity, instead of at Oxford or Cambridge.

One would think that Dean Swift, as Thomas's godfather, might have made up the lacking £14. Swift was prey to old-man's meanness. It was an awful end to such a fertile and intimate friendship.

It was at Quilca, with the Sheridans, that Swift came into closest contact with the native Irish. Two of Dr Sheridan's forebears in the previous century, mere Irish converted to Protestantism, had worked with Bishop William Bedell of Kilmore, an Englishman, on an unsuccessful project of translating the Old Testament from English into Irish. Swift's Dr Sheridan, like many Irishmen, was heir to a double culture: Gaelic and classical.

Many of the English in Ireland, especially after a generation or two, had no culture, or not of the kind that Swift would recognize. Swift characterized the (Protestant) Irish squire, 'almost to a man', as 'an oppressor of the clergy, a racker of his tenants, a jobber of all public works, and generally illiterate'.

The Irish people were commonly referred to in the Dublin Parliament as the 'domestic enemy'. An Irishman in Dublin and down the eastern seaboard might converse and do his business with Englishmen in English. But the Irish spoke what Swift called their own unpronounceable language and had their own unpronounceable place-names: 'I am confident they must be genuine', wrote Swift, 'for it is impossible that either chance or modern invention could sort the alphabet in such a manner as to make those abominable sounds.' (He was equally contemptuous of the place-names the English invented for their Irish properties, often from their own or their wives' names, such as Bessborough; he might have added, but out of loyalty did not, Dr Delany's Delville.)

The English did not seek to wipe out the living culture of the native Irish. Some of them had no idea it existed. All that ladies and gentlemen from Dublin saw, as they drove to and from country houses through the depressed and depressing countryside, were bands of ragged men and women, eking out their wretched lives, with no employment and with swarms of children whom they could not support, living in lightless mud cabins, talking a barbaric language, begging and stealing, apparently pig-ignorant and unevolved.

The apocryphal story told about Aodhagan O Rathaille – 'the Dante of Munster', and Swift's contemporary – says it all. A ragged Irish workman goes into a bookshop in Cork and picks up a large, valuable volume in Latin or Greek. Holding it upside down, he asks the price in an almost incomprehensible lilting brogue. The bookseller tells him he can have it for nothing if he can read it. Upon which the Irishman turns the book the right way up and reads off a page perfectly.

Gaelic culture, beaten down over the decades by Cromwell, the flight of leaders, the annexation of lands and homes, the disabling penal laws, and gross poverty, had declined since the days when bardic schools disciplined young aspirants in the techniques and conventions of theme, metre, assonance, memorizing and improvisation, and Gaelic big houses were centres of competitive harp-music, singing and poetry.

In Swift's day there were 'courts of poetry' still, and the exchanging and copying of precious manuscripts of old poems and music. Catholic priests and schoolteachers acquired Gaelic learning along with their Greek and Latin, and taught the Greek and Latin to their pupils – in cabins, or in the open air. The themes of new poetry narrowed from the heroic to items of local, topical interest. Practitioners, though revered in their own communities, were reduced to story-telling and singing in taverns. An élite high culture was becoming demotic. But the tradition survived. Thousands of lines of poetry, hundreds of traditional airs were stored in the memories of men, women and children living in conditions often not fit for animals, and which they shared with their animals if they had any.

Many English-speakers living in the Irish-speaking countryside understood something of this culture. It was part of the air they breathed. They necessarily picked up some Irish; and for their children, reared by local servants and nurses, Irish was a second and sometimes a first language. Irish pipers and harpists still played and sang in the houses of gentry, whether Catholic or Protestant, and the gentry took part in local festivals and went to see hurling matches. The landlord class, at its worst tyrannical, was at its best responsible and paternalistic, and social bonds were vertical as well as horizontal.

Some city people of English origins saw the fascination of Gaelic culture and, more often, the usefulness of access to the Irish through their own language in the interests of social control and Protestant proselytization. Narcissus Marsh, Provost of Trinity in Swift's undergraduate days, knew some Irish and employed a converted Catholic priest to teach it in the college. His successor, Robert Huntingdon, had the Old Testament translated into Irish. Benjamin Pratt, Provost from 1710 and a friend of Swift's, employed a lecturer in Irish. The great Irish musician Turlough O'Carolan composed an air in Patrick Delany's honour, and after he died Delany saw to the publication of a volume of his music.

There is no evidence that Swift took very much interest in any of this. He knew the Revd John Richardson, who sometimes preached in Irish and was dedicated to having the New Testament and the Prayer Book translated into Irish. Richardson was often in London in Swift's glory days. Swift facilitated him in London in 1711 because Archbishop King asked him to. He introduced Richardson to the Duke of Ormonde. But he usually only sought Richardson out when he needed him as a courier for the parcels of tea requested by Archdeacon Walls's wife in Dublin. His attitude to Richardson's project seems not so much sceptical as bored.

Yet at the Achesons', according to his own 'My Lady's Lamentation . . .', he prided himself on mixing with Irish workmen on equal terms:

> He's all the day saunt'ring
> With labourers bant'ring,
> Among his colleagues,
> A parcel of Teagues,
> (Whom he brings in among us
> And bribes with mundungus.)
> Hail, fellow, well met,
> All dirty and wet:
> Find out, if you can, whose master, whose man . . .

('Teagues' are poor Irish Catholics. 'Mundungus' is cheap tobacco. They were digging a latrine: Swift had two 'temples to Cloaca' erected in the grounds of Markethill.)

Sheridan described him fraternizing with 'Irish Teagues' at Quilca too:

> So far forgetting his old station,
> He seems to like their conversation.

Conforming to their tattered rabble
He learns their Irish tongue to gabble.

In the company of Sheridan, his clever collaborator in language-games, it would be odd if Swift did not pick up, and imitate or parody, the Irish they heard around them every day. Irish crept into *Gulliver*, probably via Sheridan: the 'luhimuhs' that the Yahoos eat are derived from 'luc', Irish for mouse, and Latin 'mus'. The land of 'Traldragdrubb or Trildrogdrib' includes elements of Irish 'triall' (slave), 'droch' (evil) and 'drib' (dirt). There is an Irish prose tale about leprechauns, the 'little people', which existed then in manuscript, which contains plot elements too uncannily similar to the adventures of Gulliver in Lilliput to be coincidental. Even if Sheridan did not know it, there were learned antiquarians and Gaelic scholars in Dublin – dons, doctors, clergymen – who could have told the stories to Swift.

Swift in a poem referred to 'blind harpers' playing at Quilca; there is a tradition that he heard O'Carolan (who was born in the neighbourhood) playing there, and that O'Carolan even came to the Deanery. Swift wrote a verse entitled 'Description of an Irish Feast, translated almost literally out of the original Irish', i.e. from a prose translation of a Gaelic poem that O'Carolan set to music.

For all that, Swift was no more concerned about ancient Gaelic culture than he was about modern technological inventions. Nor was he any longer very interested in Whig and Tory. He had come to care passionately about the state of Ireland – the subject of many of the pieces he and Dr Sheridan wrote for the *Intelligencer*, a short-lived periodical on which they collaborated in the late 1720s.

The best known of Swift's works, after *Gulliver's Travels*, is a tract he wrote in 1720 in despairing response to the gross poverty and degradation of the population. He saw that the conditions under which the Irish lived, largely due to English social and economic policies, were a transgression against common humanity. He sought to shock and shame the British government by taking their unthinking inhumanity to its logical, horrible conclusion. The *Modest Proposal* – properly *A Modest Proposal for preventing the Children of Poor People from being a Burthen to their Parents or Country and for making them beneficial to the Publick* – is still shocking today. It is also funny, which makes it doubly shocking.

He was not the only one to posit sardonically desperate remedies for a desperate situation. Archbishop King in 1721 echoed the *Modest Proposal* in his protests against the rents and taxes which pauperized the Irish population:

> They have already given their bread, their fish, their butter, their shoes, their stockings, their beds, their furniture, and houses to pay their landlords and taxes. I cannot see how any more can be got from them, except we take away their potatoes and buttermilk, or flay them and sell their skins.

Swift's onslaught begins with conventional expressions of regret for the melancholy sight, on the roads and at cabin doors, of so many female beggars surrounded by children in rags. He has a scheme for solving the problem, which he works up to methodically, as if he were an official making recommendations.

He gravely computes the number of children born, the impossibility of feeding and clothing them, and the age at which they can begin earning by stealing. Then he unfolds his scheme for children of one year old, in the same reasonable vein. He has been assured

> that a young, healthy child well nursed is at a year old a most delicious, nourishing, and wholesome food, whether stewed, roasted, baked, or boiled, and I make no doubt that it will equally serve in a fricassee, or a ragout ... A child will make two dishes as an entertainment for friends, and when the family dines alone, the fore or hind quarter will make a reasonable dish, and seasoned with a little pepper or salt will be very good boiled on the fourth day, especially in winter.

He continues with recipes and suggestions, in the polite and tentative tone of those gentlemen who wrote papers for learned societies on useful technical improvements. The thrifty, he suggested, in the present hard times, might flay the little carcasses: 'the skin of which, artificially dressed, will make admirable gloves for ladies, and summer boots for fine gentlemen'.

As for the vast number of aged, diseased or maimed poor, 'they are every day dying, and rotting, by cold, and famine, and filth, and vermin, as fast as can be reasonably expected'.

The *Modest Proposal* is a devastatingly effective piece of work. It is Swift's satirical 'final solution' – a proposal, he added, that would not disoblige England (always repressive of Ireland's exports), since the babies' flesh was too tender to bear long preservation in salt, 'although I perhaps could name a country, which would be glad to eat up our whole nation without it'.

It is horrible to have to say that Swift is hardly, in the *Modest Proposal*, being inventive. More than a hundred years before, there had been reports in Ireland of starving women lighting fires in the fields to lure children to them, and then killing and eating them. There was another early seventeenth-century report of small children living for three weeks on the roasted flesh of their dead mother, working from the feet up. The famine conditions which gave rise to such horrors were recurrent. The *Modest Proposal*, shocking in England and to us today for its outrageousness, reflected in Ireland folk-fears and folk-memories.

What definitively established Swift in the public mind as a patriot for Ireland were *The Drapier's Letters*, which came later. The ostensible issue was the coinage.

In the early 1720s, when the material conditions of Ireland were worsening, Ireland's stock of copper coins was judged to be insufficient and degraded. The coinage was privatized; a patent was issued to an iron merchant called William Wood, of Wolverhampton, to coin halfpence and farthings for Ireland, with strict specifications as to quality and quantity, and good allowance for a profit margin. The patent had actually been a gift to the King's German mistress, the Duchess of Kendal. She sold it on to Wood for £10,000. (Swift knew of this blatant jobbery, but did not go so far as to put it in the *Letters*.)

Ireland's legislators in the Dublin Parliament were extremely touchy about insensitive and damaging directives from London. The Commissioners of Revenue in Dublin protested to the proper authorities, to no avail. Both the Dublin Houses of Parliament sent addresses to King George explaining the deleterious effect the new coinage was having on the economy.

While a committee in London sat on the problem, Swift struck.

In the guise of a Dublin cloth-merchant, 'M.B., Drapier', he addressed his first published letter to 'the tradesmen, shop-keepers, farmers and common-people in general of Ireland'. In this and six more letters to different personages, one to 'the whole people of Ireland', he thunderously warned his fellow-citizens to reject Wood's coinage. All sterling would ebb from the country, since absentees and foreign merchants would never accept the coinage; Ireland would be flooded with these useless tokens; no sensible tradesmen should accept them in exchange for goods.

Sir Isaac Newton, as Master of the Mint, had Wood's halfpence and farthings assayed at the London Mint. He reported that they were as good in quality as English copper money, and that Wood had fulfilled his contract.

That was a red rag to the Drapier. 'His contract! With whom? Was it with the Parliament or people of Ireland? . . . But they detest, abhor and reject it, as corrupt, fraudulent, mingled with dirt and trash.'

The Drapier's arguments were out of order. He said the Irish people were compelled to accept the new coin in change, which was untrue. He was repetitive, bombastic and, in many of his assertions, just wrong. But he swept aside 'refinements with which we have nothing to do'. He wrote out of his towering rage against the English government's contemptuous mismanagement, corruption, carelessness, greed, coercion, and policy of sacrificing Ireland's economy to enhance England's.

His root objection was tribal: that the English in Ireland were treated as of less worth than the English in England. Elsewhere, in tracts, he made bitter comparisons between the comfortable, decently housed English country vicar, and his degraded, lonely, ill-paid, intellectually starved counterpart in an Irish rural parish – often composed of several parishes put together, the churches in ruins and the vicarage primitive and bare.

Such inequities put the status of Ireland itself in question. The Drapier found himself making a huge general point which touched a nerve not only in his own tribe, but in every Irishman who could read English:

Were not the people of Ireland born as free as those of England? How have they forfeited their freedom? . . . Are they not subjects of the same King? Does not the same sun shine on them? And have they not the same God for their protector? Am I a freeman in England, and do I become a slave in six hours by crossing the Channel?

And again:

> Those who come over hither to us from England, and some
> weak people among ourselves, whenever in discourse we make
> mention of liberty and property, shake their heads, and tell us,
> that Ireland is a 'depending kingdom', as if they would seem, by
> this phrase, to intend that the people of Ireland is in some state
> of slavery or dependence different from those of England.

'I have looked over all the English and Irish statutes', wrote the
Drapier, 'without finding any law that makes Ireland depend on
England, any more than England does upon Ireland.' The two
countries were, historically, separate kingdoms united equally under
the English Crown, and Ireland was 'a free people, in the common
acceptation of that word applied to a subject under a limited
monarch'. But 'the love and torrent of power prevailed':

> For in reason, all government without the consent of the people
> is the very definition of slavery: but in fact, eleven men well
> armed will certainly subdue one single man in his shirt. But I
> have done. For those who have used power to cramp liberty
> have gone so far as to resent even the liberty of complaining,
> although a man upon the rack was never known to be refused
> the liberty of roaring as loud as he thought fit.

The Drapier's Letters were a 'declararation of independence' in all but
their adherence to the 'limited monarch', and even on that the
Drapier sailed close to the wind, exonerating King George from his
negative response to the petition since 'it is well known, His Majesty
is not master of the English tongue', so could not have composed it
himself. The Drapier could not imagine how those who called him
disloyal, 'expedient-mongers, who shake their heads so strongly, that
we can hear their pockets jingle', could possibly be more loyal than
he himself. But England, said the Drapier, knew nothing about
Ireland, except that it was 'full of bogs, inhabited by wild Irish Papists
. . . And the general opinion is, that it were better for England if this
whole island were sunk in the sea.'
A reward was offered by the Lord-Lieutenant, Lord Carteret, to
anyone who would reveal the identity of the Drapier. No one did,
though many knew. To Swift's distress, the courageous printer-

publisher of the *Letters*, John Harding, and his wife were sent to prison. Swift had taken some precautions: the *Letters* were copied out by his butler, and delivered to Sheridan, who corrected them and got them to the printer. Swift flew into a rage with the butler because he stayed out all one night and Swift thought he had turned traitor; but he had just been drinking.

Before the last letter was written, Lord Carteret was able to announce that Wood's patent had been annulled. (Wood was given a grossly large pension in compensation.) The Drapier had won. In fact, it was the whole political establishment of Ireland, vocal in complaint, which had won this battle, the last in a series of constitutional wrangles.

But Swift had the common touch, and his talent for publicity and polemic spearheaded and popularized the protest. Afterwards, the English government was less provocative and more respectful towards Irish opinion and the Irish Parliament.

The Drapier's last letters, while animadverting to Wood, pushed some of Swift's other passionately held views, about which he wrote repeatedly in pamphlets and periodicals. He frequently wrote about the vital importance of supporting Irish manufactures, especially linens and woollens, and of making them attractive and reliable in quality in order to offset the 'affectation' of preferring goods made in England or on the Continent. He railed against ladies in Ireland who thought it smarter to import their silks instead of wearing Irish 'plaid', a speciality Irish silk with gold threads woven through it.

He had not, however, practised what he preached. Thinking of his return to Ireland, in 1712, he wrote to Stella from London that he would have to buy a 'great box' for his clothes and belongings. 'I have sent to Holland for a dozen shirts, and design to buy another new gown and hat.' That way, he said, he would come over like a gentleman, 'and lay out nothing in clothes in Ireland this good while'.

Swift's many angry state-of-Ireland pamphlets advocated the necessity of educating 'the poorer sorts of our natives'. He wrote about endemics: the evil of absentee landlords, who had their rents remitted to England, draining the country of money; the crippling list of vetoes on Irish exports to England, which protected English agriculture and manufactures; the evil of English nepotism, and of official employments in Ireland being given to men sent over from England; the evil of emigration to America (mostly Protestant emigration in his time, i.e. from the most skilled and economically useful population-group as well as rack-rented, indigent farmers); the evil of uncontrolled deforestation and random turf-cutting, which devastated the landscape.

He railed more than once at the loss of hedgerows, and the poor state of those remaining, writing in 1723 that 'nine out of ten of the quick-set hedges [were] being ruined for want of care and skill'. Another recurrent source of anger was the 'desolation made in the country' by greedy graziers taking land out of cultivation, resulting in yet more corn having to be imported.

In the euphoric aftermath of the Drapier's success he reeled off a series of poems on the halfpence business (of which 'Wood: an Insect' is a representative title). The suspect, reclusive Dean of St Patrick's was now the 'Hibernian patriot', a national hero, on his way to becoming a national monument, referred to simply as 'the Dean' throughout Ireland, as if there were no other.

He was, as Bishop William Nicolson of Derry sourly reported to Archbishop William Wake of Canterbury, 'the darling of the populace', greeted wherever he went. Public houses and shops changed their swinging signs for boards painted with the Drapier's head. A Drapier's Club was established. The Drapier's birthday was from now on annually celebrated. Faulkner's edition of Swift's works, published a decade later, carried a portrait of the Dean with the figure of Hibernia offering him a scroll, and at his feet a mother with her children, and a pauper – suffering, perhaps dead – sprawling head downwards on the steps below his chair. Over the scene hover two putti with a laurel wreath.

Swift was rightly proud of the Drapier's impact. He wrote in *Verses on the Death of Dr Swift*:

> Fair LIBERTY was all his cry;
> For her he stood prepar'd to die;
> For her he boldly stood alone;
> For her he oft expos'd his own.
> Two kingdoms, just as faction led,
> Had set a price upon his head;
> But, not a traitor cou'd be found,
> To sell him for six hundred pound.

There are limitations to Swift's claim to be an 'Irish' patriot. He was

170

singing an old song, not a new one. The most significant paragraph about Swift's attitude to Ireland in the 1720s was in a letter to the Earl of Peterborough, the Whig statesman whom he liked and esteemed. Peterborough fixed an interview for Swift with Sir Robert Walpole in London in 1726, so that Swift might set the case of Ireland's disabilities before him. He found Sir Robert, as is the way of politicians, more inclined to hold forth than to listen. Swift did not 'debate the matter with him so much as I otherwise might, because I found it would be in vain'. He set out his main complaints for Peterborough, of which the first was:

> That all persons born in Ireland are called and treated as Irishmen, although their fathers and grandfathers were born in England; and their predecessors having been conquerors of Ireland, it is humbly conceived they ought to be on as good a foot as any subjects of Britain . . .

That first aggrieved sentence – 'That all persons born in Ireland are called and treated as Irishman, although their fathers and grandfathers were born in England' – demonstrates that Swift had not made any historic shift in his perception of the English in Ireland, even though he identified nearly all the problems that were to torment the island of Ireland from that day to this.

The old claim that Ireland was an autonomous kingdom, with her own relationship with the English Crown on an equal basis with England's, had less and less meaning after the Williamite Revolution, as government by monarch gave way to government by Parliament. The phrase 'the English in Ireland' was becoming meaningless too. Leaving aside the English who had come over before the Reformation, a large number of whom were still Catholics, many English families had been established in Ireland for three generations, and had sometimes intermarried with the Catholic Irish, while some Irish families had turned Protestant in order to hold on to their lands.

Thus the demarcations between 'Irish' and 'English' were increasingly complex and blurred, and assumptions about the social status of either unsafe. As one commentator has written, Ireland was moving from 'a territory inhabited by settlers and natives to that of a single society divided along lines of religion and class'.

The Anglo-Irish – that anomalous tribe of more than dual

identity, as it arguably includes Catholic as well as Protestant gentry – who in succeeding generations furnished Ireland with patriots and leaders and, for good and ill, remained a cultural and political force until twenty-six counties of Ireland gained independence from Britain in 1922 – were foreshadowed but not defined, or foreseen, by Jonathan Swift.

He would not tolerate Ireland, where he happened to live, being pushed around and treated unjustly. He has been called 'a meteor that happened to hit Ireland', and his status as an Irish patriot 'accidental'. He can be seen as a cuckoo in the nest in Ireland, as well as in the households of his married friends. 'Had he been given a benefice in America' – and a bishopric in Virginia was indeed mooted at one point – 'he would have been the first American patriot; such was the nature of his cantankerous genius.'

By the end of 1725, sated with the Drapier's success, Swift was blasé enough to describe 'the Dean of St Patrick's sitting like a toad in a corner of his great house, with a perfect hatred of all public actions and persons'.

The Drapier had ended his last letter by recalling what he had once said to 'a great man in England':

That few politicans, with all their schemes, are half so useful members of a commonwealth, as an honest farmer; who, by skilfully draining, fencing, manuring, and planting, hath increased the intrinsic value of a piece of land; and thereby done a perpetual service to his country.

Swift reformulated this point in a memorable sentence:

And, he gave it for his opinion, that whoever could make two ears of corn, or two blades of grass to grow upon a spot of ground where only one grew before, would deserve better of mankind, and do more essential service to his country, than the whole race of politicians put together.

The 'he' speaking here is the commonsensical King of Brobdingnag in *Gulliver's Travels*, which was published the year after the patent for Wood's halfpence was withdrawn. Swift left the scene of his triumph and went back to London with the manuscript in his baggage.

Chapter Eleven

HORSE SENSE

DEAN SWIFT FOUND a very different scene on his return to London after twelve years. Thomas Parnell was dead. John Arbuthnot, in poor health, was back in his Cork Street house. Oxford, after two years' imprisonment in the Tower of London for treason, lived in retirement at Wimpole in Cambridgeshire, with a London home in Dover Street. Bolingbroke, after his flight from impeachment and a spell in France at the Court of the Pretender, lived with his French wife at Dawley, near Uxbridge. Alexander Pope had done extremely well out of his translation of Homer, and moved in 1722 with his old mother and Bounce to a pretty villa with lawns sloping down to the Thames, west of London, at Twickenham (which he wrote 'Twitnam').

Pope had about five acres of grounds with tree plantations, a vineyard, an orangery, hothouses, an orchard, a kitchen garden, beehives, and an intricate landscaping of paths and vistas. The developments were not completed when Swift visited; but Pope had already had the passage – his 'grotto' – dug beneath the house and under the main road from London to Hampton Court, opening into a further garden where the main feature was a shell-encrusted temple. Visitors came to marvel at what seemed to them the 'unaffected simplicity' of Pope's garden design.

Pope had new grand friends, too. This was the period when he was cultivating Lady Mary Wortley Montagu, the former Whig toast who held a salon for wits, poets and painters in Twickenham. She was beautiful, but marred by smallpox scars; she introduced inoculation into England, having learned of it in Turkey. Lady Mary was clever, self- educated, a traveller, a wit and a stylish writer. She said of King George that 'in private life, he would have been call'd an honest blockhead'. Pope conducted a mock-gallant epistolary affair with her. They quarrelled in the end. She took against Swift straight away.

There were other smart new friends, along the river. Lord Burlington, patron of the arts and of John Gay, had remodelled Chiswick House and laid out elaborate gardens. Not everyone admired it; Lord Hervey described Chiswick as 'too small to inhabit and too large to hang on a watch-chain'. (Lord Hervey was Lord Burlington's rival in exquisiteness. Lady Mary said the world consisted of 'men, women, and Herveys'.)

Henrietta Howard was in another brand-new Palladian villa on the Thames, Marble Hill, a few miles upriver from Pope. John Gay used a cottage in her grounds, and Pope had a hand in the design of her twenty-five-acre gardens.

Mrs Howard, who became the Countess of Suffolk, was a woman of the bedchamber to George I's daughter-in-law, the Princess of Wales. She and her husband had slipped off to Hanover just before Queen Anne died, to ingratiate themselves with the incoming regime. In this they were successful. Henrietta's (estranged) husband was now Groom of the Bedchamber to King George. She herself had a desultory ten-year affair with his son, the Prince of Wales, who had financed the building of Marble Hill.

The Prince did not get on with his father. Those out of favour and office, because of their connections with the Tories, cultivated Mrs Howard and clustered round the Waleses, forming a rival Court and hoping for better times when the Prince became King.

Swift's London visit in the spring and summer of 1726 lasted for five months. He met this whole crew. The Princess of Wales and Mrs Howard were particularly keen to see him. His old friends were delighted to have him back. At first he was in lodgings in familiar Bury Street. From April on, he stayed at Twickenham with Pope, with trips back into London; there, he stayed with Gay in his Whitehall lodgings. Gay borrowed sheets for Swift's bed from Charles Jervas, and returned them back afterwards 'mended, finely wash'd, and neatly folded up'. Gay joined Pope and Swift at Twickenham. Bolingbroke and Congreve came down for dinner.

With Dr Arbuthnot, he saw the Yahoo-like 'wild boy' who had been found in the woods in Hamelin, near Hanover, and committed to the doctor's care; the Court was greatly amused by him. Swift's judgement was: 'I can hardly think him wild in the sense they report him.' (The boy was mentally defective.)

He saw the Prime Minister, Sir Robert Walpole, not in the hope of any favours for himself from the Whig ministry, but to set before Walpole some points regarding the pitiful economic state of Ireland and the ways in which Irish affairs were mismanaged by the English government. When he got nowhere, he complained about Walpole to the Princess of Wales, 'because I knew she would tell him', and he was to lampoon Walpole in verse, making a thorough enemy of him.

The stream of long letters that followed him back to Dublin proved how much he was missed. 'Many a short sigh you cost me the day I left you', wrote Pope, 'and many more you will cost me, till the day you return. I really walk'd about like a man banish'd, and when I came home, found it no home.'

But Swift was not sorry to leave. 'I should be glad to be settled here, but the inconvenience and charge of being only a passenger, is not so easy as an indifferent home, and the stir people make with me gives me neither pride nor pleasure', he confessed to Knightly Chetwode. And to Dr Sheridan: 'This is the first time I was ever weary in England, and longed to be in Ireland.' Not that he liked Ireland any better than he did England; it was 'a wretched, dirty dog-hole and prison, but it is a place good enough to die in'.

He could not enjoy the fuss people made of him in England. *Cadenus and Vanessa* had just been published in Dublin. He was consumed with worries about its effect on Stella, who was ill, probably mortally ill, in Dublin. In August *Gulliver* went to the printer and Dean Swift prepared for home.

He made one last visit to England the following year, 1727, staying from April to September. He found the opposition resolving to 'assault the present administration', and himself much in demand by the Princess of Wales, who sent for him twice in one week to twit him about *Gulliver*.

While he was in England, King George died. 'Since then we have all been in a hurry, with millions of schemes', he wrote to Sheridan. Swift went to Court to kiss the hands of George II and the Queen, his friend. 'The talk is now for a moderating scheme, wherein nobody shall be used the worse or better for being call'd Whig or Tory.'

The Dean renewed his attentions to Henrietta Howard at Marble Hill. He gave her, and the Queen, dress-lengths of Irish silk (the gold-threaded 'plaid'). He wrote her a poem, 'A Pastoral Dialogue between Richmond Lodge [the new King's house] and Marble Hill', in which the two riverside villas compare notes about their futures. Marble Hill speaks:

> No more the Dean, that grave divine,
> Shall keep the key of my (no) wine;
> My ice-house rob as heretofore,
> And steal my artichokes no more

Richmond Lodge speaks:

> Here wont the Dean when he's to seek,
> To sponge a breakfast once a week;
> To cry the bread was stale, and mutter
> Complaints against the royal butter

And so on, with sprightly reference to Pope and 'plump Johnny Gay'. He wrote Mrs Howard letters of mock-gallantry, recommending not himself but another for a favour, but drawing attention to himself all the same: 'Thus wanting people are like drowning people, who lay hold of every reed or bulrush in their way.'

Mrs Howard was but a broken reed. If Swift really was ready to make one last throw for Church preferment in England, she was no good to him. She encouraged him to think that she could do something for him. But she no longer had any influence with her former lover, the new King.

This last visit ended wretchedly. At Twickenham, staying with Pope, Swift had an unusually bad attack of deafness, sickness and giddiness. He could not walk straight. He could not hear what Pope was saying to him. Pope's old mother was ill too. 'I am very uneasy here', he wrote to Dr Sheridan, 'because so many many of our acquaintance come to visit us, and I cannot be seen.' The King and Queen were expected at Richmond Lodge, and would want to see him. He was incapacitated. Pope too was 'sickly'. Swift determined to leave.

It is a sad picture: old Mrs Pope ill upstairs, and the deaf, tottering older man and the sickly, feeble younger one, accustomed to stimulate and amuse one another, unable to communicate, suffering together but apart in that pointlessly beautiful house. Swift was receiving even worse news about Stella, and was consumed by grief and anxiety. Pope knew about this if only from Sheridan, who wrote to him warning that 'a particular friend of the Dean's' was 'upon the brink of another world'.

Swift crawled off to London. Writing to him there, Pope made a delicate reference to Stella: 'To your bad health I fear there was added some disagreeable news from Ireland, which might occasion your sudden departure.' Pope's feelings were hurt by Swift's departure:

> I was sorry to find you could think yourself easier in any house than in mine, tho' at the same time I can allow for a tenderness in your way of thinking, even when it seem'd to want that tenderness. I can't explain my meaning, perhaps you know it. But the best way of convincing you of my indulgence, will be, if I live, to visit you in Ireland, and act there as much in my own way as you did here in yours. I will not leave your roof, if I am ill.

(Alas, poor Sheridan . . .)

Swift saw Pope in London. Afterwards, they never met again. Back in 1699, the young Swift made a comment about the sad uselessness of writing to people one never saw. 'At first one omits writing for a little while, and then one stays a while longer to consider of excuses and at last it grows desperate and one does not write at all.' That was not the case with him and his English friends. They all wrote to him, and at length, and he to them, until some of them died, and until he could write and read no more.

In September 1727 he made for Holyhead, with detours, and home.

Jonathan Swift was not a traveller. 'Abroad' was a closed book. He went from Ireland to England and back again, repeatedly. He never travelled widely even in his own island, apart from a solitary tour to the south and west after the death of Vanessa. In Ireland, as in England, he stuck to his familiar goat-paths, visiting familiar friends.

He never went to Bath for his health's sake, and for the amusing society to be found there, as his friends – literary, political, clerical, and including Archbishop King – constantly did, urging him to join them. He went occasionally to Oxford, where back in 1692 he had put in just enough time at Hart Hall (now Hertford College) to qualify for his MA.

He made a pilgrimage, at the end of this last trip to England in 1727, to Goodrich in Herefordshire, outside which still stood the house built in 1636 by his Cavalier grandfather, the Revd Thomas Swift. The eccentric design of the fourteen-room house caused Swift in his autobiographical fragment to diagnose something 'whimsical and singular' in his grandfather; the description is accompanied by four lines wildly crossed out and obliterated in the margin. A 'female relative' was in occupation when he visited. Swift saw to the erection of a memorial to his grandfather in the church of which he had been vicar, and where he was buried.

Time after time throughout Swift's life, projected trips abroad were abandoned. A month after the rift with Sir William Temple in 1694, he was angling for a chaplainship in Portugal, where Swift cousins were merchants, but it came to nothing. In 1708 he thought he might go to Vienna in Lord Berkeley's employ, and it came to nothing. In 1726 he declined an invitation to stay with Bolingbroke in France because Stella was not well.

In 1727 he requested six months' leave of absence from his deanery, proposing to go from London to Aix-en-Chapelle with John Gay. All the arrangements were made. Bolingbroke gave him letters of introduction to friends in Paris. *Gulliver* was being translated into French, and Voltaire, who had met all Swift's friends in London and who admired the book greatly, wrote to him warmly offering more introductions. Then came the news that King George had died, and Bolingbroke and Henrietta Howard advised Swift not to go, as he might miss the chance of advancement in England under the new regime. So he went to Twickenham for that last sad stay with Pope.

Dr Arbuthnot, trying in 1733 to persuade Swift to join him at a French 'spaw' (spa) for his health's sake, wrote, 'I wonder much that a person of so much good humour can let yourself grow old, or die, without seeing some other country than your own.' But he did.

There was a tacit sense of relief as each of these excursions was abandoned. In 1730, illness and low spirits disinclined him from travelling one more time from Dublin to London. In July 1732 Bolingbroke wrote about the possibility of acquiring for Swift the living of Burghfield (about twenty-five miles from where Bolingbroke lived in retirement at Dawley, and not too far from Twickenham).

The living was worth £400 a year 'above a curate paid'. To be a country vicar had no attraction for a dean who had aspired to English bishoprics. 'It would not answer', as Swift explained to John Gay:

> I am at a time of life that seeks ease and independence . . . I would rather be a freeman among slaves, than a slave among freemen. The dignity of my present station damps the pertness of inferior puppies and squires, which without plenty and ease on your side of the Channel, would break my heart in a month.

He had written to Charles Ford in April 1721: 'I am now writing a history of my travels, which will be a large volume, and gives an account of countries hitherto unknown; but they go on slowly for want of health and humor.' In April 1724, artlessly asking Ford if he had already told him 'that I sent out a small pamphlet under the name of a draper', he said he would have finished his travels very soon 'if I have health, leisure, and humor'. He was correcting and transcribing the finished work with Sheridan at Quilca in the summer of 1725.

It was Gulliver who travelled; though Swift suggested with some self-irony that any journey, however modest, had epic and Gulliver-like possibilities for a man of imagination. He reported to Pope after his return to Dublin in 1726 'what a quick change I made in seven days from London to the Deanery, through many nations and languages unknown to the civilized world. And I have often reflected how in a few hours, with a swift horse or a strong gale, a man may come among a people as unknown to him as the Antipodes.'

Gulliver is Swift's major achievement, the 'great fish' he never believed he had landed. Books that become popular classics frequently end up as books considered suitable for children. Defoe's *Robinson Crusoe*, which is, like *Gulliver*, a moral as well as an exotic adventure, is another case in point. (*Crusoe* was published in 1719. There was no copy listed in the catalogue of Swift's books sold after his death. That does not mean he had not read it.)

Swift's 'great fish' has often been cleaned and filleted to make it suitable for young readers. Yet lavatory humour is accessible and acceptable to children. Adult distaste for it only increases their pleasure. It is they who would most enjoy the episode of the Yahoos discharging their excrement on to Gulliver's head from up in the trees. Much of the crude humour in *Gulliver* belongs to the category of humour based on disparity of scale. This too has an immediacy for children, who are on the one hand dwarfed by adults, and on the other hand made giants by their toys: dolls, and minuscule boats, animals, farmyards, vehicles, castles.

Literature that lasts does not have to be 'original'. Frequently a classic is – to take a horticultural image – a prize hybrid, a stellar sport of less remarkable varieties growing out of the same cultural compost. Rabelais is a strong and obvious influence in *Gulliver*. Swift admired Rabelais extravagantly and was always pressing his merits on Pope, who would not be convinced. Folk tales and fairy tales (which Swift read with the greatest interest, calling them his 'trash') are, like fabulous traveller's tales, full of giants, dwarves, and talking animals. It did not stop with Swift either: think only of Lewis Carroll's *Alice in Wonderland* and *Through the Looking-Glass* (startlingly Swiftian in their play on scale and optical reversions) and the ingenuity of Mary Norton's *The Borrowers*. Gulliver in Brobdingnag makes himself a comb from bristle-stumps shaved off the King's chin set into a paring from the Queen's thumbnail: just the sort of thing the Borrowers would do.

In Brobdingnag, where people are as tall as church steeples, and finger-sized Gulliver is exhibited as a freak, the rats are as big as mastiffs, a cat 'three times larger than an ox', and fleas 'like swine', rooting with their snouts. The ridiculous made-up place-names and language in *Gulliver* is also the kind of humour that tickles children, and reflects Swift's own love of word-play and 'la bagatelle' in adult life. *Gulliver* is the nearest we get to Jonathan the child. But it is a book for adults.

In another context we will be looking at women's gigantic breasts through the disgusted midget-Gulliver's eyes – or rather through Swift's microscope. Stella shared his interest in magnification, because of her poor eyesight. She read his journal letters, in which he packed as many words to a line, and as many lines to a page, as he possibly could, with a magnifying-glass. When Swift was in London in 1710 he wrote asking her whether thirty shillings was too much for her to pay for a microscope of her own:

Shall I buy it or no? 'tis not the great bulky ones, nor the common little ones, to impale a louse (saving your presence) on a needle's point; but of a more exact sort, and clearer to the sight, with all its equipage in a little trunk that you may carry in your pocket.

Gulliver, describing fine old English values and attitudes to a horse, met with horrified incredulity: institutionalized corruption, irrationality and immorality in English law, religion, politics and social life are revealed for what they really are. Montesquieu's *Lettres Persanes*, which satirized French society in the same way reversed, by filtering it through the eyes of exotic tourists, was published in 1721, when Swift was beginning work on *Gulliver*. Montesquieu was in England for three years from 1729, and articulated the core tenets of Tory opposition to Walpole the Whig in *De l'esprit des lois*.

The contemporary allusiveness of some of Swift's satire in *Gulliver* is chiefly of interest to political historians of the period. The corruption of values and attitudes in public life is however, endemic, timeless and universal, and reading *Gulliver* is as comic and shocking a revelation now as it was in 1726, no matter what the reader's culture or nation. The discourse is apparently straightforward. The style is as Gulliver described the Brobdingnagians': 'clear, masculine, smooth, but not florid, for they avoid nothing more than multiplying unnecessary words, or using various expressions'.

Gulliver is a first-person narrative, but Gulliver himself does not point morals. He is 'studious of brevity' as he says, and does not extrapolate. As Michael Foot has written, *Gulliver* is 'a perpetual unfinished argument, one from which flatly contradictory morals have been and still are to be extracted'.

The full title is *Travels in Several Remote Nations of the World in Four Parts, by Lemuel Gulliver, first a Surgeon, then a Captain of Several Ships*. The 'remote nations' are Lilliput, Brobdingnag, Laputa (with Balnibarbi, Glubbdubdrib, Luggnag and home via Japan), and 'the country of the Houyhnhms'. Their location was only partly fabulous. They were situated in Australasia, deriving from William Dampier's *New Voyage round the World*, which made a huge impact on Europeans when published in 1697. (Dampier was also a primary source for Defoe's *Crusoe*.) Gulliver refers to 'my cousin Dampier' in his preliminary remarks; but it was John Hawkesworth, an intimate of Dr Johnson who edited Swift's works in the 1750s, who first spelled out the deep connection between Swift and Dampier in his biographical introduction. Swift even included maps, showing the position of Lilliput, for example, on the south-west coast of Australia.

Dampier's detailed description of aborigines – 'setting aside their human shapes they differ but little from brutes' – contributed to the creation of Swift's Yahoos.

Dampier's books began the process of replacing fantasy with fact. Swift was also picking up on previous notions of 'Terra Australis Incognita' as a locus for satirical and utopian writing. Australia – known only in garbled accounts of fantastical plants and animals and represented by speculative maps – was for Europeans the world upside down, reversing the accepted relationship between man and nature. Ideas of Australia reflected the original Eden, and the ideal worlds of classical culture: the Garden of the Hesperides, the Elysian Fields. But Swift's fantasies were given a framework of verisimilitude by laconic passages of practical seamanship, coolly lifted from books.

His technique in *Gulliver* for showing the ludicrousness of doctrinal or political conflict was to substitute some everyday thing for the real-life issue (Denis Donaghue has neatly called this 'translating down'). Thus in Lilliput the animosity between parties (Tory and Whig, for Swift, but substitute what you will) was a matter of footwear. The High-Heels and the Low-Heels 'will neither eat, nor drink, nor talk with each other'.

There was a long-standing war between the empires of Lilliput and Blesfescu, costing thousands of lives. The burning issue was how you cracked open a boiled egg. There was a ruling in Lilliput that eggs had to be opened at the smaller end. This led to rebellion and civil war. Refugees fled to Blefescu, where they opened their eggs at the bigger end. In the war between Big-Endians and Little-Endians 'it is computed, that eleven thousand people have, at several times, suffered death, rather than submit to break their eggs at the smaller end'. Big-Endians in Lilliput were 'rendered incapable by law of holding employments'.

And this mockery from Swift, who defended the Church as established by law and the disabilities of Dissenters and Catholics with repetitive, fiery, well-reasoned – and perhaps ludicrous – arguments.

There is almost no aspect of public or private life which remains unquestioned in *Gulliver*, including the education of girls and the upbringing of children. The Lilliputians' belief that parents are the least capable of rearing their young, and their practice of community parenting, foreshadowed the kibbutz ideal as well as reflecting obliquely on Swift's own lack of nuclear family.

Swift's exasperated contempt for scientific research and experiment is given free rein in Gulliver's experiences on the flying island of Laputa, where the people starved while the Academy of Projectors set forth new rules for everything, including (again Gulliver is prophetic) mechanization and 'downsiding' – 'one man shall do the work of ten' – and the production of all fruits to be ripe in all seasons.

Gulliver saw a computer designed to save time and study – a twenty-foot-square frame, its surface covered with words on dice-sized pieces of wood, which were spun round, read off and transcribed, enabling 'the most ignorant person' to 'write books in philosophy, poetry, politics, law, mathematics and theology, without the least assistance from genius or study'. In Laputa practice was sacrificed to theory. Clothes for Gulliver were tailored by calculations with a quadrant and compass, but didn't fit owing to 'a mistake in a figure of a calculation'.

Swift had visited the Royal Society in London in 1710. The experiments of the Laputan Academy of Projectors were modelled on, and in some cases actually mirrored, the experiments of that august body. Gulliver met an ancient filth-daubed academician whose life's work had been an attempt to turn human excrement back into food, 'by separating the several parts, removing the tincture which it receives from the gall, making the odour exhale, and skimming off the saliva'. Another projector

> had been eight years upon a project for extracting sunbeams out of cucumbers, which were to be put into vials hermetically sealed, and let out to warm the air in raw inclement summers. He told me, he did not doubt in eight years more, that he should be able to supply the Governor's gardens with sunshine at a reasonable rate; but he complained that his stock was low, and entreated me to give him something as an encouragement to ingenuity, especially since this had been a very dear season for cucumbers.

This man was looking, as is the way of academics, for a further research grant.

Swift's dislike of scientific enquiry mirrors his dislike of metaphysical speculation. He was closed-minded in these areas. There is, however, in many people an instinct that in matters of science one should go so far in every generation but no further, for fear of going too far and unleashing uncontrollable forces. This instinct stems from, or is expressed by, the myth of the Fall of Man. Adam and Eve were forbidden by God to taste of the fruit of the tree of the knowledge of good and evil, and from that first disobedience all their troubles sprang. Swift's writing is full of flying, floating, falling, like Lucifer falling from Heaven in Milton's *Paradise Lost* – and Milton's moral too is that we should not meddle in what does not concern us.

The Houyhnhnms were horses who could talk, though their vocabulary was small. They had no words for power, government, war, law, punishment, evil. They were like Adam and Eve before the Fall. They were mild, soft-spoken, orderly, kind. Gulliver's protector was a grey horse whom he called his master. Gulliver had to explain to him what 'lying' was. They had no word for that either. His master understood lying as 'saying the thing that was not': and why would anyone want to do that? Similarly 'doubting' and 'not believing' were virtually unknown.

Since the horses were totally governed by reason, and since passion, self-interest and self-aggrandizement were unknown to them, they had no controversies or disputes. They generalized their affections, treating all their fellows with equal decency and civility, with no partisan fondness even for their own young.

Gulliver had to explain to his master the grey horse what war was:

I gave him a description of cannons, culverins, muskets, carabines, pistols, bullets, powder, swords, bayonets, battles, sieges, retreats, attacks, undermines, countermines, bombardments, sea-fights; ships sunk with a thousand men, twenty thousand killed on each side; dying groans, limbs flying in the air, smoke, noise, confusion, trampling to death under horses' feet; flight, pursuit, victory; fields strewed with carasses left for food to dogs, and wolves, and birds of prey; plundering, stripping, ravishing, burning, destroying.

Gulliver's master then asked him why men ever went to war. Gulliver told him about the ambitions of princes, the corruption of ministers who needed a diversion from unrest at home:

> Neither are any wars so furious and bloody ... as those
> occasioned by difference of opinion, especially if it be of things
> indifferent ... Sometimes our neighbours *want* the things that
> we have, or *have* the things that we *want* ... For these reasons,
> the trade of a soldier is held the most honourable of all others:
> because a soldier is a Yahoo hired to kill in cold blood as many
> of his own species, who have never offended him, as possibly he
> can.

The Houyhnhmns shared their country with the Yahoos – hairy,
smelly, filthy, aggressive, carrion-eating, tree-climbing, savage
creatures with hooked claws on both their front and back feet –
'abominable' animals, but recognizably human in form. The horses
classed Gulliver, because of his shape, with the Yahoos, and were
surprised by his accomplishments. He was a 'clean, civil, reasoning
Yahoo'.

Gulliver could not deny his Yahoo-quality, nor the Yahoo-
characteristics of his compatriots in Europe. When he returned from
his last voyage, and 'began to consider, that by copulating with the
Yahoo species [i.e. his wife], I had become a parent of more, it struck
me with the utmost shame, confusion and horror'. It was weeks
before he could bear to sit at dinner with her, 'at the furthest end of
a long table', because of her Yahoo smell. If she is a Yahoo, so is he.
If there is disgust there is also self-disgust.

Gulliver wanted to stay for ever with the Houyhnhmns. But the
council of horses decided that a Yahoo could not live permanently
among them and he was courteously expelled from Eden.

Gulliver's idealization of the horses does not mean that they live
as we should live. (Not that Swift gives a clue as to how to interpret
all this.) The word Houyhnhmn meant in their language 'the
perfection of nature'. To be 'natural' is insufficient for an evolved
human being, and inaccessible. The Houyhnhmns had no
intellectual curiosity and so would never discover or invent anything,
nor ever have a single new idea. They would never create any great
art. Their prelapsarian passivity is a limitation, just as Swift's
rejection of scientific speculation was a limitation. But he had
intellectual passion in other directions, and he did create great art. A
human being who had no Yahoo in him would not be fully human.

185

Even the horses did not think the Yahoos wholly deplorable, because they only acted according to their natures. Their savage Eden was equally closed to Gulliver. He was inadequate even as a Yahoo, in that he had lost, as he knew, 'the few abilities nature had given us'. Humans walked 'infirmly' on their back legs, their claws were no use. We have lost our protective hair, and we cannot run fast or clamber up the branches of trees.

Swift admired and envied animals for their generic integrity. He wrote in *On Poetry, a Rapsody*:

> Brutes find out where their talents lie:
> A bear will not attempt to fly:
> A founder'd horse will oft debate,
> Before he tries a five-barr'd gate:
> A dog by instinct turns aside,
> Who sees the ditch too deep and wide.
> But man we find the only creature,
> Who, led by folly, fights with nature.

Elsewhere, Swift wrote that he thought the animal world was superior to the human world. 'Lions, bears, elephants, and some other animals are strong and valiant, and their species never degenerates in their native soil, except they happen to be enslaved or destroyed by human fraud.' Human beings, on the other hand, degenerate 'merely by the folly, the perverseness, the avarice, the tyranny, the pride, the treachery, or inhumanity of their own kind'.

He, who shunned passionate attachments and advocated in his life a horse-sense reasonableness in matters of the heart, was compelled to conclude that God 'intended our passions to prevail over reason' – first, for the propagation of the species, 'since no wise man ever married from the dictates of reason'; and second, for 'the love of life, which, from the dictates of reason, every man would despise, and wish it at an end, or that it never had a beginning'.

It was *Gulliver* that made people think that Swift was a misanthrope, a hater of his own Yahoo-species. He denied it: 'I tell you after all that I do not hate mankind: it is *vous autres* who hate them, because you would have them reasonable animals, and are angry for being disappointed.' So, often, was he. Gulliver is Everyman, not wholly bestial, not wholly reasonable, defined precisely by this quandary. We are what we are.

Gulliver was not one of those books which take time to find their readership. It was a raging success at once, and references to it dominated his friends' letters. Bolingbroke addressed one to 'the three Yahoos of Twickenham' – Pope, Swift and Gay. When Swift was back in Dublin, between his two last visits, Gay wrote to him that 'from the highest to the lowest [*Gulliver*] is universally read, from the Cabinet-council to the nursery'. He told Swift what this one said, and what that one said, and which bits of the satire were thought to be just, or too severe. It was discussed everywhere. Pope wrote many verse glosses on it, sending Swift 'some commendatory verses from a horse and a Lilliputian, to Gulliver; and an heroic epistle to Mrs Gulliver'. Pope, always with an eye to his own advancement, was jumping on the bandwagon: 'The bookseller would fain have printed 'em before the second edition of the book, but I would not approve it without your approbation . . .'

Gulliver is about morality, but it is not about Christianity. One of Smedley's verses pinned on the cathedral door ran as follows:

> The place he got by wit and rhyme
> And many ways most odd;
> And might a bishop be in a time
> Did he believe in God.

Did Swift believe in God? Many of his ecclesiastical superiors suspected he did not, because of his light way of writing about religious divisions and his conspicuous lack of professed piety. Swift thought that old Dr John Sharp, Archbishop of York, was his 'mortal enemy' and had poisoned Queen Anne's mind against him. Sharp was not the only one.

In his poem 'The Day of Judgement', cast as a nightmare of the graves giving up their dead, it is not God but the Roman deity Jove who sits in judgement. One can well understand that the Revd Dr Swift needed to distance the nightmare from Christianity; for the human race has exhausted Jove's patience and he turns judgement into a black joke – a 'bite':

> The world's mad business now is o'er
> And I resent these pranks no more.
> I to such blockheads set my wit!
> I damn such fools! – Go, go, you're bit.

He was often facetious in defence of the nominal religion which was the baseline of whatever he did believe. 'Great wits love to be free with the highest objects; and if they cannot be allowed a God to revile or renounce, they will speak evil of dignities, abuse the government, and reflect upon the ministry.' And if Christianity were once abolished, 'how could the freethinkers, the strong reasoners, and the men of profound learning, be able to find another subject so calculated in all points whereon to display their abilities?'

He saw religion as an arm of social and moral control. Human nature was such that 'the example alone of a vicious prince, will, in time, corrupt an age; but that of a good one will not be sufficient to reform it, without further endeavours'. Therefore the state should make it 'every man's interest and honour, to cultivate religion and virtue; by rendering vice a disgrace, and the certain ruin to preferment or pretensions'. In his writings on religion, and in his sermons, he referred hardly at all to Heaven or to rewards in a life to come. He was concerned with man's proper behaviour to his fellow-man in this world.

He was not one to look into metaphysics, on the grounds that he would see nothing. His common-sense attitude to the unknowable is reflected in the poem 'On Dreams'. They are sent neither from Jove above, nor from the 'infernal mansions' below,

> But all are mere productions of the brain,
> And fools consult interpreters in vain.
> For, when in bed we rest our weary limbs,
> The mind unburthen'd sports in various whims,
> The busy head with mimick art runs o'er
> The scenes and actions of the day before.

In a piece on freethinking, he asks, 'How can a man think at all, if he does not think freely? Christ himself told us to be freethinkers, and Socrates was a freethinker'. However, 'the bulk of mankind is as well qualified to flying as to thinking, and if every man thought it his duty to think freely, and trouble his neighbour with his thoughts . . . it would make wild work of the world'.

All 'men of sense' depart from received opinion, and are more or less men of sense, according as they depart more or less from the opinions commonly received. Keep it to yourself, though, the implication is, unless you want to be persecuted or worse.

Christ himself 'is nothing but reason', and Socrates 'never made notions, speculations, or mysteries, any part of his religion, but demonstrated all men to be fools who troubled themselves with enquiries into heavenly things'. 'I do not find that you are anywhere directed in the canons or articles, to attempt explaining the mysteries of the Christian religion', he wrote in *A Letter to a Young Gentleman, lately entered into Holy Orders.*

His sermon on the Holy Trinity supports this view. One must have faith. 'How little do those who quarrel with mysteries, know of the commonest actions of nature! The growth of an animal, of a plant, or of the smallest seed, is a mystery to the wisest among men.' How then can we expect an explanation of the doctrine of the threefold God? Even if He were to reveal the mysteries, 'we should not be able to understand them', unless he gave us at the same time 'some new powers or faculties of the mind'.

In his 'Thoughts on Religion', disconnected notes not I think intended for publication, he acknowledged doubt and endorsed nominal Christianity:

> The want of belief is a defect that ought to be concealed when it cannot be overcome . . . I am not answerable to God for the doubts that arise in my own breast, since they are the consequence of that reason which He hath planted in me; if I take care to conceal those doubts from others, if I use my best endeavours to subdue them, and if they have no influence on the conduct of my life.

Swift is not like Gulliver's grey horse. He knows what 'doubt' and 'not believing' is.

Thomas Sheridan, quoting Bolingbroke's description of Swift as a 'hypocrite revers'd', thought him 'a man of very great piety and true religion', who always wore a mask. His cast of mind was more suited to politics than to religion. Yet having conceded as much, Patrick Delany believed Swift was 'truly orthodox' but 'without any parade, or colour of ostentation'. Swift loathed false piety. 'I hate Lent; I hate different diets . . . and sour devout faces of people who only put on religion for seven weeks', he told Stella, wishing her 'a merry Lent'.

Deane Swift bears this out, describing his great-uncle as 'really a man of high religion, without grunting, groaning, canting, hypocrisy, or making wry faces ... He beat all his contemporaries many thousands of leagues in the race of Christianity.' Delany had known the Dean a long time before he learned that he read prayers to his 'family' – as he called his household of servants – 'at a fixed hour every night, in his own bed-chamber'.

Dean Swift renewed what Dr Delany saw as the 'primitive practice' of celebrating the sacrament of Holy Communion every Sunday, consecrating and administering it himself; St Patrick's was the only Anglican church in Dublin where this took place weekly. He had never thought much of his own abilities as a preacher, advising his successor at Kilroot to throw away a bundle of sermons he had left there; they were never very much good to him, he said. In his London years, his Tory friends said he should preach a sermon before the Queen; nothing ever came of it, and he did not mind. He wrote out his sermons in clear print-like writing, double spaced; at least he would not stumble; he instructed the clergymen in his cathedral to do the same.

Surviving sermons show that he addressed his mixed congregations of gentry and tradesmen's families with simplicity, without expressions of wit, but with occasional fierceness. The titles convey the sermons' nature: 'On Brotherly Love', 'On Doing Good', 'On False Witness', 'On the Poor Man's Contentment' in which there is a nice half-expressed image of nagging uneasiness as a bluebottle:

> Business, fear, guilt, design, anguish, and vexation are continually buzzing about the curtains of the rich and the powerful, and will hardly suffer them to close their eyes, unless when they are dosed with the fumes of strong liquors.

Nominal religion required a more than nominal act of presence. His sermon 'On Sleeping in Church' must have had the congregation shifting uncomfortably in their pews:

> A preacher cannot look around from the pulpit, without observing, that some are in a perpetual whisper, and, by their air and gesture, give occasion to suspect, that they are in those very minutes defaming their neighbour. Others have their eyes and imagination constantly engaged in such a circle of objects,

perhaps to gratify the most unwarrantable desires, that they never once attend to the business of the place . . . But, of all misbehaviour, none is comparable to that of those who come here to sleep; opium is not so stupefying to many persons as an afternoon sermon.

He often used the generalized term 'Providence' instead of 'God': a common evasion. I think he wanted to believe. A long 'Evening Prayer' – too long, maybe, to have been read aloud in the cathedral, or to his servants at the Deanery – was found among his papers after his death. It is like an urgent personal letter to God, asking for mercy, for the protection of His angels, for a realization of 'the happiness of that blessed state of living for ever with thee', for the ability to pray, and for the ability to sleep.

In the meanwhile, we beseech thee to take us, and ours, and all that belongs to us, into thy fatherly care this night . . . Lord, grant that the sense of this wonderful love of thine to us, may effectually encourage us to walk in thy fear . . . that so when we shall put off this mortal state, we may be partakers of that glory that shall then be revealed . . .'

Expressions like 'wonderful love', 'thy fatherly care', 'happiness' have poignancy for the student of Jonathan Swift's life and work. I would give anything to know whether the hopes they evince were fulfilled, and glory revealed, in the embers of his brave mind at the end. Comfort is not enough for Swift's intemperate spirit. One wants for him revelation, integration, an epiphany. 'Surprised by joy – impatient as the wind . . .'

Chapter Twelve

DEATH OF LOVE

GULLIVER HAS BEEN travelling throughout these pages, and will go on doing so till the end. When he was in the land of the giant Brobdingnagians, he was protected and looked after, as if he were a doll or a pet, by his 'little nurse' – though still a giant to him – called Glumdalclitch. She loved him tenderly. She made him miniature clothes, and a doll's bed, and set out his tiny dishes and forks. She was nine years old.

I think Swift played with Hetty Johnson's doll's house with her when they both lived at Moor Park. He taught her reading and writing. In *Gulliver* the roles are reversed. It is Glumdalclitch who is the 'grown-up', though still a child, and who teaches him to read and write the language of Brobdingnag. The roles were reversed sometimes, with the adult Hetty – Stella. She eased his domestic routines, and cared for him when he was ill. Stella loved him in a reasonable, useful way – or so he always hoped and trusted. We do not know her thoughts and inner feelings.

In the land of the Houyhnhmns Gulliver, bathing naked, attracted the attention of a female Yahoo. 'Inflamed with desire . . . she embraced me after a most fulsome manner.' Terrified, Gulliver escaped, while she stood 'gazing and howling' as he put on his clothes. The point about this incident, for Gulliver, was that it proved he was 'a real Yahoo in every limb and feature', since he was recognized by the desirous female as one of her own species. She could not, he thought, 'be above eleven years old'.

Why is she a child-Yahoo? Either because he had a view about the dangerous sexuality of girl-children; or because he could not bring himself to depict Gulliver being desired by an adult Yahoo. Both Stella and Vanessa were his girl pupils, however much time had passed, and even though he traced in his verse, quite brutally, the grey in Stella's hair and the lines on her face. Perhaps he harped on her advancing age to stress the insignificance of her appearance for him; or to put her out of court, sexually.

He felt that Vanessa's burning passion for him was irrational. He offered friendship, 'which gently warms, but cannot burn'. But the Yahoo in Vanessa was calling out to the Yahoo in him, and he responded in spite of himself before he left her on the further shore.

These parallels are seductive, whether Swift in *Gulliver* was making them consciously or not. It has been all to easy, too, for contributors to the Swiftian myth to see Stella and Vanessa as angel and devil, virgin and whore. Thackeray was particularly mawkish about Stella: 'Who does not love her? fair and tender creature; pure and affectionate heart! . . .You are one of the saints of English story.'

Stella was a more muscular character than that. Swift's poems to her are full of teasing references to her flashing eyes, her boldness, and her regrettable passions – in the sense of 'tempers'. Thackeray considered the link with Vanessa as just 'a little episodical aberration'. (It lasted more than twelve years.) Lord Orrery dismissed Vanessa as 'a miserable example of an ill-spent life, fantastic wit, visionary schemes and female weakness'. As Delany more charitably wrote, 'her only misfortune was that she had a passion for Dr Swift'.

Patrick Delany fairly remarked that there was nothing wrong in Vanessa's falling in love with Swift, nor in her telling him so. 'He was a single man, she was a single woman: and her first view was evidently marriage.'

A poem attributed to her would confirm this; and would suggest that she believed that it was precisely because Swift desired her that he would or could not marry her. (One might infer from the following lines that it was precisely because he did *not* desire Stella that he would or could not marry her, either.) Vanessa apostrophizes 'curs'd discretion, all the fault is thine':

> Cupid and Hymen thou has set at odds,
> And bred such feuds betwixt those kindred gods,
> That Venus cannot reconcile her sons,
> When one appears, away the other runs.

Vanessa was not an abandoned woman, but a woman 'unhappily

intoxicated by love', thought Dr Delany. Deane Swift too stood up for Vanessa. 'Is there any crime in love? Far from it . . .'

Vanessa's mother had died in early 1714, leaving her a considerable heiress if only she could lay her hands on the money. She came over to Dublin, in spite of Swift's warnings, later that year – quite soon after Swift moved in to the Deanery – with her younger sister Mary (called Moll, and Malkin), who was already ill with the tuberculosis that would kill both of them. They settled into lodgings in Turnstile Alley, just off College Green. Vanessa also had a house which had belonged to her father, ten miles out at Celbridge. As soon as she arrived, she sent for Swift.

The new Dean had been panic-stricken. 'I ever told you, you wanted discretion . . .' He would come and see her when he could. 'A fig for your letters and messages.' It was one thing to see Vanessa in England, quite another to have her within half a mile of himself, and of everyone he knew, including Stella, in Dublin. In one of the poems attributed to Vanessa, she railed against 'curs'd discretion', the enemy of love. He did go and see her, and often, but never often enough for Vanessa. 'You once had a maxim', she wrote to him, 'which was to act what was right and not mind what the world said . . . Your frowns make my life unsupportable.' He did mind horribly what the world said in this case, and the world would say what it could. Vanessa felt herself to be among 'strange, prying, deceitful people'. She and Swift had rows. ''Tis impossible to describe what I have suffered since I saw you last', she wrote to him; 'those killing, killing, killing words.'

Swift hated receiving a letter (delivered by her servant) when there was company with him at the Deanery; it put him in 'such confusion' that he didn't know what to do, probably because Stella was present. Vanessa never came to the Deanery, and she never mentions Stella in her surviving letters. It is not thought that they ever formally met. But the centre of Dublin and the intersecting circles of acquaintances were both so small that no one could be on the streets for more than five minutes without meeting someone they knew, or who knew who they were. Dublin has always been a goldfish bowl.

'I ever feared the tattle of this nasty town, and told you so; and that was the reason why I said to you, long ago, that I would seldom see you in Ireland', wrote Swift to Vanessa. He said that 'a woman who does business for me' – I guess he was avoiding mentioning Dingley, or Stella – 'told me she heard I was in love with one – naming you, and twenty particulars, that little master and I visited you, and that the A[rch]B[ishop] did so; and that you had an abundance of wit, etc.'

It has been argued, on the basis of a tale that Swift had a son (whose mother was either Vanessa or Stella, depending on the teller), that the 'little master' referred to in that letter was their love-child. I don't think so. I think he was a dog. Vanessa had a pampered dog. Swift kept spaniels at the Deanery (and used an ancient 'dog-doctor' who was also a cobbler).

Swift had no intention of endangering the long-established intimacy with Stella: the shared friends and shared dinners, the almost daily visits, the co-dependency growing out of deep knowledge of one another's history, health, habits, needs and weaknesses. He had to lead a double life. He used a 'doubling' image in a poem for Stella's birthday, asking the gods to 'split' her virtues and graces into two equal nymphs,

> And then before it grew too late
> How should I beg of gentle fate,
> (That either nymph might have her swain,)
> To split my worship too in twain.

His best hope was to weave Vanessa into his Dublin life on a normal social level, while keeping her apart from Stella. There was some overlapping. Archbishop King had known Vanessa's father, and befriended her in Dublin. Patrick Delany knew both Vanessa and Stella, and Charles Ford was a particularly good friend to both women, though even here there was a doubling. Ford was nick-named 'Glass-Heel' by Swift and Vanessa, and 'Don Carlos' by Swift and Stella. Vanessa, in Dublin, had more and smarter friends than Stella. Calling at Turnstile Alley in her absence, Swift left a note:

I dined with the Provost [of Trinity, Dr Pratt] and told him I was coming here . . . He said you had been with him, and would not be at home this day, and went to Celbridge tomorrow. I said I would however go try. I fancy you told him so that he might not come tonight. If he comes you must piece it up as you can, else he will think it was on purpose to meet me, and I hate anything that looks like a secret.

There is a four-year gap in the surviving letters. Deane Swift and Thomas Sheridan both say that Swift took the well-off Revd Sankey Winter, Archdeacon of Killala, to meet Vanessa, hoping to deflect her passion, and that she was not at all amused. Deane Swift said it was in the year 1716; if he is right, that could be significant, as we shall discover.

The next letter in this correspondence that has survived is from 1719, the year in which Swift wrote so gloomily about his deafness, and age, and boringness, and piles. When he was ill, Stella and Dingley moved into the Deanery, so that Stella could look after him. A poem written for her in 1720 records how Stella

> My sinking spirit now supplies
> With cordials in her hands, and eyes.
> Now, with a soft and silent tread,
> Unheard she moves about my bed.

She was, to a sick and ageing man, a more 'useful friend', to use a favourite expression of Swift's, than the younger and amorous Vanessa. As he wrote in *Cadenus and Vanessa*:

> What planter will attempt to yoke
> A sapling with a falling oak?
> As years increase, she brighter shines,
> Cadenus with each day declines,
> And he must fall a prey to time,
> While she continues in her prime.

But he was hooked on Vanessa, and on her passion for himself which he so savagely deplored. It was dangerous; but there was with his recovery a resurgence of intimacy with her, and an escalation. 'Cadenus' (an anagram of 'decanus', Latin for dean) was the name he (and Vanessa, who abbreviated it to 'Cad') used of himself in poems and letters. He instructed her to use dashes for the endearments they must not spell out, for 'everything that may be said to Cad, at beginning or conclusion'. He used dashes too. Repairing their relationship in 1720, he wrote to her, in French, a long, conciliatory letter praising her intelligence, her good sense, her character, her gifts of expression, her lack of affectation: how was it possible for him not to value her above the rest of the human race?

In tacit betrayal of Stella, he wrote that all women apart from her were 'beasts in petticoats'. He ended with four dashes.

It was never plain sailing. She was always depressed and beseeching him to come to her,

> for I'm sure you'd not condemn anyone to suffer what I have done, could you but know it. The reason I write to you is because I cannot tell it to you . . . for when I begin to complain, you are angry, and there is something in your looks so awful, it strikes me dumb.

He called her 'Governor Huff' when she was in that mood. 'I am confident you came chiding into the world, and will continue so while you are in it.' She could be imperious and a little threatening:

> I believe you thought I only rallied [joked] when I told you, the other night, I would pester you with letters . . . Now, because I love frankness extremely, I here tell you that I have determined to try all manner of human arts to reclaim you . . . Pray think calmly of it. Is it not much better to come of yourself than to be brought by force . . . But there is one thing that falls out very luckily for you, which is that, of all the passions, revenge hurries me least, so that you have it in your power to turn all this fury into good humour . . .

Vanessa's desperate letters exist only in her own drafts. It is possible she toned them down in the fair copy, as one does. Swift took this one lightly, in any case: 'If you write as you do, I shall come the seldomer, on purpose to be pleased with your letters, which I never look into without wondering how a brat, who cannot read, could possibly write so well.' When feeling fond, he called her 'Skinage', 'little Heskinage'.

In July 1720 Vanessa was at Celbridge. Writing to her there, enclosing a note for her sister, who was mortally ill: 'I reckon by this time the groves and fields and purling streams have made Vanessa romantic, provided poor Malkin be well . . . So drink your coffee and remember you are a desperate chip . . .' The wrangling went on and on. 'I shall promise you no more, and rather choose to be better than my word, than worse . . . You do not find that I answer your questions to your satisfaction. Prove to me, first that it was ever possible to answer anything to your satisfaction.' Yet his tone was wistful; he ended with four dashes. Vanessa, hopefully reading words of passion into his dashes, replied ecstatically:

> ——, ——, ——, ——, ——, Cad ——, you are good beyond expression
> ... I am now as happy as I can be without seeing ——, ——, ——.
> Cad. I beg you'll continue happiness to your own Skinage.

And the Dean, in August, asked what she would give to have 'the history of Cad and ——, exactly written, through all its steps, from the beginning to this time: I believe it would do well in verse, and be as long as the other [i.e., as *Cadenus and Vanessa*]:

> It ought to be an exact chronicle of twelve years, from the time of spilling the coffee to drinking coffee, from Dunstable to Dublin, with every single passage since. There would be the chapter of the blister; the chapter of Madam going to Kensington; the chapter of the Colonel's [her brother] going to France; the chapter of the wedding, with the adventure of the lost key; of the strain; of the joyful return; two hundred chapters of madness; the chapter of long walks; the Berkshire surprise; fifty chapters of little times; the chapter of Chelsea; the chapter of swallow and cluster; a hundred whole books of myself and 'so low'; the chapter of hide and whisper; the chapter of Who made it so?

We cannot know quite all the references. It doesn't matter. The tender litany is indication enough of Swift's absorbed enthralment. For Vanessa, Swift was the magus: 'What marks are there of a deity but what you are known by?'

> My guide, instructor, lover, friend,
> (Dear names!) in one idea blend . . .

He began going to Celbridge to see her that summer. Her house (later named Marley Abbey) is on the river Liffey. When Sir Walter Scott was writing about Swift, there was still an old gardener living who had worked for Vanessa, 'and his account of her corresponded with the usual description of her person, especially as to her *embonpoint*'. The garden was full of laurels; Vanessa planted another one for each of the Dean's visits, said the gardener. There was an arbour of close-planted shrubs and trees with two seats and a table inside, and a view over the river. Here the Dean and Vanessa would sit, with their books and writing materials. He was working on *Gulliver*, and shared what he was writing with her.

In October, Swift was writing her a diary-letter from Dublin, as he once had to Stella from London. He and Vanessa are still using the coffee-code:

> I am getting an ill head in this cursed town, for want of exercise.
> I wish I were to walk with you fifty times about your garden,
> and then – drink your coffee. I was sitting last night with half a
> score of both sexes for an hour, and grew as weary as a dog.

He would far rather, he said, 'hear the Governor [Huff] chide two hours without reason'. And in cryptic reference to some dream or erotic fantasy: 'The Governor was with me at six o'clock this morning, but did not stay two minutes, and deserves a chiding, which you must give when you drink your coffee next.'

Stella was unhappy. She wrote a poem called 'Jealousy'. For his birthday in November 1721 she wrote him a poem repositioning herself as the adoring pupil of the magus – knowing that he had another. I should like to think her lines, which would have been read out at the birthday dinner in the Deanery, carried a cryptically ironic message. It is more likely that she was just trying to give him what he wanted.

> St Patrick's Dean, your country's pride,
> My early and my only guide,
> Let me among the rest attend,
> Your pupil and your humble friend.

The poem recalls how he had taught her to trust in her moral and mental strengths and not to envy the conquests of young coquettes; their day would pass,

> While Stella holds her station still.
> Oh! Turn your precepts into laws,
> Redeem the women's ruined cause,
> Retrieve lost empire to our sex,
> That men may bow their rebel necks.

199

The Dean was in a dilemma. Filling his time with writing, and cathedral duties, and country visits, he detached himself again from Vanessa. He did not see her for ten weeks, and unleashed a spate of anguished letters.

> You endeavour by severities to force me from you; nor can I blame you, for with the utmost distress and confusion, I behold myself the cause of uneasy reflections to you. Yet I cannot comfort you; but here declare that 'tis not in the power of art, time or accident to lessen the unexpressible passion which I have for ---, ---, ---.

She spent all her days and nights thinking of him:

> Oh! that I could hope to see you here, or that I could go to you. I was born with violent passions, which terminate all in one – that unexpressible passion I have for you . . . You are present everywhere; your dear image is always before my eyes; sometimes you strike me with that prodigious awe I tremble with fear; at other times, a charming compassion shines through your countenance, which revives my soul.

Vanessa, no longer the artless girl that Swift had first known, was so articulate that any commentary on her letters is unnecessary. She was an intelligent woman irrevocably and self-destructively fixated on Swift: in love. She was on her own in the world, and in charge of a dying sister. Moll was buried in March 1721. Swift did not desert Vanessa in the bad time, but preserved an emotional distance. He hated deathbeds and mourning. 'I observed [Moll] looked a little ghastly on Saturday, but it is against the usual way for one in her case to die so sudden. In God's sake get your friends about you . . . I want comfort myself in this case, and can give little.'

Afterwards Vanessa was more often in Dublin, to pursue her lawsuits, and to be near the Dean.

Writing to her from the Rochforts' at Gaulstown in July 1721, he assured her that 'Cad' continued 'to esteem and love and value you above all things, and so will do to the end of his life, but at the same time entreats that you will not make yourself or him unhappy by imaginations'.

She was to live in the moment, and avoid the spleen. 'Shall you, who have so much honour and good sense, act otherwise, to make Cad – and yourself miserable?' Once she had settled her affairs she should 'quit this scoundrel island, and things will be as you desire'. He had drunk no coffee since he left her, 'nor intend to till I see you again. There is none worth drinking but yours . . .'

This is a double-sided letter. It is a declaration of love. He ended by saying: 'Rest assured that you are the only person on earth who has ever been loved, honoured, esteemed, adored by your friend.'

'Loved . . . adored'. These are unique admissions, from Jonathan Swift. But the letter is also a declaration that nothing – no marriage, nothing – was to be hoped for from him. He is bent on renunciation.

Subsequent letters from him begin with common sense. 'Remember I still enjoin you reading and exercise for the improvement of your mind and health of your body, and grow less romantic and talk and act like a man of the world.' He was not really cured of her. He wrote to her that riches were nine parts of the good in the world, and health the tenth:

> Drinking coffee comes long after, and yet it is the eleventh; but without the two former you cannot drink it right; and remember the china in the old house, and Ryder Street, and the Colonel's journey to France, and the sick lady at Windsor . . .

And he's off again on a litany of reminiscence. He is trying to establish that although the affair is over, what they were to one another, and the precious memories, are intact. 'We differ prodigiously in one point: I fly from the spleen to the world's end, you run out of your way to meet it.' She, unable to accept finality, continued to write, and to plead for visits, and to justify her passion. The last letter that survives from the correspondence is from Swift, in August 1722, and it contains another would-be comforting litany:

> Go over the scenes of Windsor, Cleveland Row, Ryder Street, St James's, Kensington, the Sluttery, the Colonel in France etc. Cad thinks often of these, especially on horseback . . . But I will not proceed at this rate, or I am fast writing myself into the spleen, which is the only thing I would not compliment you by imitating.

The tradition is that Vanessa heard a rumour that Swift was secretly married to Stella, and took action. Dr Delany said she 'gave herself up to Bacchus . . . from the day she was deserted', that is, she took to the bottle. Hawkesworth perpetuated this story. Perhaps it is true, he wrote, 'that in the anguish of disappointed desire, she had recourse to that dreadful opiate which never fails to complicate diseases with trouble, to leave the sufferer more wretched when its operation is at an end . . .', and more in the same sententious vein. Why wouldn't Vanessa drink? Not only had her sister died, and the only man she had ever loved detached himself. Her own terminal illness now had her in its grip.

Various contemporary writers in the circle of friends, and Sir Walter Scott, tell the same story: that Vanessa wrote a letter to Stella, asking her outright if she was married to the Dean. We don't know what else she said. This was not an immoral act but it broke every taboo, and had consequences. Both Swift and Stella were 'shocked and distressed (tho' it may be differently)', wrote Patrick Delany. That was an understatement.

Stella, outraged, had Vanessa's letter sent over to Swift. She herself immediately left Dublin with Dingley and took refuge with Charles Ford at Woodpark. The Dean of St Patrick's, in a rage the like of which even Vanessa had never seen before, rode out to Celbridge, threw down Vanessa's own letter in front of her, rode straight back to Dublin, and never had anything to do with Vanessa again. The lurid theatricality of this anecdote – which can only have acquired currency through Vanessa – ensures its immortality. Poets and novelists have latched on to it ever since. Here, for example, is Thomas C. Unwin in 1869:

> She enters – springs to meet him. God!
> Can passion demonize a brow
> Of spirit-splendour! In a breath
> The letter's thrown; and he, like death,
> Is gone; Hark! Ringing from the road
> His horse's trampling echoes now.

Upon which Unwin's Vanessa drops dead on the spot, 'Brain-blasted by his silent scorn.'

In May 1723 Vanessa, not dead but indeed dying, made her will. She named as her executors Robert Marshall, a lawyer, and the philosopher Dean (later Bishop) George Berkeley, whom she had met with Swift in London but not seen since. Swift respected Berkeley, and recommended him to Lord Carteret, the year after Vanessa died, as 'one of the first men in this kingdom for virtue and learning'. She left small bequests to Erasmus Lewis (the discreet friend of Swift, Stella and Vanessa, who had forwarded Vanessa's letters to Swift from London under his own cover), Archbishop King, and Bishop Theophilus Bolton of Clonfert (whom Swift visited two months after Vanessa's death: what did they talk about?). Her main legatee was Dr Berkeley, but his £3,000 was reduced by her debts and the remainder took a long time to materialize. Swift was not mentioned in her will.

She died on 2 June. Swift, hearing the news, wrote a note, 'past twelve at night', to Knightly Chetwode, who was seeking to involve Swift in his own problems: 'I am forced to leave the town sooner than I expected.'

He then disappeared on a two-month fugue through the south and west of Ireland. This was something he had planned to do, and the visit to Bishop Bolton at Clonfert in Co. Galway had long been arranged. Vanessa's death gave the journey a different colour. 'I go where I was never before, without one companion, and among people where I know no creature; and all this to get a little exercise, to cure an ill head.' And an ill heart. He had plenty of time to get his thoughts in order.

'Anecdote and folklore', as one who traced his lone itinerary has written, now take the place of factual documentation. It is said that he stayed with the vicar at Myross, and at Castletownshend, both in West Cork, and went out in a boat; he certainly wrote his Latin poem 'Carberiae Rupes' about that wild rocky coast. Further anecdotes attach to a visit to Sixmilebridge in Co. Clare and other places. It is known that Part IV of *Gulliver*, about the Yahoos and the Houyhnhnms, was finished by the end of 1723. He said afterwards that he traversed, on horseback, four hundred miles in all, and that he visited many clergymen and heard their views on the state of the country. The contrast between the ragged, degraded and, to him, savage peasantry and the clean civility of (some) parsons' houses may have helped to shape what he was writing.

When he returned he became reconciled – with relief, no doubt –

with Stella. He wooed her back with a poem, 'Stella at Woodpark', in which he teased her for acquiring luxurious tastes in food and wine in Charles Ford's hospitable house. It was time to go back to Dublin and the lodgings on Ormond Quay. She must return

> From ruling there the household singly
> To be directed here by Dingley:
> From ev'ry day a lordly banquet,
> To half a joint, and God be thank it . . .
> From Ford, who thinks of nothing mean,
> To the poor doings of the Dean.

When she sighed to leave Woodpark,

> We think you do mistake the case;
> The virtue lies not in the place:
> For though my raillery were true,
> A cottage is Woodpark with you.

His birthday poem for her in March 1724 referred to his recurring illness, but perhaps not only to that:

> Whatever base returns you find
> From me, dear Stella, still be kind.
> In your own heart you'll reap the fruit,
> Tho' I continue still a brute.
> But when I once am out of pain,
> I promise to be good again.

Vanessa did leave Swift a legacy, of an unwelcome sort. His poem *Cadenus and Vanessa* was written for her eyes only, in 1712 or 1713, though probably tinkered with later. Patrick Delany said she had instructed her executors to publish it after her death.

The poem is, in essence, an analysis of their relationship – from his point of view. He presents Cadenus as the dedicated tutor of this exceptionally lovely, modest and promising young pupil. She, suddenly struck with Cupid's dart, feels passionate desire for him, to which he cannot respond:

He now cou'd praise, esteem, approve,
But understood not what was love.
His conduct might have made him styl'd
A father, and the nymph his child.
That innocent delight he took
To see the virgin mind her book,
Was but the master's secret joy
In school to hear the finest boy.

He stressed the same lack of romantic impulse in a birthday poem to
Stella:

Without one word of Cupid's darts,
Of killing eyes, or bleeding hearts:
With friendship and esteem possesst;
I ne'er admitted love a guest.

Unfortunately he never gives a clue as to Stella's vulnerability to
Cupid's darts. I guess that she suffered. Hence the tempers. Swift's
highest praise of both Stella and Vanessa is that they are not as other
women. Their virtues, for him, are the masculine ones of courage,
honour, sense, and wit. Of Stella:

She thinks that Nature ne'er designed
Courage to man alone confin'd . . .
Say, Stella, was Prometheus blind,
And, forming you, mistook your kind?
No: 'twas for you alone he stole
The fire that forms a manly soul;
Then to complete it every way,
He molded it with female clay.

Similarly, with Vanessa: in her babyhood, Pallas Athene the goddess
of wisdom

Down from Olympus comes with joy,
Mistakes Vanessa for a boy;
Then sows within her tender mind
Seeds long unknown to womankind,
For manly bosoms chiefly fit,
The seeds of knowledge, judgement, wit.

In each case, forcing the 'female clay' of both of them into the same mould, he sought to compliment them on their doubleness of gender – and to de-sex them.

When, in *Cadenus and Vanessa*, the 'nymph' Vanessa confesses her passion, Cadenus feels 'Shame, disappointment, guilt, surprise'. Vanessa defends her love by reasoned argument, according to the system he has taught her:

> Cadenus, to his grief and shame,
> Cou'd scarce oppose Vanessa's flame;
> But tho' her arguments were strong.
> At least, could hardly wish them wrong . . .

because they were based on what she had learned from him: that it was right to love wisdom, wit and learning, the qualities embodied in Cadenus. The tables are turned. Vanessa is now the teacher, teaching Cadenus the art of love, and he the pupil – a reversal summed up in a passage which has teased readers of the poem ever since:

> But what success Vanessa met,
> Is to the world a secret yet:
> Whether the nymph, to please her swain,
> Talks in a high romantic strain;
> Or whether he at last descends
> To like with less seraphic ends;
> Or, to compound the business, whether
> They temper love and books together;
> Must never to mankind be told,
> Nor shall the conscious Muse unfold.

What 'must never to mankind be told' is, clearly, whether they became lovers or not. Patrick Delany said that the poem's insinuations 'were not perhaps so much intended to wound her reputation, as to save that of her admirer'. There is complacency, disingenuousness, self-deception in Swift's presentation. Delany condemned Swift's 'idle vanity' in 'these vile verses' – a vanity which the poet conceded:

'Tis an old maxim in the schools.
That vanity's the food of fools.
Yet now and then your men of wit
Will condescend to take a bit.

He 'let himself be loved', as Leslie Stephen wrote.

No one can know whether Swift and Vanessa were actually lovers. It doesn't really matter; they were linked; and there are sufficiently intoxicating caresses which stop short of intercourse. No one reading 'Cad's' letters or hers could believe that he was immune to the attraction. Sometimes it overwhelmed him. Their letters are not written in the 'high romantic strain' of lovers who have no physical connection. They 'tempered love and books together' in states of suspended arousal, in the way that they drank their emblematic coffee. If I were forced to make a judgement, I would say that maybe they somehow consummated their affair once, and that the act established Vanessa's lasting fixation; and that Swift regretted it. His moment of human weakness, if that's how he saw it, put him somewhat in her power, and left the door open for more. When she was not cravenly beseeching, she made bids to 'claim' him. I think Swift was always a little afraid of what she might do.

Swift, in London in 1726, responded to a warning from Knightley Chetwode that manuscript copies of *Cadenus and Vanessa* were circulating, and that it was to be published, by covering his tracks:

As to the poem you mention, I know several copies of it have been given about, and Lord Lieutenant told me he had one. It was written at Windsor near fourteen years ago, and dated. It was a task performed on a frolic among some ladies, and she it was addressed to died some time ago in Dublin, and on her death the copy [was] shown by her executor [Robert Marshall]. I am very indifferent what is done with it, for printing cannot make it more common than it is . . .

Not even the 'gravest character', he wrote, could be held responsible for 'a private humorsome thing' which, by 'the baseness of particular malice', was made public.

That kind of diplomatic flannel was not going to appease Stella. Whether as a result of the poem or not, she deteriorated in health and spirits.

Swift had never wanted to be near Stella when she died. When he was in England in the summer of 1726 he heard that she was seriously ill, and told John Worrall that if he thought Mrs Johnson 'could not hold out until my return', he would stay away in retirement somewhere, 'till I can be in a disposition of appearing after an accident that must be so fatal to my quiet . . . I would not for the universe be present at such a trial of seeing her depart.' He is thinking of himself, not of her.

> Self-love, in Nature rooted fast
> Attends us first, and leaves us last.

He impressed on Worrall the absolute undesirability of her dying at the Deanery; she should be moved to an 'airy healthy part, as it would be a very improper thing for that house to breathe her last in'. Worrall was to burn this letter immediately 'without telling the contents of it to any person alive'. Secrecy about his personal life had become a priority.

Five days later he wrote to a parson friend, James Stopford, in Dublin, that 'there is not a greater folly than entering into too strict and particular a friendship, with the loss of which a man must be absolutely miserable; but especially at an age when it is too late to engage in a new friendship'.

His pain and distress were greater even than his letters to Worrall would suggest. He added a sentence which is unusually intimate and as close as we get to a definition of his feeling for Stella: 'Dear Jim, pardon me, I know not what I am saying; but believe me that violent friendship is much more lasting, and as much engaging, as violent love.' This concept of 'violent friendship' is worth pausing to think about. Its primacy for Jonathan Swift is to be respected. His brief spontaneous declaration to 'dear Jim' is more moving than any protestation of romantic love.

He wrote what was to be his last birthday poem to Stella.

> This day, whate'er the fates decree,
> Shall still be kept with joy by me:
> This day, then let us not be told,
> That you are sick, and I grown old,
> Nor think on our approaching ills,

And talk of spectacles and pills;
Tomorrow will be time enough
To hear such mortifying stuff . . .

O then, whatever heav'n intends.
Take pity on your pitying friends;
Nor let your ills affect your mind,
To fancy they can be unkind.
Me, surely me, you ought to spare,
Who gladly would your suff'rings share;
Or give my scrap of life to you,
And think it far beneath your due;
You, to whose care so oft I owe,
That I'm alive to tell you so.

The lovingness of this, and the hint that she expressed resentments, should be remembered when we are trying to assess the accounts of what happened between them. He was the most important person in her life. She was the most important person in his life. His happiest, easiest times were with her. Yet the 'violent friendship' laboured under strains and constraints. Something remains eternally unresolved between Swift and Stella, which leaves one sad.

On the evening that he heard of her death, he had friends with him at the Deanery. It must have taken a superhuman effort to sit talking with them for another three hours, until they departed. Maybe Patrick Delany and the others did not want to leave him alone too soon. The note was probably from Dr Sheridan. Later, Swift sat down and began to write:

This day, being Sunday, January 28, 1727–8, about eight o'clock at night, a servant brought me a note, with an account of the death of the truest, most virtuous, and valuable friend, that I, or perhaps any other person, ever was blessed with. She expired about six in the evening of this day; and as soon as I am left alone, which is about eleven at night, I resolve, for my own satisfaction, to say something about her life and character.

She was sickly until she was about fifteen, he wrote, but afterwards had perfect health, 'and was looked upon as one of the most beautiful, graceful, and agreeable young women in London, only a little too fat. Her hair was blacker than a raven, and every feature of her face in perfection.'

Swift did not get very far that night. He tried to pick up where he left off the following night, but only managed one line: 'My head aches, and I can write no more.' He tried again the next night, writing not in his own bedroom overlooking the cathedral but in another one, at the front of the house, to avoid torturing himself:

> January 30. Tuesday. This is the night of the funeral, which my sickness will not suffer me to attend. It is now nine at night, and I am removed into another apartment, that I might not see the light in the church, which is just over against the window of my bed-chamber.

The best thing in his life had gone out of it. There never was, there never could be, a replacement for Stella. In so far as Swift had a life companion, it was she.

Night-funerals were common, there was nothing secretive about that. Stella was buried beneath the great aisle of St Patrick's. She had left money for a monument. Her executors waited in vain for the inscription which Swift promised to compose, but never did. It was probably just too difficult. Some years after his death, a marble slab was erected, with a long inscription (no one knows by whom) which begins:

> Underneath lie
> interred the mortal Remains
> of Mrs. HESTER JOHNSON better
> known to the World by the name of STELLA,
> under which she is celebrated in the Writings of
> Dr. JONATHAN SWIFT Dean of this Cathedral.
> She was a Person of Extraordinary Endow-
> ments and Accomplishments in Body, Mind and Be-
> haviour; justly admired and respected, by all who
> knew her, on account of her many eminent vir-
> tues, as well as for her natural and
> acquired Perfections.

Death, Swift told Bolingbroke a year later, was rarely out of his mind, but 'it terrifies me less'. He loved 'la bagatelle' more than ever. 'I am always writing bad prose, or worse verses, either of rage or raillery, whereof some few escape to give offence, or mirth, and the rest are burned.' He wished to get into a better frame of mind, 'and not die here in a rage, like a poisoned rat in a hole'. He found curious ways to assuage his rage.

After Stella died, social life at the Deanery changed. Swift made new female friends – Dublin women with literary aspirations or interests, delighted by the famous Dean's favour. They were unthreatening, and sufficiently amusing, and he could treat them as badly or as well as he felt inclined.

The cleverest of these women friends was Constantia Grierson, the very young and self-educated wife of a Dublin printer, who published editions of Terence and of Tacitus before dying in her late twenties. Mrs Grierson's close friend was Mary Barber, an older woman and a woollen-draper's wife. She was a published writer, ambitious and difficult, but Swift admired her, and she was a friend of the Delanys. There was also Mrs Sican, a prosperous grocer's wife and a second-rate versifier 'but a good reader and a judge', according to Swift. Her son went to Dr Sheridan's school, and on to Trinity. Mrs Sican went shopping for Swift, who wrote about her as 'Psyche':

> To please you, she knows how to choose a nice bit;
> For her taste is almost as refin'd as her wit.

There was also Laetitia Pilkington, of whom more shortly.

Lord Orrery only became acquainted with Swift at this stage in his life. He was a regular caller. Swift told Charles Ford that Orrery seemed 'in every way a most deserving person, a good scholar, with much wit, manners and modesty'. Orrery was a snob, as Swift was not. Although he became quite a friend of Mrs Barber, Orrery disapproved of both the type and class of these women, and of Swift's wasting his time with them. 'He trifled away many hours in their conversation, he filled many pages in their praise, and by the power of his head, he gained the character of a lover, without the least assistance of his heart.'

He stressed the command Swift had over 'all his females', that 'seraglio of very virtuous women who attended him from morning till night, with an obedience, and awe, and an assiduity, that are seldom paid to the richest, or the most powerful lovers'.

Orrery exaggerates. He was probably irritated by never having the Dean to himself, and by having to make conversation to women who did not interest him. They, said Orrery, were responsible for the printing of many pieces 'which should never have been given to public view'. Swift showed them everything he wrote, and they took copies. He was still corresponding copiously with Pope, Gay (until his death in 1732), Arbuthnot (until his death in 1735), and Bolingbroke, who he was never to see again – but his real life was becoming confined to this small domestic circle.

It was the 'despotic power' that he exercised over this circle, said Orrery, which permitted him to give free rein to 'passions that ought to have been kept under proper restraint'.

Perhaps we can learn something from the testimony of Laetitia Pilkington, née Van Lewen. She was the daughter of a distinguished obstetrician practising in Dublin, whose Dutch father had settled in Ireland. She was much with Swift between 1730 – when she was only eighteen and recently married to the thirty-year-old clergyman Matthew Pilkington – and 1737, when her marriage collapsed in adultery, scandal, mutual acrimony, and divorce.

Both the Pilkingtons were diminutive, with ambitions in inverse ratio to their stature. Dr Delany, who had been at Trinity with Laetitia's father, befriended the tiny pair and entertained them at Delville. Laetitia had the ability to write tolerable verse by the yard and at speed. Hearing that Delany was to attend the Dean's birthday dinner, she composed a poem for the occasion which gratified the Dean sufficiently to admit the young lady to his acquaintance. He already knew her little husband.

Swift took a fancy to the childlike, saucy, fearless Laetitia. He took her alone into his library, and showed her his treasures, and teased her. He abused her as a 'damned, insolent, proud, unmannerly slut'. The Pilkingtons, 'Tom Thumb and her Serene Highness of Lilliput', became habitués of the intimate suppers at the Deanery. In his fits of deafness, their high, thin voices got through to him. Laetitia spent days alone with him, pasting his correspondence with the great into an album at his request (and reading the letters). He trotted round Naboth's Vineyard with her, and he showed her unpublished poems – running, she said, into the parlour at the Deanery to throw bundles of manuscript into her lap. He dined with her and her husband in what he called their 'Lilliputan Palace', and inspected it from garret to kitchen, not omitting Laetitia's bedroom.

'I doubt not', she wrote in her extraordinary memoirs, 'but that the world will expect to hear from me some of the Dean's amours, as he has not quite escaped censure on account of his gallantries.' She was referring to the notoriety of *Cadenus and Vanessa*. But, she continued, 'I really believe it was a passion he was wholly unacquainted with, and which he would have thought it beneath the dignity of his wisdom to entertain.'

Laetitia Pilkington acquired wide experience of men, being forced by circumstances into exploiting her attractions for gain. Her memoirs are filled with dark diatribes against the sexual opportunism and outrageous hypocrisy of bishops, deans and clergymen. Swift, like Delany, is always specifically exempted from these accusations.

What gave the Dean pleasure, she went on to say, was to instruct women – 'though to tell the truth, he was a very rough sort of tutor for one of my years and sex; for whenever I made use of an inelegant phrase, I was sure of a deadly pinch, and frequently received chastisement before I knew my crime'. She does not specify where the 'blue and black flowers' of the bruises she described were bestowed. On her upper arms? Had Stella, the first young girl he instructed, received similar punishment? Had Vanessa?

She tells even more curious stories. Dining at Delany's house one Christmas, Swift set the wine before a hot fire, which melted the pitch and resin that sealed the corks. Swift rubbed his fingers in the black sticky mess and smeared it on Laetitia's face. She merely told him he did her great honour in 'sealing me for his own'. Determined to get a reaction out of her, he asked the company if they had ever seen 'such a dwarf', and insisted she take off her shoes ('Why, I expected you had either broken stockings or foul toes, and in either case should have delighted to have exposed you') and stand against the wainscot. He pressed his hand down hard on her head until she half-crumpled, 'then making a mark with a pencil, he affirmed I was but three feet two inches high'. Laetitia was unable to eat her dinner. She was pregnant at the time.

Laetitia also recalls Swift summoning her to the Deanery very early one morning, and after two hours' badinage but no breakfast instructing her to open a low drawer in his cabinet and take from it a flat bottle containing rum. She knelt down and tried to open the drawer,

but he flew at me, and beat me most immoderately; I again

made an effort, and still he beat me, crying: 'Pox take you! *open* the drawer!' I once more tried, and he struck me so hard that I burst into tears, and said: 'Lord, sir, what must I do?' 'Pox take you for a slut!' said he; 'would you spoil my lock, and break my key.' 'Why, sir, the drawer is locked.' 'Oh! I beg your pardon', said he. 'I thought you were going to pull it out by the key: well, open it and do what I bid you.'

Laetitia found the flat bottle. Swift produced a piece of gingerbread and tried to make her eat some. He always breakfasted between the Deanery and the cathedral, he said, 'and I carry my provision in my pocket'. As the pregnant Laetitia was 'terribly afflicted with the heartburn', she declined, but he insisted; also that she took a sup from the bottle. She held it to her mouth, pretending to drink. He then 'threw me down, forced the bottle into my mouth, poured some of the liquor down my throat, which I thought would have set my very stomach on fire'.

'He then gravely went to prayers' – presumably munching on his gingerbread – 'and I returned home, not greatly delighted, but, however, glad to have come off no worse.' Laetitia is writing of events a quarter of a century earlier. Yet the very pettiness and inconsequentiality of the scenes she describes lend them verisimilitude. (The cabinet is still in the Deanery. The one lockable drawer is the bottom left-hand one.)

If Stella had lived, the Deanery would not have been the scene of such sadistic silliness. What of the report that Stella and Swift had been secretly married? Were they really husband and wife?

Chapter Thirteen

WIFE?

THE ONLY WRITERS it is worth consulting for information about Swift's rumoured marriage are those who knew him, or who knew people who did. Sir Walter Scott was the last of these. No more recent researcher has found new evidence either for or against.

After Scott, writers on Swift have simply chosen what to believe, basing the belief on their own idea of his nature and the statements of whoever has most convinced them among earlier writers whom they may have consulted.

The opinions of even the earliest writers have been undercut in advance by Swift himself, or rather by his Gulliver, who expressed contempt for 'the roguery and ignorance of those who pretend to write anecdotes, or secret history [the 'inside story']', and who 'have the perpetual misfortune to be mistaken'.

Tentatively, then, we proceed.

Laetitia Pilkington was first into print about the Dean; but it was only in the third volume of her memoirs, posthumously published in 1754, that she refers to the marriage. Stella, she wrote, 'was actually his wife, though they never, I am convinced, tasted even the chaste joys which Hymen allows'.

Mrs Pilkington never passed up any opportunity for a dramatic reconstruction of a remembered incident or conversation. The uncharacteristic brevity and discretion with which she writes of the marriage suggests that the Dean never spoke in her presence about it, and that she was simply picking up on what other people told her.

Lord Orrery published his *Remarks on the Life and Writings of Dr Jonathan Swift* in 1752, seven years after Swift's death. Orrery asserts unambiguously that Stella was 'the concealed, but undoubted wife of Dr Swift . . . If my informations are right, she was married to Swift in the year 1716, by Dr Ashe then Bishop of Clogher.' He does not say from whom he got his 'informations', but he was familiar with Swift's Dublin circle. In Swift's lifetime he was more circumspect. During the Dean's last illness he wrote to Deane Swift saying how different things would have been for the sick man in this difficult time 'had he been married, or, in other words, had Stella lived'.

Orrery is always shrewd about Swift, and generally deflationary. He was condescending about Swift's band of friends in Dublin, and they resented his book deeply. No sooner was it published than Orrery heard news of ripostes. His friend Dr Edward Barry of Cork reassured him that if Swift's dependants printed an 'answer' to the book, ''tis likely their splenetic resentment will evaporate in words'. Barry added a rider, apt for all biographers writing about literary contemporaries: 'it is impossible so early to write just criticism on the life and writings of an eminent author without giving offence to some of his dependents and admirers'.

Orrery was very grand about the criticism. He found the adverse comments he had already seen 'low in style, erroneous, impotent, malicious'. He treated them 'as a friend of mine [Swift?] used to treat silly and absurd books of devotion. I just looked into them, shrugged up my shoulders at the folly and threw them into the window seat among the foul linen and various unseemly utensils.' (He means, among the soiled tablecloths and napkins, and the chamber-pots – which were commonly kept in the dining-parlour for the convenience of gentlemen at dinner.)

Orrery wrote to Dr Johnson: 'I cannot wonder that the book should be obnoxious in Ireland. Many of Swift's sycophants are still living. Many expected to be flattered, for all who flatter love flattery.' Dr Barry had heard that Mrs Barber was leading the opposition. 'I am told Sheridan is at the head of all the cavillers', replied Orrery. 'But silence, the strongest symptom of contempt, is my rule. The book that cannot defend itself ought to die. The book that can, ought not to be defended.'

The Sheridan to whom Orrery refers was Thomas Sheridan the younger, Swift's godson. It was not until 1784, twenty-three years after Orrery's death, that Thomas Sheridan went public with *The Life of the Rev Dr Jonathan Swift, Dean of St Patrick's, Dublin*. In between Orrery and Sheridan, others had their say: Patrick Delany, John

Hawkesworth, Deane Swift and Samuel Johnson.

Patrick Delany came in with his *Observations on Lord Orrery's Remarks*, two years after the *Remarks* appeared. Delany poured scorn on Orrery's informants; their purpose, he said, was 'to banish the Dean's best friends from about him, and make a monopoly of him to themselves'.

There is something disagreeably familiar going on here. There is always that jostling competition, after the death of an eminent person, between claimants to the closest friendship.

But Orrery's account of the marriage to Stella, wrote Delany, 'is, I am satisfied, true'. Delany found Swift's failure to acknowledge Stella as his wife paradoxical and extraordinary – 'a woman, who would have done honour to the choice of the greatest prince upon earth'.

Delany's theory was that Swift had meant to acknowledge her when he had saved enough money to set up a marital household. Poverty was also the reason for 'his abstaining (as undoubtedly he did) from all marital commerce with that lady for a considerable time; to prevent the increase of a family under such circumstances'. Before circumstances were sufficiently favourable, writes Delany, 'various accidents intervened' which made the couple continue to live separately.

These accidents, according to Delany, were the collapse of Swift's political life in London, the disappointment arising from his truncated career prospects, and the death of friends. The change in Swift – his bad temper, his 'attention to money', gave Stella 'inexpressible uneasiness'. Her health was deteriorating. She just could not take him on. It was *she*, Delany thought, who refused, in the end, to own the marriage. It was too late. Her resolution was confirmed by the publication of *Cadenus and Vanessa*, which deeply shocked both her and its author, Swift, for their different reasons. Vanessa left instructions with her executors to publish it: a revenge, or a posthumous claiming.

Delany, an uxorious man himself, just wished that his two friends could have lived together as man and wife at the Deanery, and avoided the scandalous speculation of posterity: 'How much happier had he lived! how much more honoured had he died!' Yes.

Samuel Johnson and Jonathan Swift never met; the twenty-seven-year-old Johnson only moved to London in 1737. In his piece on Swift for his *Lives of the English poets*, Dr Johnson was writing at second-hand, but he had sat with Lord Orrery and old Erasmus Lewis while they reminisced about the Dean, and he was an intimate of Dr Hawkesworth, whose life of Swift, originally a prefix to his twelve-volume edition of the works, was issued as a single volume in 1755. Hawkesworth accepted the story of the marriage. Dr Johnson has yet another source: 'Soon after 1716, in his forty-ninth year, he was privately married to Mrs Johnson, by Dr Ashe, Bishop of Clogher, as Dr Madden told me, in the garden. The marriage made no change in their mode of life . . .'

Dr Madden is the Revd Samuel Madden, a rich man twenty years younger than Swift and closely connected with the group that founded the Dublin Society in 1731, of which Dr Delany was an early member. In the small world of clerical-intellectual Dublin, Dr Madden and Swift were acquainted. But they were not particular friends. There is no evidence that they were on visiting terms. If Dr Madden told Dr Johnson about the marriage, it means that the story had wide currency in Dublin, and was widely believed.

Thomas Sheridan the younger remembered the change in Swift as he grew older and became 'peevish, fretful, morose, and prone to sudden fits of passion'. Yet he was always kind to Thomas the schoolboy, and Thomas was never afraid of him. Thomas's line on Swift and Stella can only have been derived from family lore. His father, after all, died when he was still a boy.

Thomas's story is that when Stella (aware of Swift's attachment to Vanessa and suffering miserably from jealousy) showed signs of physical decline and 'spiritual dejection', Swift employed a common friend to discover the cause. (One might consider this to be more than a little disingenuous.) Stella told the friend how unhappy she was about her ambiguous position in Swift's life, and about the resulting gossip, and about his recent coldness towards her.

Swift replied to the friend that he had always determined never to marry unless he had means to provide for a family; and even then, only if he were young enough to see his children grown up and settled in the world. As it was, he was still in debt, never likely to make his fortune, and 'had already passed that period of life, after which it was his fixed resolution never to marry'.

If he had married anyone, he said (as he had remarked long ago to her suitor William Tisdall), it would have been Stella. He conceded that he was prepared to go through a ceremony of marriage with her, on condition that they still lived separately, and that it remained an absolute secret. This of course would not answer Stella's anxiety about her reputation. But it would relieve her of jealousy, in that he could not then marry Vanessa.

Accordingly, wrote Thomas, they were married by St George Ashe, then Bishop of Clogher, in 1716. Ashe, who had been Swift's tutor at Trinity College, was also the 'common friend' who had acted as go-between. Thomas was not just following Orrery here. He writes that he has this information directly from Mrs Sican, 'a lady of uncommon understanding, fine taste, and great goodness of heart', the good friend of both Swift and Stella.

Thomas followed Orrery to the extent that he posited ambition as the single driving force behind Swift's behaviour. He thought that Swift, when Stella first came to live in Ireland, 'knew not what the passion of love was', and that Swift's fondness for her was 'only that of an affectionate parent to a favourite child; and he had long entertained a dislike to matrimony'. (It was Thomas who remembered that saying of Swift's, that 'he never yet saw the woman, for whose sake he would part with the middle of his bed'.)

But Swift did know what the passion of love was, when Stella first came to live in Ireland. He was then just recovering from the fever of his involvement with Varina.

Thomas also has a story that when Stella was dying she asked Swift, in the presence of Dr Sheridan, to acknowledge her publicly as his wife. 'Swift made no reply, but turning on his heel, walked silently out of the room, nor ever saw her afterwards during the few days she lived.' After 'unspeakable agonies' of mind, Stella drew up her will as a single woman, in her own name: Esther Johnson.

That part of the story, about her will, is true. That Stella's patience and submission cracked, towards the end, may be inferred from one of the prayers Swift composed to read at her bedside: 'Forgive every rash and inconsiderate expression, which her anguish may at any time force from her tongue . . .' Dr Sheridan, according to his son's account, was with her when she died. 'His grief for her loss was not perhaps inferior to the Dean's.'

Dr Sheridan was one of her executors. Even his son concedes that Sheridan was 'a perfect child as to the knowledge of the world', which makes him not the ideal witness to Swift's complex emotional accommodations. But there can be no doubt as to Dr Sheridan's humane qualities and his tender heart – except where his own marriage was concerned.

Sir Walter Scott's biography of Swift, which constitutes the first volume of his edition of Swift's works and correspondence, was published in 1814. Scott's object was, as he wrote, 'to condense the information afforded by Mr Sheridan, Lord Orrery, Dr Delany, Deane Swift and Dr Johnson ... into one distinct and comprehensive narrative'. Thus he reproduces the sequence of events related by Thomas Sheridan about Stella's unhappiness, St George Ashe's intervention and Swift's response; and he accepts the story of the marriage: 'They were married in the garden of the deanery, by the Bishop of Clogher, in the year 1716.'

But Scott did some research of his own as well, among the survivors of those days and their descendants. He had the benefit of 'the most liberal communications' from Deane Swift's son Theophilus. Between the first edition of Sir Walter Scott's memoir and the second (in 1824), Theophilus Swift died in furnished lodgings in London, and his Swift material fell into hands 'totally incapable of estimating their value'. Most, writes Sir Walter, was treated as 'ordinary waste paper' until the remains of the cache were found by a Mr Smith, who was 'much grieved and surprised at the condition in which he discovered the correspondence of Swift, and of Pope . . .'

It is infuriating for the late twentieth-century student of the early eighteenth century to realize how many letters and manuscripts became 'ordinary waste paper' and used for various homely purposes in the ensuing century. Sir Walter Scott was just in time. Thomas Steele, nephew of the Dr Lyon who was involved in the administration of Swift's affairs in his final years, showed Scott a collection of papers 'concerning Swift and his affairs' which he had inherited from his uncle. The Revd Edward Berwick, the literary vicar of Leixlip, not far from Vanessa's country house at Celbridge, let Scott use correspondence between Swift and Vanessa which had come into his possession.

'Only a woman's hair.' Sir Walter Scott reports that those words were written in Swift's hand on an envelope containing a lock of Stella's hair. The envelope was, when Scott was writing, in the possession of Dr Tuke of Dublin in his house on St Stephen's Green. 'Only a woman's hair': Scott sees this as evidence of Swift's way of veiling his 'most bitter feelings' under the guise of 'cynical indifference'.

The laconic phrase 'Only a woman's hair' contains, for me, a suppressed intensity of heartbreak. But as so often, Swift's statement of bare fact lands the reader with the responsibility of inferring its significance.

When Swift himself died, and the public filed into the Deanery to pay their respects to his body lying in an open coffin, and the woman in attendance was momentarily absent, someone cut off a lock of his soft white hair as a souvenir. After that the public were excluded.

I don't suppose that purloined lock of hair was the same one that Swift's guardian Dr Lyon, twenty-three years later, sent as a present to the second Earl of Shelburne – along with Lyon's copy of Gilbert Burnet's *History of His Own Time* annotated by Swift in 1739, and Swift's own Book of Common Prayer 'which he used in his private devotions, tho' an old one, and of no value, but shewing the prayers he most used', according to Lyon's accompanying letter. The prayer book has disappeared, but Burnet's book and the lock of hair have remained with the Shelburne family ever since. Jonathan Swift's hair – a lock about three inches long, its whiteness yellowed by time – is twisted into an open-ended figure of eight and secured by a stitch to the paper in which Dr Lyon had enclosed it. 'Only a man's hair.'

Someone – he doesn't say who – told Sir Walter Scott that St George Ashe, the Bishop of Clogher, confided to Dr (later Bishop) George Berkeley that he had indeed conducted the secret marriage; and that Berkeley's widow passed the information on to his young relative George Monck Berkeley. Sir Walter thinks, since Dr Berkeley was in Italy from the time of the supposed marriage until after Ashe's death, that the communication could not have taken place.

But it could have been transmitted by letter. Correspondence between Berkeley and Ashe was inevitable, as Berkeley was in Italy as companion and tutor to Ashe's son. Unfortunately Ashe had little time to confide the truth to anyone else. The February following the supposed marriage, he died.

Martha Whiteway, the widowed cousin who looked after Swift and kept him company in his last years, also believed in the marriage, according to Sir Walter. As he says, 'a report so directly traced to Sheridan, Delany and Mrs Whiteway, Swift's nearest intimates and friends, will have great weight with persons who consider the question without prepossession'.

Sir Walter, however, also acknowledged the voices that spoke against the marriage to Stella. Dr Lyon did not believe in it, and he had had access to Swift's private papers. William Monck Mason did not believe in it: he set out his views forcibly in his *History and Antiquities of the Collegiate and Cathedral Church of St Patrick, near Dublin*, which he published four years before Scott's second edition.

Monck Mason reports that an unnamed friend of Swift's, 'who was intimate with Mrs Dingley for ten years before she died', broached with the old lady the subject of the rumoured marriage, 'and she only laughed at it as an idle tale, founded only on suspicion'. Mrs Brent, Swift's housekeeper for many years, and who was 'much confided in' by the Dean, did not believe in it either. She thought it was 'all platonic love', as she told her daughter Anne Ridgeway, who succeeded her as housekeeper at the Deanery, and with whom Rebecca Dingley boarded in her old age. Anne Ridgeway was probably the 'unnamed friend' who quizzed old Dingley about what she knew.

If Rebecca Dingley was sincere in her disbelief, and Swift and Stella really had gone through a marriage ceremony, we have to rethink the often-stressed view that Stella never went anywhere without Dingley as a chaperone, and that she was always present when Stella was with the Dean. As for Mrs Brent and Mrs Ridgeway, they were servants – even if trusted and familiar ones – and there is no reason why they should have been privy to Swift's secrets.

Swift's London friends certainly knew of no marriage. Dr John Arbuthnot ended a letter to Swift in 1718 by sending him Mrs Arbuthnot's love, '& which is the first thing to occur to all wives, wishes you well married'. Bolingbroke, writing in 1727, said that his wife was sending Swift some fans 'just arriv'd from Lilliput' – presumably miniature ones – 'which you will dispose of to the present Stella, whoever she may be'. Bolingbroke knew the poems to Stella, and was using the name as a generic. Swift cannot have spoken to him of his private life.

Swift always defended himself against emotional dependency, and preached that gospel to others. In 1727 he wrote a chilling letter from the Deanery to the wife of a clergyman who was grieving for the loss of a daughter, urging her against 'too strong attachments' to her children, which was 'a weakness God seldom leaves unpunished'.

Children may have posed, potentially, the greatest threats to his own emotional independence. As a young man of twenty-two he had made a list of resolutions for 'when I come to be old'. Mostly they are conventional, but one isn't: 'Not to be fond of children, or let them come near me hardly.' He may have been frightened, then, by his own dangerously strong feelings for Stella the child. His prescribed strategy for emotional survival is flight from all risk of grief, pain or disappointment – at the price of fleeing also from the pleasure and sweetness which make life worth living for most people.

Swift's expressed views on marriage and children are like those of Francis Bacon, writing more than a century before him. Most men who remain single, wrote Bacon, do so from love of liberty, 'especially in certain self-pleasing and humorous minds ... Unmarried men are best friends, best masters, best servants; but not always best subjects, for they are light to run away, and almost all fugitives are of that condition.' Swift, self-pleasing and humorous, is also fugitive – not only as a personality, but geographically, a guest in friends' houses, on the move between Dublin and Laracor, between Dublin, Leicester and London.

One cannot tell whether by a single life Bacon also meant a chaste one. I think not. In the 'Digression on Madness' in *A Tale of a Tub* Swift describes a great prince who raised a fleet and an army and a great fortune and carried all before him, performing gratuitous acts of conquest with inexplicable force and energy. 'What secret wheel, what hidden spring could put in motion so wonderful an engine?' The answer was sexual frustration aroused by 'an absent female, whose eyes had raised a protuberancy'.

Undischarged semen, this argument goes, turns into a vapour and ascends to the brain. (We would call it sublimation, or displacement activity.) 'The very same principle that influences a bully to break the windows of a whore, who has jilted him, naturally stirs up a great Prince to raise mighty armies, and dream of nothing but sieges, battles, and victories.'

Conversely, there was a general belief in Swift's day that losing semen was debilitating and damaging. Marriage manuals preached moderation. A balance must be maintained. It was equally damaging to retain semen indefinitely. Periodic discharge was essential or the vital fluid turned poisonous, leading to mad over-achievement, as in the case of Swift's great prince, or something more sombre.

If indeed Swift – over-fastidious, wary, defensive – lived chastely for most of his life, his own drive, and his genius, can be explained according to these theories, of which he made play in his writing. And so, of course, on the negative side, can his anger and spleen. We adopt the currently dominant myths and models both of ease and of disease, as Sir William Temple had pointed out years before in 'Of Health and Long Life'. At any period, psychologically and physically, we produce symptoms and behaviours which are culturally recognized, and attribute their cause to concepts that are to hand.

It is no good, anyway, thinking about Swift's putative marriage with any model of modern marriage in mind.

A marriage held not in a church, and without banns, or witnesses, or a ring, or a licence, or registration, was perfectly legal. Swift is believed to have conducted at least one such marriage himself, on one of his journeys between London and Chester, and to have issued this rhyming marriage certificate:

> Under an oak, in stormy weather,
> I join'd this rogue and whore together;
> And none but he who rules the thunder
> Can put this whore and rogue asunder.

These 'private marryings' and clandestine marriages were not restricted to 'whores and rogues'. They were not uncommon middle- and upper-class practice too. A marriage without a clergyman present – a 'contract marriage', over which canon law had no jurisdiction – was also legal. This was the general law throughout western Europe. It pertained in England until 1753, and in Ireland even longer.

For ordinary people, bigamy was the accepted way out of marital discontent. There were few prosecutions. Defrocked or sham clergymen, notably in and around the Fleet prison in London, would marry – for a fee – any couple who applied to them, often in a tavern, and no questions asked. A deserted spouse had no recourse but blackmail.

When the actor-playwright Colley Cibber read Laetitia Pilkington's racy memoirs, he wrote her a candid letter suggesting that she might have made something good out of her parson husband's taking another wife when he was on his own in London: 'For, had he picked up a fortune, the hush, hush of your prior claim to him, might have been worth a better maintenance than you are now likely to get out of him . . .' Defoe's fictional adventuress Moll Flanders, though she moved in less genteel circles, received a practical sort of decency from one of her husbands; he discharged her from all obligation, and 'if you can marry to your advantage do not decline it on my account . . . I will never disturb your repose if I should know of it, which however is not likely.'

Clandestine marriages, however, although perfectly legal, were already beginning to cause unease among the clergy, especially when clergymen themselves exploited the custom. At the turn of the century, fifteen years or so before the alleged marriage of Swift and Stella, St George Ashe was in correspondence with Dr King (later Archbishop of Dublin), about the 'mischief of clandestine marriages'. There was a need, he wrote, to 'discourse with some lawyers, whether a clandestine marriage be not a sufficient cause of deprivation [i.e. of a parish or living, from a clergyman]'.

Swift was a very senior clergyman. Was Ashe, the man who professed such opinions, likely to conduct a clandestine marriage for the Dean of St Patrick's?

Ashe himself was a married man. Archbishop King never married. Maybe Ashe softened his views. In the summer of 1716 – the year Swift's marriage is said to have taken place – Ashe was writing about clandestine marriage again to King, in a more liberal as well as a more jocose vein: 'I cannot think you so good a judge in matrimonial matters as in others. I find you would strip mankind of all inclinations, that are not agreeable to the strictest reason, that is, you would introduce a kind of stoical apathy, fit only for old philosophical bachelors like your Grace.' The 'nicest prudence', wrote Ashe on this occasion, was rarely to be met with in the 'course and variety of human affairs'.

One might deduce that Ashe was referring to the secret marriage of Dean Swift – as maybe he covertly was, though his letter only makes specific reference to a Mr Molyneux.

If Swift remained unmarried, it would be no special cause for comment. Statistics for the early eighteenth century are unreliable. But they are pointers. The median age of marriage was rising in his lifetime. It has been calculated that around twenty per cent of the sons of the English aristocracy born in the year 1675 (i.e. eight years younger than Swift) never married. The figure was even higher for women. Another authority asserts that at the end of the seventeenth century about twenty-five per cent of the general adult population never married at all.

The correlation between a high level of singleness and chastity cannot be known. Lawrence Stone, the historian of the family, thinks that there was less sexual activity then than now. Although I do not agree with him, I can see why one might think that. Other people's bodies were likely to smell and look disgusting.

It was normal to wash face, neck, hands and feet from time to time, but rarely the whole body. The bridegroom Strephon, in Swift's poem 'Strephon and Chloe', was anxious not to give offence to his stainless bride, and so took unusual precautions:

> His hand, his neck, his mouth, and feet
> Were duly washt to keep 'em sweet;
> (With other parts that shall be nameless,
> The ladies else might think me shameless.)

Swift's personal cleanliness was legendary simply because he washed more of his person and more frequently than was usual. Thomas Sheridan wrote: 'He was one of the cleanliest men that ever lived. His hands were not only washed, as those of other men, with the utmost care, but his nails were constantly kept pared to the quick . . . As he walked much, he rarely dressed himself without a bason of water by his side, in which he dipt a towel and cleansed his feet with the utmost exactness.'

Orrery has an anecdote about a new Bishop of Meath recommending his clergy to wear 'numms', which were scraps of linen hanging from the neck to conceal dirty shirts. In public, at the synod in Trim, Dr Swift the vicar of Laracor savagely 'fell upon' the Bishop on the subject of numms. 'I would have you know', he said, pushing up the sleeves of his cassock and tearing open the front of his waistcoat, 'that you have gotten into a diocese of gentlemen, who abhor dirt, and filth, and nastiness.' On and on he went, 'lashing the Bishop, and making him feel his sarcasms'.

The use of forks and handkerchiefs betokened a growing concern with 'delicacy' and 'civility' and with keeping one's own body products to oneself. But to be clean was an idiosyncratic luxury, and dependent on being able to afford servants to carry water and dispose of waste. The bisexual Lord Hervey, whom Pope in his satirical verse called 'Lady Fanny', is the first Englishman on record to have bathed daily, and he was considered remarkably eccentric. When Pope referred to Hervey as 'this painted child of dirt, that stinks and stings', he meant it figuratively.

Naturally, poor people smelled strongly, and so did most rich ones. Swift, well washed himself, was hypersensitive to smells. He wrote in his 'character' of Archbishop Narcissus Marsh: 'He is so wise as to value his own health more than other men's noses, so that the most honourable place at his table is much the worst, especially in summer.' He was altogether less restrained in the way he wrote about women who smelled bad.

Powerful sexual attraction can override disgust, and in any case Stella was as clean and neat as a pin. But sexual attraction was not a necessary component of marriage. Even though it was increasingly argued that the young should choose their own partners, within reason, a man did not normally marry in order to secure an intense physical relationship, but to have an establishment and a family – and, whenever possible, a 'fortune' and a chunk of real estate, settled on the couple by the bride's father. Physical attraction was not a safe basis for choice of partner, being 'unreasonable'.

Thus the sexual life of the passionately inclined operated outside marriage. This brought with it the fear of pregnancy. Some precautions could be taken. There were vaginal sponges, and condoms made of sheep-gut, secured by red ribbons. They were worn for protection against disease even more than pregnancy.

The prevalence of venereal infections, especially syphilis, was a disincentive for the cautious. Pamphlets and periodicals of the politest sort carried advertisements for publications on treatment. Cures, in the form of pills and unguents, were available at some coffee-houses.

Swift frequently referred to the physical and moral devastation brought about by syphilis. Female Yahoos – as Gulliver described the prostitutes of England to his master the Houynhnhnm – suffered from 'a certain malady, which bred rottenness in the bones of those who fell into their embraces', producing a great variety of symptoms, and 'propagated from father to son, so that great numbers come into the world with complicated maladies upon them'.

Swift suffered from a 'complicated malady', his giddiness and deafness, for which he found neither diagnosis nor prognosis. Perhaps he sometimes wondered. If so, it was a dark burden of anxiety to carry, and a definite disincentive to procreation.

I think it is possible, I think it is probable, that Swift and Stella did go through some ceremony in the summer of 1716 with their old and close friend St George Ashe, behind the high walls of the Deanery garden. Perhaps Rebecca Dingley was in the house having a lie-down. After all, since Bishop Ashe was there, the alleged rule of Swift never being alone with Stella was not broken. It was maybe a tender, indulgent play-ceremony, in the spirit of make-believe games played in the garden at Moor Park when Stella was a child, and of their private 'little language'. It comforted and reassured Stella. Then the moment passed. They went on as before. For a long time they did not talk about it. Both were left with the uneasy option of regarding what had happened as a grown-up legal marriage – or not.

I cannot prove that this was how it was.

Chapter Fourteen

FATHERS

IF SWIFT DID marry Stella, was there some real and pressing reason for keeping it secret? There need not have been. Secret marriages were still quite common.

Gossip about them was common too. There was a rumour, for example, that Alexander Pope was secretly married to Martha Blount. When Pope died, those who imagined they were in the know were surprised that he did not acknowledge her as his wife in his will – though he did bequeath to her the use of his Twickenham estate for her lifetime.

In the case of Swift and Stella, however, explanations for the secrecy of the supposed marriage have constantly been sought. Apart from speculation about his health fears, and the possibility that he was cold or sexually underpowered, the rival theories centre on his paternity, and hers.

Orrery thought the marriage was kept secret because Stella was the daughter of servants, and that this 'flaw' in an undoubted jewel prevented Swift from acknowledging their alliance. 'Ambition and pride will, at any time, conquer reason and justice, and each larger degree of pride, like the larger fishes of prey, will devour all the less; thus the vanity of boasting such a wife was suppressed by the greater vanity of keeping free from a low alliance.'

This is not a pretty explanation. Deane Swift thought the same thing – and that Swift was quite right to keep the secret. Deane thought that Stella, to whom he attributed every good quality except a love of music (a lack she shared with the Dean), was, as the daughter of one of Sir William Temple's servants, 'by no means worthy to have been the acknowledged wife of Dr Swift'; Swift had 'more wisdom than to acknowledge this beautiful, this accomplished woman for his wife'.

He would also have had to cope, Deane Swift suggests, with bitter retaliations from his sister Jane Fenton (whose marriage to a tradesman he had so violently opposed) if he had acknowledged 'a wife so meanly extracted, and particularly that individual person whom she despised and hated beyond all the inhabitants on earth'.

Why did Swift's sister hate Stella so much? I don't know. Maybe the girl who had waited on Jane 'in the character of her little servant' on Jane's first visit to Moor Park had, as she grew older, patronized Jane when she became one of Martha Giffard's waiting-women. Stella fetched and carried for Martha Giffard too, but from a privileged quasi-daughterly position, at Moor Park.

The arguments that Stella was not socially up to Swift have a shaky basis. They hold water, in so far as they do hold water, only after he became Dean of St Patrick's. Macaulay, after describing the position of a clergyman of the period in his patron's house, wrote that once he found a living, and a means of support, the clergyman could marry: 'The wife had ordinarily been in the patron's service ... A waiting-woman was generally considered as the most suitable helpmeet for a parson.'

If Macaulay is right, Stella could hardly have been more suitable. Swift could have married her at any time after Sir William Temple's death, or when she came to live in Ireland and he was vicar of Laracor with a prebend in St Patrick's Cathedral.

Indeed, it was what people expected in those early days. Deane Swift quoted from a letter written by Swift's cousin Thomas, comfortably ensconced as vicar of Puttenham, enquiring 'whether Jonathan be married? or whether he has been able to resist the charms of both those gentlewomen that marched quite from Moor Park to Dublin (as they would have marched to the North or anywhere else) with full resolution to engage him'. Yet Swift maintained, for public consumption at least, his tutelary, teasing, semi-paternal persona.

There is something snagging in my mind from cousin Thomas's question about Swift resisting the charms of 'both those gentlewomen' who followed him to Dublin. The second gentlewoman is of course Rebecca Dingley.

No one has ever imagined that Swift could have been interested in *her*. Her secondary character as Stella's companion, and her reputation as a scatty and limited woman, is too well established. Stella's 'English friend, who was eternally buckled to her girdle', wrote Deane Swift, 'was by all accounts a very insipid companion'. Be this as it may, Dingley would have been a socially acceptable wife for Swift. She was gently born and, as the granddaughter of Sir John Dingley of the Isle of Wight, Sir William's uncle, a near kinswoman of his.

Because of Dingley's status as poor relation at Moor Park, earning her keep by dancing attendance on the exigent Martha Giffard, and because she was fifteen years older than Stella, one thinks of her as an elderly body from the beginning. It is a bit of a shock to check the dates and discover that she was exactly the right age for Swift – in fact, a year younger than he.

Perhaps she had her hopes when she came to Ireland, as well as Stella. Perhaps the indissoluble dyad 'MD' of the *Journal to Stella*, and the inseparable domestic triad of Swift, Stella and Dingley, had more emotional tension in it than has been recognized. If Dingley ever considered her own relationship with Swift to be as significant as Stella's, there is little wonder that she was happy to play her chaperone's part so well that Swift and Stella were never alone together, nor that she rubbished the very idea of Swift's marriage to Stella; nor, if it indeed took place, that they kept it from her.

Stella's handwriting was like Swift's, but Dingley's was even more so, according to him. His letters from London were always addressed to Mrs Dingley, and occasionally they were written for her alone, though generally to both Ladies, or for Stella alone under the guise of a double letter. The most anxious enquiries, the tenderest, fondest messages, are for Stella alone. But the *Journal to Stella* is also a journal to Rebecca Dingley.

Stella's eyes were bad. Swift wrote small in his letters to them to save paper, and it was usually Dingley who read the letters out. 'Don't read this, you little rogue, with your little eyes; but give it to Dingley, pray now.' Stella was to dictate her letters to Dingley too, and not strain to write herself. He teased Rebecca, as he did Stella, about losing money at cards. Swift doubted the truth of Dingley's accounts of their exploits; though she did not tell as many fibs as Stella, 'she tells thumpers'.

He fulfilled in London Dingley's shopping commissions as he did Stella's: for Dingley, a pair of hinged spectacles, and 'the finest piece of Brazil tobacco that ever was born', and an ivory snuff-rasp, salad dishes, and plates, and a pocket-book, but not the linen she asked for, it was too costly. 'Dingley is well enough. Go, get you gone, you naughty girl, you are well enough.' She made and sent him a fur cap, which he found too hot to wear. Sometimes she was 'little Dingley', or 'Madam Dinglibus'.

His servant Patrick bought a singing bird, a linnet, 'to bring over to Dingley: it cost him sixpence and is tame as a dormouse ... I suppose in a week he will die of the spleen.' Patrick kept the linnet in a closet in Swift's lodgings, 'where it makes a terrible litter; but I say nothing: I am tame as a clout'.

Dingley fussed over both Swift and Stella.

> Now, mistress Dingley, an't you an impudent slut to expect a letter next packet from Presto, when you confess yourself, that you had so lately two letters in four days? Unreasonable baggage! No, little Dingley, I am always in bed by twelve; I mean my candle's out by twelve, and I take great care of myself.

Dingley was in charge of practical matters: 'I reckon you are now preparing for your Wexford expedition; and poor Dingley is full of carking, and caring, scolding ... Love one another, and be good girls.' In a New Year poem he wrote for her in 1723, which suggests she feels weighed down by cares and responsibilities, he apostrophizes her familiarly as 'Bec'.

Stella, he comments approvingly in the *Journal*, is a good walker, even in bad weather, 'and Dingley would do well enough if her petticoats were pinned up; but she is so embroiled, and so fearful, and then Stella scolds, and Dingley stumbles, and is so daggled. Have you got the whalebone petticoats among you yet? I hate them; a woman here may hide a moderate gallant under them.'

In the summer of 1726, when Stella was ill and Swift was staying with Pope in Twickenham, receiving only bad news from Dublin, he wrote of the Ladies to John Worrall:

> We have been perfect friends for 35 years. Upon my advice they both came to Ireland and have been ever since my constant companions, and the remainder of my life will be a very melancholy scene when one of them is gone whom I most

esteemed upon the score of every good quality that can possibly recommend a human creature.

But in this crisis Rebecca Dingley was not rising to the occasion. She had done, or omitted to do, something which disillusioned Swift entirely: 'I have these 2 months seen through Mrs D's disguises, and indeed ever since I left you my heart hath been so sunk, that I have not been the same man . . .'

It's worth noting here the opinion of Dingley given by Thomas Sheridan the younger, bearing in mind that his father, Dr Sheridan, attended closely on Stella in her last illness and was her confidant: Dingley was 'one of the common run of women, of a middling understanding, without knowledge or taste; and so entirely selfish, as to be incapable of any sincere friendship, or warm attachment'.

This is harsh. It may be that what Dingley overheard in Stella's last unhappy months – between Stella and Dr Sheridan, between Stella and Swift – made her realize that she herself had all along been the marginal member of the trio, and to some extent the dupe of Swift and Stella; and that she made her bitterness apparent. Or it may be that she just collapsed like a jelly in time of crisis. In one of the prayers Swift wrote to read at Stella's bedside, he prayed on behalf of her 'sorrowful friends': 'Let not our grief afflict her mind, and thereby have an ill effect on her present distempers. Forgive the sorrow and weakness of those among us, who sink under the grief and terror of losing so dear and useful a friend.'

In September 1727, when he had just left Pope after his last and wretchedly unsuccessful stay at Twickenham, knowing that Stella was now mortally ill, Swift wrote to Dr Sheridan: 'I brought both those friends over, that we might be happy together as long as God should please; the knot is broken, and the remaining person, you know, has ill answered the end; and the other who is now to be lost, was all that is valuable.' He instructed John Worrall, however, to 'answer all calls of money power to Mrs Dingley, and desire her to ask it', so she must still have been in place and in charge of Stella.

Swift did continue to see Rebecca Dingley after Stella died, and sent her wine, and still courteously looked after her finances. He had always subsidized her, tactfully. She had an annuity of £16 a year; Swift, who administered the payments, personally made up the sum to fifty-two guineas (a guinea was £1. 1s.).

Dingley remained affectionately attached to Mrs Brent, Swift's housekeeper, and lodged with Mrs Brent's daughter Anne Ridgeway in Grafton Street. Swift remained devoted to Mrs Brent too, and a year after Stella's death sent via John Worrall his 'most humble service' to Mrs Worrall and Mrs Dingley, but 'love' to Mrs Brent. Four years earlier, in happier times, he had written a little song called 'Dingley and Brent'. The first and last verses go like this:

> Dingley and Brent
> Wherever they went
> Ne'er minded a word that was spoken;
> Whatever was said,
> They ne'er troubled their head,
> But laugh'd at their own silly joking.
>
> You tell a good jest,
> And please all the rest,
> Comes Dingley, and asks you, What was it?
> And curious to know,
> Away she will go
> To seek an old rag in the closet.

In the 1720s, before Stella became ill, Swift's fondness for Rebecca Dingley was as strong as ever. He wrote a poem for 'Bec's Birthday' in 1726, and a couplet for the collar of her spoiled lapdog, Tyger:

> Pray steal me not, I'm Mrs Dingley's
> Whose heart in this four-footed thing lies.

But those days were over. However she had behaved in Stella's last illness, Swift's feelings towards her soured. But Rebecca Dingley had been essential to the dynamic of his relationship with Stella. In public, her presence lent respectability. In private, her inclusion in the intimacy diffused the intensity, and in itself gave him pleasure. The close threesome had amused and sustained him. He wrote in the *Journal*: 'Stella, Dingley, Presto, all together, now and for ever all together.'

Rebecca Dingley's tragedy was that ultimately she never came first with anyone. Except with Tyger. Swift wrote a doggerel obituary for Tyger, noting that she died leaving two puppies.

Rebecca went to Swift for advice when she was making her will. The Revd Dr John Lyon, Swift's own assistant at the time, was her executor; she also left Lyon some money, plate, books, and papers. (Anne Ridgeway was her residuary legatee.) Writing in his old age to Deane Swift, Dr Lyon claimed he had no more Swift material left in his possession, 'though many things did fall into my hands as executor of Mrs Dingley'. I wish I knew what had been in her papers.

Archbishop King was among those who were on friendly terms with the Ladies. When in 1713 Swift was briefly back in Laracor to be installed as Dean, depressed by events in London, corresponding with Vanessa, and suffering from a serious bout of his chronic sickness and giddiness, King wrote to him kindly about his illness. King added that 'an odd thought came into my mind on reading that you were among your willows imagining that perhaps your mistress had forsaken you and that was the cause of your malady. If that be the case cheer up, the loss may be repaired, and I hope the remedy easy.'

This is unusually intimate, from King to Swift. It is the sort of letter one only writes when one has heard some rumour – of a break in the friendship with Stella, of an involvement in London? No one, least of all this particular archbishop, would broach such a delicate matter out of the blue, and King was writing from Bath, a hotbed of gossip. The letter also suggests that King accepted Stella as Swift's beloved – for that is the sense in which 'mistress' is to be understood. In this context a strange story told by Sir Walter Scott becomes slightly less strange.

Immediately after the date of the supposed marriage, 'Swift's state of mind appears to have been dreadful'. Patrick Delany was so concerned about his friend's gloom and agitation that he went to consult Archbishop King in his Palace of St Sepulchre's, next door to the Deanery. As Delany was entering the Archbishop's library he encountered Swift himself rushing out, distracted, not even able to speak.

Delany went in to the Archbishop and found him in tears, and was told: 'You have just met the most unhappy man on earth; but on the subject of his wretchedness, you must never ask a question.'

Swift shut himself up in the Deanery for the next few days; and then picked up his link with Stella and Rebecca Dingley as before, with no change in their intimate, decorous routines.

Delany does not refer to the scene in the Archbishop's library in his own memoir. Scott had it from a friend of Mrs Delany, a lady 'distinguished for high rank, eminent talents, and the soundest judgement'. He regrets that he is unable to name her. If the story is true, then speculation about some dark secret is justified.

It is possible that Vanessa, devoured by jealousy, threatened to publicize their relationship and make any honourable marriage to Stella a scandalous impossibility. But according to the anonymous distinguished lady, Delany inferred that Swift, after going through the marriage ceremony, had discovered that there was 'too near a consanguinity' between himself and Stella to allow of their living together as man and wife.

How Swift suddenly discovered this was not explained. A notice of Orrery's book in the *Monthly Review* for November 1751, however, repeats the story, with additions:

> It has generally been asserted, that Swift received a letter from England, the day after his marriage, the purport of which was, that the writer thereof hoped that it would not come to his hands too late to prevent the consummation of a match which it was rumoured was intended betwixt Dr Swift and Mrs Johnson, for that they were both the natural children of one father: and gave the doctor sufficient reason to believe that this information was true.

Stella's mother could have been the informant, it seems to me; but as the anonymous reviewer says, 'whether the Dean ever did receive or credit such information, or not, it may be impossible for anyone now living to prove or disprove'.

There was certainly speculation, in Swift's lifetime, that he was the natural son of his patron, Sir William Temple. 'I am not quite certain', wrote Lord Orrery, 'that Swift himself did not aquiesce in the calumny.' Perhaps, suggested the malicious Orrery, Swift preferred the fantasy of an illustrious illegitimacy to the unimpressive reality.

There were also rumours that Stella was Sir William Temple's daughter. This would make Swift her half-brother. Orrery thought, again maliciously, that Swift could not have believed the latter story, 'because the same false pride that induced him to deny the legitimate daughter of an obscure servant, might have prompted him to own the natural daughter of so eminent a man as Sir William Temple'.

A good case can be made for believing that Stella was Sir William Temple's daughter. Why else, for a start, should Rebecca Dingley, an older woman and a close relation of the Temples, be the companion and carer of Stella, ostensibly the daughter of an 'obscure servant', rather than vice versa? Sir William was back in England, and at a low ebb as far as his career was concerned, in the summer of 1680, when Stella was conceived. The previous year, his only remaining daughter Diana had died. Sir William and his family were at the house in Sheen, just outside Richmond, when the baby registered as Esther Johnson was baptized in Richmond parish church.

The little girl received very special treatment in the Temple household. There was an extraordinary article in the *Gentlemen's Magazine* of November 1757, written in response to the books by Orrery and Deane Swift. No one knows who wrote it; it it is signed with the initials C.M.P.G.N.S.T.N.S. Let us call him the Gentleman.

The Gentleman reports that Stella's 'appearance and dress so far exceeded the rank and fortune of her mother, and her mother's other children, that the world soon declared Miss Johnson to be Sir William's daughter'. In his will, in which Sir William left her the leases on his lands in Co. Wicklow, he described her simply as 'Esther Johnson, servant to my sister Giffard'. But John Evans, the Bishop of Meath, referred to her in her lifetime (in a letter to the Archbishop of Canterbury) as 'a natural daughter of Sir William Temple, a very good woman'.

Bishop Evans did not like Swift. He retailed other gossip about his private life, including a story about Vanessa refusing violently to see a priest when she was dying. Swift did not like Bishop Evans, either. They had a quarrel about Swift's non-appearance, in 1719, in his capacity as vicar of Laracor (a living he retained, employing a curate), at the Bishop's annual visitation; in the course of which Swift requested his Lordship 'please to remember in the midst of your resentments that you are to speak to a clergyman, and not a footman'. However, the wide currency of the rumour about Stella being Temple's daughter is proven by Orrery's comment that Swift's sister Jane Fenton used to contradict the aspersion, 'whenever she heard it made'.

But even if Stella was Temple's daughter by Bridget Johnson, it may be irrelevant to the consanguinity issue, as there is absolutely no way in which Swift could have been Sir William Temple's son. Swift was born in Dublin in November 1667. Temple was continuously on diplomatic business in the Low Countries from April 1666 until January 1668.

There is another, more recent, hypothesis about Swift's paternity. That is, that Swift's father was Sir William Temple's father – Sir John Temple, Master of the Rolls in Ireland, Uncle Godwin's powerful friend. This would make Swift Sir William Temple's half-brother – and, if Stella was Sir William's daughter, her uncle.

Sir John would have been in his sixties at the time of Swift's conception. The case rests on the precise date of the death of Swift's legal father, Jonathan Swift the elder, of which there is no record. It has to be deduced from the Black Book of King's Inn in Dublin, wherein Jonathan senior, an attorney in his early twenties, entered accounts and the minutes of the benchers' meetings as Steward of the Inn.

No minutes at all were kept between mid-November 1666 and mid-April 1667, when they recommenced in a different hand. It may reasonably be inferred that Jonathan the Steward died in that interim. A ruling on a petition to the benchers from Abigail Swift about her deceased young husband's finances is dated 15 April.

Laetitia Pilkington frequently heard Dean Swift say that his father had died suddenly, poisoned by mercury he took for 'the itch' (which usually signified nothing more sinister than scabies) contracted while on circuit – Deane Swift asserted that the circuit was for the spring assizes of 1667. If he died in March or April, he would have had time to father our Jonathan, born at the end of November.

Nor does it sound, from Laetitia's account, as if Swift led friends to suppose his paternity was anything other than legitimate. In early 1712, in his glory days in London, he was planning a personal coat of arms for himself based on Swift family emblems. He asked Stella to go and see his aunt (Uncle Godwin's wife), and to take a look at his great-grandfather's portrait:

> you know he has a ring on his finger, with a seal of an anchor
> and dolphin about it; but I think there is besides, at the bottom
> of the picture, the same coat of arms quartered with another,

which I suppose was my great-grandmother's . . . My reason is, that I would ask some herald here, whether I should choose that coat, or one in Guillim's large folio of heraldry, where my uncle Godwin is named with another coat of arms of three stags. This is sad stuff to write; so nite, MD.

'Sad stuff' maybe, but he clearly was not rejecting his Swift heritage. In summary, the case for disbelieving the obvious rests on Jonathan the Steward's absence from his clerical duties from the previous November, and an arbitrary assumption that he died well before March. But it is quite unprovable, either way.

There is nothing in Sir John Temple's will to support the theory that he was Jonathan Swift's father. He died in 1705, leaving everything to his four legitimate children. If he was Swift's father, he was not going to acknowledge it, or help him any more than he already, perhaps, had.

For every scenario about Swift's and Stella's origins there is just enough material to make a case, and not quite enough to make it conclusively. That is why the speculation has gone on for two and a half centuries, with biographers scouring the available documentation for evidence to fit a pet theory.

Stop. There is another hypothesis concerning Stella's parentage that no one, so far as I know, has come up with. It is this: that Stella was not Bridget Johnson's daughter, but Martha Giffard's. Widowed almost as soon as she was married, Martha had many admirers. You can take this extravagantly further, incorporating the prevailing belief that Stella was Sir William Temple's daughter. What if Stella were Sir William's daughter by his own sister, brought up under their roof as the daughter of Bridget Johnson?

What evidence can be adduced for this incest theory? Enough. Martha Giffard spent much time with her brother acting as his hostess, companion and confidante when he was en poste in the Low Countries, while Lady Temple was at home in England with the children. Martha Giffard's biographer, Julia Longe, the epitome of genteel Edwardian discretion, went so far as to stress the unusually close bond between brother and sister.

Lady Temple lost all her children. After her son John's suicide, she lived away from her husband and sister-in-law, at their house in London.

Sir William, as he boasted, had an amorous temperament. Lady Temple died in 1695, aged sixty-six. Lady Giffard stayed on at Moor Park with her brother, whom she always referred to as 'Papa'. She remained for his sake, since she never liked what she called 'this desolate place', and left it after his death.

What of Bridget Johnson, Stella's de facto mother? The Gentleman, clearly a Farnham man, said that when Sir William came to live at Moor Park he brought with him from Sheen a gentlewoman, 'in the character of a housekeeper'. This was Bridget Johnson. The Gentleman says that although she had a fat, squat figure, her face was lovely; she was charming, well educated, well read, and must surely have known 'a more genteel walk in life' than her present situation allowed. She professed, apparently, to be the widow of the master of a ship trading between England and Holland, where he died, leaving her with three children.

This story about Bridget Johnson's husband, presumably the father of her two younger children, is no less intrinsically likely than the others in print. But the father of her children was not Sir William Temple's steward, as was averred elsewhere; she only married a previous steward of the Temples, named Mose, in her later years, when Stella was grown up. Neither was Bridget Johnson a distant relation of Lady Temple, another and particularly 'wide shot into a very thick fog', as one commentator has remarked. Nor has any proof been found that Stella's father was 'a cadet of a good old Nottinghamshire family', as Swift said in the painful piece he wrote about Stella on the night of her funeral – curiously connecting her with his fictional Lemuel Gulliver, who was born in Nottinghamshire where his family had 'a small estate'.

Swift wrote nothing that would support the Gentleman's view of Bridget Johnson as a cultivated woman living below her proper station in life. He knew her very well from his Moor Park days, obviously liked her, and continued to see her when he was in England, 'without hazarding seeing Lady Giffard, which I will not do until she begs my pardon', as he told the Ladies. He wondered how Stella's mother could 'confine herself so much to that old beast's humour'. Bridget Johnson took a motherly interest in him, sending plum cakes and candles to his London lodgings, and medicine when he was ill.

Stella's mother, Swift wrote, 'was of lower degree [than the unverifiable Nottinghamshire gentleman]; and indeed she had little to boast of her birth'. Does that last 'she' refer to Stella or to Bridget Johnson? In either case, it seems gratuitously derogatory. If he did have any better information, he was taking pains to see that posterity should not know it.

Stella was the eldest of the three Johnson children. Her sister Anne ('a good modest sort of girl', according to Swift) was reared not at Moor Park but in London, and at the age of seventeen married a baker called Filby. The boy, Edward, went to school in Farnham, and died young abroad.

Bridget Johnson's two younger children were fair, says the Gentleman. Stella, as we know, was black-haired, and bore a 'striking resemblance' to Sir William. Martha Giffard was black-haired too, and bore a striking resemblance to her brother. The Gentleman is 'positive' that when Stella went to Ireland to live near Swift, 'her mother parted from her as one who was never to see her again'. Which would seem reasonable if Bridget Johnson was not in fact her mother.

Bridget Johnson remained with Martha Giffard until the latter's death in 1722, and then, says the Gentleman correctly, went back to Farnham, having married Ralph Mose, a widower previously married to a Moor Park cook. When Mose died she remained in Farnham, in the same lodgings as Swift's sister Jane Fenton, with whom she was on intimate terms, and died there in 1743. 'I saw her myself', writes the Gentleman, 'in the autumn of 1742, and although far advanced in years she still preserved the remains of a very fine face.'

Why did Bridget Johnson marry Mose, a man apparently far below her in cultivation and status? Because, says the Gentleman, he was 'privy to certain secrets that she was unwilling to have divulged', i.e. he had a blackmail hold on her. 'The lady to whom I am obliged for many of these anecdotes assured me that she had heard Mrs Mose, in her freer hours, declare that she was obliged by indispensible necessity to marry the man, whose servile manners her soul despised.'

That Mose kept a stern hold on his wife is suggested from a letter that Martha Giffard wrote to a Temple relation from London in 1715, saying that 'Mrs Mose has prevailed with her husband to let her pass so many days here once in three years.' Bridget Mose was on Lady G.'s payroll as late as 1721, when she is listed in an account book as receiving £20 p.a. That could have been a pension.

241

The Gentleman assumes that Bridget's dark secret was the fact that Stella was Sir William Temple's daughter. But Mr Mose could have known an even darker secret: that Stella was also Martha Giffard's daughter.

There was a portrait of Lady Giffard in Swift's possession in Dublin in early 1737, when he offered it to her pet nephew, Jack Temple, who had taken over Moor Park. Swift wrote that his painter friend Jervas assured him the portrait was 'in Sir Peter Lely's best manner, and the drapery all in the same hand'. He was not looking for payment for the picture: 'I shall think myself very well paid for it, if you will be so good as to order some marks of your favour to Mrs Dingley. I do not mean a pension, but a small sum to put her for once out of debt.'

There is reproach in this. Mrs Dingley was 'a little mortified that you did not mention or enquire after her. She is quite sunk with years and unwieldiness; as well as very scanty support. I sometimes make her a small present, as my abilities can reach; for I do not find her nearest relations consider her in the least.' He had made 'small presents' to her for decades. Dingley, to all intents and purposes, was dumped on Swift in her – and his – declining years. She died two years before him, but by then he was beyond caring for anybody. Some lines from his old poem 'Bec's Birthday' have a sad irony:

And, when she's in another scene,
Stella long dead, but first the Dean,
May fortune and her coffee get her
Companions that will please her better . . .

Why did Swift have at the Deanery this fine portrait of Lady Giffard, whom he did not like and who did not like him? Maybe it came to him after Stella died, when Dingley moved into more modest lodgings. When he was in London, in 1713, he had written to Stella: 'Yes, I have Lady Giffard's picture sent me by your mother. It is boxed up at a place where my other things are.' If one is making a case for the incest theory, it is reasonable to suppose that Stella should be sent the portrait by her alleged mother, as a gift from her unacknowledged real mother.

In this scenario, there would need to be an early acquaintance and a close bond of trust between Bridget Johnson, the foster-mother, and Martha Giffard, the real mother. This too can be adduced.

Monck Berkeley, in his *Relics,* wrote that it was Martha Giffard who knew Bridget Johnson first, well before the latter came to work at Moor Park, and that it was Martha Giffard and not Sir William who brought her (and Hetty/Stella, her elder daughter) into the household:

> Whilst Mrs Johnson lived at Richmond, she had the happiness of first becoming acquainted with Lady Giffard . . . *As they were seldom apart* [my italics], and Lady Giffard lived much with her brother Sir William, it was through her that Mrs Johnson and her two daughters (her son dying young) were brought to the knowledge and friendship of Sir William Temple and his lady . . .

Monck Berkeley is inaccurate on many small points. It does not follow that he was inaccurate on all points.

In her will, Martha Giffard left small sums to Dingley relatives, and 'to Mrs Hester Johnson [Stella] I give ten pounds with the hundred pounds I put into the exchequer for her life and my own and declare the hundred pounds to be hers which I am told is there in my name upon the survivorship and for which she has constantly sent me her certificate and received the interest, I give her beside my silver chocolate pot . . .' The capital on this investment, in the event, was worth £400.

Stella's alleged mother, now Mrs Mose, was left £20, 'my largest silver saucepan', and 'the wrought iron bed in the largest room at Sheen with the largest chair those of my own work [i.e. tapestry or embroidery]'.

Stop again. You do not have to believe the incest story. I had much rather you did not. It is a wilful biographical vagary. Readers confronted with a sufficiency of puzzles will find it just one too many. I am absolutely not putting it forward as the truth, nor even as a possible truth.

My point is this: by showing that the case can be made, I am demonstrating how almost any hypothesis about the parentage of Stella – or Swift – can be reasonably well documented and, momentarily, knock the rest out of the water.

As Orrery wrote of the concealment of the marriage, 'There are actions of which the true sources will never be discovered. This

243

perhaps is one.' I am prepared to accept that, and to accommodate this mystery as a mystery, along with others.

Yet there is something in us which makes us want to form a view, or to have one convincingly formed for us. The right solution is often the unremarkable one. Swift's father may well have been his mother's lawful husband, the young man who died some time in spring 1667.

Or not. What one chooses to believe about other people's private lives is a matter of temperament. For example, in any question as to whether two people were actually lovers (i.e., Swift and Vanessa), the world is divided between those who assume they were, and those who assume they were not.

The belief, whichever way, derives from one's own experience and practice and from a defensive hope that one's own experience and practice is the norm. There is a similar divide, for the same reason, between those who latch on to conspiracy theories and complications, and those who take life and events at their face value. We can make up our own minds, from the evidence, whether Stella and Swift were married, and whether there was anything unorthodox about his parentage, or hers, and if so, what.

But no one can know for certain. We are left in the flurry of Swift's passage as he rushes from the Archbishop's library, his clerical robe askew, deeply upset, brushing past his friend Patrick Delany without a word, and leaving the Archbishop disturbed and honourably unable, ever, to reveal what the unhappy Dean had confided.

Chapter Fifteen

FILTH

GIVEN SWIFT'S KEENNESS on personal cleanliness, which in the eyes of his contemporaries amounted to an eccentricity, it is hardly surprising that he minded very much about the cleanliness of those he was close to. All contemporary commentators stress how neat and clean Vanessa and Stella were, both in their clothes and in their persons. This distinction between the clothes and the body they clothed was necessary, in that it was common practice to put on smart new clothes over never-washed bodies.

Congenital abnormalities went uncorrected. Chronic disorders of the skin or the digestion were untreatable, or functionally untreatable. People had fleas and lice and bad teeth or no teeth and few did much washing of themselves. Laundering cost money. Some articles of women's clothing were unwashable anyway. Their corsets, made of leather and bone, lasted for years, until they rotted. Wadded or quilted petticoats were worn until they disintegrated.

Laetitia Pilkington described in her memoirs her landlady in Fleet Street, a milliner, who had not combed her hair for three years. This unsavoury lady wore dirty shifts which were sleeveless: 'no matter for that; she sold ready made cambric sleeves, and could easily pin on a pair, for she never took any further trouble about them'. Mrs Pilkington referred her readers to Swift's poem 'The Lady's Dressing Room' (of which more later): 'I really, till I saw this wretch, imagined the Dean had mustered up all the dirty ideas in the world on purpose to affront the fair sex, as he used humorously to style old beggar-women and cinder-pickers'.

Swift's passion for cleanliness, as we have seen, was mirrored by an equally intense horror of its opposite: 'dirt, and filth, and nastiness'. It was not only dirty clothes and dirty bodies that he hated, though he did. Human waste products loomed even larger. His notoriety as a scatological and apparently misogynistic writer has overshadowed his literary reputation.

When Gulliver is a prisoner of the tiny Lilliputians, his bodily functions cause concern. 'When I made water, which I very plentifully did, to the great astonishment of the people, who conjecturing from my motions what I was going to do, immediately opened to the right and left on that side, to avoid the torrent which fell with such noise and violence from me.'

Gulliver has a similar problem, delayed as long as possible, in 'disburthening' himself of his 'uneasy load' of excrement. But when the Emperor of Lilliput's palace is on fire, Gulliver is happily able to extinguish the blaze in three minutes with the great stream of his urine.

Among the Brobdingnagians, who are giants, a woman's 'monstrous breast' comes under Gulliver's scrutiny. 'It stood prominent six foot, and could not be less than sixteen in circumference. The nipple was about half the bigness of my head, and the hue both of that and the dug so varified with spots, pimples and freckles, that nothing could be more nauseous.' The Queen's maids of honour 'would often strip me naked from top to toe, and lay me at full length in their bosoms; wherewith I was much disgusted; because, to say the truth, a very offensive smell came from their skins; but I conceive that my sense was more acute in proportion to my littleness . . .' Gulliver sat on their dressing tables and experienced further 'horror and disgust' on seeing 'a mole here and there as broad as a trencher, and hairs hanging from it thicker than pack-threads'.

There is a running metaphor, so faint as to be ignorable, of tiny Gulliver as an unhappy phallus, forced into entering disgusting places. He was plunged into a bowl of cream in which he stifled and nearly drowned. There was an empty marrow-bone set erect on a plate, and his giant child-nurse Glumdalclitch 'took me up with both hands, and squeezing my legs together, wedged them into the marrow-bone above my waist, where I stuck for some time . . .'

What about the scatalogical poetry, mostly written in the 1730s, after Stella was dead? 'Celia shits.' There is nothing very odd about an amazed awareness that an exquisite and desirable person shits. This amazement too is childlike; children (and some adults) find lavatory jokes funny, because of the shocking incongruity and the breaking of taboo. Most adults learn to compartmentalize, keeping separate the awareness of the desirability, and the awareness of the shitting. But the inevitability and universality of the bodily functions, the fact that – as Pope wrote – 'some folks read, but all folks sh––t', do not temper the incongruity of it.

> Swift and St Augustine
> Lived in centuries
> When a stench of sewage
> Ever in the nostrils
> Made a strong debating
> Point for Manichees.

Pollution came from below and around and above. The rivers were open sewers. John Gay's poem *Trivia, or The Art of Walking the Streets of London* describes the hazards of a city centre: uneven cobbles, gaping open cellars; overflowing gutters of stinking water (and blood from slaughter houses) and more filthy water flung from the overhanging upper storeys of houses; spatterings of mud and dung from streets choked with carts and coaches, further congested by herds of animals on their way to market or to slaughter; plus the danger of being kneecapped by the protruding poles of sedan chairs.

Foulness seeped out of the ground and into the lower parts of houses. (That is why drawing-rooms were on the upper floor.) Around the edges of London lay a welter of decomposing matter in a wasteland of stagnant ponds, dunghills and ditches – material which fertilized the market gardens, and on which bands of rooting hogs grew fat. The urban population was increasing at an unprecedented rate. Smoke from coal fires and human exhalations (it was thought) poisoned the air: Swift's friend Dr Arbuthnot calculated that 'the sweat of less than 3,000 human creatures would make an atmosphere 71 feet high, over an acre of ground, in 34 days'.

It was hard to forget about human filth, except in the countryside where the spacious privacy of fields and woods made human animality acceptable. The turds of the population lay around in the gutters, courts and alleys, wastegrounds and parks, and in the angles of churches, palaces and great institutions. It is reported that even at Versailles, the grandiose palace of the King of France, the passages and courtyards were treated as public lavatories.

'Every person who walks the streets', wrote Swift in Dublin in 1732, 'must needs observe the immense number of human excrements at the doors and steps of waste houses, and at the sides of every dead wall.' He was making a comic-serious point about Irish poverty: he had heard it said 'that these heaps were laid there privately by British fundaments, to make the world believe, that our Irish vulgar do daily eat and drink'. The joke spirals into a mock-scientific investigation of the bore and odour of the British as opposed to the Hibernian product, and for once I will spare you the details.

The politer kind of people had cesspits on their premises, and commodes in their bedrooms, closets or dressing-rooms, which were emptied by servants and the contents tipped into the carts of the night-soil men – only to be deposited on to some convenient nearby wasteground or dunghill.

All in all, eighteenth-century people could not afford to be too squeamish. It is easy, except when the drains become blocked, for most modern people to 'not think' about these things. In the developed countries our bodily functions have been privatized by public-health measures. Most readers of this book will have bathrooms, and running water, and every device technology has come up with to deal with the problem of human waste. We can compartmentalize both mentally and geographically. What we'd rather not think about happens behind the closed door.

'Dirt, and filth, and nastiness' is matter in the wrong place. It is messiness. It epitomizes disorder. It is disgusting. The compartmentalizing keeps it in its place. Swift stood on the threshold between compartments, unable or unwilling to avert his mind or his senses or his imagination from smells and stains.

His poem *The Lady's Dressing-Room* is an account of what Celia's admirer Strephon finds there after his 'goddess' finishes her toilette and '. . . from her chamber issues,/ Array'd in lace, brocades and tissues.' It is not a short poem. Here are some of the more notorious lines:

> And first a dirty smock appear'd,
> Beneath the arm-pits well besmear'd . . .
> Now listen while he next produces,
> The various combs for various uses,
> Fill'd up with dirt so closely fixt,

No brush could force a way betwixt.
A paste of composition rare,
Sweat, dandriff, powder, lead and hair . . .
Hard by a filthy bason stands,
Fowl'd with the scouring of her hands;
The bason takes whatever comes
The scrapings of her teeth and gums,
A nasty compound of all hues,
For here she spits, and here she spues.
But oh! it turned poor Strephon's bowels,
When he beheld and smelt the towels,
Begumm'd, bematter'd, and beslim'd
With dirt, and sweat, and ear-wax grimed.
No object Strephon's eye escapes,
Here pettycoats in frowzy heaps;
Nor be the handkerchiefs forgot
All varnish'd o'er with snuff and snot.
The stockings why shou'd I expose
Stain'd with the marks of stinking toes . . .

Finally Strephon lifts the decorative lid of her 'reeking chest', her commode, whose contents

Send up an excremental smell
To taint the parts from whence they fell.
The pettycoats and gown perfume,
Which waft a stink round every room.

Thus finishing his grand survey,

Disgusted Strephon stole away
Repeating in his amorous fits,
Oh! Celia, Celia, Celia, shits!

Strephon's misery is that he can no longer see the loveliness of Celia *without* thinking of her shit:

His foul imagination links
Each dame he sees with all her stinks:
And, if unsav'ry odours fly,

249

Conceives a lady standing by:
All women his description fits,
And both ideas jump like wits:
By vicious fancy coupled fast,
And still appearing in contrast.

Swift is careful at the end of the poem to separate its author from
Strephon, and expresses pity for him.

Should I the Queen of Love refuse,
Because she rose from stinking ooze?

If Strephon would only 'stop his nose',

He soon would learn to think like me,
And bless his ravish't sight to see
Such order from confusion sprung,
Such gaudy tulips rais'd from dung.

The horticultural image is characteristic, and apt. 'Only connect', he
is saying, like E. M. Forster. 'Only connect the monk and the beast.'
We are what we are. His personal peculiarity is his insistence on this
particular aspect of our Yahoo animality, and on its female
manifestations. He chooses his words exactly. Plain speaking may
not be the easy option. Reporting to Stella from London that the
Queen had 'the gout in her bowels', he added, '(I hate the word
bowels)'.

The Lady's Dressing-Room was among the poems whose rights he
gave to Matthew Pilkington, who published it. Thus although Swift
assured Pope that it had been taken from a 'stolen' manuscript copy,
he cannot have been averse to its public appearance. But, as with
many of his political tracts as well, he wanted to avoid seeming to
endorse it.

The poem appeared in a sixpenny collection of his verse in
London in 1732, and was reprinted at least twice by other publishers
in the same year, with variants – suggesting that more than one
manuscript copy was in circulation. With the same batch went *A
Beautiful Young Nymph Going to Bed*, which describes Corinna, a whore,
returning to her garret and stripping off all the artificial aids to
appearance – false hair, false teeth, glass eye, make-up, padding.

Corinna in the cold light of dawn is 'a dreadful sight!': 'Who sees, will spew; who smells, be poison'd.'

Strephon and Chloe, another in this vein, is about a wedding night. The exquisite Chloe is caught short in bed:

> Twelve cups of tea, (with grief I speak)
> Had now constrain'd the nymph to leak.

Strephon's tragi-comic disillusion, on this and related lavatorial matters, may be imagined.

The poems are cast as a plea for female modesty and concealment – 'decency', as Swift calls it. Some contemporaries found this a perfectly reasonable strategy. Lord Orrery's second wife, after reading her husband's book about Swift, wrote to him:

> Your observation that tho' he sometimes appears indecent yet there is much wisdom in even his dirty Dressing Room, is certainly right, and I make no doubt has been of service to many a fair lady, and as all women wish to be thought goddesses, why should we take it ill to see what is disagreeable set in so strong and striking a light as may make us avoid it?

Those who knew him said that his conversation was not 'dirty', and that he did not tolerate dirty talk from others, certainly not from women. Patrick Delany, who attributed Swift's 'defilement' of style and wit to the bad influence of Alexander Pope, recalled him 'falling into a furious resentment' with Stella once on account of 'a very small failure of delicacy'. There is however some mild indelicacy in the *Journal to Stella*. He is cruelly crude about the appearance of other women, especially as they looked just after childbirth: 'the ugliest sight I have ever seen', he told Stella, 'pale, dead, old and yellow, for want of her paint. She has turned my stomach.'

He was affectionately sensual towards Stella herself. 'Stay, I'll answer some of your letter this morning in bed: let me see; come and appear, little letter . . .' When he finds the letter in the mess of papers on his bed, he begins to talk to Stella: 'Faith, if I was near you, I would whip your [arse] to some tune, for your grave saucy answer' (to some query about Dean Stearne). Again, writing in bed in the early morning, before Patrick has lit his fire, and fantasizing about the similar scene in Dublin: 'Stella is just now showing a white leg, and putting it into the slipper.'

Lady Mary Wortley Montagu, a shrewd commentator, was of the opinion that obscene speech and writing was a fashionable 'depravity of manners', with 'many *talking* lewdly who *live* soberly'. One could take her thought further. Those who talked most lewdly might well be precisely those who lived most soberly, as with (some) men in groups today, boasting of sexual prowess and concealing fears of sexual inadequacy.

In the years after Stella's death, when most of the scatological writing was done, Swift's language in public was less nice. Laetitia Pilkington told a story about a supper at the Deanery: 'The Dean was giving us an account of some woman who, he told us, was the nastiest, filthiest, most stinking old b—ch that ever was seen – except the company, ladies! except the company! for that you know is but civil. We all bowed; could we do less?'

But it was on paper that the mental controls imposing delicacy, decency and discretion were chiefly abandoned. He was not alone. Pope too used explicitly 'dirty' language in private letters and public verse. Swift published *Gulliver* without a qualm; and later he read his scatological poems to the circle at the Deanery, and lent them, or left them around to be copied out, or memorized, or published.

Some anxiety-ridden men, over-controlled and over-controlling in most areas of their lives, have the impulse to expose themselves physically. In expressing so graphically that dualistic view of female humanity which in Strephon he condemned as 'foul imagination', 'vicious fancy', Swift wilfully exposed himself to moral, critical and aesthetic disapproval: the Dean of St Patrick's was behaving like a Yahoo.

Even the broad-minded Mrs Pilkington remarked that 'with all the reverence I have for the Dean, I really think he sometimes chose subjects unworthy of his Muse, and which could serve for no other end except that of turning the reader's stomach, as it did my mother's, who, upon reading the 'Lady's Dressing Room', instantly threw up her dinner'. Not that Laetitia Pilkington had any time for her mother, or valued her opinions.

However, many readers since then have felt like throwing up their dinner after reading Swift's scatological verse, and if not their dinner, then their hands in pious horror. Relatively few people read in order to be disturbed, disgusted, or shaken up.

Gulliver's Travels provoked nearly as much disgust as the

scatological poems. An early history of fiction, published in 1814, pronounced *Gulliver's Travels* to be 'evidence of a diseased mind and lacerated heart'. Augustine Birrell, man of letters and chief secretary for Ireland 1907–16, wrote in 1894: 'No fouler pen than Swift's has soiled our literature. His language is horrible from first to last.' Birrell wrote a great deal more, in the same vein. Most late nineteenth-century critics, Jekyll-and-Hyde to a man, loathed Jonathan Swift for his scatology. A small anthology could be composed of their pompous, prudish protestations of distaste and horror. Here is that good man Thackeray, to take just one example, in an incontinence of adjectives: 'horrible, shameful, unmanly, blasphemous . . . filthy in word, filthy in thought, furious, raging, obscene'.

The early twentieth century was a little more perspicacious, but not much. Post-Freudian critics have had a field day with Swift's 'diseased mind'. Their classic position was encapsulated by A. L. Rowse: 'It is a well-known fact of psychology that complete sexual repression is liable to compensate itself with a marked scatological fixation, and this is the direction Swift's mind took.' The psychoanalytically inclined reader should also note that Swift kept detailed accounts of everything he spent, and remember his costiveness about parting with money.

D. H. Lawrence, naturally enough, had something to say. 'Think of Swift's *But* of horror at the end of every verse of that poem to Celia. But Celia shits! – you see the very fact that it should horrify him, and simply devastate his consciousness, is all wrong, and a bitter shame to poor Celia.' It was all, he wrote, 'a question of conscious acceptance and adjustment – only that'. Quite so. Here Lawrence is referring to another and more jocular Celia poem from the same group, *Cassinus and Peter*, which is about one Cambridge under-graduate, insane with grief, bewailing to another how heart-breakingly his passion for Caelia (as she is spelled this time) has been betrayed. It is only in the last four lines that he confides in his friend:

> And yet I dare confide in you;
> So, take my secret, and adieu.
> Nor wonder how I lost my wits;
> Oh! Caelia, Caelia, Caelia sh——.

Elsewhere, Lawrence wrote of Swift: 'He couldn't even see how much worse it would be if Celia didn't shit.'

Quite so, again. It's much easier for us, now, to laugh, while raising a speculative eyebrow at Swift's turn of mind and imagination. It's not that we are no longer shockable, but we are shocked by quite different things, some of which our forebears knew too but never gave a thought to, and some of which not even Swift, in his most inventive fantasies, could have imagined. (Though Michael Foot saw a prophecy of nuclear warheads in the capacity, designed by scientists, of the flying island of Laputa to crash down on the rebellious city, instantaneously wiping out buildings and population. It was never attempted, because it would have destroyed not only the city but the island, the king and the scientists as well.)

It is important to remember that Swift is writing within an established convention. He is dealing in something of a literary commonplace. As Pope wrote:

> Now wits gain praise by copying other wits
> As one hog lives on what another sh—.

If Swift's scatological writing is pathological, then what of Aristophanes, Juvenal, Catullus, Horace, Martial, Montaigne, Rabelais, Dante, Scarron, Oldham, let alone Gay and Pope? What, moving ahead of Swift, about James Joyce? What about painters, from Goya to Gilbert and George? Are they all pathological too? The shock of bodily reality has been a recurring topic for artists and writers. And what, in the generation before Swift, of the only other writer who has been the recipient of a similar degree of moral opprobrium – the Earl of Rochester? This is a sample of Rochester's manner:

> By all love's soft, yet mighty powers,
> It is a thing unfit
> That men should fuck in time of flowers
> Or when the smock's beshit.

('Flowers' was the contemporary term for a woman's monthly periods.)

The excrement problem, and the smell problem, were topics of discussion, like air pollution today. They were also favourite subjects for humour. Examples of lavatory humour in Swift's contemporaries are easy to find. Pope wrote 'On a Lady who P--st at the Tragedy of Cato' (a political play by Addison):

> While maudlin Whigs deplored their Cato's fate,
> Still with dry eyes the Tory Celia sat,
> But while her pride forbids her tears to flow,
> The gushing waters find a vent below.

John Gay, in 'The Fan', and 'La Toilette', and 'Work for a Cooper', was as lavatorially explicit as Swift ever was. But Swift was the better writer, which is why he and his work are remembered. Swift and his friends wrote in apposition and opposition to the more conventional verse of their contemporaries, travestying the pastoral effusions from languishing swains to unattainable and ineffably pure nymphs and shepherdesses, with names such as Chloe, Dorinda, Selinda, Phyllis, Delia – and Celia.

Swift's cultural background was Latin prose and poetry, and his dirty women were as classically conventional as the pastoral maidens. They refer back to the polluted and polluting harpies, the foul bird-women of classical mythology. The tone, however, is Swift's own. There is an edge of anger and pain and blame in Swift's verses – for the human condition, and for Strephon, whom Swift makes his scapegoat and the carrier of his obsession. 'A nice [i.e. fastidious] man is a man of nasty ideas', wrote Swift. The nicer the man, the nastier the ideas.

Sometimes it seems these poems are acts of exorcism: as if Swift were doing what analysands call 'work' on a neurosis. But Norman O. Brown, in his psychoanalytical essay 'The Excremental Vision', universalized the issue in a humane and I believe the correct way: Swift's scatological writings are not to be explained away as 'mere epiphenomena of his individual neurosis'. We should rather 'seek to appreciate his insight into the universal neurosis of mankind'. Psychoanalysis should be a tool for explicating Swift, not for explaining him away.

It is always Swift's way to look closely at whatever it is that angers or disturbs or upsets him, so that his focal range becomes narrowed and tunnel vision excludes all countervailing values. Obsession leaves out everything that does not feed it. As Swift the poet told Strephon, his alternative self, nauseated by observing the natural functions of his lovely bride Chloe:

> For fine ideas vanish fast
> While all the gross and filthy last.

Other lubricious writers include the sexual act and the sexual organs in their repertoire. Rochester's poems were full of pricks and cunts. Swift never mentioned them. Is this because the Dean of St Patrick's allowed himself the quasi-conventional indulgence of anatomizing 'dirt, and filth, and nastiness' but drew the line at the central issue, out of some residual sense of self-preservation and clerical modesty? Or because what for most people is the central issue was, for him, a scary blank? Or because the sexual organs are sacred? Or because what they represent is inexpressible horror, the heart of darkness? The nearest he gets to the sexual act is in 'The Problem' (about Lord Wharton farting during intercourse), and in the rollingly repeated last line of each stanza of a ballad expressing his savage indignation about the appointment of yet another grossly unworthy Englishman to an Irish deanery:

> Our brethren of England, who love us so dear,
> And in all they do for us so kindly do mean,
> (A blessing upon them!) have sent us this year,
> For the good of our church, a true English dean.
> A holier priest ne'er was wrapt up in crape,
> The worst you can say, he committed a rape.

(The rapist was Thomas Sawbridge, Dean of Ferns.)

There is one other way of getting Swift's scatological writing into perspective, and that is to look at the proportion of all his writing that it represents. There is simply *not* what Orwell called an 'endless harping on disease, dirt and deformity'.

The dirty poems, all written in the early 1730s, are *The Lady's Dressing-Room, A Beautiful Young Nymph Going to Bed, Strephon and Chloe,* and *Cassinus and Peter* – four poems out of the 270 assumed to be his. Other mildly improper poems belong more to the mode of 'la bagatelle', and should be treated as such. Even if you count in 'The Problem' and 'Apollo, or a Problem Solved' (about an impotent lover) and 'The Gulph of All Human Possessions' (a riddle or fable based on the digestive tract), it has been calculated that all this only constitutes 3.33 per cent of all his poetry. The proportion of scatological matter in *Gulliver* is about the same.

*

Since female virginity, at least among the upper and middle classes, was officially protected until marriage, the kind of men with the leisure to write poetry acquired their sexual experience from women of easier virtue – all the way down the scale, from society women already married, to whores or 'women of the town'. The most striking thing about Swift's writing about women, whether in prose or poetry, is its graphic, shocking immediacy. His women are not notional. The man who described the 'monstrous breast' of the woman of Brobdingnag had looked closely at a real woman's breast; indeed, Gulliver adds at that point that 'our English ladies' appear beautiful because their defects can only be seen through a magnifying glass, 'where we find by experiment that the smoothest and whitest skins look rough and coarse, and ill coloured'.

The poetry too has to be based on observation, heightened but not supplied by imagination. A woman at her dressing table, half-dressed and beautifying herself for the day with every cosmetic art, was a conventional subject for verse. In Gay's contribution to the genre, 'The Fan', he dwells with voyeuristic self-titillation on all the details. (He once worked as a draper's assistant, and indulged a fascinated familiarity with the female toilette.) There is a 'camp' archness about Gay's tone, but very little animus. Pope's *The Rape of the Lock* epitomizes the genre, with its cataloguing of perfume-bottles, salves and potions, pins, combs of tortoiseshell and ivory, and all the paraphernalia of the dressing table – 'Puffs, powders, patches, bibles, billet-doux.'

This focus on the toilette is due to the fact that it was the custom for a woman to receive male visitors in her dressing-room. Swift has seemingly watched that Beautiful Young Nymph preparing for bed, he has surely been in that Lady's Dressing-Room. What sort of woman, or women, had he been watching? What was his relationship with them?

Certainly Pope's friend (and later, enemy) Lady Mary Wortley Montagu, in her riposte, assumed that the lady in question was a whore. She retold the 'Dressing-Room' tale suggesting that Swift wrote his poem as a revenge because he had been impotent with her, blaming the dirt and smells of her room and person for his inability to perform, and demanding his money back (£4, quite a lot). The lady, in riposte, called him a 'fumbler':

I'll be reveng'd you saucy quean
(Replys the disappointed Dean)
I'll so describe your dressing room
The very Irish shall not come.
She answer'd short, I'm glad you'll write,
You'l furnish paper when I shite.

(Lady Mary, when she lived in Venice, used to show privileged
visitors her commode. On the bottom of this receptacle were painted
the faces of Pope, Swift, and Bolingbroke.)

Swift's contemporaries and near-contemporaries (and biographers
and critics ever since) have speculated on the nature of his sexuality.
George Orwell thought him 'a diseased writer': 'Swift was
presumably impotent, and had an exaggerated horror of human
dung.' Impotence has been a favoured explanation of the scatology.

'Impotent' does not seem to me to be a sufficient explanation, or
any explanation at all. Impotence would be a result, rather than a
cause. The modern mind may leap to the conclusion that his disgust,
focusing on women, was the reverse face of an attraction that he
would not acknowledge. Aldous Huxley, while more maidenly in his
language than D. H. Lawrence ('The monosyllabic verb, which the
modesties of 1929 will not allow me to reprint, rhymes with "wits"
and "fits"), was more sophisticated in his view that 'the horrifying
and the disgusting are sources of strong emotion, therefore the
horrifying and disgusting are pursued as goods. Most of us, I
suppose, enjoy disgust and horror, at any rate in small doses.'

Or one may wonder whether Swift was, in the modern sense, gay
– a word which in his day, to confuse the issue, simply meant sexually
active, while 'effeminate' meant excessively pleasure-loving and
(heterosexually) promiscuous.

Edward Hyde, the Earl of Clarendon, as governor of New York in
Queen Anne's reign, 'had caused some consternation by appearing
at state functions in women's clothes, in order, so he said, to
represent the Queen more exactly'. Cross-dressing was a spectator
sport, and a gesture of liberation; The Female Tatler in 1709 was
reporting reprovingly on upper-class girls who dressed up as men
and romped about the streets at night drinking, and breaking
windows.

But early eighteenth-century sexual orientations cannot be

defined or categorized in hard-edged terms. *The Female Tatler*, again in 1709, reported on five young baronets who met at the Smyrna coffee-house, talked only to one another, and did needlework. They were collaborating on a floral embroidered waistcoat for a brother beau's wedding, while eating sweets. The writer blamed the parents. She cited the spoiled son of a doting mother who 'goes a visiting with my Lady, where he imbibes all effeminacies, lies with my Lady's woman till she begins to make complaints', and then has a wife provided for him.

Sodomy was a capital offence, though there were few prosecutions, and the permissiveness that had characterized the reigns of the latter Stuarts survived, though not uncriticized, throughout Swift's lifetime. Steele and Addison were suspected of being lovers. There was a male gay subculture in London, centring on the back rooms of taverns and male brothels called 'molly-houses'. The poets of the late seventeenth century, including Rochester, celebrated the pleasures of sex with boys and with women with equal enthusiasm, and non-exclusively. Given the amount of venereal disease, pleasure with young boys may have been the healthy option, for men. Towards the end of Swift's life, attitudes were hardening; in 1731 his friend William Pultney publicly accused Lord Hervey of being a homosexual.

The most interesting aspect of the fluidity of sexual orientation lay in what has been called 'sentimental sodomy', i.e. homosocial behaviour, homoeroticism which stopped short of physical contact. Men who were friends wrote to one another in very warm terms. Educated men, however much they liked women's company, found their soul-mates in one another, since – with notable exceptions – the women whom they knew were poorly educated, and conditioned to devote their energies to card-playing, gossip, and their own appearance. Men desperate to make their way in the world, or to secure an income, fawned flatteringly – and sometimes homoerotically – on men who had the power to oblige them.

All this made for an emotionally inflated style of discourse between men. John Gay (who on Swift's recommendation got a job as secretary in Hanover to the Lord Clarendon who had represented the Queen 'so exactly') is a case in point. Gay ingratiated himself with men and women of influence. He cultivated Lord Burlington with an extraordinary emotional intensity, as he did William Pultney.

Gay was equally assiduous in his flattering attentions to influential women. There is no evidence that he was sexually involved with anyone, ever. He was a household pet, like a dog or a cat, though 'hermaphroditic tendencies' were diagnosed in his work. ('Hermaphrodite', just to add another strand to the pattern of linguistic shift, was the contemporary term for 'queer'.)

Swift has to be observed in this context. Laetitia Pilkington graphically recorded an episode which could be interpreted as Swift being 'camp' (though he was, perhaps, just re-enacting the intimate raillery of coffee-making with Vanessa). He was making coffee after dinner over his fire at the Deanery and,

> the fire scorching his hand, he called to me to reach him his glove, and changing the coffee-pot to his left hand, held out his right one, ordered me to put his glove on it, which accordingly I did; when, taking up part of his gown to fan himself with, and acting in character of a prudish lady, he said: 'Well, I do not know what to think. Women may be honest that do such things, but, for my part, I never could bear to touch any man's flesh except my husband's, whom perhaps', says he, 'she wished at the Devil.'

He was closely observed in his lifetime. There was an oblique hint (hinting by denying) of a homosexual link in *Dr S——t's Real Diary*, an anonymous parody and follow-up to Smedley's malicious spoof-diary, in which the mock-dedication to Lord Oxford referred to the happy days 'when I was to your Lordship *a mensa & secretis* [privy to your table and your secrets] (the world was never so wicked as to say, *a thoro* [to your bed])'. But as Robert Mahony has written, 'the whispery hint of homosexual association did not get picked up'.

Swift's attachment to Sheridan amounted, at its height, to a dependency. His devotion to both Harley and Bolingbroke was unconditional. He valued his other English friendships – especially with Pope, Gay and Arbuthnot – almost as much. In later life he was helpful, watchful and tender towards the many young men who were his protégés while on the lower rungs of the ladder of success. All these friendships were tinged with a 'normal' and insignificant eroticism. Many same-sex friendships were (and are).

The longer physical intimacy is eschewed, the more impossible it becomes. Inhibition can become total. Use it or lose it. There is, to use an anachronistic image, nothing wrong with the engine, but the ignition has seized up. That was Thomas Sheridan's slant on a theory of functional impotence. He thought that owing to 'a constant habit of suppressing his desires', Swift 'at last lost the power of gratifying them: a case by no means singular, as more than one instance of the kind has fallen within my knowledge'.

What we are left with is the image of Swift watching. It is not what one looks at that determines what one sees, it is the lens that one looks through and the perspective from which one sees it. *Gulliver* is full of references to telescopes and spectacles. Strephon in *The Lady's Dressing-Room* looks into Celia's magnifying glass:

> It shew'd the visage of a giant.
> A glass that can to sight disclose,
> The smallest worm in Celia's nose,
> And faithfully direct her nail
> To squeeze it out from head to tail.

Perception, hence judgement, becomes a problem in optics.

Swift's is an age of voyeurism: watching people at Court and in public places, to see who is whispering to whom in the anterooms of power; watching to see who is weak or sick, and soon to be vacating a desirable position in church or ministry; watching to see who is in favour with which great man, and which lady has bedroom-influence over him, and is therefore to be cultivated.

We cannot know whether Swift lived chastely for most of his life or not. But given his pride, and his caution, his screwed-up attitude to women, and his patterns of emotional defence, it is probable that he did live for much of his life as a celibate. And he watched.

We are watching too, from a distance, through the distorting lens of time. Writing and reading about Swift is watching a movie about watching.

Chapter Sixteen

ENDGAME

IN 1731 Swift, in reasonably good health, had written some prophetic *Verses on the Death of Dr Swift*:

> The time is not remote when I
> Must in the course of nature die;
> When I foresee my special friends,
> Will try to find their private ends:
> Tho' it is hardly understood
> Which way my death will do them good;
> Yet, thus methinks, I hear 'em speak;
> See how the Dean begins to break:
> Poor gentleman, he droops apace,
> You plainly find it in his face:
> That old vertigo in his head,
> Will never leave him, till he's dead:
> Besides, his memory decays,
> He recollects not what he says;
> He cannot call his friends to mind;
> Forgets the place where he last dined . . .

When he showed it to Laetitia Pilkington, her eyes filled with tears. 'Pooh, I am not dead yet,' he said.

> . . . He gave the little wealth he had,
> To build a house for fools and mad . . .

Madness, to Swift's mind, was a matter of 'wrong' or unorthodox

262

associations of ideas; a personal, unacceptable logic. What seemed sanity at one time is perceived as 'mad' in another person at another time or in another context. In a sense we are all mad: 'if the wisest man would, at any time, utter his thoughts in the crude indigested manner as they come to him in his head, he would be looked upon as raving mad'. There were quite as many madmen, to Swift's divergent mind – politicians, lawyers, generals, scientists, philosophers – outside Bedlam as within its walls, and as many shrewd men within as without:

> Yet many a wretch in Bedlam, knows,
> How to distinguish friends from foes;
> And though perhaps among the rout,
> He wildly flings his filth about,
> He still has gratitude and sap'ence,
> To spare the folks that gave him ha'pence
> Nor, in their eyes at random pisses,
> But turns aside like mad Ulysses . . .

London's Bedlam – short for St Mary of Bethlehem – was on the edge of the open space called Moorfields, the high railings around the building lined with stalls for old books and old clothes. Bedlam was open to the public, who entered through a gateway fourteen feet high and topped by two vast, agonized stone figures (sculpted by Colley Cibber's father) representing 'Raving Madness' and 'Melancholy Madness'. The unhappy and filthy inmates, chained and caged, were on show as in a zoo, to be marvelled and laughed at, and wilfully provoked by some visitors into frenzy. The more savage their behaviour, the greater the frisson for the voyeur. Yahoos in captivity.

A visit to Bedlam, like a visit to the lions kept in the Tower of London, was a completely normal part of a sightseeing tour of the capital. On a rainy day in December 1710, Swift himself had gone out with three fine ladies, and a bunch of their children and servants, in three coaches, 'and saw all the sights, lions, etc, and then to Bedlam', ending the day with a puppet show in Moorfields. In 1714 Swift, along with Bishop Atterbury, was appointed a governor of Bedlam, but the political crisis intervened and he left England without ever attending a meeting.

In 1732 he was in correspondence with Sir William Fownes, Lord

Mayor of Dublin, about the problems of charitable institutions for 'lunatics' in Ireland. Sir William was cynical, fearing 'we should be overloaded with numbers under the name of mad ... Wives & husbands trying who could first get the other to Bedlam. Many who were next heirs to estates, would try their skills to render the possessor disordered & get them confined, and soon run them into real madness.' Sir William was, however, instrumental in the founding of a hospital for 'incurables' (mental defectives), endowed by Mary Mercer. He wanted Swift to abandon his own scheme, which he had already been outlining to interested parties. Swift did become a governor of Mercer's Hospital (which still exists).

Swift's attitude to the 'mad' was not sentimental. Dr Delany remarked that he did not have the kind of compassion for others 'that urges us, by relieving their distresses, to relieve our own'. His generosity was dispassionate. In his will, he left – apart from certain small bequests – his whole estate for the building and endowment of 'an hospital large enough for the reception of as many idiots and lunatics as the annual income of the said lands and worldly substance shall be sufficient to maintain', and to provide 'for ever after ... victuals, clothing, medicines, attendance, and all other necessaries' for the inmates. If a sufficient number of idiots and lunatics could not be found, incurables might be admitted.

The hospital was to be called St Patrick's. There was not enough money in Swift's estate for the running costs, and the governors had to raise more, and apply to the government for a subsidy. St Patrick's Hospital survives to this day as a modern psychiatric hospital, fulfilling Swift's wishes.

A time was to come when the Dean seemed, to Lord Orrery, suitable as 'the first proper inhabitant for his own hospital'.

Jonathan Swift did not 'go mad'. He grew old, and his mind went.

Gulliver, on the island of Luggnagg, heard that a small number of the population, known as Struldbruggs, were born immortal, and never died. He thought with pleasure of what he would do were he to be so fortunate. He would never marry after the age of sixty, and 'live in a hospitable manner, yet still on the saving side', educating younger and mortal men with the fruits of his eternally lengthening experience, and enjoying an inner circle of choice companions which would change as the normal cycle of life continuously replaced them.

The reality, he discovered, was different. After the age of eighty, Gulliver was told, the Struldbruggs

> had not only all the follies and infirmities of other old men, but many more which arose from the dreadful prospect of never dying. They were not only opinionative, peevish, covetous, morose, vain, talkative, but incapable of friendship, and dead to all natural affection . . . Envy and impotent desires are their prevailing passions.

At ninety the Struldbruggs lost their teeth, hair and sense of taste. Their diseases continued without increasing or diminishing.

> In talking they forget the common appellation of things, and the names of persons, even of those who are their nearest friends and relations. For the same reason they can never amuse themselves with reading, because their memory will not serve to carry them from the beginning of a sentence to the end; and by this defect they are deprived of the only entertainment whereof they might otherwise be capable.

A group of Struldbruggs was brought in for Gulliver to look at. 'They were the most mortifying sight I ever beheld, and the women more horrible than the men . . . The reader will easily believe, that from what I had heard and seen, my keen appetite for perpetuity of life was much abated.'

Swift had always been afraid of losing his mind. He had witnessed, in youth, the senile decay of his Uncle Godwin. Famously, he said to the poet-clergyman Edward Young, on a walk, seeing a blighted tree: 'I shall be like that tree; I shall die first at the top.'

When he had indeed begun to die 'at the top', Lord Orrery wrote to Deane Swift: 'It is the more melancholy to me, as I have heard him often lament the particular misfortune incident to human nature, of an utter deprivation of senses many years before a deprivation of life. I have heard him describe persons in that condition, with a liveliness and a horror, that on this late occasion have recalled to me his very words.' He used, wrote Orrery in his published *Remarks . . .*, to cite as examples the Duke of Marlborough (who suffered a disabling stroke six years before he died) and Lord Somers, sighing heavily, 'and with gestures that showed great uneasiness, as if he felt an impulse of what was to happen to him before he died'.

Swift was well enough to 'feast his clergy' on St Patrick's Day, as usual, in 1737, with 'ladies, music, meat and wine', as Lord Orrery reported. He still went out to dine in the houses of his regular circle of friends. Since these were not rich people, and also because he was fussy, the two servants who accompanied him often took along a sort of picnic: a small joint, or a fowl, or a fish, with bread, wine, and even a tablecloth and napkins, 'which no one took amiss, but gave him his way'.

But he had lost weight during 1736, his sixty-ninth year, writing to a new friend, William Richardson of Coleraine, Co. Londonderry: 'I have not an ounce of flesh about me, and cannot ride above a dozen miles a day without being sore, and bruised, and spent. My head is every day more or less disordered by a giddiness: yet I ride the strand here constantly when fair weather invites me.' To Pope, again about his emaciation: 'my skin comes off in ten miles riding because skin and bone cannot agree together'.

That year, however, he produced one scarifying piece of satire against the Irish House of Commons, *The Legion Club*, inspired by his habitual rage against any threatened despoliation of the Anglican Church. Parliament was meeting in its brand-new building (what remains is now the Bank of Ireland) beside Trinity College:

> As I stroll the city, oft I
> Spy a building large and lofty.
> Not a bow-shot from the College,
> Half the globe from sense and knowledge . . .
> Tell us, what this pile contains?
> Many a head that holds no brains.

The issue was Parliament's vote to deprive the Church of the tithe of pasturage, called 'agistment'. Landowners, wanting to lay more fields down to grass for cattle, felt abused by this tax. Swift was against increasing pasturage on economic grounds, believing that food for humans should be grown, and that pasturage depopulated the countryside and increased unemployment. Even more strongly, he feared it was the thin end of the wedge, which would lead to further losses of what he saw as the Church's rightful patrimony. He knew the huge importance to ill-paid clergy of their tithes. Referring to his own project of a house for 'lunatics and fools' (which was written into his will that same year), he transformed the smart new Parliament House into a madhouse for its members:

> Let them, when they once get in
> Sell the nation for a pin;
> While they sit a-picking straws
> Let them rave of making laws;
> While they never hold their tongue.
> Let them dabble in their dung;
> Let them form a grand committee
> How to plague and starve the city;
> Let them stare and storm and frown,
> When they see a clergy gown . . .
> We may, while they strain their throats,
> Wipe our a[rses] with their v[otes].

There follows a lot more: *ad hominem* invective of an outrageous fluency. This was his last blast, and published immediately.

Swift retained his obsession with exercise, which he believed preserved him from disease. His doctors thought he overdid it. 'I seldom walk less than four miles, sometimes six, eight, ten, or more . . . or, if it rains, I walk as much through the house, up and down stairs.' Laetitia Pilkington saw him doing this: 'The Dean then ran up the great stairs, down one pair of back-stairs, up another, in so violent a manner that I could not help expressing my uneasiness lest he should fall and be hurt.' The endorphin-rush which results from hard exercise probably relieved his melancholy.

He asked Pope to send his best wishes to young Lord and Lady Oxford, whom he loved dearly 'but we seldom correspond of late because we have nothing to say to each other'. And to another correspondent: 'I am now at the age of blundering in letters, syllables, words, and half sentences, as you see, and must pardon.'

> . . . For poetry, he's past his prime,
> He takes an hour to find a rhyme:
> His fire is out, his wit decay'd,
> His fancy sunk, his muse a jade . . .
> I'd have him throw away his pen;
> But there's no talking to some men . . .

His verses on his own death were becoming all too apt. Describing his state to Dr Sheridan in spring 1737, he complained he could 'hardly write ten lines without blunders, as you will see by the numbers of scratchings and blots before this letter is done. Into the bargain I have not one rag of memory, and my friends have all forsaken me, except Mrs Whiteway, who preserves some pity for my condition, and a few others, who love wine that costs them nothing.'

His widowed cousin Martha Whiteway, aged around fifty, was now the most important person in his life. She became his companion, confidante and carer, spending every day at the Deanery. His friends began to direct their letters and enquiries directly to her. She answered on his behalf and, increasingly, in her own arch and lively persona.

Young Deane Swift sent what his great-uncle Jonathan called 'gimcracks of cups and balls' – actually a box with soap and a brush – to make shaving easier. He was shaving himself these days. 'I cut my face once or twice, was just twice as long in the performance, and left twice as much hair behind.' He sent the novelty back.

But he also gave Deane a present of his five-volume *Works*, published by Faulkner in Dublin; and an introduction to Pope when Deane went to England, explaining that the young man was 'heir to the little paternal estate of our family at Goodrich in Herefordshire' and expressing his esteem for him as 'much the most valuable of any in his family'. Deane Swift married Mrs Whiteway's daughter by her first marriage, his cousin Mary Harrison, in 1739.

Swift put on flesh again but continued to deteriorate mentally. The last St Patrick's Day party at the Deanery was in 1739. When in the unusually icy winter of 1739–40 Mrs Whiteway was ill and could not be with him – she lived across the river in Capel Street – Swift missed her badly and did not leave his bedroom. He appointed the Revd Dr John Wynne, one of his precentors, as sub-dean, to take the chair at meetings of the Chapter in his stead. For the first couple of years under this arrangement, the meetings were held at the Deanery so that Swift could be present. After that, there was no point.

Around the time of Mrs Whiteway's illness, the Revd Dr Francis Wilson, rector of Clondalkin and a prebendary in the cathedral, took up part-time residence in the Deanery. He also was responsible for collecting the deanery tithes. Swift must have taken strongly to Dr Wilson, who was in his mid-forties. He made him one of his executors in the last version of his will, signed in May 1740, in which

Dr Wilson was also left a generous legacy: the works of Plato in three volumes, Clarendon's *History of the Rebellion* peppered with Swift's annotations, his 'best Bible', the thirteen Persian pictures from the drawing-room, and a silver tankard engraved with the names of the friends who donated it. Just how important Wilson had become to Swift can be judged by the fact that John Worrall was left just 'my best beaver hat', Dr Delany only a silver medal depicting Queen Anne, and Deane Swift only his silver standish.

In 1739 Bindon painted his last and great portrait of the Dean, and his own *Verses on the Death of Dr Swift* were published. In his last will, Swift described himself as 'of sound mind, although weak in body'; but in that same month of May 1740 Mrs Whiteway was telling Pope that the Dean's memory was so bad that he could not finish or correct any written work; also that a few years previously he had burned most of his unpublished writings, 'except a few loose papers, which are in my possession'. She told Orrery she was looking after 'the book of letters stitched together by the Dean' – his treasured correspondence with Oxford, Bolingbroke, Addison, Gay and Congreve among others. 'There is one treatise in his own keeping, called *Advice to Servants*, very unfinished and incorrect, yet what is done of it, hath so much humour, that it may appear as a posthumous work.' As indeed it did.

Swift's last surviving note to Mrs Whiteway (26 July 1740) is heartrending.

I have been very miserable all night, and today extremely deaf and full of pain. I am so stupid and confounded, that I cannot express the mortification I am under both in body and mind. All I can say is, that I am not in torture; but I daily and hourly expect it. Pray let me know how your health is, and your family. I hardly understand one word I write. I am sure my days will be very few; few and miserable they must be.

But there were five more years to go.

Swift's correspondence with Pope was mysteriously appearing in print. Pope, assiduously constructing his own posthumous reputation, was behind this, while denying and pharisaically deploring it. Orrery wrote to Mrs Whiteway in concern about the possibility of precious books, letters and papers being pinched from the Deanery by unscrupulous friends or employees. He was extremely courteous to her, but keen to get the material into his own hands – or to give it to Pope for publication. 'He [Swift] has not yet put the letters into my hands', he had written to Pope in June 1737, 'they are reserved for the *dona extrema* [last gift].'

Orrery was manipulative. He was supportive of Mrs Whiteway and discussed with her the unpleasant possibility that the favoured Dr Francis Wilson was cheating the Dean of his tithes and stealing his books. But Orrery, despising and distrusting Swift's circle of friends, and always longing to 'snatch him from his little senate', privately resented the influence of Mrs Whiteway too.

'We hear often of him [the Dean], but seldom from him', he wrote to Pope, with his usual facetious pompousness, in 1740:

> The lady's power (one may say it without hurting one part of his reputation) increases daily: at night her influence ends, that is, she retires to her lodgings and the Dean to his bed: but returning light brings her back to her station, which she quits not, till, as she poetically expresses it (for now she scarce deigns to call for small beer in prose) the goddess Luna . . . borrows light from her brother Phoebus.

By the end of 1742 Mrs Whiteway's reign was over, anyway. She wrote to Orrery that the Dean's understanding was quite gone. He was sometimes violent. He had turned against even her (as demented people sometimes do against those closest to them).

'I was the last person whom he knew, and when that part of his memory failed, he was so outrageous at seeing anybody, that I was forced to leave him.' All she could do now was to call at the Deanery twice a week 'to enquire after his health, and to observe that proper care was taken of him, and durst only to look at him while his back was turned towards me, fearing to discompose him'. He walked ten hours a day (around the house), would not eat or drink if his servant stayed in the room. His meat was served up ready cut, and sometimes it would lie an hour on the table before he would touch it, and then eat it walking.

Mrs Brent's daughter, Anne Ridgeway, who lived with her cabinet-maker husband in Grafton Street, remained as housekeeper. The Dean developed a boil on his eyelid which swelled up as big as an egg, with more boils on his body and arms, which caused horrible pain. The infection passed and he was himself again for a day or two. He probably suffered some minor strokes. He shortly became utterly lethargic, and no longer walked about much, or understood anything. 'I rejoice to hear he grows lean', Orrery wrote to Mrs Whiteway. 'I am sorry to hear his appetite is good . . . In one word, the man I wished to live the longest, I wish the soonest dead. It is the only blessing that can now befall him.'

Three more years to go.

Dr John Lyon, a young curate, looked after Swift's business affairs. He did not live at the Deanery. Swift had liked him, trying unsuccessfully to get him a lectureship at Trinity, and recommending him to Dr Delany in 1736 as one who 'hath been employed as assistant to Mr Worrall in visiting the sick of our Liberty, hath a general good character, and is not married'. Dr Francis Wilson turned out to be more problematical. 'Good God!' wrote Orrery, having heard a horrid rumour. 'Dr Swift beaten and marked with stripes by a beast in human shape, one Wilson.' Deane Swift then told Orrery all he knew.

Apparently in June 1742 Dr Wilson had invited the Dean to dine with him at his own house at Clondalkin, and took him out of town in a hackney coach – with the Dean's servant Richard Brennan, but without Anne Ridgeway, who always accompanied the Dean on excursions outside the house since he began to lose his memory.

Dr Wilson, at dinner, got the Dean drunk. 'Now the Dean's stint, for about half a year before, was two large bumpers of wine, somewhat more than half a pint.' When Wilson pressed him to take more, the manservant whispered that a third glass would affect his master's head. Wilson not only made the Dean drink the third glass, but called for another bottle, and made him take some of that too. The Dean, quite incapacitated, had to be supported back to the coach. On the way back Wilson stopped at an ale house 'and forced the poor Dean to swallow a dram of brandy'.

As they came back into Dublin through Kilmainham, Wilson began to curse and swear and 'to abuse the Dean most horribly'. The coach was stopped, and a small crowd collected to gawp at the scandalous brawling of two clerics. 'Whether he struck the Dean or not is uncertain, but, one of the Dean's arms was observed, next morning, to be black and blue.'

That was the story for official consumption. According to other accounts, it was the Dean – Jonathan Swift, demented, drunken, disoriented, terrified, aware only of indignity and outrage – who went for Dr Wilson, pulling off his wig; and that Wilson, also drunk, had to defend himself violently. Personally, I hope it was that way round.

The piteous thing about this hideous episode is that as soon as Swift was back at home, 'he asked for this fellow with a kind of surprise, saying "Where is Dr Wilson? Ought not the doctor to be here this afternoon?" So absolutely was he then lost to all reason and memory.'

No one knew quite what Dr Wilson's motive was, though the servant Richard Brennan reported overhearing him ask Swift, in the coach, to give him the influential position of sub-dean in place of Dr Wynne; and Swift refusing. In any case, the general outrage was so great that Dr Wilson never showed his face at the Deanery again. He never collected his legacy either. He died before the Dean.

It was two months after this that a Commission in Lunacy investigated the Dean's mental condition – an event precipitated, according to one early biographer, by Swift's distressingly obscene language.

The Commission was formally applied for by a group of doctors, lawyers and clergy which included personal friends – Alexander McAuley, John Rochfort, Charles Grattan. Their task was to appoint a jury, and report their findings to Chancery. Twelve Dublin tradesmen – chandlers, hosiers, carpenters, and including John Sican, the grocer-husband of Swift's literary friend Mrs Sican – assembled at the house to assess whether the Dean 'be a person of unsound mind and memory and not capable of taking care of his person and fortune' and to determine 'who is his next heir'.

Did the twelve crowd awkwardly into his study, or did the Dean receive them in the dining-parlour? Did they, or the gentlemen who accompanied them, set questions to the Dean about the day of the week or the name of the reigning monarch, to test his understanding? Did he know what was happening? Was he lethargic and silent, or a beast at bay?

They all signed their names to a statement finding him to be of unsound mind and memory, etc., but 'it does not appear to us who is his next heir'. As part of the procedure his worldly possessions had to be valued: he was possessed of 'lands, tithes and tenements' worth £800 a year, and goods and chattels worth £10,000.

A committee of guardians was appointed, who put Dr John Lyon in overall charge at the Deanery. Anne Ridgeway was 'very faithful to her trust', according to Deane Swift, and treated the Dean with care and tenderness, as did Richard Brennan. 'Their wages are high, and it is in their interest to preserve him. The Dean is always as clean and decent, as if twenty people were employed about him.' He had a clean shirt and clean underlinen every day. He was 'an object of pity to every good man', said Dr Lyon.

> . . . Behold the fatal day arrive!
> How is the Dean? He's just alive.
> Now the departing prayer is read:
> He hardly breathes. The Dean is dead . . .

Jonathan Swift died on 19 October 1745, aged seventy-eight.

Dr Lyon had a death mask made. 'After the Paris plaster had continued one night on his countenance, it was taken off by the artist, and left to dry in the study.' (From the mask a mould was made, which Dr Lyon deposited in Trinity College.)

The bells of St Patrick's tolled, muffled, for four days, His body lay in an open coffin in the hall of the Deanery and crowds came in to pay their respects. The Dean was already a legend.

> . . . Why do we grieve that friends may should die?
> No loss more easy to supply.
> One year is past: a different scene;
> No further mention of the Dean;
> Who now, alas, no more is missed,
> Than if he never did exist . . .

Not so, Dr Swift. That is what you wrote in your verses on your own death. But you never fell into the trough of oblivion into which so many great reputations disappear.

Shortly before Swift died, Deane Swift told Orrery that 'a thousand stories have been invented of him within these two years, and imposed upon the world'. A thousand more stories were to be imposed upon the world in ensuing decades.

His immortality is not only a matter of 'stories'. In his will he bequeathed his soul to God. Alexander Pope had sent from Twickenham in 1738 a prophetic message, telling his sick friend of the many young men 'who love you unknown, who kindle at your fire, and learn by your genius. Nothing of you can die, nothing of you can be obscured, or locked up from esteem and admiration, except what is at the Deanery; just as much of you only as God made mortal.'

Swift had frequently said he wanted to be buried at Holyhead on the coast of Anglesey in north Wales, the point of embarkation and disembarkation, his bridgehead between England and Ireland. In 1727 he had been held up there for several days, desperately anxious about Stella dangerously ill in Dublin, waiting for a favourable wind for the crossing to Ireland. He sat in an inn parlour at Holyhead, 'with muddy ale and mouldy bread', passing the time scribbling verses:

> I never was in haste before
> To reach that slavish hateful shore
> Before, I always found the wind
> To me was most malicious kind
> But now, the danger of a friend
> On whom my fears and hopes depend
> Absent from whom all climes are curst
> With whom I'm happy in the worst
> With rage impatient makes me wait
> A passage to the land I hate.
> Else, rather on this bleaky shore
> Where loudest winds incessant roar
> Where neither herb nor tree will thrive,
> Where nature hardly seems alive,
> I'd go in freedom to my grave,
> Than rule yon isle and be a slave.

Ireland had become home. He changed his mind about sailing into his rest on a distant 'bleaky shore'. He left precise instructions that he was to be buried in the 'great aisle' of St Patrick's, 'on the south side, under the pillar next to the monument of primate Narcissus Marsh, three days after my decease, as privately as possible, and at twelve o'clock at night'. On a black marble slab 'seven feet from the ground, fixed to the wall' the following inscription was to be carved 'in large letters, deeply cut, and strongly gilded':

> Hic depositum est corpus
> JONATHAN SWIFT, S.T.D.
> hujus ecclesiae cathedralis
> Decani
> ubi saeva ignatio
> ulterius cor lacerare nequit.
> Abi, viator
> et imitare, si poteris
> strenuum pro virili libertatis vindicatorem

Swift's elliptic Latin may be translated thus: 'Here lies the body of Jonathan Swift, Doctor of Divinity, dean of this Cathedral Church, where savage indignation can no longer lacerate his heart. Go, traveller, and imitate if you can one who with all his might championed liberty'. The poet W. B. Yeats composed a graceful free version:

> Swift has sailed into his rest;
> Savage indignation there
> Cannot lacerate his breast.
> Imitate him if you dare,
> World-besotted traveller; he
> Served human liberty.

Chapter Seventeen

MIDNIGHT

WHILE I WAS writing the previous chapter I went to an exhibition of the paintings of Georges de La Tour at the Grand Palais in Paris. Georges de La Tour has nothing to do with Jonathan Swift. He died fifteen years before Swift was born.

The exhibition gathered together virtually all the known paintings by La Tour. Sometimes he painted the same subject several times – a sequence, for example, of Mary Magdalene; and of 'le Vielleur', the viol-player, painted from an elderly model, wearing the same cloak, in different positions and with different props, but always the same man.

In one version the viol-player is playing and singing, his mouth distorted, his sparse grey hair awry, his bleary eyes half-closed: a street-performer, you would imagine, and one who liked a drink. In another version the model is in handsome profile, with neat hair and beard: a gentleman amateur.

The same man is not always the same man. It depends on how you look at him and on what you want to see, and on how he sees himself, and on what day of the week it is, and any number of other variables.

Some of La Tour's paintings have been lost over the years. They survive at one remove. There were, in the exhibition, copies of lost originals done by other artists, some made by La Tour's contemporaries, others much later, the paintings having disappeared later. Some of the copies achieve a simulacrum of La Tour's formal and luminous quality; others are clearly inept travesties. But one deduces something of the lost original from each, even the bad ones. Seeing a variety of copies brings one nearer to the original than seeing a single, unique copy.

Biographical writing is like that. There is no such thing as a definitive biography. All the versions of Jonathan Swift – from the gossip and Chinese whispers of his contemporaries and near-contempories, to the wilder flights of speculative fancy and the sober gleanings of scholarship and historical research – contribute something to our understanding of him.

But the same man is not always the same man. The living, breathing, joking, suffering Swift remains a lost original. Biographical writers can do their utmost to avoid saying, to quote his Houynhnhnms, 'the thing which was not'. To say the thing which *was* is harder.

We know quite a lot about Jonathan Swift by now. It is time to draw in the threads.

Start from his perception that in childhood and youth he was humiliated and unloved, and that in maturity he was repeatedly disappointed. The most fruitful friendship of his life was with Alexander Pope. Pope betrayed him by publishing what should have been private, in his determination to control his own immortality, but that was par for the course. Swift's former schoolfriend William Congreve ('whom I loved from my youth', as Swift wrote on his death in 1729) wrote in his last poem:

> Believe it, men have ever been the same,
> And all the Golden Age is but a dream.

Believe it, and don't believe it. Something may not be less true for being a dream. Pope and Swift worked and played together, and they talked. In Pope's poetry one finds a mirror image of Swift. 'Search then the ruling passion', wrote Pope in the first epistle of his *Moral Essays*. 'This clue once found, unravels all the rest.'

Swift's ruling passion may be his pride. All those who knew him commented on his pride. 'His pride, his spirit, or his ambition, call it by what name you please, was boundless', says Lord Orrery. His pride was 'not to be conquered'. 'In pride, in reas'ning pride, our error lies', writes Pope in *An Essay on Man*.

Swift's Gulliver too excoriates pride: 'I am not in the least provoked at the sight of a lawyer, a pickpocket, a colonel, a fool, a lord, a gamester, a politician, a whoremonger, a physician, an evidence, a suborner, an attorney, a traitor, or the like.' Their existence was 'according to the due course of things'. But 'when I behold a lump of deformity and diseases both in body and mind, smitten with *pride*, it immediately breaks all the measures of my patience'.

Pride is a double bind. Pride may preserve a man from error. But pride is, in itself, error. In Swift's 'Day of Judgement' Jove addresses sinners thus:

> Offending race of human kind,
> By nature, reason, learning, blind;
> You who thro' frailty stepp'd aside
> And you who never fell – *thro' pride* . . .

The Houyhnhnms in *Gulliver's Travels*, naturally, had no word for and no idea of pride. Yahoos in the wild showed signs of it (as also of greed, selfishness and jostling for place). Gulliver entreated those human Yahoos who had 'any tincture of this absurd vice, that they will not presume to appear in my sight'. These are the very last words of *Gulliver's Travels*.

Long before, Sir William Temple had written: 'Of all passions, none so soon or so often turns the brain, as pride.'

In what directions does pride turn the brain? More than the brain is at stake. Pride seals off the deeper feelings. The humiliated and unloved build around themselves a wall of pride and solitude, too distanced from hope to entertain dreams of private happiness.

To dream of happiness you must have vestiges of expectation, or to have experienced it, even briefly. With no idea and no model of private contentment, you remain dry-eyed. It is the sense and knowledge of loss that give rise to intense grief. So, intense grief is as distant an emotion as intense happiness, to those who have nothing to lose. Swift has something to lose on losing Stella. To the extent he expresses grief, and he does, he acknowledges what she meant to him.

In *A Tale of a Tub* he defined happiness as 'a perpetual possession of being well deceived'. He formulates this definition a second time, adding that happiness is 'the serene peaceful state, of being a fool among knaves'. 'How fade and insipid do all objects accost us that are not conveyed in the vehicle of delusion! How shrunk is everything that appears in the glass of nature!' Were it not for 'artificial mediums, false lights, refracted angles', there would be a 'mighty level [i.e. a levelling down] in the felicity and enjoyments of mortal men'.

278

To express the superficiality of the attractiveness of other human beings, he picked an image cruel and unusual even for him: 'Last week I saw a woman flayed, and you will hardly believe how much it altered her person for the worse.'

What remains to the pride-bound man is an intelligence untempered by indulgence towards others or oneself, and a vision of the behaviour of others which is both accurate and skewed: accurate because observed through the clear lens of reason; skewed because any perception of motivation other than self-interest is beyond focal range.

The love or desire of someone else for your own person cannot be taken at face value, nor can the praise of critics: 'because I am wonderfully well acquainted with the present relish of courteous readers, and have often observed with singular pleasure, that a fly driven from a honey-pot will immediately, and with very good appetite, alight and finish his meal on an excrement'. The face value, like that of Wood's Halfpence, is perceived as illusory. The currency is debased. Passion for another person is, observably, fragile and, frequently, short-lived. Only when it consumes you does it fill the horizons of consciousness. If you have made yourself unavailable – not only to the passion of the other, but to the attaching emotion that would put you yourself in thrall – love can only seem ridiculous, frightening, or demeaning.

So what remains, in addition to intelligence, is a sense of the ridiculousness of human passion, and its inappropriateness. Reason, understood as practical common sense, is the true enlightenment. Reason makes limited associations and connections from observable evidence and from nature. Yet God, Swift conceded, is on the side of passion – without which there would be no sexual congress and therefore no propagation of our species, and none of the 'love of life' which preserved Gulliver in his worst moments and which prevents us, said Swift, from committing suicide. God has made us Yahoos. Our task in life is to be clean, civil, reasoning Yahoos.

The other kind of reason, which is based on abstract logic, and on a belief that by using logic we can ascertain the inascertainable – 'things agreed on all hands impossible to be known', in Swift's phrase – is a form of madness. This was what Pope meant when he wrote of man's error lying in 'reas'ning pride'. Swift did not have that sort of pride. There is more than one kind of pride, as there is more than one kind of reason.

Rochester, born twenty years earlier, also saw false illumination in the wrong kind of reason:

> Reason, an *ignis fatuus* in the mind,
> Which leaves the light of nature, sense, behind.

And at the end of life, wrote Rochester, in lines that are tragically applicable, later, to Swift, reason's limitation is all too obvious:

> Huddled in dirt, the reasoning engine lies,
> Who was so proud, so witty, and so wise.

Swift's negative attitude to scientific or metaphysical investigation and speculation can be seen as a reversed form of the intellectual pride he diagnosed in projectors and natural philosophers. What else remains, for Swift? A keen eye for bullshit, hypocrisy and injustice, since allowances are not made in the name of charity, or history, or circumstances.

Pope wrote,

> And, spite of pride, in erring reason's spite,
> One truth is clear, 'Whatever is, is RIGHT.'

That is not something Swift can really sign up to. He sees too much madness and wrong thinking in the world around him. His work as a government propagandist can be seen as a sell-out of his integrity. But I think the capacity, or compulsion, to argue in any direction, or to play the devil's advocate, is not merely the opportunistic exercise of wit and ingenuity, in Swift's case or anyone else's. It is the result and the penalty of having a sharp intelligence, and the expression of an ambivalence provoked by the knee-jerk certainties that end in ideological bigotry – even if those certainties reflect in exaggerated form what one quietly believes oneself.

Swift is immoderate, a man of intense responses, provoked to towering rage: *saeva ignatio*. Anger is energy, or an energy. There is uncontrollable anger in him, originating in some early outrage one cannot precisely determine. He reports the consequences of immoral actions and the abuse of power, taking all to its logical – and therefore outrageously illogical, and mad – conclusion. (The *Modest Proposal*: if there is too large a population for the supply of food, why not eat the babies?)

Swift is not unique in some of his conflicting qualities. The spiritual harmony of Mozart's music has to be reconciled with the scatology of his letters. Most people shrug their shoulders and get on with muddling through their lives, instinctively doing their best to be clean, civil, reasoning Yahoos. Yet we would not respond to Swift as we do if we did not recognize the conflict in him, which recurs in art because it is intractably there in ourselves. We are what we are.

Swift's black imagination is like that of the Spanish painter Francisco de Goya, who a century after the publication of *Gulliver's Travels* (which he may or may not have read in translation – perhaps he was just told about it) produced something which looks like an illustration for Gulliver in Lilliput – the head of a giant, with a mass of tiny figures climbing all over it with the aid of ladders. Goya, who like Swift suffered from deafness, drew women as witches lighting their braziers using children as bellows, and eating new-born babies. He drew women searching their shifts for fleas and using chamber-pots, he drew bedizened whores, bird-faced harpies, monsters, grotesquely shaped human bodies, enemas, beatings, tortures. He caricatured lewd and gluttonous men, the pillars of Church and state. He painted that great, horrible picture of Saturn bloodily tearing at and devouring his own child.

Swift's effect can be compared too with that of the twentieth-century director Quentin Tarantino in the film *Reservoir Dogs*. Denis Donoghue, the best analyst of Swift's mind and style, has written that 'a mind possessed by paradox is not necessarily brought to a halt, but it is unlikely to move smartly from point A to point B'. Swift's refusal to resolve the conflicting arguments in his narratives seems unsatisfactory to some readers. Joe Orton, for example, who was reading Swift systematically in the 1960s, thought that the scheme of *A Tale of a Tub* was 'clever, but not sufficiently worked out'. But with Tarantino, as with Swift, there is a brutal logic. If 'A', in Tarantino's case, is childish thieving and bullying, then 'B' is horrific adult violence, still childish because its perpetrators are unevolved. Like Swift, Tarantino neither endorses nor condemns. He creates a black entertainment, and leaves it with you.

In Tarantino's film, characters made one-dimensional perform horrific acts like children enacting fantasies. We do not enter their emotional hinterlands, as we do not enter Gulliver's. They are given comic-strip pseudonyms. The only moment of redemption and humanity in *Reservoir Dogs* occurs when two men near death reveal to

one another their own real names. Names are magical. Folk-tales –
Rumpelstiltskin is an example – abound in cases where malign power
is maintained only so long as the tyrant's real name is not spoken.
Swift gave everyone he loved or hated (including himself) pretend
names, distancing and diminishing and infantilizing them. The Earl
of Oxford, when things began to go very wrong, became 'the
Dragon'.

Those who find their validity in the love of God, or in work that fulfils
their aspirations, in the affection of a close companion or in the
(illusory?) security of love may not even notice that the bed is hard or
the bread is stale or a great man offhand. Their priorities are other.
For the man wrapped in the web of pride and solitude, small things
are large, as they were for Swift. Minor snubs and irritations are
major assaults on the citadel of pride and self-protection.

At the flashpoint where a curving line becomes a circle, extremes
meet and revolution becomes Revolution. East becomes West. Day
becomes night. Idealization looks like misanthropy. 'One cannot
hate humanity to that extent unless one has believed in it; one must
have thought man a little lower than the angels before one can
concentrate on the organs of elimination.' Fastidiousness becomes
an obsession with filth. Reason becomes insanity. Chaos, pursued by
mathematics, reveals its rules.

Sir Isaac Newton, the great scientist, built the first reflecting
telescope the year after Swift was born. (He also practised alchemy.)
Swift's protégé George Berkeley, to whom Vanessa left her money,
published his *Essay towards a New Theory of Vision* in 1709. Swift's
Gulliver in Lilliput concealed about his person a pair of spectacles
and a pocket telescope. The spectacles saved his sight from the hails
of tiny arrows from the Blefescu navy. Celia's magnifying glass made
the bogey in her nose enormous. Swift exploited the implications of
contemporary developments in optics, and the surreal absurdities of
magnification and reduction. Joe Orton thought that 'Lilliput and
Brobdingnag amount merely to trick photography.' Since
photography had not been invented, 'merely' may quite fairly be
translated back into the sense in which Swift would have understood
it.

When Swift grew long-sighted and he found it hard to read, he
refused to use his spectacles. He himself is a problem in optics. In the
world upside down, paradox is the norm. Who is to say whose

version or vision is correct? You see what you see. As Orrery understood of Swift, 'you must never look upon him as a traveller in the common road. He must be viewed through a *camera obscura* that turns all objects the contrary way. When he appears most angry, he is most pleased; when most humble, he is most assuming. Such was the man, and in such variegated colours must he be painted.'

Swift sees everything and identifies himself wholly with nothing that he sees, though out of his passion for justice he champions underdogs and out of his insecurities he is pleased to consort with top dogs. He cannot comply, be like other people. They notice this. How can he possibly have expected, while writing as he did, that he would be given a bishopric in Ireland, let alone in England?

Towards the end, he saw his dilemma with clarity: 'My invention & judgement are perpetually at fisty cuffs, till they have quite disabled each other', he wrote to Bolingbroke in 1731.

Like his Gulliver, and like Lewis Carroll's Alice, Swift is always too big or too small for the company he keeps. He longs for the world's rewards but cannot respect the world's rules, and cannot be quiet. Every man, he wrote, ought to 'be content with the possession of his own opinion in private, without perplexing his neighbour or disturbing the public'. He perplexed and he disturbed, and he meant to, and he still does. That's another knot he couldn't disentangle in himself. He urged discretion on Vanessa; but discretion, he wrote elsewhere, is 'a species of lower prudence'.

Swift is out of tune. For there is, he wrote in *A Tale of a Tub*, 'a peculiar string in the harmony of human understanding' which, 'if you can dexterously screw up to its right key and then strike gently upon it, whenever you have the good fortune to light among those of the same pitch they will, by a secret necessary sympathy, strike exactly at the same time'.

But if on the other hand 'you chance to jar the string among those who are either above or below your own height, instead of subscribing to your doctrine they will tie you fast, call you mad, and feed you with bread and water'. He returns to the same thought with yet another image: 'Thus one man, choosing a proper juncture, leaps into a gulf, from thence proceeds a hero and is called the saver of his country; another achieves the same enterprise but, unluckily timing it, has left the brand of madness fixed as a reproach upon his memory.'

There are rents in the web of pride and solitude. The man who feels little but distaste for his family of origin, and who has no children of his own whom he might love, projects the feelings most people have for their families on to institutions, or on to friendships. Swift was quick to combat with verbal savagery and active politicking any threat to the established Church, with which his own relationship was ambivalent. In his later years he identified himself with Ireland, which was where he did not want to be.

As in family relationships, for such a man the lesser personal friends may be abused and exploited, the greater ones idealized. A corresponding intensity is expected from the friends. Unaware of the invisible mantle that has been thrown over them, and immersed in their own concerns, the friends may betray or disappoint, provoking a corresponding reinforcement of disillusion. Swift compiled a list of people he had known, putting beside each name the letters 'u' for ungrateful, or 'g' for grateful. ('Grateful', then, carrying an additional meaning of pleasant and agreeable, as well as of having come up to scratch.)

But to abandon belief in his greatest friendships, which were his friendships with the greatest men, would be to abandon all sense of self-worth. Swift's respectful love – it is not too strong a word – for Oxford and Bolingbroke was sustained to the end. Bolingbroke for one would not have accepted the common perception of Swift as a misanthrope. Touched by Swift's expressions of tender affection for him, Bolingbroke wrote that 'the bitterest satire which can be made on the present age, is this, that to think as you think, will make a man pass for romantick. Sincerity, constancy, tenderness are rarely to be found. They are so much out of use, that the man of mode imagines them to be out of nature.'

Swift did not have for anyone, except perhaps Stella, and for Dr Sheridan before they fell out, the kind of tolerant, amused affection that values a person for, rather in spite of, their failings. Swift valued highly certain individuals. He had no illusions about the generality of the species. He advised Dr Sheridan to 'expect no more from man than such an animal is capable of, and you will every day find my description of Yahoes [*sic*] more resembling. You should think and deal with every man as a villain, without calling him so, or flying from him, or *valuing him less* [my italics]. This is an old true lesson.'

If that is misanthropy, it is the measured misanthropy of Montaigne and la Rochefoucauld, 'who is my favourite because I found my whole character in him'. Swift's friend Pope would not have recognized the common perception of Swift as a misogynist, either. 'Never imagine', Pope wrote to Mrs Whiteway in 1740, 'that I can do otherwise than esteem that sex, which has furnished him [the Dean] with the best friends.'

Swift had 'normal', affectionate, concerned friendships with several women who have been squeezed out of these pages. One example is Mrs Barber, a member of the Deanery circle, whose small literary talent he fostered. A letter she wrote to him from Bath in 1736 suggests that he was encouraging her to return to Dublin; she thanked him for his kindness in 'generously offering to support me there'. She felt she should support herself, and rejected his plan: 'I need not tell you that I am not able to pursue the scheme of *letting lodgings*. Your goodness and compassion for my unhappy state of health has made you think of it for me; 'tis impracticable.' What she really wanted, she said, was a present of his manuscript of the unpublished satire *Polite Conversation* 'and a few of your original poems', to sell to a printer for publication. All this, generously, he let her have.

With women who were closer to him, the permafrost of the emotions was maintained. A thaw cannot be risked. No one must have power over him – the power to melt self-possession, the power to hurt. Vanessa's frank display of desire is less alluring to him – because so obvious an assault on the walled citadel – than Stella's patience. As a defence against naked emotion from either, he becomes the minatory schoolmaster. Nakedness of any kind is to be fled from.

A man like this would have to be smoothed and soothed into unselfconsciousness and self-abandon. But some men will never be sufficiently soothed, and there never was a man quite like Swift.

The only possible emotional outlets are limited, unthreatening ones with powerless and submissive women, such as Stella, who was and remained his dear pupil; or superficially flirtatious friendships with other men's wives or with politically influential women; or with the women of minor attractions and talents with whom he passed his time, and whom he made his pets, in Dublin. With all of them he was often an emotional bully, through a mixture of deflected desire, and contempt, and self-contempt.

He comes at some semblance of intimacy from the opposite and negative direction, through insults and 'la bagatelle'. When he plays, he plays like a little boy. His sense of humour can be completely puerile. Irvin Ehrenpreis rightly stresses what he calls Swift's 'prankishness'. He is prankish even when he is most serious. In his intolerance of the foolishness, corruption and hypocrisy of the great world, he is the child in the story whose clear voice announces to the deferential populace the thing that everyone knows but no one says: the emperor is wearing no clothes. Genius which does not retain something of the anarchic misrule of play is only talent.

Literary theoreticians are comfortable with talent – so gratifying to deconstruct – and often reductionist in the face of genius. 'But I know not how it comes to pass', wrote Swift, 'that professors in most arts and sciences are generally the worst qualified to explain their meanings to those who are not of their tribe.' General readers respond without preconceptions, and are unafraid of rejecting canonical reputations. 'I'm inclined to think', Joe Orton wrote in his diary, 'that the main fascination of Swift (as with Dylan Thomas, Brendan Behan and many other writers and artists) is with his life.' Maybe. But if it were not for the work, none of those three would have had the lives that they did.

Swift's intensity is channelled into words, words, words, and always to a purpose. His work is his own monument. His mythologized personality is the world's monument to him. Thomas Harley, a cousin of Lord Oxford, told him in 1714 that he had 'formed a new character which no one is vain enough to pretend to imitate'.

A deeper, silent refuge was his depression and impatient ill-humour. There is reason for this, in his physical illness – his recurrent deafness, giddiness and nausea – though the illness may have been exacerbated by the distortions of his emotional life. We may think an understanding of psychosomatic illness to be, in the West, a post-Freudian development. We are only retrieving something previously understood. Sir William Temple reported talking to a physician who told him that 'in the fanatick times' of the seventeenth century he found his patients so emotionally disturbed that he 'had to play the divine with them before he could begin the physician'. For 'divine' (clergyman), read today's psychiatrist or counsellor. Sickness was not just a bodily ailment. 'A disappointed hope, a blot of honour, a strain of conscience, an unfortunate love, an aching jealousy, a repining grief, will service the turn, and all alike.' Swift is subject to most if not all of these misfortunes.

Locked within himself, he loves no one more than himself. Therefore he is that rare thing, a just man, unswayed by the alluring refuge of private happiness, or the overwhelming value to him of any other human being. There is a point on the circle where justice meets mercilessness and the two become terrifyingly indistinguishable.

For many women, whose psychic and physical boundaries tend to be diffuse, most men seem astonishingly, even enviably, self-centred. I mean 'self-centred' to be taken literally, and not as a synonym for selfish or inconsiderate. At a time when obsessional romantic love was hardly yet a gleam in any young poet's eye, still less the modern notion of 'sharing', Swift's walled-in self-centredness hardened, unchecked. Out of this centre poured his polemics, out of this centre his imagination blackly flowered, his ambition grew and was thwarted by the world's rules. But he turned his disappointment and anger to useful ends:

> The same ambition can destroy or save,
> And make a patriot as it makes a knave.

His pride protected him from furthering his ambition by unworthy means. In an age when corruption was endemic and expected, his worst enemies never accused him of that fault. Orrery, quick to point out Swift's shortcomings, said he was 'above corruption', and that was 'a virtue in itself sufficient to cover a multitude of human failings'.

Swift does not love himself. But himself – adamantine, *mere* – is all that there is. He has no idea of curbing his behaviour, his expressions or his opinions. He cannot function in deference or reference to others. He is Jonathan Swift.

One day during the sad last months – it was Sunday 17 March 1744 – sitting in his chair, he put out his hand to snatch at a knife lying on the table. Anne Ridgeway moved it out of his reach. He shrugged his shoulders, and rocked himself, and said, 'I am what I am.' He repeated the words. 'I am what I am. I am what I am.'

CHRONOLOGY

1664	Jonathan Swift (senior) marries Abigail Erick.
1666	Jane Swift born.
1667	Jonathan Swift (senior) dies – before April, but date unknown. JONATHAN SWIFT born (30 November).
1669	Swift taken by his nurse to Whitehaven in Cumbria for ? three years.
1673	Swift goes to board at Kilkenny School.
1677	Sir John Temple dies.
1681	Esther Johnson (Stella) born.
1682	Swift enters Trinity College, Dublin.
1685	John Gay born.
1686	Swift graduates BA.
1688	Hester Vanhomrigh (Vanessa) born. Alexander Pope born.
1689	Protestant monarchs William of Orange and his wife Mary crowned in London. The deposed Catholic King James II flees to France. Swift leaves Ireland because of the Troubles consequent to James II's attempt to regain his crown by first reclaiming Ireland. Swift goes to his mother in Leicester and then into the employ of Sir William Temple, in whose house at West Sheen he meets Esther Johnson (Stella), then eight years old.
1690	Swift returns to Ireland. William III's forces definitively defeat James II's at the Battle of the Boyne in Co. Meath.
1691	Swift returns to England and to the Temple household, now at Moor Park. His first work in print: 'Ode to the Athenian Society'.

1692   Swift obtains his MA from Hart Hall, Oxford, after a short period in residence.

1694   Swift goes back to Ireland to take holy orders. Ordained deacon.

1695   Swift ordained priest and appointed to the parish of Kilroot in Co. Antrim. Becomes involved with Jane Waring (Varina). Uncle Godwin Swift dies. In England, Lady Temple dies.

1696   Swift proposes marriage to Varina. She prevaricates. Swift returns to Sir William Temple at Moor Park.

1699   Sir William Temple dies (January). Swift returns to Dublin in August as chaplain to the Earl of Berkeley.

1700   Swift becomes vicar of Laracor in Co. Meath and prebendary of St Patrick's Cathedral in Dublin. Relationship with Varina petering out.

1701   Swift visits England and publishes his first political pamphlet. Stella and Rebecca Dingley come over to live in Ireland.

1702   Death of William III and accession of Queen Anne. War declared by England and her allies on France and Spain. Swift takes degree of Doctor of Divinity at Trinity College, Dublin; is henceforth known as Dr Swift.

1704   Swift's *Tale of a Tub* and *Battle of the Books* published. He visits England. Robert Harley is in the Cabinet as Secretary of State and Henry St John as Secretary-at-War. (Swift does not meet them yet.) The Captain-General the Duke of Marlborough triumphs at the Battle of Blenheim.

1705   British general election leaves Whigs and Tories roughly equal in House of Commons.

1706   Victory of the Allies at Ramillies.

1707   Bad defeat for the Allies in Spain. Tory attacks on the conduct and cost of the war begin in Parliament. Swift returns to England with commission from Anglican Irish bishops to seek remission of the 'First Fruits' tax from Queen Anne. Swift becomes friendly with Addison and Steele, and publishes *Bickerstaff Papers* and tracts on church and state topics.

1708   Harley and St John resign from the Cabinet. General election, with clear majority for the Whigs. Whig 'Junto' under Lord Godolphin dominates the Cabinet.

1709   Swift in Ireland, at Laracor.

1710   Swift's mother Abigail (Erick) Swift dies (April). In September, Swift returns to England. Whig lords dismissed by Queen Anne. Landslide victory for Tories in general election. Swift meets Robert Harley, head of the new Tory government, and is taken up by him. Swift begins to write the *Examiner* in the Tory interest, and against continuance of the war with France. Swift begins to write diary-letters to Stella (*Journal to Stella*) and to visit Hester Vanhomrigh (Vanessa).

1711   Assassination attempt on Robert Harley (March). In May, Harley created Earl of Oxford and Lord Treasurer. Swift writing in support of the ministry, notably *The Conduct of the Allies*. His intimacy with Lord Oxford (Harley) growing. Twelve new Tory peers created in order to get peace proposals through the Lords (December). Duke of Marlborough dismissed. Bridget Johnson (Stella's mother) marries Ralph Mose.

1712   Swift's propaganda writing continues, notably *Some Remarks on the Barrier Treaty*. Lord Oxford's peace policy endorsed by Parliament, but Lord Oxford and Henry St John getting on badly. Swift getting to know Pope, Gay and Arbuthnot and quickly establishing with them convivial friendship and literary collaboration.

1713   Peace of Utrecht signed (March). Henry St John created Viscount Bolingbroke. In June, Swift returns to Dublin to be installed as Dean of St Patrick's. By September, Swift back in London vainly trying to reconcile Lords Oxford and Bolingbroke, who struggle for control of the ministry and are suspected by Steele and others of Jacobite sympathies.

1714   Swift publishes *The Public Spirit of the Whigs* and is threatened with prosecution. Cabinet split and personal antagonism between Lords Oxford and Bolingbroke now terminal. Swift takes refuge at Letcombe Bassett in June. His relationship with Vanessa fraught and intense. On 1 August, Queen Anne dies. Elector of Hanover proclaimed George I. Sir Robert Walpole heads his first Whig administration. Swift returns to Dublin to take up his duties as Dean. Vanessa follows him to Ireland.

1716 Swift's alleged marriage to Stella.

1718 Swift's close friendships with Dr Thomas Sheridan and Dr Patrick Delany established.

1720 Swift becomes involved in Irish politics with the publication of *A Proposal for the Universal Use of Irish Manufacture*. Archbishop William King dies.

1722 Lady (Martha) Giffard dies.

1723 Vanessa dies. Swift takes himself off on a tour of south and west Ireland.

1724 Publication of Swift's *The Drapier's Letters*, protesting against the introduction of Wood's Halfpence. Lord Oxford (Robert Harley) dies.

1725 Wood's Halfpence cancelled and Swift becomes celebrated as an Irish patriot.

1726 Swift visits London, taking with him manuscript of *Gulliver's Travels*, published this year. He also sees Walpole over Irish matters. Swift's *Cadenus and Vanessa* published. Stella is seriously ill.

1727 Swift's last visit to England. Death of George I, accession of his son George II.

1728 Stella dies (28 January). Swift's first visit to the Achesons at Markethill. Writes *The Intelligencer* with Dr Sheridan. The circle of female friends at the Deanery established.

1729 Second long visit to Markethill. *A Modest Proposal* published.

1730 Third and last long visit to Markethill.

1731 Swift writing poetry, including the scatological poems and *Verses on the Death of Dr Swift*.

1732 John Gay dies.

1733 Swift writing and publishing poetry including *On Poetry, a Rapsody*.

1735 Dr John Arbuthnot dies.

1736 Swift writes *The Legion Club* against the agriculture policies of the Irish House of Commons.

1738   Dr Thomas Sheridan dies.

1742   Swift found to be of unsound mind by a Commission of
        Lunacy.

1743   Rebecca Dingley dies. Bridget Johnson dies.

1744   Alexander Pope dies.

1745   JONATHAN SWIFT dies (19 October).

Trainspotting

NOTES AND SOURCES

S WIFT BIOGRAPHIES: The first and chief sources for Jonathan Swift's life are the biographical writings of those who knew him, and, in the next generation, of those writers who knew Swift's surviving friends or family, or had access to their relicts and immediate descendants:

Memoirs of Mrs Letitia Pilkington, Written by Herself, 3 vols 1748–1754; edited in 2 vols by A. C. Elias as *Memoirs of Laetitia Pilkington*, 1997.

Orrery, 5th Earl of (John Boyle), *Remarks on the Life and Writings of Dr Jonathan Swift*, 1752.

Patrick Delany, *Observations upon Lord Orrery's Remarks on the Life and Writings of Dr Jonathan Swift*, 1754.

Deane Swift, *An Essay upon the Life, Writings and Character of Dr Jonathan Swift*, 1755.

John Hawkesworth, *Life of Dr Jonathan Swift*, 1755 (originally the first volume of Hawkesworth's edition of Swift's correspondence, 1741).

Samuel Johnson, *Lives of the English Poets*, 1779.

Thomas Sheridan, *The Life of the Rev Dr Jonathan Swift, Dean of St Patrick's, Dublin*, 1784.

Sir Walter Scott, *Memoirs of Dr Jonathan Swift*, 1814 (the first volume of his 19-vol. edition of the works and correspondence).

Unless otherwise indicated, quotations in the text from these writers are from the books cited above.

The most important subsequent biographical works are:

John Forster, *Life of Swift* (first volume only), 1876.

Leslie Stephen, *Swift*, 1882.

Henry Craik, *The Life of Jonathan Swift*, 1894 (2nd ed.).

Stephen Gwynn, *The Life and Friendships of Dean Swift*, 1933.

John Middleton Murry, *Jonathan Swift: A Critical Biography*, 1954.

Denis Johnston, *In Search of Swift*, 1959.

Irvin Ehrenpreis, *Swift, the Man, his Works, and the Age*, 3 vols 1962, 1967, 1983. (This is the 'standard biography'.)

A. L. Rowse, *Jonathan Swift, Major Prophet*, 1975.

David Nokes, *Jonathan Swift, A Hypocrite Reversed: A Critical Biography*, 1985.

Other authorities are acknowledged in the notes, which have been kept to the minimum and are intended for the general reader. Wherever it is convenient, sources are indicated in the text. The list of books at the head of the notes to some chapters may be of use for further reading as well as to indicate sources for the text.

With the exception of his letters to Stella from England, all quotations in the text from letters both from and to Swift (including Vanessa's drafts), and all correspondence between his friends, unless otherwise indicated, are from *The Correspondence of Jonathan Swift*, ed. Harold Williams, 5 vols, 1963–5.

Swift's letters to Stella from England 1710–1713, collected under the title *Journal to Stella*, are most conveniently read in the 2-vol. annotated edition by Harold Williams, 1948.

Swift's poems, plus those attributed to Stella and Vanessa, and Swift-related verses by Dr Thomas Sheridan, Patrick Delany, Jonathan Smedley and other contemporaries, are collected in *The Poems of Jonathan Swift*, ed. Harold Williams, 3 vols, 1958. Verse quotations are from this source unless otherwise indicated. A good though not comprehensive single-volume edition of the poems is *Swift: Poetical Works*, ed. Herbert Davis, 1967. At the time of writing, a 'hypertext' of Swift's poems is in preparation.

Swift's surviving account books, all but one in the Forster

Collection at the V&A, are published as *The Account Books of Jonathan Swift*, ed. Paul V. Thompson and Dorothy Jay Thompson, 1984.

There are numerous collections and editions of Swift's prose writings, which as well as the major works and his political, religious and historical writings comprise sermons, prayers, pamphlets, ephemera, memos, 'characters', and rough notes. They can most conveniently and comprehensively be studied in *The Prose Works of Jonathan Swift*, ed. Harold Williams, 14 vols, 1939–1968. I happened to use *The Prose Works of Jonathan Swift, D.D.*, ed. Temple Scott, 12 vols, revised ed. 1902–1911, with the bookplates of the old Kildare Street Club in Dublin. I bought the set from the Bantry Bookshop in West Cork early in my research, and became attached to it.

Chapter One: Beginning

2   'always just round the next corner': W. B. Yeats, preface to 'Words upon the Window Pane', in *Wheels and Butterflies*, 1934.

4   in which we could meet and be alone': Elizabeth Bowen, *Bowen's Court*, 1942.

5   'One young woman . . . "pure affection"': Laetitia Pilkington. Stories of Swift's babyhood are complicated by the fact that 'the cradle of Jonathan Swift' is in the parish church of Brede, in Sussex, purchased at a local sale by a former rector.

6   'all my future disappointments': JS to Bolingbroke and Pope, 5 April 1729.

7   'nothing but the name': Stephen Gwynn, op. cit.

8   'into easy-going verse': Leslie Stephen, op. cit.

8   '. . . in too literal a sense': JS, 'The Sentiments of a Church of England Man, with respect to Religion and Government'.

     'incoherent piece of patchwork': JS, 'A Letter to a Young Clergyman, lately entered into Holy Orders'.

9   'If nam'd with scorn, gives just offence': JS, 'To Mr Delany'.

     'Yet still was at the tables of the great': JS, 'The Author Upon Himself', written 1714.

10   'only some of the most remarkable': quoted in Bishop Gilbert Burnet, *History of His Own Time*, 2 vols, 1724 and 1734. Available in Everyman's Library edition.

14   'of flattery and cringing': JS, 'Considerations upon Two Bills
      . . . relating to the Clergy of Ireland', 1732.

Chapter Two: Young

Principal sources for this chapter:

William Wilde, *The Closing Years of Dean Swift's Life*, 2nd edn 1849
·Maurice Craig, *Dublin 1660–1860*, 1952.
R. F. Foster, *Modern Ireland 1600–1972*, 1988.
Irvin Ehrenpreis op. cit. vol I.
John Nichols, *The History and Antiquities of the County of Leicester*, 1898.
Leicestershire Record Office: *Transactions* of the Leics. Architectural
    and Archaeological Society; Parish Records, Registers of
    Freemen.
Victoria History of the County of Leicestershire, 1954–5.

19   'chiefly in Co. Carlow': see Jimmy O'Toole, *The Carlow Gentry*,
      privately printed 1993.

23   '. . . with this iron project': JS, 'On Barbarous Denominations
      in Ireland'.

      'to his family and friends': Deane Swift, op. cit.

24   'village of Wigston Magna': Denis Johnston, *In Search of Swift*,
      1959.

25   'John Nichols, a local historian': op. cit. Nichols was also a
      printer and a man of letters, the editor of the *Gentleman's
      Magazine* and of volumes of anecdotes.

29   'A list, compiled by himself': in his account book, which he
      used also as a memo book and sometimes as a diary.

32   'We have a description of Jane': from Deane Swift.

Chapter Three: Temples

Principal background sources for the Temples, in this chapter and
subsequently:

Sir William Temple, *Miscellanea*, 1680, 1692, 1701.
Richard Faber, *The Brave Courtier: Sir William Temple*, 1983.
Julia Longe, *Martha Giffard, Her Life and Correspondence*, 1911.

John Cloake, *Palaces and Parks of Richmond and Kew* Vol. II, 1996.
Temple Prime, *Some Account of the Temple Family* 3rd edn 1896.
A. C. Elias, *Swift at Moor Park*, 1982.

Additional sources:

Lord Macaulay, *History of England*, 4 vols, 1848–61.
Simon Schama, *The Embarrassment of Riches: An Interpretation of Dutch Culture in the Golden Age*, 1987.

34   'Her letters to him have been published': *The Osborne Letters*, ed. G. C. Moore Smith, 1928.

35   '. . . I believe will not part with it': Temple Prime, op. cit.

36   'as quietly and innocently as I can': Sir William Temple to his father Sir John, Sept 1671.

38   'about forty cherries': Sir William Temple, 'Of Health and Long Life'.

      'little balls with fresh butter': idem.

40   'against truth only a little while': Samuel Johnson, *Lives of the English Poets*.

      'practising moderation in a garden': Cyril Connolly, *Horizon*, February 1935.

41   'looks kindly upon every body that comes in': Sir William Temple, 'Heads designed for an Essay on Conversation'.

      'had nearly killed him': Earl of Rochester to his brother Lord Clarendon, quoted in Faber, op. cit.

42   'due by her before our marriage': Temple Prime, op. cit.

      'peaceful, wise and great': JS, ode 'Occasioned by Sir William Temple's Late Illness and Recovery', written 1693.

43   'France against England': Sir William Temple, 'A Survey of the Constitutions and Interests of European States'.

45   'like the plagues of Egypt': Keith Feiling, *History of the Tory Party 1640–1714*, 1924.

46   'male and female': Bishop Burnet, in *History of His Own Time*, wrote that King William 'had no vice, but of one sort, in which he was very cautious and secret'. Swift wrote in pencil in the margin of John Lyon's copy: 'it was of two sorts, male and female, in the former he was neither cautious nor secret'.

49   'who suffered a good deal from the gout': Desmond Clarke, *Arthur Dobbs Esquire 1689–1765*, 1957.

50   'or a papist': ibid.

'no long time to determine': JS, 'A Letter concerning the Sacramental Test'.

51   'partition between us': *The Orrery Papers*, ed. Emily Charlotte Boyle, Countess of Cork and Orrery, 2 vols, 1903.

Chapter Four: The Ladies

54   'he had been excluded': Macaulay, op. cit.

55   'honest man in the kingdom': JS to Thomas Tickell (Chief Secretary in Ireland) 18 Sept 1725.

'height of her ambition': Lange, op. cit.

'superiors to countenance': quoted in Elias, *Swift at Moor Park*.

57   'alter them a hundred times': JS to Thomas Swift 1691.

'extraordinary at fifteen': JS, 'A letter Concerning the Sacramental Test'.

58   'to take care of him': Sir William Temple to Sir Robert Southwell, Secretary of State for Ireland, 29 May 1690. Forster Collection, V&A.

59   'openness of my nature': Sir William Temple, *Memoirs* III, 1709.

60   'any of his good qualities': Lange, op. cit.

'either of honour or religion': idem.

62   'and I always take his part': JS, 'The Humble Petition of Frances Harris', written 1700.

63   'the happy composition, Floyd': JS, 'To Mrs Biddy Floyd', 1708.

Chapter Five: Questions

Chief background sources for this chapter:

The London Encyclopaedia, ed. Ben Weinreb and Christopher Hibbert, revised edn 1993.

Eighteenth Century English Literature: Modern Essays in Criticism, ed. James Clifford, 1959.

From Dryden to Johnson, vol. 4 of the New Pelican Guide to English
  Literature, ed. Boris Ford, revised edn 1991.
David Piper, *The English Face*, 1992.
Mairead Dunleavy, *Dress in Ireland*, 1989.

69   'With Swift came the voice': Elizabeth Bowen, review of Brian
      Fitzgerald, *The Anglo-Irish* (1952) in *The Mulberry Tree: Writings of
      Elizabeth Bowen*, ed. Hermione Lee, 1986.

      'although of English parents': JS, 'On Barbarous Denomi-
      nations in Ireland'.

72   'in their proper pitch': Thomas Sheridan, *A Course of Lectures on
      Elocution*, 1762.

      'perspicuous pronunciation, Sir': quoted in Fintan O'Toole, *A
      Traitor's Kiss: The Life of Richard Brinsley Sheridan*, 1997.

      'to us, irretrievable': the word 'irretrievable', used by Roy
      Foster, concluded a private discussion about Swift's accent.

73   'crammed into his mouth': Thomas Sheridan, *Intelligencer* no.
      XIII, October 1728. See *Jonathan Swift and Thomas Sheridan: The
      Intelligencer*, ed. James Woolley, 1992.

      'a particular easy smile': Joseph Spence, *Observations, Anecdotes
      and Characters of Books and Men* (mss compiled 1728–44), ed.
      J. M. Osborn, 2 vols, 1966. Commonly referred to as 'Spence's
      Anecdotes'.

75   'in the search of truth': Francis Atterbury, 'A Scorner
      Incapable of true Wisdom', *Fourteen Sermons*, 1708.

      'but ne'er so well expressed': Pope, 'An Essay on Criticism'.

      'what it hurts with wit': Pope, 'The First Epistle of the Second
      Book of Horace Imitated'.

      'for one that hits': JS, 'On Poetry, a Rapsody'.

76   'funnier, but feared': Alistair Cook, 'Letter from America',
      BBC Radio 4, 26 April 1996.

      'the greatest fools': *The Female Tatler*, ed. Fidelis Morgan,
      Everyman Library, 1992.

77   'Instructing Members how to vote': JS, 'On Poetry, a
      Rapsody'. Swift used a classical pseudonym ('Battus') for
      Dryden, in the second line quoted.

78   'in any other man': Spence's *Anecdotes*.

79   'each of them me and each other': *Journal to Stella*.

81   'a wild work': Samuel Johnson, *Lives of the English Poets.*

82   'an exceeding agreeable mouth': quoted in John Hawkesworth, *Life.*

      'hard as a hog's bristles': John Lyon, note in Hawkesworth's *Life*, Forster Collection, V&A.

83   'an uncommon archness in them': Spence, op. cit.

84   'Swift ... dreaded the rain': 'The wig is wet' was a catch-phrase for the young Fanny Burney (born 1752) and her siblings, signifying 'It can't be helped'. See Kate Chisholm, *Fanny Burney: her Life*, 1998.

86   'the life of a spider': JS, 'Thoughts on Various Subjects'.

87   'with indefatigable pains': JS, *Tale of a Tub.*

Chapter Six: Teapot

Principal background sources for this chapter, for Chapter 7, and the political story as it subsequently unfolds:

Paul McQuail, 'Swift and the Politicians 1710–1714' (private paper, unpublished, 1997).
Keith Feiling, *The History of the Tory Party 1640–1714*, 1924.
Michael Foot, *The Pen and the Sword*, 1957.
Geoffrey Holmes, *British Politics in the Reign of Queen Anne*, 1957.
John Kenyon, *The Stuarts*, 1958.
J. H. Plumb, *The Growth of Political Stability in England 1675–1725*, 1967.
J. A. Downie, *Robert Harley and the Press*, 1979.
Edward Gregg, *Queen Anne*, 1980.
Pat Rogers, *Hacks and Dunces: Pope, Swift and Grub Street*, 1980.
Brian Hill, *Robert Harley, Speaker, Secretary of State and Premier Minister*, 1988.
Geoffrey Holmes, *The Making of a Great Power 1660–1722*, 1993.

88   'Dr White Kennett...': Given as an Appendix in *Correspondence of Jonathan Swift* vol. 5.

89   'even a teapot to convey': Anthony Trollope, *Travelling Sketches*, 1866.

91   'entirely approve of either': JS to Archbishop King.

92   'unbias his mind as much as possible': JS, 'The Sentiments of

a Church of England Man . . .'.

'all good and ill qualities are included': JS, idem.

'a venomous, vulgar-minded woman': Sir Charles Petrie, *The Jacobite Movement*, 1959.

93   'shifting the Queen': this procedure is described by Swift's later friend Henrietta Howard, Countess of Suffolk, in *Letters of Henrietta Countess of Suffolk*, 1824.

94   'vice serviceable to the cause of virtue': Spence's *Anecdotes*.

Chapter Seven: Public

Principal sources for this chapter, additional to those listed for Chapter 6:

Ian Hamilton, *Keepers of the Flame*, 1992.
Maynard Mack, *Alexander Pope*, 1985.
David Nokes, *John Gay: A Profession of Friendship*, 1995.
John M. Beattie, *The English Court in the Reign of George I*, 1967.
And, *passim*, the *Journal to Stella*. Swift's accounts of his activities, where not otherwise indicated, are from this source.

100   'wrap them together in a paper': John Lyon's letter is in John Forster's copy of Hawkesworth's biographical first volume of his edition of Swift's correspondence (1741), now in the V&A. Forster compiled an impressive archive of Swiftiana for the biography he never completed. The Hawkesworth volume has the bookplate of Sir Arthur Acheson (see Chapter 10), and is packed with eighteenth-century annotations, notes, memos and letters.

'not many of his genius': McQuail, op. cit.

102   'weasel-toothed, sharp-sighted Robin Harley': Kenyon, op. cit.

104   'before or since': David Lloyd George, Liberal Prime Minister 1816–1922, had the idea of creating five hundred new peers in an attempt to reform the hereditary House of Lords, but did not do it. Labour Prime Minister Tony Blair, in August 1997, created 41 'working' peers, of which 31 took the Labour Whip – but to balance the parties in the House of Lords, not to facilitate the passing of a particular measure.

106 'the thoroughbred levee-haunter': Lady Mary Wortley Montagu, *Essays and Poems*, ed. Halsband and Grundy, 1977.

107 'And so proceed *ad infinitum*': JS, 'On Poetry, a Rapsody'.

111 'and Secretary for Jamaica': the public offices held by men of letters are usefully listed by W. M. Thackerary in *The English Humourists of the Eighteenth Century*, 1853.

115 'employed in public affairs': JS, 'An Enquiry into the Behaviour of the Queen's last Ministry'.

116 'to make any new experiments': Sir William Temple, *Memoirs* III, 1709.

117 'Whose chariot's that upon the road?': JS, 'Horace, Lib.2 Sat.6 [Book 2, Satire 6], Part of it imitated', written 1714.

Chapter Eight: Private

Principal additional background sources for this chapter:

Sybil le Brocquy, *Cadenus*, 1962.
Denis Johnston, *In Search of Swift*, 1959.

121 'the most morbid of his writings': Cyril Connolly, *Horizon*, February 1935.

'brightened as they saw them': Frederick Ryland, introduction to *Journal to Stella*, ed. Temple Scott, 1908.

130 'a more delightful spectacle': *The Complete Letters of Lady Mary Wortley Montagu*, ed. Robert Halsband, 1966.

131 'I think it plain he lay with her': Horace Walpole to Lady Mary Wortley Montagu, 1766, quoted in *The Correspondence of Jonathan Swift* vol. II.

'Raptur'd he lies': Lady Mary Wortley Montagu, *Essays and Poems*.

'I could scarce have forgot it': Spence's *Anecdotes*.

'exaggerated teasing style of gallantry': Maynard Mack, *Alexander Pope*.

132 'and praise shall last!': Pope, 'Lines on Coffee'.

'prolong the rich repast': Pope, *The Rape of the Lock*, Canto III.

133 'senior clerical appointments': Swift had also hoped strongly for a secular appointment, as Historiographer Royal, and

pressed his case relentlessly with Lord Oxford. The post, which was in the gift of the Lord Chamberlain, the Earl of Shrewsbury, was given to Thomas Madox.

Chapter Nine: Deanery

Principal additional sources for this chapter:

Harold Williams, *Dean Swift's Library*, 1932.
Louis A. Landa, *Swift and the Church of Ireland*, 1954.
H. J. Lawlor, 'The Deaneries of St Patrick's', *Proceedings of the Royal Society of Antiquaries of Ireland*, 1932.
As By Law Established: The Church of Ireland since the Reformation, eds A. Ford, J. McGuire and K. Milne, 1995.

140   'at present as things stand': JS to Knightley Chetwode, 20 October 1714.

142   'Without a tear will tend my hearse': JS, 'In Sickness, Written soon after the author's coming to live in Ireland . . .', October 1714.

     'Of land set out to make a wood': JS, 'Horace Lib.2 Sat.6 [Book 2, Satire 6], Part of it imitated'.

145   'This day month I had clean sheets': *An Hue and Cry after Dr S–––t*, 'occasioned by a True and exact Copy of Part of his own Diary, found in his Pocket-Book, wherein he has set down a faithful Account of himself, and of all that happened to him for the last week of his life'; this pamphlet (1715) is the third printing of the 'diary', and includes Smedley's verses which were fastened to the gate of St Patrick's Cathedral on the day of Swift's installation, plus 'Dr S––––s real Diary . . . His entire Journal, from the Time he left London, to his settling in Dublin': another comic pastiche.

147   'an awkward way of address to ladies': King to JS, 16 February 1712.

149   'the Grameen Bank in Bangladesh': for a fuller account see interview with Muhammad Yunus, *The Bangladesh Times*, 28 February 1997.

150   'His new book on polygamy': Patrick Delany, *Reflections upon Polygamy*. In his second edition, 1739, he refuted criticism by

claiming that although polygamy had been abolished by Christianity, 'how long it may continue so, under the present increase of infidelity and licentiousness, is not easy to pronounce'.

Orrery's letter to Mrs Barber is from *The Orrery Papers*.

150   'from one place to another' and 'like reasonable creatures': vol. I of *The Autobiography and Correspondence of Mary Granville, Mrs Delany*, ed. Lady Llanover, 6 vols 1861–2.

Chapter Ten: Cuckoo and Patriot

Additional sources for this chapter:

Joseph McMinn, *Jonathan's Travels*, 1994.
Daniel Corkery, *The Hidden Ireland*, 1924.
Vivien Mercier, 'Swift and the Gaelic Tradition', *Review of English Literature*, July 1962, and reprinted in *Fair Liberty was all his Cry*, ed. A. Norman Jeffares, 1967.
S. J. Connolly, *Religion, Law, and Power: the Making of Protestant Ireland 1660–1760*, 1992.

155   'in a friend, or in his house': William Temple, 'Heads designed for an Essay on Conversation'.

156   'As if I were a darling child': JS, 'A Panegyrick on the D———n, in the Person of a Lady in the North', written 1730.

157   'Like the tusk of a boar': JS, 'My Lady's Lamentation and Complaint against the Dean', 28 July 1728.

'Tho not a soul would have him stay': JS, 'Lady Acheson Weary of the Dean'.

158   'And leaves a lifeless corpse behind': JS, 'The Dean's Reasons for not Building at Drapier's Hill'.

'green notebook . . . and one that has never been published': the unpublished poem in the green notebook (in private hands), 'An excellent new Panegyrick on Skinnibonia August 12, 1728', does not differ in kind from the other Markethill poems, though cruder.

159   'the dirtiest place I ever saw': JS to Mrs Whiteway, 8 November 1735.

160 'and never entered it again': this story is retailed by Thomas Sheridan the younger.

161 'and generally illiterate': JS, 'The Character of an Irish Squire'.

'those abominable sounds': JS, 'On Barbarous Denominations in Ireland'.

162 'and reads off a page perfectly': this story is told in Corkery's *The Hidden Ireland*, an inspired, inspiring but over-romantic book, unreliable in some of its emphases.

164 'He learns their Irish tongue to gabble': Dr Thomas Sheridan, 'To the Dean of St Patrick's'.

'Irish crept into *Gulliver*': I am indebted for this information to Fintan O'Toole, *The Traitor's Kiss*, 1997.

165 'or flay them and sell their skins': Archbishop William King, 'Some Observations on the Taxes pay'd by Ireland to support the Government', ms in Trinity College Dublin and printed by James Woolley in *Jonathan Swift and Thomas Sheridan: The Intelligencer*, 1992.

166 'working from the feet up': a scene reported by Fynes Moryson in *An Itinerary . . . of ten years' travel through twelve European countries*, 1617, and reproduced by James Woolley, op. cit.

171 'lines of religion and class': S. J. Connolly, op. cit.

172 'his cantankerous genius': Terence de Vere White, *The Anglo-Irish*, 1972. Note also Elizabeth Bowen: 'To burn for Ireland is not to burn for truth: Swift never buried for Ireland the quality that he had.' (Review of Elizabeth Longford, *A Biography of Dublin*, in *The Mulberry Tree*.)

Chapter Eleven: Horse Sense

Gulliver's Travels is available in the Penguin World Classics series.

174 'an honest blockhead': Lady Mary Wortley Montagu, *Essays and Poems*.

'to hang on a watch-chain': quoted by Marianne Bruce and Ernest Frankl, *London Parks and Gardens*, 1986.

175 'in the sense they report him': JS to Thomas Tickell, Secretary of State for Ireland, 16 April 1726. A pamphlet about the 'wild boy', *It Cannot Rain but it Pours; or, London Strow'd with Rarities*,

was a satire on the Court, and probably by Swift. Another, *The Most Wonderful Wonder that ever Appeared to the Wonder of the British Nation* may have been a collaboration between Swift and Arbuthnot. *See* Mary Medlicott, *Wild Children*, 1998.

'because I knew she would tell him': JS to James Stopford, 20 July 1926.

182   'notions of "Terra Australis Incognita"': see W. T. James, 'Nostalgia for Paradise: Terra Australis in the Seventeenth Century', *Australia and the European Imagination*, ed. Ian Donaldson, 1982.

'translating down': Denis Donoghue, *Swift: A Critical Introduction*, 1969.

186   'inhumanity of their own kind': JS, 'Further Thoughts on Religion'.

'or that it never had a beginning': JS, 'Thoughts on Religion'.

'angry for being disappointed': JS to Bolingbroke.

188   'and reflect upon the ministry': JS, 'An Argument Against Abolishing Christianity'.

'to display their abilities': JS, idem.

'ruin to preferment or pretensions': JS, 'A Project for the Advancement of Religion and the Reformation of Manners'.

'opinions commonly received': JS, 'Mr Collins's Discourse of Freethinking; put into Plain English, by Way of Abstract, for the Use of the Poor'.

191   'Surprised by joy – impatient as the wind': William Wordsworth, first line of sonnet 'Desideria'.

Chapter Twelve: Death of Love

193   'Which gently warms, but cannot burn': a poem by Stevie Smith, 'Francesca in Winter', echoes the spirit and phrasing of parts of *Cadenus and Vanessa* so strongly that she must have been reading Swift around the time she wrote it.

195   'their love-child': see Sybil le Brocquy, *Cadenus* and *Swift's Most Valuable Friend*.

203   'to cure an ill head': JS to Robert Cope, 1 June 1723.

'Anecdote and folklore': Joseph McMinn, in *Jonathan's Travels*

(1994), which traces Swift's Irish journey as closely as is possible. See also P. J. Kavanagh, *Voices in Ireland*, 1994.

207 'let himself be loved': Leslie Stephen, *Swift*.

208 'Attends us first, and leaves us last': JS, *Cadenus and Vanessa*.

Chapter Thirteen: Wife?

Additional sources for this chapter:

Maxwell B. Gold, *Swift's Marriage to Stella*, 1937.
Sybil le Brocquy, *Swift's Most Valuable Friend*, 1968.
W. M. Faloon, *The Marriage Law of Ireland*, 1881.

Both for this chapter and for Chapter Fifteen, 'Filth':

Lawrence Stone, *The Family, Sex and Marriage in England 1500–1800*, 1977.
Richard Davenport-Hines, *Sex, Death and Punishment*, 1990.
Alain Corbin, *The Foul and the Fragrant: Odour and the Social Imagination*, 1994

216 'dependants and admirers': *The Orrery Papers*.

'various unseemly utensils': ibid.

'ought not to be defended': ibid.

217 'Samuel Johnson and Jonathan Swift never met': it is impossible to be equally the devotee of both men; one must choose, perhaps for the reason given by Macaulay in his essay 'Sir William Temple', *Edinburgh Review*, October 1838: 'A person may possibly think Johnson a greater man than Swift. He may possibly prefer Johnson's style to Swift's. But he will at once acknowledge that Johnson writes like a man who has never been out of his study. Swift writes like a man who has passed his whole life in the midst of public business, and to whom the most important affairs of state are as familiar as his weekly bills.'

221 'the prayers he most used': the lock of Swift's hair, and John Lyon's accompanying letter, are at Bowood in Wiltshire – the home, now as in the eighteenth century, of the Earls of Shelburne.

223 'fugitives are of that condition': Francis Bacon, 'Of Marriage and Single Life', *Essays*.

225 'likely to get out of him': *The Orrery Papers*.

'reference to a Mr Molyneux': Ashe's letters to Archbishop William King are among King's unpublished correspondence in the Library of Trinity College, Dublin.

'It has been calculated that . . . never married': statistic from Lawrence Stone in *The Family, Sex and Marriage in England 1500–1800*.

226 'Another authority asserts . . . never married at all': Peter Earle, *A City Full of People: Men and Women of London 1650–1750*, 1994.

227 'That stinks and stings': Pope, 'Epistle to Dr Arbuthnot'.

Chapter Fourteen: Fathers

235 'as executor of Mrs Dingley': letter interleaved in Hawkesworth's *Life* in the Forster Collection, V&A.

238 'more recent hypothesis about Swift's paternity': see Denis Johnston, *In Search of Swift*, for the full argument about Sir John Temple. Johnston made a study of the Black Book of King's Inn, as no one had done since Sir Walter Scott. Johnston's hypothesis that Swift's father was Sir John Temple is persuasive but by no means watertight.

240 'into a very thick fog': Sybil le Brocquy, *Swift's Most Valuable Friend*.

241 'once in three years': quoted in Lange, op. cit.

244 'no one can know for certain': we could know. Today's DNA matching techniques would determine the genetic relationship between Sir John Temple and Swift, and between Sir William Temple and Stella. Graves would have to be opened – or re-opened. During the nineteenth century, Swift's coffin was opened twice.

Chapter Fifteen: Filth

247 'but all folks sh-t': Pope, 'Verses to be prefix'd before Bernard Lintot's New Miscellany', written 1711.

'Point for Manichees': W. S. Auden, 'Thanksgiving for a Habitat', 1964.

248 'do daily eat and drink': JS, 'An Examination of Certain

Abuses, Corruptions, and Enormities in the City of Dublin'.

250 'the monk and the beast': E. M. Forster, *Howard's End*, 1910.

251 'as may make us avoid it?': *The Orrery Papers*.

252 '*talking* lewdly who *live* soberly': Lady Mary Wortley Montagu, *Essays and Poems*.

253 'diseased mind and lacerated heart': John Dunlop, *The History of Fiction*, 1814.

'horrible from first to last': Augustine Birrell, review of J. Churton Collins's 1893 biography of Swift, *Essays about Men, Women and Books*, 1894.

'furious, raging, obscene': W. M. Thackeray, *English Humourists of the Eighteenth Century*, 1853.

'the direction Swift's mind took': A. L. Rowse, *Jonathan Swift, Major Prophet*.

'acceptance and adjustment – only that': letter to Lady Ottoline Morrell, 28 Dec 1928, in *D. H. Lawrence: Selected Literary Criticism*, ed. Anthony Beal, 1961.

'if Celia didn't shit': D. H. Lawrence, introduction to privately printed edition of his *Pansies*, 1929.

254 'and the scientists as well': Michael Foot, introduction to *Gulliver's Travels*, Penguin World Classics.

'Or when the smock's beshit': Earl of Rochester, 'Song'. For further examples see John Wilmot, Earl of Rochester, *The Complete Works*, ed. Frank H. Ellis, Penguin Classics, 1994.

'like air pollution today': the comparison is made by Alain Corbin, *The Foul and the Fragrant*.

255 'the universal neurosis of mankind': Norman O. Brown, 'The Excremental Vision', *Life Against Death: the Psychoanalytical Meaning of History*, 1959.

256 'The proportion . . . is about the same': these calculations are from Hermann J. Real and Heinz J. Vienken, in an excellent article to which I am much indebted, 'Psychoanalytical Criticism and Swift', *Eighteenth-Century Ireland*, Vol. I, 1986.

258 'an exaggerated horror of human dung': George Orwell, 'Politics vs. Literature', *Shooting an Elephant*, 1950.

'at any rate in small doses': Aldous Huxley, *Do What You Will*, 1929.

'to represent the Queen more exactly': David Nokes, *John Gay*.

259 'sentimental sodomy': the phrase is Davenport-Hines's, op. cit.

260 'did not get picked up': Robert Mahony, *Jonathan Swift: The Irish Identity*, 1995.

Chapter Sixteen: Endgame

I am indebted to Jenny Uglow, *Hogarth: A Life and a World*, 1997, and Pat Rogers, *Hacks and Dunces*, 1980, for information on Bedlam.

263 'looked upon as raving mad': JS, 'Some Thoughts on Freethinking'.

'but turns aside like mad Ulysses': JS, 'Traulus, Part One'.

265 'I shall die first at the top': story told by Stephen Gwynn, *The Life and Friendships of Dean Swift*, 1933, and elsewhere.

'ladies, music, meat and wine': *The Orrery Papers*.

266 'but gave him his way': Hawkesworth, *Life*.

267 'But there's no talking to some men': JS, 'Verses on the Death of Dr Swift'.

270 'light from her brother Phoebus': *The Orrery Papers*.

272 'a Commission in Lunacy': the Commission document, issued 12 August 1742, and the report executed the same day, are in the Forster Collection at the V&A.

273 'object of pity to every good man': John Lyon's note in Hawkesworth's *Life*, Forster Collection V&A.

'He hardly breathes. The Dean is dead': JS, 'Verses on the Death of Dr Swift'.

'and left to dry in the study': John Lyon's note in Hawkesworth's *Life*.

'Than if he never did exist': JS, 'Verses on the Death of Dr Swift'.

274 'Than rule yon isle and be a slave': JS, poem headed 'Holyhead. Sept 25, 1727'.

Chapter Seventeen: Midnight

278 'so often turns the brain, as pride': Sir William Temple, 'Heads designed for an Essay on Conversation'.

279 'finish his meal on an excrement': JS, *A Tale of a Tub*.

279 'on all hands impossible to be known': idem.

280 'so proud, so witty, and so wise': Rochester, 'A Satyr against Mankind'.

'Whatever is, is RIGHT': Pope, *Essay on Man*.

281 'from point A to point B': Denis Donoghue, *Swift: A Critical Introduction*, 1969.

'not sufficiently worked out': Joe Orton, *The Orton Diaries*, ed. John Lahr, 1986.

282 'revolution becomes Revolution': 'Every joke is a tiny revolution ... "clean fun" is a general unwillingness to touch upon any serious or controversial subject ... To be funny, indeed, you have to be serious': George Orwell, 'Funny, but Not Vulgar', *Leader* 28 July 1945.

'organs of elimination': Cyril Connolly, *Horizon*, February 1935.

'amount merely to trick photography': *The Orton Diaries*.

283 'or disturbing the public': JS, 'Thoughts on Religion'.

'a species of lower prudence': JS, 'An Essay on the Fates of Clergymen'.

285 'found my whole character in him': JS to Bolingbroke; and NB the first lines of JS, 'Verses on the Death of Dr Swift':

> As Rochefoucault his maxims drew
> From Nature, I believe 'em true:
> They argue no corrupted mind
> In him; the fault is in mankind.

'a few of your original poems': letter from Mrs Barber in Forster Collection, V&A.

286 'those who are not of their tribe': JS, 'A Letter to a Young Clergyman, lately entered into Holy Orders'.

'will serve the turn, and all alike': Sir William Temple, 'Of Health and Long Life'.

287 'And make a patriot as it makes a knave': Pope, *Essay on Man*.

'I am what I am': this story was told by Deane Swift in a letter to Lord Orrery, 4 April 1744.

INDEX

safe. We royl was all against the Dutch, who ridled here with the knaves
Foole and Medinen Mr Secrety is soon to be made a Viscount: He desird I would
draw up Preamble of his Patent; but I excused my self from a Work that
might lose me a great deal of Reputation, and get me very little: we would fain
have to constitute him an Earl, but it will not be, & and therefore he will not
take the title of Bullenbrook, which is lately extinct in the elder Branch of his
Family. I have advisd him to be called Ld Pomfret; but he thinks that
title is already in some other Family, and besides he objects that it is in
Yorkshire where he has no Estate, but there is nothing in that. And I love Pomfret,
Don't you love Pomfret? why, tis in all our Historyes, they are full of Pomfret Castle:
But what's all this to you: you don't care for this. Is goody Stoit come to London? I
have not heard of her yet. you dream of St Pch—never had the manners to
answer my Letter. I was tother day to see Sterne and his Wife: she is not half
so handsome, as when I saw her with you in Dublin. They Design to pass the Sum̃er
at a House near Ld Somers's about a dozen miles off. You never told me how
my Letter to Dr Tucer passes in field. I suppose y are drinking at this
time Templse—something waters. Steel was arrested tother day for
making a Lottery, directly agst an Act of Parlat. He is now under Prosecution,
but they think it will be dropt out of Pity. I believe he will very soon lose
his Employmt, for he has been mighty impertinent of late in his Spectators, and
I will never offer a Word in his behalf. Reynds writes me Word, that the Bp
of Meath was going to Summon me in order to Suspension for absence; if the
Provost had not prevented him. I am prettily rewarded for getting them their
first fruits with a P—— We have had very little Rd ivralle during the whole
montl of June; And for a Week past we have had a good deal of rain, tho not
every day, Kesterday I am just now told that the Garison of Dunkirk has
not orders yet to deliver up Ye Town to Stick Hill and his Forces, but expect
them daily, this must pull off Hills Journy awhile, and I do not like these
Stoppings in such an Affaire— Go get a gam & drink a water if this Rein
has not spoild them securidori. I hear no more to say to oo at present but
var Pdfr: & wish me & Podeb will van Pdfr if thd & me— I wish y had taken
say Accord which y sent mony to gum Bums, I believe y hant don it a grad while
and pray tad no adieu when
Farewell dearest MD FW FW. FW me mr me.